Debating the Global Financial Architecture

SUNY Series in Global Politics
James N. Rosenau, editor

DEBATING
THE
GLOBAL
FINANCIAL
ARCHITECTURE

Edited by
Leslie Elliott Armijo

State University of New York Press

Published by
State University of New York Press, Albany

© 2002 State University of New York

For information, address State University of New York Press
90 State Street, Suite 700, Albany, NY 12207

Production by Judith Block
Marketing by Michael Campochiaro

Library of Congress Cataloging-in-Publication Data

Debating the global financial architecture / edited by Leslie Elliott Armijo.
    p.   cm. — (SUNY series in global politics)
    Includes index.
    ISBN 0-7914-5449-5 (alk. paper). — ISBN 0-7914-5450-9 (pbk. : alk. paper)
    1. International finance.   I. Armijo, Leslie Elliott.   II. Series.

HG3881.D3434 2002
332'.042—dc21   2002017743

For Kaizad, Zubin, and Chitra

CONTENTS

ACKNOWLEDGMENTS

Chapter 1 contains some material from Leslie Elliott Armijo, "The Political Geography of World Financial Reform: Who Wants What and Why?" which appeared in *Global Governance: A Review of Multilateralism and International Organizations* 7, no. 4 (2001), copyright by Lynne Rienner Publishers. Permission to reprint is gratefully acknowledged.

Chapter 3 is a slightly revised version of Benjamin J. Cohen, "Capital Controls: Why Do Governments Hesitate?" which appeared in *Revue Économique* 52, no. 2 (2001). Permission to reprint is gratefully acknowledged.

We thank the Institute for International Economics, which retains the copyright to the material in chapter 4, for permission to include it in this volume.

Chapter 10 was first published as "Motivation: Insulation and the Welfare State" in Erik Jones, *The Politics of Economic and Monetary Union* (Lanham, MD: Rowman and Littlefield Publishers, 2002). Reprinted by permission.

TABLES

INTRODUCTION

Leslie Elliott Armijo

Most of the contributors to this book labor in ivory towers, though a few are policymakers and policy advisors. The contributors, of course, agree neither with me nor with one another on all points, though we share a belief that the future shape of the global financial architecture is of crucial importance to world economic growth and thus also for international political stability. With the exception of my own essays, the chapters, most written expressly for inclusion in this volume, were last revised in 2000.

I use the first chapter to identify core questions and mental categories employed by scholars from different disciplines to conceptualize the international financial architecture. Economists think in terms of adjustment, liquidity, and stability, while economic historians organize the world in periods: the prewar gold standard era, the interwar period, the Bretton Woods regime, and the post Bretton Woods era since the early 1970s. Political scientists, meanwhile, ask about the international balance of power, employing concepts such as hegemony and multipolarity—while dreaming of greater democracy and institutionalization at the international level. Political scientists may also be sensitive to the peculiar irony of policymakers in the wealthy democracies, which largely have insulated themselves from exogenous financial and monetary shocks, demanding that policymakers in newly democratic emerging market countries expose their populations to the rigors of full integration with volatile world capital markets. I close with a summary of four influential policy positions in the current debate over reform of the international financial architecture.

Chapters two through four address issues of leadership and the politics of global finance. Mark Brawley takes up the question of hegemonic stability. While endorsing the view that a pro-market hegemon may provide useful system management for other participants, he yet reminds us that hegemons can find it convenient to destroy as well as to create and maintain existing structures of international governance (also known as international regimes). Brawley further observes that the U.S. willingness to provide leadership has always been driven by perceptions of the national economic interest. Benjamin J. Cohen notes that the mainstream of the discipline of neoclassical economics in the 1990s became much more skeptical about the virtues of wholly free international capital flows, yet most incumbent politicians and policymakers have not yet picked up on this message. He wonders why, and speculates on the barriers to policy relevant learning, reluctantly concluding that continued U.S. government opposition to even interim capital controls is the most likely explanation of their rarity.

C. Fred Bergsten, director of the eminent Washington, D.C., think tank, the Institute for International Economics, reports on his experience as a member of two rival expert committees on reform of the international financial architecture. One was sponsored by the Council on Foreign Relations, whose consensus report represents the position that chapter one terms that of the transparency advocates, with a few nods to the financial stabilizers. The second, popularly known as the Meltzer Committee after its chairman, was commissioned by the Republican-dominated United States Congress in late 1998, at the height of the Asian financial crisis. Its majority views are those of laissez-faire liberalizers. The reason that the conservative majority was joined by Harvard economist Jeffry Sachs, sometime transparency advocate turned idiosyncratic financial stabilizer by his experience advising Russia in the 1990s, may be Sach's agreement with the left anti-globalizers on the dim possibilities for genuine democratic reform of the IMF and World Bank.

Chapters five to seven address issues of stability, equity, and the economics of global finance. David Felix takes the main theses of the laissez-faire liberalizers' canon and debunks them, one by one. Eduardo Fernández-Arias and Ricardo Hausmann were at the time of writing the senior and chief economists, respectively, of the Inter-American Development Bank, here writing in their private capacity. Their greatest concern is that the regulatory fixes to the current post–Bretton Woods financial architecture that seem most likely to be implemented address several of the important concerns of the advanced industrial countries, such as their fears of taxpayer-funded bailouts and financial contagion from emerging markets crises, but are unresponsive to the concerns of many developing countries, such as maintaining the access to global capital markets to which their relatively rapid growth and attractive investment possibilities would seem to entitle them. Fernández-Arias and Hausmann—like Cohen, Felix, and other contributors to this book, but unlike most of the influential expert commissions on international financial reform created in the past decade—would explicitly include issues of currency choice and exchange rate regimes in the debate over the global financial and monetary architecture. Ashima Goyal, a senior economist at one of India's premiere economic think tanks, takes issue with Fernández-Arias and Hausmann on a number of specifics, for example arguing in favor of loan contracts that bail in private creditors, an arrangement about which the Latin Americans are dubious. But like them, she laments the paucity of lender of last resort facilities for developing countries confronting liquidity crises due to financial contagion, and the sad reality that the views of emerging market countries are typically marginalized in the high-level committees most likely to influence actual reforms.

The three final chapters directly tackle the political conundrum of multilateral reform. Henry Laurence's highly entertaining account of Japan's not yet successful efforts to exercise international monetary leadership illustrates the degree to which policymaking in this international arena remains extraordinarily hegemonic. His discussion also spotlights the multiplicity of views—and rising regional multipolarity—in Asia, an area still largely sidelined in global financial governance, despite its wealth. Tony Porter and Duncan Wood, based in the "other" NAFTA countries of Canada and Mexico, respectively, trace the progress of global negotiations over reform of the rules governing international financial flows. They do not hide their frustration over the structural inequities of the process, though they choose to end on a hopeful note, predicting a trend of greater inclusiveness in the future. Erik Jones writes of, and from, the region of the world that has pursued monetary and financial integration the furthest: Western Europe. Jones's essay explicitly confronts and critiques a defining worry of many in both of the broad, and in most respects dissimilar, alliances that I have labeled laissez-faire liberalizers and anti-globalizers. This is the fear of both conservative "new sovereigntists," on the one hand, and organized labor and other interests hurt by globalization, on the other, that faceless and unresponsive supranational institutions will come to determine their fates if multilateral economic and financial cooperation continues and even deepens. Jones asserts, on the contrary, that the European Monetary Union is on its way to becoming the greatest aid to buffering national economies from international shocks since the postwar Bretton Woods regime. He does not, however, directly address the closely related question of how monetary union in a single region might affect the future of monetary and financial multilateralism across geographic and cultural areas, although the existence of the EMU makes this question urgent.

To close the book, Laurence Whitehead's lighthearted yet provocative afterword considers reform of the financial architecture in light of enduring themes of political philosophy, revisiting the issues of democracy and representativeness also raised explicitly in chapter one.

We leave the reader, and ourselves, with a number of unresolved questions, among the most significant of which are these: Can the international financial system safely be left to "the markets," or are intentional regulation and supervision necessary to ensure adjustment, liquidity, and/or stability? Does the United States merit praise or blame for its dominance in global monetary affairs since the Second World War? Is U.S. monetary hegemony now exhausted, or nearly so? Is the frustration with, and vulnerability to, the international monetary status quo felt by newly enfranchised publics in Russia, Indonesia, Argentina, Turkey, and South Africa merely a cause for regret and crocodile tears in the advanced capitalist democracies, or are there critical implications for managing future global financial crises? Finally, is representative multilateralism in the financial sphere even remotely possible?

I thank the Political Science Department of Reed College for extending to me the privileges of a Visiting Scholar while this volume was in preparation, and hope that the included essays amplify the continuing debate.

I. CORE QUESTIONS AND MENTAL CATEGORIES

Chapter 1

THE TERMS OF THE DEBATE: WHAT'S DEMOCRACY GOT TO DO WITH IT?

Leslie Elliott Armijo

At the dawn of the twenty-first century, reform of the global financial architecture has become a burning issue, albeit almost exclusively within an extraordinarily narrow circle of policymakers and interested parties. The current debate results from a series of high-profile financial crises in the 1990s. In 1992 and 1993 troubles in Western Europe's Exchange Rate Mechanism (ERM) cost the German government at least $1 billion and the Swedish government as much as $26 billion and brought fame and wealth to financier George Soros, who correctly bet against the British pound sterling. In 1994 and 1995 the Mexican peso crisis and subsequent "tequila effect" devastated emerging markets throughout Latin America and other countries as far flung as Canada and the Philippines. And from 1997 to 1999 the East Asian financial crisis brought down Indonesia's Suharto after thirty years in power, and exposed the feet of clay of several of the much admired Asian tigers. Front page pictures of Indonesian President Suharto signing a loan agreement with International Monetary Fund Managing Director Michel Camdessus looking over his shoulder, and of newly elected Korean President Kim Dae Jung exchanging a hearty handshake and photo opportunity with George Soros, defined the moment. Less noticed outside financial circles was the eleventh-hour weekend rescue of Long-Term Capital Management, a little known American hedge fund, in the fall of 1998, just after the Russian financial crisis and just prior to the Brazilian one. The rescue relied on "voluntary contributions" of funds from major private U.S. banks, but was urgently coordinated by Gerald Corrigan, Chairman of the New York Federal Reserve Bank. These events spawned a flurry of commissions and studies.

This book, written in 1999 and 2000, contains observations on both the process and the content of proposed reforms. The authors are political scientists and economists. These disciplines not being as close as they once were, my overview chapter sets itself definitional as well as analytical tasks. I also hope to suggest that neither the economic perspective (more oriented toward the *con-*

tent and economic results of the global financial architecture), nor the political one (typically focused on actors, perceptions, preferences, power, and decision-making *processes*) is alone adequate to comprehend or make policy for international monetary and financial relations. At the same time, I argue a substantive thesis: an international financial architecture that is *consistent with underlying global political and social realities* will be both more effective and more enduring than one that is not.

Section one reviews the functions of an international financial architecture. Section two summarizes the main institutions of the four historical financial architectures since the mid-nineteenth century, briefly evaluating each. Section three explores the implications of three secular trends in the international political economy for understanding the performance of past and potential future international financial architectures. *Technological advancement* can render what were once perfectly adequate regulatory frameworks newly incompetent. Gradually *declining United States hegemony* seems to make greater multilateral cooperation over reform of the global financial architecture imperative—though never easy to achieve. The *spread of mass democracy* to so-called emerging market countries implies that any international monetary regime that does not provide at least minimal buffering to the domestic economies of developing countries will be inherently unstable and unsustainable for those countries, with potentially dangerous consequences for the advanced capitalist countries as well. The uncomfortable conclusion of the section is that a debate over the future financial architecture that continues to be overwhelmingly dominated by the preferences of interests located within the United States may not produce a reform blueprint that can last. I note that this statement is positive, not normative. Section four summarizes the ideas and interests behind four dominant contemporary perspectives on global financial reform. Unfortunately, the most influential positions in the contemporary debate largely ignore the questions of international political feasibility and long-term political sustainability raised in this book.

THE FUNCTIONS OF AN INTERNATIONAL FINANCIAL ARCHITECTURE

The global financial architecture is what contemporary international relations theorists term an "international regime," designating a set of "principles, norms, rules, and procedures" in an international issue arena (Krasner 1982).[1] The international financial architecture consists of a loose set of multilateral agreements and understandings, among a core group of powerful capitalist states, about the rules and norms that govern, and/or should govern, cross-border money and credit transactions of all kinds. These understandings may be informal, written, and/or embodied in shared expectations about the normal operations of ongoing international or transnational organizations. The most obvious and influential actors in the international financial and monetary regulatory arena are nation-states, which are the primary focus of my analysis. Private actors, from multinational banks to nongovernmental organizations, also are intermittent players at the international level, as well as working actively within national borders to influence the global economic policy stances of governments. The international financial institutions (IFIs) and various multilateral forums are simultaneously locations within which bargaining occurs and independent participants in their own right.

An initial and often overlooked observation is that an international financial architecture only becomes necessary where two conditions hold. First, international trade is primarily through purchase, not barter. Second, some significant portion of the money in circulation within and between the major economies of the system is of uncertain value or entirely lacking in intrinsic worth, the latter being the case with all paper currency. In order to accept currency, or even coins of ambiguous provenance and quality, in settlement sellers need to believe that this money will retain its value when they in turn spend it. Maintaining the value of international money is thus the most essential point of the exercise. It is noteworthy that the world progressed from a nineteenth-century situation in which major currencies were redeemable in gold at a fixed rate, to a system in which major currencies were redeemable at a fixed rate in a key currency, the U.S. dollar, itself redeemable at a fixed rate in gold. Since the early 1970s, however, major currencies have been redeemable at a floating—and thus fundamentally uncertain—rate in a key currency, typically the U.S. dollar. The U.S. dollar meanwhile is itself redeemable at a floating, and thus fundamentally uncertain, rate in other major currencies. One begins to understand the overwhelming importance of credibility to the system.

International economists typically assess alternative international financial arrangements in terms of the way they fulfill three tasks: *adjustment, liquidity,* and provision of a lender of last resort, or more generally, *stability.*

Adjustment

The core meaning of adjustment is coping with the adverse domestic economic consequences of structural trade imbalances. The underlying assumption is that international trade is good. Free trade allows beneficial specialization via each country's comparative advantage, as given by its relative endowments of factors of production such as labor, capital, and land. Trade raises world income and benefits each country, at least as an aggregate, and is thus worth preserving and expanding. However, in the real world a country's exports and imports to the rest of the world frequently will not balance, either in the short-term or over a longer period such as a year, the latter situation constituting a "structural" im-

Table 1.1 Functions of an International Financial Architecture

Task	Adjustment	Liquidity	Stability
Main Purpose	Rebalance external accounts, making trade possible	Support growth	Prevent international crises
Main Processes	• Exchange rate regime • Regulation (or not) of private capital flows	• Reserve standard • Regulation (or not) of private capital flows • IFI investment and lending (or not)	• Lender of last resort • Data collection and dissemination • Regulation (or not) of private capital flows
Major Institutional Alternatives	• Fixed exchange rates • Intermediate regimes (adjustable peg, crawling peg, managed float) • Freely floating exchange rates	• Reserve standard: (a) gold (b) gold exchange (c) key currency (d) multiple key currencies • Private capital flows (a) laissez-faire (b) purely national regulation (c) multilateral regulation	Crisis management is: • Ad hoc • Partially institutionalized • Both institutionalized and explicitly representative

balance. Unless trade is by barter, accounts are settled in money, with exporters in any given country usually preferring to be paid in their national currency. A trade deficit implies a demand at home for foreign goods, which must ultimately be purchased with foreign money, that is greater than the offsetting demand of foreigners for the home country's goods, and thus for the home country's money. This generates a net outflow of the first country's stocks of foreign money, or foreign exchange reserves. A trade surplus in the second country meanwhile provokes the accumulation of reserves. A trade imbalance cannot continue indefinitely. Either the parties somehow must adjust, or trade itself will cease.

Capital account flows, or cross-border investments unconnected to the exchange of goods or services, may also generate trade-inhibiting external imbalances. For example, persistent net inflows may result when a country's real domestic interest rate (the price that large borrowers, such as private banks or the government, pay for the loan of funds) exceeds that prevailing in global markets. Under floating exchange rates, such net capital inflows may result in a currency that is overvalued relative to its domestic purchasing power. Alternatively, capital flight (that is, large net capital outflows unwanted by the national authorities) may put unsustainable downward pressure on a fixed exchange rate. Both of these problems may occur even when the country's underlying trade accounts remain in rough balance.

There are three principal institutional alternatives for solving an external imbalance through the global financial system. In a world of freely convertible national monies, exchange rates may either be fixed or float. Under *fixed exchange rates* a deficit nation is, in principle, automatically on a diet or a budget. When the foreign exchange is gone, nothing more can be imported. As the quantity of reserves (gold and foreign exchange held by the central bank as backing for the paper currency) shrinks, the monetary authority withdraws credit from the national economy, provoking a fall in overall economic activity.[2] Less money for the same amount of goods soon results in reduced consumption and investment, including diminished demand for imports, and/or falling prices. Meanwhile, the trading partner with a surplus has an economic expansion; as its central bank uses the excess reserves to expand credit, its import demand rises. Voilà, equilibration has occurred. The gold standard, in which all major currencies are pegged to and convertible in gold, is a special case of a fixed exchange rate regime. A gold exchange standard means that a dominant currency, such as the U.S. dollar, is convertible in gold; other major currencies freely convert into dollars.

The most serious implementation problem for fixed exchange rates is that national governments resist the supposedly automatic discipline of allowing the country's trade position to determine the level of domestic activity. The cure, economy-wide recession (less frequently expansion) seems worse than the disease, so adjustment is postponed, perhaps indefinitely, while the deficit country keeps the problem from worsening by employing trade barriers and/or capital controls. Yet when an objective need for adjustment is finessed, fixed rates become risky. Speculators, recognizing an unsustainable trade imbalance, usually a deficit, "bet against the currency," engaging in a "war" with the central bank to force an emergency devaluation. When it arrives, such a devaluation provides a deep shock to the domestic economy, dramatically and with no warning reducing the country's purchasing power as imports, and by implication domestic products that compete with imports, now suddenly become much more costly. The depth of the shock depends upon the country's degree of trade integration. Larger, more insular countries have less to fear from sudden, unexpected exchange rate movements than do smaller, more internationalized economies.

Under *floating rates* the relative prices of currencies are set in a market in which prices can change at any pace from monthly to every few seconds, depending upon the trading technology. In principle, a trade deficit causes the price of a currency to fall relative to one or more trading partners, making exports cheaper and thus more desirable abroad, while the reverse is true for imported goods, thus provoking a rebalancing of the country's trade account. The mechanism is simple and elegant and requires no centralized decision making or oversight. The drawbacks of floating exchange rates appear mainly in practice. Although floating rates are meant to facilitate trade, they actually can discourage it, as sellers and buyers resist entering into contracts with their local prices unspecified. Floating rates also allow for, and perhaps render irresistible, currency speculation, in which individuals hoard (or sell) national monies, not for the purpose of purchasing goods or services, but on a bet that exchange rates will rise (or fall). A little such speculation usefully greases the wheels, but when the volume of foreign exchange trading vastly outstrips the money value of total trade, as has increasingly been the case in the world since the 1980s, adjustment to an underlying trade imbalance is no longer what actually is driving foreign exchange markets (see the chapters by Benjamin J. Cohen and David Felix). A principal drawback to freely floating rates, particularly in a world of rapid and deep foreign exchange trading, is that they are vulnerable to speculative overshooting. The relative prices of currencies become delinked from countries' present, or likely future, relative trade positions. In other words, the intended solution to external imbalances instead worsens the problem.

A third institutional possibility for achieving adjustment to trade imbalances is some form of *intermediate regime*, such as an "adjustable peg" (that is, fixed rates until the objective need for readjustment can be ascertained by some authoritative and prespecified decision process, whether multilateral or purely national) or a "managed float" (in which central bankers intervene in foreign exchange markets with the purpose of countering speculation around the "true" value of a given currency).

The preceding paragraphs assumed that all major countries in the system would adopt the same exchange rate regime. Both fixed and floating rates function more smoothly if governments in all of the major economies adhere to similar rules. Yet given the absence of world government, there is of course no military or other overt political sanction that major independent powers can exercise against one another in order to force compliance. Moreover, different adjustment mechanisms may favor one or another country. Generally, however, floating rates tend to drive out fixed rates, as in the short run a national government that can readily manipulate the value of its currency has an advantage, causing currency traders to shun fixed rate monies unless they can be very confident of the incumbent government's determination not to devalue, and to foreswear domestic economic policies that might later provoke an unwanted devalution.

National governments may also employ controls and regulations on private capital flows as an aid to balancing their external accounts, ranging from the creation of desirable financial assets available only to those with foreign exchange to quantitative controls on cross-border flows. Finally, national governments may borrow, or lend (that is, invest), abroad. We are accustomed to conceiving of capital controls or inducements, and of government decisions to borrow or lend internationally, as purely national decisions. However, there is no inherent technical reason why such policies cannot be the subject of international bargaining, agreement, and implementation.

Liquidity

An international financial architecture also must ensure liquidity, or make available money and credit. In a national economy additions to liquidity come about through injections of cash or credit into the domestic money supply, as when a central bank purchases outstanding government bonds or lowers interest rates. If a nation's money supply fails to increase gradually over time, then any incipient increase in production of goods and services will be stifled by insufficient financing, as the price of money is bid up and investment slows. Similarly, the provision of net additions to liquidity in the global system is an important determinant of world economic growth.

An international financial architecture sets several kinds of standards that have critical implications for systemic liquidity. First, what money will be used for payments across borders? That is, what is the architecture's implicit or explicit reserve standard? Second, what, if any, constraints will individual states, or the international community as a whole, impose on private decisions to transport funds across borders? Third, does the international community as a whole— or do leading members of it—take any explicit collective responsibility for the provision of systemic liquidity? For providing credit and investment funds to individual countries?

International payments can be based on a *money of intrinsic value*, such as gold or silver, or on a paper currency credibly redeemable in precious metals. Under this system, of which the gold standard was an example, the world's money supply increases only when there are new discoveries of precious metals, which unavoidably leaves international liquidity growth to chance. Under a *gold exchange* system, a country willing to convert its home paper currency into gold on demand becomes the key currency country of the system. In this case, new additions to global liquidity can result either from the discovery of gold or the individual decisions of foreign private citizens and foreign central banks to increase their holdings of the key currency outside the country of its origin.[3] The advantage of this arrangement is that expansion of the world's money supply is not left entirely to chance. A crucial disadvantage, from the viewpoint of non–key currency countries, is that the key currency country may use its monetary influence to enhance its overall national power.

A third possibility is a straightforward *key currency* system, in which other countries hold quantities of the key currency as their main reserve asset—even though the key currency country no longer agrees to redeem this currency in gold. This is a risky system in that there is little to fall back on if the key currency is ever seriously questioned. Fortunately, participants in a pure key currency system each have a strong individual incentive to maintain the stability of the system.[4] The fourth alternative is a system of *multiple key currencies,* in which two or more currencies are widely held as reserves, perhaps by different regional blocs. It is hard to know whether such a system is more or less risky than one in which a single reserve currency dominates. However, as long as most countries perceive key currency status as a power resource, such a multipolar system is quite likely to be less stable in configuration than a hegemonic monetary system, as the leaders of rival blocs compete (Cohen 2000). A move toward regional trading blocs could reinforce a trend toward regional monetary blocs, and vice versa.

Like both adjustment and stability, liquidity also is affected by the ways in which national governments regulate private international capital flows. On the one hand, this is an issue of substance: are there no controls, few controls, many controls? What kind of controls are there: taxes, quantitative ceilings, preferential interest rates for foreign exchange? On the other hand, and perhaps more fundamentally, it is an issue of process: who decides and how? We have then three broad institutional alternatives. First is a system norm of *few or no controls*, with most limits to private freedom of capital movement being defined as illegitimate. Second is a system norm of *national decision making* about barriers to private cross-border financial flows (a prescription about process), perhaps combined with another system norm about the acceptable range of capital freedoms or capital controls (a prescription about substance). The third alternative is a system norm, and its attendant institutions and procedures, for *collective or multilateral decision making*, possibly bundled with a substantive prescription as well.

Finally, once there is a precedent for collective negotiations or simply authoritative discussion about regulation of private, voluntary capital, then the subject of jointly managed and publicly funded flows may arise. If multilateral public funds are proposed only to serve as an occasional lender of last resort, then such funds have only incidental implications for liquidity. Since the midtwentieth century, however, permanent multilateral bureaucracies, collectively known as the international financial institutions (IFIs), have been assigned the tasks of managing global liquidity (mainly through the International Monetary Fund) and, at least fitfully, of ensuring a supply of development credit to individual countries (via the World Bank and regional development banks).

Stability

The third function of an enduring international financial architecture is providing stability by preventing major systemic crisis and reducing "financial contagion," that is, the cross-border transmission of national crises. The need to encourage stability follows from the unique nature of financial markets, which are infinitely more prone than goods markets to bubbles and crashes (Kindleberger 1978). Individual firms in financial markets, such as banks, are uniquely vulnerable to one another in that the bad fortunes of one bank, rather than being a source of joy to its competitors, instead may threaten other initially healthy banks, either because of interlinked deposits or simply because depositors in general panic and begin a run on all financial institutions in that market. Because credit is an essential input to all modern business activity, a banking collapse brings the entire economy to a halt. All of these characteristics of purely domestic financial markets also hold internationally as soon as national financial markets become interdependent, with the added complications in the international arena of exchange rate issues and a multiplicity of regulatory authorities, national and perhaps also multinational.

Many analysts discuss the stability function in terms of alternative institutional arrangements for provision of a *lender of last resort* (LLR) (see Eichengreen [1989] 2000). An LLR is an entity willing to make a judgment that a particular financial institution or borrower (note that all commercial banks borrow from their depositors) facing bankruptcy is in a condition of *illiquidity*, or a temporary inability to repay debt, and not one of *insolvency*, or a fundamental and more or less permanent inability to repay. In practice, and not only in the contemporary era, the distressed borrower often has been a sovereign state. Once a finding of illiquidity is in, the LLR extends an emergency loan to the distressed debtor, hoping to avert panic withdrawals while giving the debtor some breathing space. In addition, in some circumstances the LLR may decide to rescue an insolvent and thus unworthy debtor, not for its own sake but to preserve the health of the larger financial system—or, in the case of countries, for the sake of the strategic value of the borrowing country to the state or states that control the LLR decision. Other substantive responses to the ever present possibility of financial crises are international prudential regulations (a type of capital control, it should be clearly noted), and mechanisms for full and transparent disclosure of national, often government, financial information to the global markets, which is supposed to reveal incipient problems before they arise.

One way to think about alternative institutional frameworks for ensuring stability would be to list different possible international institutions that might be created, from the currently existing International Monetary Fund to proposed new institutions such as a world bankruptcy court, global credit rating institution, or an expanded IMF formally tasked with acting as the world's lender of last resort (Eichengreen 1999 and Blecker 1999 review many of these proposals). A world bankruptcy court, for example, could be empowered to forbid creditors from seizing a borrower's assets while it restructured and tried to devise a viable plan for paying the debt.[5] The sheer multiplicity of options, however, suggests a categorization based on process. Novel and unexpected financial crises will arise occasionally in any system, the interesting question is how the implicit or explicit regulatory architecture shapes the system's responses to crisis.

The first alternative is *ad hoc crisis management* by the great power(s) of the era. Under this scenario, there are no permanent international institutions or even standing committees. Crises are dealt with by the most powerful state, or hegemon, which acts in what its leaders perceive to be its own national interests, perhaps with the assistance of other great powers. A second model is that of *partially institutionalized crisis prevention and management* by the great powers. The key difference from the preceding alternative is that in this case collective efforts have been made, and ongoing, formal, multilateral institutions and mechanisms constructed, prior to the onset of crisis. Partially institutionalized crisis prevention and management by definition coexists with ad hoc crisis response. A third institutional alternative has not yet existed in practice, yet is possible. This is *institutionalized and explicitly representative multilateral crisis prevention and management*. The third model differs from the second in two particulars. First, at least limited supranational authority for crisis management exists, to which national governments in principle are prepared to defer. Second, the process through which individuals are selected to direct the supranational regulatory institution(s) is both transparent and explicitly representative of member states. The new European Central Bank approximates this model at the regional level.

HISTORICAL FINANCIAL ARCHITECTURES

There have been four major international financial architectures since the mid-nineteenth century. The earliest and most recent periods have enjoyed the reputation, if not always the reality, of having evolved naturally in response to market mechanisms rather than resulting from heavy-handed interference by national governments, while the middle two periods saw self-conscious multilateral attempts at architectural design. The most accessible, entertaining, and current source on the evolution of the international financial architecture is surely that of Barry Eichengreen (1996; revised in 1998 for the paperback edition cited here), from whom many of my facts are borrowed, but who is of course not responsible for my interpretations. This section briefly describes the major institutions each architecture employed. I also risk a personal, but perhaps not uninformed, judgment on the overall efficacy of the architecture during each period, in terms of the goals set for it by politically dominant contemporaries.

Table 1.2 Historical Financial Architectures

Financial Architecture	*Adjustment*	*Liquidity*	*Stability*
Classical Gold Standard ~1870–1914	• Fixed exchange rates • Flexible domestic prices	• Gold • Free capital flows	• Ad hoc crisis management
Interwar Drift 1919–1939	• Free float, then fixed rates, then managed float • Increasing capital controls in period	• Gold and gold exchange • De facto national regulation of private flows	• Ad hoc crisis management
Bretton Woods System 1944– ~1971	• Quasi-fixed ("adjustable peg") • Capital controls	• Gold exchange (U.S. dollar) • National regulation of private flows • Some collective responsibility for liquidity in world (IMF) and individual states (WB)	• Partially institutionalized crisis management (IMF)
Post–Bretton Woods System ~ 1973–Present	• Progressively freer float (major states) • Decreasing capital controls in period, although domestic prices remain inflexible (major states)	• U.S. dollar • System norm of national (de)regulation of private flows • Some collective responsibility for liquidity	• Partially institutionalized crisis management (G7, IMF, and so forth) • Limited joint re-regulation of private flows for international prudential reasons

Classical Gold Standard (1870–1914)

In 1717 the English mint set a relative price for gold and silver that undervalued silver, thus driving this alternative money out of circulation. Set along one path by this historical accident, over the subsequent century England gradually adopted the gold standard. By 1821 England, the major economy in

Europe, was fully on gold. Portugal, whose major trading partner was England, had followed by midcentury. When Germany, the second largest economy and a rising power, chose to tie its marks to gold in 1871, others soon followed. The classical gold standard was an implicit international regime, without written rules or formal multilateral agreements, yet possessed of rules, norms, and expected behaviors well understood in the finance ministries of participating countries (Simmons 1994, 21–40). Eichengreen (1996, 13–25) attributes both the slow start and subsequent rapid spread of the gold standard to network externalities, whereby smaller countries reaped transaction and other advantages from choosing the same monetary arrangements as the major powers.

Adjustment under the gold standard was via fixed exchange rates, as each currency was convertible into gold at a preset rate. Adjustment also required free movement of gold; importers into the trade deficit country would take the local currency they received as payment and redeem it for gold, supplied by the central bank of the trade deficit country. As the gold backing for the domestic money supply in the trade deficit country shrank, credit would tighten, the economy would slow, and prices would fall. Since unionization had not yet made wages sticky downwards, deflation could begin relatively rapidly. The classical gold standard thus also needed flexible prices, and citizen tolerance of sometimes dramatic swings in the level of domestic economic activity, in order to function. Moreover, national central banks, and the political authorities to which they were subject, had to be willing to retain an immutable domestic exchange rate between the national currency and gold; that is, participant countries had to resist the lure of domestic inflation to solve public revenue problems. During the four and a half decades in which this financial architecture regulated international monetary relations, countries adhered to gold standard norms with remarkable fealty. When the requirements of gold standard participation strained national economic management, countries instead drew back from the concurrent free trade regime, with chronically trade deficit countries erecting tariffs to avoid the necessity for subsequent adjustment through the monetary system. Thus Germany, France, and many other European countries at the core of the world economy began to increase tariffs in the 1880s and the 1890s, following two long decades in which trade barriers had generally fallen (Krasner 1976). But they remained on the gold standard.

As gold was the ultimate unit of value, new discoveries of gold were the source of *liquidity* for the world monetary system. Such a rule had the advantage of being automatic, that is, of not requiring active management by any state or institution. The amount of liquidity in the system was not subject to political control by a hegemon or cabal of dominant states. During the nineteenth and very early twentieth centuries, there were some new discoveries of gold. Nonetheless, the shift from bimetallism (a combined gold and silver standard) to a purely gold standard was deflationary in most countries. In Britain itself the domestic price level fell by 37 percent between 1873 and 1886 (Eichengreen 1996, 19). The worldwide deflation of the 1870s was quite probably heightened, if not caused, by the widespread shift to the gold standard by the major economies of the time. During these decades, private investors often provided liquidity for countries with trade deficits; so long as monetary management was credibly tight, providers of inward capital flows could expect to be rewarded with higher interest rates in the trade deficit economy (Eichengreen 1996, 31–32). Maintenance of convertibility remained a powerful norm of the system, so currency risk for foreign investors was minimal. Net foreign investment flows, well above what was needed to rebalance trade, also grew, arguably adding to the global efficiency of investment. The total dollar value of world foreign investment in 1914 was more than five times that of 1870 (Pollard 1985, 492).

The regime's implicit prescriptions for achieving *stability* were more vague. Under the classical gold standard the markets (that is, private financial actors, each acting in a decentralized, self-interested fashion) expected that national authorities (central banks and finance ministries) would intervene procyclically in order to hasten the deflation, or less often the inflation, needed to reequilibrate the trade balance. Because they believed this, private investors were willing to bring capital into a country with a trade deficit, in the expectation of making a profit as the money supply tightened and interest rates rose. Though not based on written international covenants, the classical gold standard regime also led to informal and productive consultation and subsequent mutual adjustment among key countries, especially in times of crisis.[6]

In its own terms the classical gold standard performed excellently. Adjustment to trade imbalances was typically rapid and effective. Less happily, the rapid and effective adjustment mechanism of the classical gold standard, which reequilibrated trade imbalances through sharp shifts in domestic prices and levels of economic activity, was harsh for ordinary citizens, many of whom lost employment during an era in which there was no social safety net, and for businesses, which experienced waves of bankruptcies during economic downturns. In terms of the financial architecture's own goals, however, these seeming drawbacks were virtues, as they demonstrated the credibility of the financial framework. The gold standard—along with the world's first widespread regime of mostly free trade—coincided with tremendous and sustained expansion in the world economy. As compared to the period from 1820 to 1870, both world gross domestic product (GDP) and GDP per capita rates nearly doubled from 1870 to 1900, reaching rates of 1.9 and 1.1 percent respectively. Growth and per capita growth rose further to 2.2 and 1.2 percent from 1900 to 1929 (Maddison 1995, 227–228). Finally, the financial architecture, though not without crises among both core and peripheral members, yielded remarkable stability in the system. Rule following plus periodic central bank coordination resulted in most threatened financial crises in the advanced economies of the day being blunted or avoided.

Interwar Drift (1919–1939), including the Restored Gold Standard (1926–1931)

The established systems for trade, payments, and foreign investment all broke down during the Great War, partly because shipping was subject to enemy attack, but also because belligerent governments commandeered both goods and their citizens' savings for the war effort. Following the end of the war in 1919, governments were anxious to reestablish international trade and payments. The gold standard, which apparently had worked so well before the war, was the obvious choice for the financial architecture. Yet it could not be reestablished immediately, as most governments recognized that an early commitment to exchange their national monies for gold would result in a loss of their remaining gold reserves. Only the U.S. dollar was convertible in the early 1920s.

There were three distinct de facto financial architectures during the two interwar decades (Eichengreen 1996, 45–92; Kindleberger 1986; Simmons 1994). From *the War's end through 1925* most currencies of the major economies floated freely, their prices set by market supply and demand. Private capital moved easily among the major economies. Under this system, *adjustment* to trade imbalances worked reasonably well in a narrow and technical sense, in that the prices of national currencies (and thus of goods and services denominated in those currencies) were set by market supply and demand. However, exchange rates were notoriously volatile, leading to great uncertainty for both importers and exporters, and thus depressing trade. *Liquidity* meanwhile suffered from two problems. The more serious and structural systemic flaw was the global shortage of gold—the only store of value that most governments and markets ultimately trusted—which imposed a deflationary bias not only on the early 1920s but throughout the interwar period. Added to this fundamental bind were several related imbalances in international capital flows that resulted from the short-sighted reparations and official debt repayment arrangements constructed by the victors of World War I.[7]

The floating rate, laissez-faire system of the early 1920s performed worst of all in the task of *stability*. The problem was not simply that exchange rates were volatile. Under floating rates and open capital flows currency traders responded not only to realized trade imbalances but also to expectations about the domestic economy, in particular its inflationary potential. At the end of the Great War, returning servicemen had embarrassed their governments into granting, for the first time in much of Western Europe, universal male suffrage, including in Britain, long the financial center of the global economy. Working men, now the majority in the electorate, preferred jobs to a stable currency. Private investors responded accordingly, fleeing countries whenever left-leaning politicians appeared to be scoring even minor victories. International financial credibility, previously mainly a problem for hard-pressed monarchs fighting expensive wars, in the 1920s became an ever present worry for finance ministers in all broadly democratic polities, a designation that then included all of the core capitalist states, even Germany. Private investors' lack of confidence in governments—even when actual budget and trade deficits were perfectly reasonable—rendered the floating rate system of the early 1920s highly volatile and thus fatally unstable.

Policymakers and pundits thought the solution was to reestablish predictability by bringing back the gold standard, or at least a gold exchange standard. Countries in Central Europe that had experienced hyperinflation in the immediate postwar years were the first to re-peg to gold.[8] In 1925 Britain, under a Conservative government, restored sterling convertibility at the prewar parity, a decision that left the pound objectively overvalued, somewhere between 5 and 15 percent, reducing the competitiveness of British industry and pushing already troubling unemployment even higher (Eichengreen 1996, 59–60). France restored convertibility the following year, but only after devaluing relative to the franc's prewar value.

Between 1926 and 1931 all four of the major economies—the United States, Germany, Britain, and France—plus most of their close neighbors and allies, adhered to a restored gold standard, one whose only noticeable technical difference from its illustrious prewar predecessor appeared to be the intentionally expanded reserve role for foreign exchange. But the interwar gold exchange standard flopped. The first problem was that *adjustment* to trade imbalances was no longer rapid, automatic, and smooth: labor unions, and occasionally even their employers, resisted the drop in the nominal wage that was supposed to begin the necessary cycle of domestic deflation. Despite the gold standard, therefore, domestic price levels did not adjust to re-equilibrate trade imbalances. Instead, gold drained from Britain, for example, and entered both France and Germany, whose central banks in the late 1920s enjoyed domestic political support for tight money policies because of popular memories of high inflation in the early 1920s. *Liquidity* was problematic for the same reason it had been in the freely floating days of the early 1920s: investors declined to trust currencies backed by foreign exchange, preferring only gold, but there was insufficient gold to support the expansion in the world economy that had occurred since the early twentieth century. Countries whose central banks held foreign exchange as reserves, or foolishly expanded the domestic money supply in response to domestic economic conditions, were punished by private capital flight. The overall result was a purely monetary drag on world economic growth (Friedman 1992).

The restored gold standard also failed to deliver *stability* (Kindleberger 1986). The combination of the French franc's devalued rate plus the Bank of France's extremely tight and conservative domestic monetary policy exacerbated Britain's competitive problems. In 1928 and 1929 the banking systems of Austria, Hungary, and then Germany crashed as industrial borrowers could not meet their nominal debt obligations under conditions of deflation. In 1929 the U.S.

stock market also crashed, despite the efforts of the Federal Reserve Bank prior to the crash to induce investors to switch out of corporate stocks by setting high interest rates. The combination of the dramatic fall in banks' own net worth (because of their large holdings of corporate stocks) and tight money generated a huge banking crisis in the United States. Britain suspended convertibility and devalued in 1931. The United States went off of gold under newly inaugurated President Franklin Delano Roosevelt in early 1933, and the dollar fell almost 40 percent in nine months.

From 1932 to 1939 most countries followed a managed float—a term that here denotes the efforts of individual countries, through foreign exchange intervention by their central banks, to stabilize their exchange rates, but does not imply that coordinated, multilateral efforts were common. From the beginning, the managed float of the 1930s was a system that limped. *Adjustment* was minimal. Currencies were not convertible and few governments permitted free movement of capital. Under floating rates, trade rebalancing was supposed to happen via exchange rate movements. Yet the bad experience with high exchange rate volatility in the early 1920s initially led most governments in the 1930s to intervene to counter market movements, hoping to dampen wild exchange rate swings. In addition, the lack of trust and coordination among the governments of the major economies rendered such national exchange rate interventions both expensive and ineffective.[9] The other strategies for re-equilibration were "competitive devaluation"[10] and trade protectionism, as in the United States' infamous Smoot-Hawley Tariff of 1930. *Liquidity* remained uncertain and insufficient: the markets trusted only gold, and occasionally U.S. dollars, yet there was not enough gold to support economic expansion. Empirically, the system was *stable* in that it did not generate major crises before it was broken up by the coming of the Second World War. However, the lack of financial crises largely resulted from the degree to which most countries had isolated themselves from previously open international financial markets: these costs were felt everywhere in reduced trade and growth. Most of the putative stability, that is, came from nationally imposed capital controls, which exacted a high efficiency cost in terms of both foregone trade and investment.

Despite the best intentions of finance ministers and central bankers, none of the financial architectures of the interwar years was a success, though contemporaries had a hard time understanding exactly why.

Bretton Woods Regime (1944–73)

The experiences of the Great Depression and the Second World War, not to mention the theories and persuasive efforts of crucial individuals such as John Maynard Keynes, altered the reigning ideological parameters in the major powers of the international system (Hall 1989). After the war, Western Europe embraced national economic planning and even the United States began to rely on Keynesian demand management by the federal government. Moreover, influential intellectuals blamed the war itself on isolationism and lack of mutual cooperation among the major powers. The hostility between the Western Allies and the Soviet Union at the war's end also aided multilateralism among the capitalist democracies by giving the West an enemy to unite against. For all of these reasons, financial and economic policymakers in the soon-to-be-victorious Allies supported the convening of a multicountry conference at Bretton Woods, New Hampshire, in 1944 to work out a new, cooperative, and explicit financial and economic architecture for the postwar era (Helleiner 1994). The biggest change from the past, therefore, was not in any of the specific arrangements per se: the interwar period had seen experimentation with a great many permutations of particular rules. Rather, intentional multilateral management by the representatives of sovereign states— with decision power concentrated in the great powers of the time, particularly the United States and Britain—was the bedrock of the new international financial regime. The United Nations, a resurrection and rethinking of the failed League of Nations of the early 1920s, embodied a similar cooperative and multilateral understanding about how to ensure world peace.

Harry Dexter White and John Maynard Keynes, negotiators for the United States and Britain, respectively, dominated the talks that led up to the Bretton Woods agreement. With respect to *adjustment*, neither floating rates nor the gold exchange standard of the interwar years had proved effective. The proposed solution was an "adjustable peg," that is, a fixed rate system (which it was hoped could avoid the instability of floating rates), with major currencies convertible into U.S. dollars, these in turn to be convertible at a fixed par value into gold. To avoid the phenomenon of countries entering seemingly permanently into either surplus or deficit, exchange rates were to be periodically adjustable—but only when a country was willing to request multilateral permission, in the form of acceptance by the International Monetary Fund. The IMF was a new institution charged with the ongoing tasks of monitoring international trade and payments, providing incentives for good monetary and fiscal behavior by member countries, and extending relatively short-term assistance to member countries experiencing temporary balance of payments problems.[11]

In the long run, the worst performance of the BW architecture was in the arena of adjustment. The intended reason for IMF pre-certification of currency devaluations or revaluations was to prevent countries from engaging in them frivolously, such as for the purpose of gaining a temporary trade advantage from devaluation vis-à-vis a competitor. However, in practice countries seldom consulted the IMF ahead of time, as they reasonably feared that news of the planned devaluation might leak beforehand to the financial markets. Moreover, most countries proved very reluctant to devalue, which was perceived as a loss of prestige and credibility for the government. So the "adjustable" pegs behaved like firmly fixed rates, and were not really available as an instrument to adjust national economies to trade imbalances through shifts in trade prices. At the same time, governments in the post–World War II era were even less interested than those in the interwar years in implementing the technically appropriate adjustment mechanism for fixed exchange rates: tight money and austerity to reduce domestic economic activity and thus shrink a trade deficit, and the reverse for a trade surplus. So adjustment was finessed by trade barriers and/or postponed by capital inflows.

The United States, at the core of the system, did not have balanced trade accounts. For approximately the first fifteen years, the United States ran a continual trade surplus and Western Europe and the rest of the world a corresponding deficit. This was so even though most European currencies were not even convertible on current account until 1959, meaning that these governments rationed all access to foreign currency, even for permissible merchandise imports. Up through the early 1960s, large net capital outflows from the United States made this structural imbalance possible by relieving pressure on the currencies of trade deficit countries. Thereafter, the positions reversed, with the U.S. merchandise trade surplus steadily shrinking to nothing in 1971. Moreover, and utterly perversely from a purely technical viewpoint, the United States continued to be a large net exporter of capital. Consequently, U.S. official reserve assets of gold and foreign exchange shrunk steadily after 1957, eventually provoking the unilateral American actions that ended the Bretton Woods regime (Odell 1982, 203–206 and passim). Further stories of persistent non-adjustment could be told of many other core countries. The fundamental problem was that national policymakers were unwilling to subordinate domestic macroeconomic policies to the goal of defending the exchange rate, a necessary component of a fixed exchange rate regime with even limited free private capital flows (Mundell 1960).

The postwar agreement on *liquidity* was pragmatic: the dollar was the only currency strong enough to be immediately convertible after the war. IMF member countries, including all of the core capitalist states (and soon the major defeated states as well, though not the Soviet bloc) were encouraged to hold their reserves in the form of both gold and U.S. dollars, so that global growth would not be entirely dependent upon new gold discoveries. As compared to earlier decades (or the present!), policymakers had scant faith in the ability of private voluntary capital flows to provide liquidity either for easing temporary balance of payments pressures in specific countries or for greasing the wheels of global growth more generally. The IMF, therefore, would have at its disposal quotas of the national currencies of all member countries. It could lend foreign exchange out to countries with temporary trade imbalances at prespecified rates of interest and with increasingly tough "conditionality," that is, requirements for domestic policy reform, typically fiscal and monetary tightening. The BW financial architecture, meanwhile, left decisions about controls on private cross-border financial flows up to national governments. Although IMF member countries were encouraged to restore current account convertibility quickly, the IMF Articles of Agreement explicitly legitimated enduring national barriers to cross-border capital flows. Interestingly, the designers of the BW architecture also viewed the intentional promotion of long-term international investment as a legitimate core goal of a successful financial architecture. The IMF's sister organization, today known as the World Bank, used its initial capital subscriptions from member countries to borrow long-term in private capital markets, while loaning long-term to governments for specific capital investment projects.

Over the subsequent three decades the provision of liquidity under the Bretton Woods system was generally satisfactory, although the actual arrangements were not quite those initially envisioned. The U.S. dollar so effectively augmented monetary gold that world growth hummed (see the chapter by David Felix). There was no liquidity constraint at the system level. In many respects dollar holdings were even more attractive for central banks than gold, in that dollar holdings frequently took the form of interest–earning Treasury securities. This highly effective solution to the global liquidity dilemma, a major problem under the interwar financial architecture, of course was intimately linked to the failure of the United States to equilibrate its trade and payments imbalances. The world economy needed liquidity, and the United States was a large net emitter of dollars. As early as 1960, dollars held outside the United States exceeded the total American stock of monetary gold (Eichengreen 1996, 116). A rush by foreigners to convert their dollars in principle would have bankrupted the key currency country. In the 1960s, the U.S. government also began to worry about the large sums of U.S. private investment abroad and tried to limit it with outward capital controls (Hawley 1987). Naturally the Europeans, the other major players in the postwar decades, were not unaware of the power this unique ability to print and spend money abroad gave the United States. They tried unsuccessfully to place the function of global liquidity provision back with the IMF, first through obligatory quota increases and later through the creation of a new international "currency" backed by the basket of national currencies held by the IMF.[12] Like it or not, the Bretton Woods key currency system both required and perpetuated U.S. financial hegemony.

Perhaps the most important function initially envisioned for the IMF, meanwhile, was that of ensuring *stability* in international financial markets. If countries followed procedure and checked with the IMF's board of governors before they devalued, then the waves of "competitive devaluations" that were perceived to have generated so much trouble in the 1930s could be avoided. Moreover, the BW conferees expected that the IMF could and should function as the world's lender of last resort, extending credit to national central banks whose gold and foreign exchange reserves were under threat, perhaps due to a panic that went far beyond any objective domestic or international economic policy flaws. White, Keynes, and their peers from less dominant countries agreed that many of the financial, currency, and banking crises that spread rapidly from neighbor to neighbor in 1928 through the early 1930s might have been avoided had a decisive LLR stepped in to stem the panic at any of several crucial stages.

Governance of the International Monetary Fund, it should be noted, was designed to reflect, at least roughly, the economic—and, less explicitly but no less surely, the military and strategic—strength of the member countries, with votes on the governing board being proportional to financial contributions. This scheme of representation, similar to the veto of the permanent members of the Security Council in the United Nations, was intended to give powerful countries a reason to believe that they received a net benefit from the creation of multilateral institutions, even though they could not wholly control them. The big differences between the BW system and the previous financial architectures, it bears reemphasizing, lay in the new architecture's emphasis on continuous, regularized, multilateral cooperation and international monetary governance.

The BW financial architecture in fact provided satisfactory international financial stability for nearly thirty years. Of course there were various crises, including a run on sterling in 1947, an emergency devaluation of the pound in 1949, and large capital outflows in the United States following the election of Democrat John F. Kennedy in late 1959. But all were handled by means of partially institutionalized crisis management by the great powers, particularly the United States, Britain, France, and Germany, who in each case supported one another's currencies and/or arranged a consensual exchange rate realignment. Interestingly, the governments of the core capitalist states soon discovered that they had more freedom of action if they simply bypassed the IMF, in which numerous small states also held membership, and dealt directly with one another. The United States set this pattern early on.[13] That is, ad hoc crisis management became more important than originally envisioned, and institutionalized multilateral monetary governance somewhat less so, over the years.

Even the end of the Bretton Woods financial architecture, which generally is referred to as a "crisis," can instead be understood as illustrating the regime's remarkable ability to handle serious disagreements among key actors, and to finesse fundamental economic disequilibria. The lack of a well–functioning adjustment mechanism, plus the U.S. dollar's key role in providing liquidity, meant that trade imbalances and their attendant stresses were bound to accumulate. The United States argued that it should not have to devalue the dollar in relation to gold: American leaders wanted to keep their decades old relationship of $35 to the ounce of gold 9/10 fine—even though nonmonetary gold was by the late 1960s worth considerably more than this. The Europeans, particularly the French and the Germans, were unwilling to revalue their currencies, which had transactional and reputational costs, when they viewed the problem as principally of American making.[14]

Just as the U.S. trade balance was dipping into deficits in 1971, President Richard Nixon and Treasury Secretary John Connolly acted to avert a run on the dollar by announcing that it was no longer automatically convertible into gold. They addressed the trade problem directly by imposing a temporary across-the-board import surcharge of 10 percent, an instance of using the United States huge market power as a blunt weapon to force its major trading partners to revalue. In the end they did revalue, while the United States also agreed to devalue (Odell 1982). There was some acrimony, but no crisis. The major powers announced a new, more balanced system of fixed rates in 1973. However, in the absence of any significant alterations in the financial architecture, the markets found the new parities not credible, and runs on various major currencies forced them to float in the mid-1970s. In other words, the stability framework of partially institutionalized consultations (sometimes through the IMF, other times outside), along with ad hoc management by the major players (a designation that covers both the United States' dramatic but not wild decision to break the link with gold and other countries' considered responses), was remarkably successful in avoiding breakdowns of international trade or payments and in protecting domestic financial systems.

Post–Bretton Woods Financial Architecture (1973–Present)

With the shift of major countries to floating exchange rates, the adjustment (or non-adjustment) mechanism of the Bretton Woods financial architecture was gone. The big contrast between the subsequent architecture, often unimaginatively designated the "post–Bretton Woods" (PBW) system, and its famous predecessor was that the newer architecture was not, at least initially, carefully negotiated among the contracting parties. The current arrangements have been termed a "non-system," though this is not quite the case. Soon after the decisions to float, the major powers formed the Group of Seven (G7), a forum of finance ministers and central bank governors from the United States, Germany, Japan, Britain, France, Italy, and Canada, with a brief to consult regularly on monetary and economic affairs of mutual interest (Bergsten and Henning 1996). During the next decades, other partially intersecting groupings also provided informal system management, including the Bank for International Settlements (BIS), the central bankers' organization founded in 1930, which since the early 1960s has brought together central bankers in the core economies on a monthly basis. The IMF, moreover, continues to receive regular reports from all of its members, and to offer them regular advice, though only borrowers are obliged to accept it!

On the surface, the *adjustment* mechanism differs dramatically from that of the BW regime. Since the mid-1970s, most of the major economies have had floating exchange rates, while smaller countries most often have pegged, either to the currency of their major trading partner or to a trade-weighted basket of currencies. In principle, this means that adjustment comes via shifts in relative prices of imports and locally produced goods. There has been considerable exchange rate volatility, even among the major economies (see the chapters by David Felix and Erik Jones). The G7 countries on occasion have engaged in joint intervention to manage exchange rates, such as via the so-called Plaza Accord in 1985 to push the dollar down (Henning 1994) or, more recently, in the autumn of 2000 to support the euro. Many international economists would like to see the exchange rates of major currencies managed more actively, arguing that much of the volatility is unnecessary and harmful to economic growth (for example, Bergsten 1998; Coeuré and Pisani-Ferry 1999). Nonetheless, the yen rose 45 percent against the dollar and 65 percent against the euro between its lowest point in 1998 and its highest one in the first half of 2000, suggesting that exchange rate volatility is not abating (BIS 2000, 84).

As noted, in the past capital controls frequently have substituted for domestic price flexibility in periods of floating exchange rates. One principal trend for the post–Bretton Woods "non-system" has been toward national deregulation of private international capital flows, as well as a complementary breaking down of barriers among previously distinct segments of domestic financial markets in the major industrial countries. The United States had implemented fairly free external private capital flows by the late 1970s, and since the 1980s has lobbied hard for other countries to do likewise (Armijo 2000). Had it not been for the 1997–1999 Asian financial crisis, the IMF in 1998 would have followed through with its intended rewriting of its Articles of Agreement to incorporate, for the first time, a formal obligation of all members to move rapidly toward full capital account convertibility. The quantity and volatility of capital circulating in global financial markets has ballooned enormously since the late 1970s, in tandem with the relaxation of capital controls worldwide (see the chapters by Felix and Cohen below). However, the combination of floating exchange rates and increasingly free capital movements has not made adjustment to external imbalances easy or automatic. Among the more serious problems are inflexible domestic prices and incomes (especially in the industrial countries) and huge speculative swings in the capital account, delinked from any plausible changes in the trade balance or the real domestic economy (especially in the developing countries).

Overall, adjustment under the post–Bretton Woods financial architecture frequently has been unsatisfactory. Because both foreign central banks and foreign private citizens want to hold dollars, the U.S. currency has remained overvalued, thus rendering imports into the United States artificially cheap and provoking an ever larger trade deficit. Private capital flows were supposed to ease the adjustment process, not postpone it indefinitely, but this seems to be what has happened. After about 1971 the U.S. trade balance was steadily negative. In 1981, the entire current account became negative, thus transforming the United States into a net capital importer. In 1998, the U.S. net foreign asset position became negative for the first time since World War II, indicating that foreigners owned more U.S. real and financial property than American citizens did abroad (BIS 2000).

The reserve standard in the PBW era has been the unadorned U.S. dollar, which today is convertible only into goods, services, or other currencies, at real rates that fluctuate with the market. *Liquidity* has been much less problematic than adjustment for the system, in that the United States' external deficits have provided ample credit for the global economy most of the time. The global financial architecture proved adequate to the task of recycling the so-called "petrodollars" accumulated by oil exporting countries in the 1970s and "solving" the Latin America debt crisis of the 1980s, at least from the viewpoint of the major creditor banks, whose insolvency would have threatened the economies of the G7 countries and thus the global economy (Kapstein 1994). At the same time, the credibility of international finance continues to be tightly wedded to the fortunes of the U.S. dollar, which remains the world's key currency. In the late 1990s a few pundits began seriously questioning whether the dollar's dominance could or should last (see Cohen 2000, as well as the chapters by Henry Laurence and Erik Jones in this volume). Yet the technical, not to mention the political, challenges of a world of multiple key currencies remain nebulous. A worrisome thought is that a regime of competing reserve currencies might provide much weaker incentives on the part of any given participant to support the value and credibility of any given key currency.

It is largely because of doubts about the current regime's ability to continue to ensure *stability* that the contemporary debate over reform of the international financial architecture has arisen. As in the Bretton Woods period, crisis management under the PBW financial architecture has been partially institutionalized. Since its formation in the mid–1970s the G7 has performed most of the global economic steering functions that ostensibly were to have occurred within the IMF. The seemingly odd transformation of the G7 into the G8 with the addition of Russia in the 1990s merely reflects the fact that the G7 is an organization of core capitalist states, who use it to manage the global political economy as they see fit.[15] The European Community, after 1979 through the European Monetary System, has played a similar collective crisis management role in monetary affairs at the regional level (see Eichengreen 1996, 152–181 and this volume's chapter by Erik Jones). System management in times of acute crisis, however, has in most instances fallen to the United States, or to Germany for European panics. For example, U.S. treasury secretaries coordinated the rich country responses to the 1980s Latin American debt crisis, the 1994–95 Mexican and Latin American peso crisis and the 1997–1999 Asian financial crisis (see the chapter by Mark Brawley). At the close of the twentieth century, the global financial and monetary system remained infinitely more centralized in its resources and governance practices than, for example, the global trading system.

In somewhat uneasy coexistence with the emerging PBW norm of capital account deregulation is a recent trend by the major advanced industrial countries to re-regulate, through multilateral channels, certain global capital flows that they consider dangerous. Those capital controls that might protect industrial country banks, depositors, and investors tend to be conceived of as "prudential regulation," which makes them ideologically acceptable. For example, bank regulators from the major advanced industrial countries negotiated through the BIS to arrive in 1988 at consensual standards for regulating transational commercial banks, the "Basle Capital Adequacy" ratios (Kapstein 1994). National securities regulators, some public and some private, in the 1980s and 1990s began meeting under the auspices of the International Organization of Securities Commissions (IOSCO) to standardize domestic capital markets legislation worldwide (Porter 1999). In mid-2000, negotiators from the Organization for Economic Cooperation and Development (OECD) countries finally seemed to have agreed on a comprehensive set of capital controls, with stringent penalties for noncompliance, to reduce global money laundering through small, financially open tax haven countries, such as Bermuda or the Cayman Islands—although the laissez-faire administration of U.S. President George W. Bush was unwilling to support these multilateral controls until after the September 11, 2001 attacks on the United States. However, there is no agreement—and precious little high-level discussion within forums controlled by the G7—on collective institutional innovations to curb the kinds of volatile capital flows that in the 1990s ravaged the economies of so many developing countries. Despite limited multilateral cooperation on "prudential" norms and greater data sharing ("transparency"), the dominant trend today is for external financial liberalization.

There are good reasons to question the future stability of the post–Bretton Woods international financial architecture. The volatility and sheer quantity of private capital in the international system continue to increase rapidly. Moreover, the size of emergency financial bailout packages increased markedly in the 1990s. For example, in December, 2000, the IMF coordinated a credit line of $37 billion for Argentina, representing an extraordinary 13 percent of that country's GDP. In the previous five years, even larger packages in terms of absolute amounts or their weight in the recipient's economy had gone to Mexico, Thailand, Korea, and Indonesia. At the same time, both opinion leaders and the attentive portions of the public around the world—but most significantly in the core capitalist states—since the mid-1990s have been increasingly dissatisfied with the crisis management performance of the IMF, the "markets," and dominant governments such as that of the United States. One consequence has been the present debate over reform of the international financial architecture.

A Rough Assessment

Table 1.3 assays a more formal rating exercise. It should not be taken too seriously, but at the same time its ranking of the four historical architectures is unlikely to be very controversial. I subjectively judge each historical financial regime in terms of how well it fulfilled the basic functions of adjustment, liquidity, and stability, *as understood by policymakers and opinion leaders of the time.* In other words, the standards of judgment explicitly are not constant—which is more than half of the point of the exercise. Politically relevant contemporary observers of the classical gold standard, who were of course members of the elite, found domestic deflation an acceptable means of adjustment to a trade deficit, and recognized that flexible prices, incomes, and capital flows, along with Bank of England leadership, provided the system with considerable stability, even when particular actors, or markets, experienced crises. Astute finance ministers, however, recognized that leaving liquidity growth entirely to chance was not optimal. On a scale of 0 (unsatisfactory), 1 (mostly unsatisfactory), 2 (mostly satisfactory), or 3 (satisfactory) for performance in each important function of a financial architecture, one might award the classical gold standard a score of "excellent," or roughly 89 percent satisfactory, as shown in the table. It is no wonder that the financial architecture of the gold standard was fervently professed at the time, stood as a beacon of stability for envious interwar policymakers, and retains committed adherents even today.

In contrast, the monetary experiments of the interwar period have had few defenders, then or now. I assess the interwar financial and monetary experiments as a group as "mostly unsatisfactory" in terms of both adjustment and liquidity, and "unsatisfactory" in the provision of stability, for a score of 2/9 or only 22 percent satisfactory performance. Most observers, I believe, would rate the Bretton Woods financial architecture as a success, though perhaps not quite as seamless a triumph *in terms of the goals of incumbent policymakers in the major states* as the pre–World War I architecture. The BW architecture provided liquidity and stability, though imperfect adjustment was a constant source of friction among the major industrial states. I award it 7 of 9 possible points, for an overall score of "good."

In the final quarter of the twentieth century, as in the third quarter, global liquidity growth has not been a problem, as the world has remained willing to absorb any overhang of U.S. dollars. But, despite the shift to floating exchange rates, adjustment to trade imbalances has been neither easy nor automatic, while

Table 1.3 Performance of Historical Financial Architectures

International Financial Architecture	Adjustment Satisfactory?	Liquidity Satisfactory?	Stability Satisfactory?	Overall*
Classical Gold Standard ~ 1870–1914	Yes	Mostly yes	Yes	Excellent (89%)
Interwar Drift 1919–1939	Mostly no	Mostly no	No	Poor (22%)
Bretton Woods System 1944– ~1971	Mostly no	Yes	Yes	Good (78%)
Post–Bretton Woods System ~ 1973–Present	Mostly no	Yes	Mostly yes to 1990, but less so thereafter	Good to Fair (67% and falling)

*Overall score calculated on the basis of equal weights for satisfactory perfomance in each function, with "no" = 0, "mostly no" = 1, "mostly yes" = 2, and "yes" = 3. Note that the assessment, while subjective, is intended to reflect the views of national policymakers in key countries during each period.

imbalances originating in the capital account seem to have become a permanent feature of the system. Moreover, maintaining stability has required much more active intervention and management by the major states than their leaders initially expected or would have preferred. By the late 1990s, the PBW architecture's ability to prevent or ameliorate future crises was enough in question that an authority such as Paul Volcker, a former chairman of the U.S. Federal Reserve Bank, could write in the conservative *Financial Times*, "The problems we see with such force today are systemic—they arise from within the ordinary workings of global financial capitalism" (1998, n.p.). In the view of many contemporaries, the performance of the post–Bretton Woods financial architecture was, by the turn of the twenty-first century, rapidly slipping from "good" to "fair."

THE SOCIAL EMBEDDEDNESS OF FINANCIAL ARCHITECTURE: THE TERMS OF THE DEBATE THAT MIGHT BE

What makes for a successful financial architecture? Suppose we accept the rough relative judgments of the preceding section. What explains these outcomes? This section reviews several attempts to account for the variable performance of past financial architectures, in the hope that they might prove enlightening for understanding present challenges. My conclusion is that an international monetary framework that is inconsistent with underlying political and social realities is unlikely to work very well or last very long. Today's significant world political trends are, first, increasing multipolarity in the interstate system and, second, the rise of mass procedural political democracy as the dominant form of organizing domestic political life. An international financial architecture that ignores these global shifts will be precarious.

The Perfect Set of Rules?

One answer is that there is a *single best financial architecture* for all historical circumstances, at least if we limit ourselves to the modern industrial world. Quite a number of reasonable people accept this notion, mostly those with an overriding faith in free markets not only as a panacea for world economic troubles, but as a solution for many political disagreements as well. As noted, the majority of policymakers during the interwar years believed that the classical gold standard financial architecture would work automatically and elegantly, if only governments would be responsible and recreate it forthwith. The failures of the interwar monetary experiments did much to discredit this faith. However, the belief that a restored gold standard, or perhaps a rigorous gold exchange standard with little to no monetary policy discretion for individual countries, could solve today's myriad problems of adjustment, liquidity, and stability is far from dead. The editors of the *Wall Street Journal*, a far from inconsequential media outlet, frequently lament the loss of the certainties of the gold standard, and even advocate a return to such a financial architecture or its close equivalent. By the logic of the "one best design" hypothesis, international financial instability is explained by the imperfect policies adopted by national leaders, who need to be educated to the error of their ways: the political realm tends be viewed primarily as an impediment to sensible reform. This teleology is popular with those whom I identify in section four as laissez-faire liberalizers, and with a few anti-globalizers, but remains unconvincing to the majority of observers.

Technological Determinism

An alternative view holds that the global stage of *economic and technological advancement* determines the appropriate financial architecture. There is no one best set of monetary rules and institutions for all time; instead, financial regulation must be modernized along with our modes of transport and communication. The principal argument of contemporary technological determinists is that today's globalization of capital flows is fundamentally a result of advances in telecommunications and computers, enabling such innovations as nearly instantaneous settlement of market trades and twenty-four-hour global trading.

Interestingly, this thesis can lead to two somewhat different conclusions. The first and more widespread is that external financial markets liberalization and ever deepening global integration is inevitable and not really controllable by governments. If one kind of capital movement is prohibited, those desiring it will simply find disguised ways to perform the same transfer, and these subterfuges will be both more destabilizing and less efficient than the prohibited flow itself would have been (see, for example, Bryant 1987). By this logic, adjustment and liquidity will be autonomously provided by the markets, and the only recourse for governments wishing to regulate for purposes of stability is to press one another for publication of more timely and accurate accounting of capital flows and related macroeconomic indicators. Neither control nor regulation of jet speed international capital flows may be possible, but better, more timely, more transparent information can help the markets to cope, perhaps reducing overshooting or even irrational panics.

Yet the same facts can lead to the opposite conclusion. Perhaps the heightened contemporary interdependence of previously national markets enhances both the necessity for and the possibility of achieving cooperative multilateral regulation. As countries' national strategies for achieving trade adjustment, smooth monetary expansion at a rate commensurate with real economic growth, and monetary and financial stability all become more vulnerable to exogenous shocks, the logical response is increasingly to relocate regulation from the national to the international level. After all, this reasoning seems to be reflected in the decision of most of the members of the European Community to move to outright monetary union (see the chapter by Erik Jones). Where once national, or even subnational, financial regulation was technically appropriate, over the past two or three decades it has become increasingly inappropriate.

Alternatively, one might view the problem less as an economist would (asking what the appropriate set of regulations should be) and more through the lens of a political scientist (by inquiring into the decision process and its legitimacy). That is, we might instead proceed within a different intellectual framework, one which emphasizes the fundamental and inescapable implications of the social systems within which international financial architectures operate. Political and other social scientists have long argued that social and economic institutions that are congruent with underlying distributions of social and political power tend to function more smoothly than regulatory or legal frameworks that presuppose a different set of actors, preferences, and capabilities. Both of the remaining two interpretations of the performance of alternative historical financial architectures discussed in this section share the view that different social systems require distinct types of international rules for money and credit.

Hegemonic Stability

The *theory of hegemonic stability*, also discussed at some length in the chapter by Mark Brawley below, focuses at the international level of analysis.[16] The label has been applied, usually by third parties, to the work of scholars such as Charles Kindleberger ([1973] 1986, 1981), Stephen Krasner (1976), and Robert Gilpin (1987, 2000). The core hypothesis suggests that an open international political economy, including an international financial architecture supportive of vibrant trade and free markets, will run most smoothly and effectively when a single dominant state, the *hegemon,* steps forward to manage the system, identifying success or failure with its own national assumptions. Abstracting from specific approaches and analyses, the argument rests on two broad assumptions (Conybeare 1984; Snidal 1985; Lake 1993). The first is that no market, including financial markets, operates automatically. Instead, markets operate within a socially constructed framework of expectations and protections for participants, a framework which does not exist within a state of nature and cannot ever be taken for granted. For example, markets depend on expectations of continued free trade, universalistic rather than particularistic treatment of buyers and sellers ("everyone's money is the same color"), expectations that written contracts will be honored, and an understood network of consequences for noncompliance. Markets thus require a scaffolding of rules and institutions which, in turn, need conscious, active management.

A crucial second assumption is that hegemonic management, or decision making by a single leader or single dominant state, is considerably easier and more efficient than collective management, all other dimensions being equal.[17] System management requires expenditure of scarce resources. If there are multiple managers, not only may they disagree about policy design and implementation, but each may be tempted to "free ride," or to contribute little to the joint regulatory effort, while reaping the collective benefits of financial adjustment, liquidity, and stability, from which it is difficult to exclude any participant. A hegemon can make decisions more quickly. At the same time, a hegemon typically also can skew an international economic regime so that it receives a larger than average share of the benefits, as an (implicit) return for paying the lion's share of regime maintenance costs.[18] For example, a country that maintains the global financial architecture probably also provides the key reserve currency and has the dominant and most profitable international financial sector. The main implication of hegemonic stability theory for our purposes is its hypothesis that the international financial architecture, whatever its specific institutional arrangements, will work best when the international balance of power is such that one country is considerably more influential and possessed of resources than its fellows, and when that country desires, for its own reasons, to manage a reasonably open international financial architecture.[19]

The theory of hegemonic stability thus has something important to say about why and when financial architectures fail or succeed. Suppose we define a hegemon as a country whose total capabilities—including both standard "power resources" such as military strength, population, and gross national product, as well as such difficult to measure qualities as the "credibility" of its institutions with international investors—are enough larger than those of its nearest competitors that, when it expresses a decisive preference in the international sphere, other countries feel obliged to go along, either because the hegemon somehow compels them to, or simply because the hegemon provides a convenient means for solving problems of coordination.[20] Realized hegemony is actual international leadership. This, in turn, is a function of a state's capabilities, its desire to exercise leadership, and, to some extent, how others in the system perceive such leadership, which is to say, whether others find leadership useful or onerous.

Instances of realized international hegemony have coincided with those historical financial architectures that commonly are judged to have been the greatest successes, as shown in the first column of table 1.5.[21] The pre–World War I era was a period of British hegemony, both economic and, to a lesser extent, military. Britain's ability to lead in the economic and monetary arena was based upon its share of world overseas investments, still 44 percent in 1914, its leadership in trade, London's role as the international financial center, the overwhelming dominance of sterling in international transactions and global foreign exchange reserves, the credibility of the Bank of England, and, last but hardly least, on its government's demonstrated willingness to manage a relatively open global trading and financial regime among the major capitalist states of the time.[22] That is, I assess the period as hegemonic, even though by the turn of the century the United States, and on some dimensions both the United States and Germany, had overtaken Britain on several objective measures of economic and military capability, including share of world industrial production, iron and steel consumption, energy consumption, and GDP (Lairson and Skidmore 1997, 45–48; Maddison 1995, 182). The classical gold standard architecture arguably worked because Great Britain stood ready to defend the pound, the integrity of the currencies of its major trading and strategic partners in Europe, and to maintain open markets even while others reimposed protectionism in the very late nineteenth-century.

In contrast, the tragedy of the interwar years was that the only state that might have possessed the capabilities to assume a global leadership role, the United States, was uninterested in doing so. The U.S. refusal was evidenced in the security realm by its failure to join the League of Nations, and in the economic realm by its inability to see the possible value, both for itself and for the interstate system, of paying some of the upfront costs of maintaining a liberal international economy. Such costs to the United States might have included more open domestic markets, more liberal capital exports (private or if necessary public, as was the case following World War II), and greater willingness to risk inflation to maintain growth of the U.S. economy, which even then was the engine for much of the rest of the world (see especially Kindleberger [1973] 1986). Britain tried to reconstruct the gold standard in the 1920s, but was not up to the task, particularly given its prestige-driven decision to restore sterling's prewar gold parity, despite England's considerable wartime inflation. Overall, the interstate system during the interwar years was multipolar, not hegemonic. There were three strong powers: the United States, Germany, and Britain. Unfortunately, there was no leadership during the 1920s and 1930s that was both sufficiently strong and committed to the maintenance of an open global economy. Consequently, both the liberal trading system and the financial architectures that might have supported it collapsed.

By the close of World War II, the question of international primacy across a range of both military and economic capabilities had been settled in favor of the United States. The United States accepted its position of leadership and was willing to exercise it, if not altruistically then at least responsibly. Moreover, the security threat to the capitalist democracies from the Soviet Union and its allies served as a powerful incentive for both Western Europe and Japan to accept U.S. leadership in the Cold War, which was waged through military, economic, and political means. Through the Bretton Woods agreement, and successive actions both cooperative and unilateral, the United States thereafter imposed its economic preferences upon the international system, but also acted to stabilize the world economy, opening its markets to foreign imports by debtor countries, sending large amounts of capital abroad, and providing the liquidity needed for global expansion (Gilpin 1987). One consequence was unprecedented global growth.

The hegemonic stability hypothesis also offers a potentially straightforward explanation for the breakdown of the BW regime. Just as the international monetary framework created at Bretton Woods was cracking, proximately impelled by the self-interested policy choices of the Nixon Administration, the United States' relative primacy in the economic sphere also was declining. As shown in Table 1.4, the American share of the total gross domestic product (GDP) of all of the high-income members of the OECD fell from 52 percent in 1960 to 47 percent in 1970. In other words, what really happened in the early 1970s was that the United States, no longer possessed of the abundant resources necessary to lead, had opted to try to protect itself, even though this undercut a global financial architecture that had proven extremely felicitous, at least from the viewpoint of ensuring global economic growth (see the chapter by David Felix). Nonetheless, it is controversial to suggest that the Bretton Woods international financial architecture broke down in the early 1970s because of a decline in U.S. capabilities relative to those of the other great powers. Mark Brawley in this volume, for example, argues not that the United States was less hegemonic, but that its self-interest in providing global monetary leadership had changed. One could just as easily be surprised that a fixed rate regime endured as long as it did, given its difficulties in providing adjustment (Eichengreen 1996, 123).

In any case, by the yardstick for recognizing hegemony suggested in this chapter, which is effective international leadership on issues chosen by the putative hegemon, the United States in the final decades of the twentieth century arguably was as much a hegemon in the monetary and financial arena as ever.[23] So is the United States today a declining or a reigning hegemon? Two observations seem clear. First, as an economic power, the United States in the first decade of the twenty-first century continues to be first among equals, and its policymakers succeed in shaping international agreements an extraordinary share of the time, particularly in the monetary and financial arena. Second, however, the degree by which American capabilities today exceed those of its allies and potential rivals is substantially less than it was during the immediate postwar decades. I suggest that the current international balance of power represents a case of gradually declining U.S. dominance, and consequently a situation of rising global multipolarity. If the theory of hegemonic stability is valid, then designing and managing an effective international financial architecture for the twenty-first century therefore will be a more difficult task than constructing and maintaining the Bretton Woods regime was. Some partisans of the theory would stop here. However, one also could go beyond this prediction to reason that, given declining hegemony, future world financial governance will be particularly problematic if the United States resists the orderly replacement of unilateral leadership with institutionalized, multilateral, and somewhat representative decision making in global monetary relations. (It is not as though a new, as yet reluctant, hegemon were waiting in the wings, as arguably was the case during the interwar years.)

Table 1.4 shows that the U.S. share of the GDP of the advanced capitalist countries fell from 52 percent in 1960 to only 35 percent in 1980, declining more slowly through the 1980s to reach 34 percent in 1990. In the 1970s and especially the 1980s there was every evidence that the relative primacy of the United States was declining; America was becoming, in the words of Richard Rosecrance (1976), an "ordinary country." A spate of scholarly analyses in the late 1980s and early 1990s tried to understand the sources of America's apparent decline, with many predicting increased economic and political uncertainty, not only for the United States but also—and this point is the crucial one—for the global postwar international political and economic system(s) as well. Robert Gilpin (1987) and others, for example, worried over the growing prominence of Japan in global capital markets, wondering whether the share of total new U.S. Treasury issues purchased by Japanese financial institutions was lulling the United States into a dangerous state of dependency. Paul Kennedy (1987) also concluded

Table 1.4 Rising Multipolarity? GDP at Market Prices

	1960	1970	1980	1990	1998
U.S. as % of GDP of High Income OECD Members*	52	47	35	34	38
5 EMCs** as % of GDP of High-Income OECD Members	13	11	12	10	13
5 EMCs as % of GDP of U.S.	25	24	34	30	35

* High income OECD includes the United States.
** The 5 emerging market countries (EMCs) are Brazil, China, India, Korea, and Mexico.
Source: World Bank, World Development Indicators 2000, CD-ROM.

that the relative power of the United States in the world was bound to decline. Others, such as Joseph Nye (1990), emphasized the myriad dimensions along which the United States remained overwhelmingly dominant.

In the 1990s the angst in U.S. policymaking circles over hegemonic decline quieted.[24] During this decade, the United States experienced a resurgence in international influence across a range of indicators. The breakup of the USSR, and Russia's rapid demotion from superpower to great power to big emerging market, suddenly left the United States as the sole superpower in the military and security arena, which was a sobering experience for the other advanced capitalist democracies. Moreover, the American economy was buoyant with astonishingly low inflation in the 1990s, a success story that strongly contrasted to stagnation in Japan and adjustment rigidity and high unemployment ("Eurosclerosis") in France, Germany, and most of the rest of Western Europe. The United States' share of the GDP of high-income OECD countries rose again, going from 34 percent in 1990 to 38 percent at the end of the decade. As recently as 1995, the U.S. economy was 103 percent of that of the eleven countries that in 1999 jointly formed the European Monetary Union. Yet by the close of 1999, this ratio had risen to 136 percent, partly due to the surprising weakness of the new currency, the euro, since its introduction in January, 1999.[25] Even in the international monetary and financial sphere, an arena in which the U.S. dollar's dominance had declined steadily for decades, the dollar rode a power surge. The share of the United States in total world official foreign exchange reserves had fallen from over 90 percent in the 1950s to only 50.6 percent by 1990. Yet the financial turmoil of the 1990s, along with the strong dollar and opportunities for investors in the U.S. stock market, caused the dollar share of world reserves to swell to 66.2 percent by the end of 1999 (IMF Annual Report 2000). As of the dawn of the twenty-first century, the United States was still enjoying what Ethan B. Kapstein and Michael Mastanduno (1999) called its "unipolar moment" (see also Cohen 2001). Therefore, the hypothesis that rising international financial instability in the 1990s might be partly explained by the *weakness* of the United States seems on the surface implausible.

But is it? What are reasonable expectations for relative shifts in a variety of international political and economic capabilities over the medium term? Despite the impressive shadow of the United States in the 1990s, there are good reasons to believe that the gradual shift to multipolarity will continue. Since Japan and the countries of Western Europe now have mature postindustrial economies, there is no reason to suppose that their long-term growth trajectory will outpace that of the United States, except temporarily, perhaps in a reversal of the United States' relatively faster growth in the 1990s. However, European Monetary Union, to the surprise of many, came into being on schedule in 1999. Also probable is continued progress toward stronger political union, such as forging of a common foreign policy. Were the EMU to evolve toward anything like a political federation of Europe, then today's unipolar moment surely would be over.

Moreover, new major powers may arise. Although the relative combined share of five large emerging-market economies in the world economy has not yet changed in the postwar period as a whole (see table 1.4), the combination of democratic government plus market reforms could change this result.[26] Economic theory suggests that late industrializers should grow faster than mature economies. More immediately, the greater relative influence of Western Europe and Japan, in 2000 as compared to 1970 or even 1980, suggests that developing countries have a greater value as allies—either for the United States or for a combination of other great powers aligned against the United States on a given issue—in various international bargaining relationships than ever was the case before. In a situation in which coalitions are necessary to prevail, relatively weak swing players sometimes exercise disproportionate influence, as any student of parliamentary government knows.

I conclude that increasing multipolarity, rather than continued U.S. hegemony, is the dominant underlying trend over the medium term. If it is also true that a well functioning global financial architecture, whatever its specific institutions, requires ongoing active management, then the theory of hegemonic stability suggests that we should be concerned, because effective collective or cooperative management always is more difficult to carry through than are clear commands emanating from a single authoritative leader. The function of maintaining system stability in the post–Bretton Woods era has been shared between formal institutions of collective responsibility, the IMF and especially the G7, and ad hoc crisis management by the continuing monetary hegemon, the United States. So far this mixed arrangement has operated reasonably smoothly, but only because the United States has been willing to play a leading role in the several emerging market financial crises of the 1990s (see Mark Brawley's chapter). In the absence of an obvious external security threat such as that provided by the Soviet Union during the Cold War, however, domestic politics in the United States became increasingly hostile to U.S. international leadership, especially when foreign policy involved either commitment of U.S. resources or formal multilateral cooperation. As this book was in press, the terrorist attacks of September, 2001 dramatically heightened the salience of international affairs for the U.S. Congress and the American public, leading the United States to attack Afghanistan and openly ponder extending the war to Iraq. Structurally, however, the international distribution of economic power continues to shift toward multipolarity. For example, as the world's largest debtor nation, the United States implicitly is vulnerable to the willingness of foreign individuals and central banks to continue to hold U.S. dollars. Recent American military assertiveness may imply an enhanced willingness to lead. Still, the unipolar moment cannot be prolonged indefinitely.

The theory of hegemonic stability provides a plausible, if hardly conclusive, understanding of the relative success of the four international financial architectures over the past century and a half, suggesting that the two periods in which there was a clear hegemon had more effective international financial architectures. If we also take the conclusions of the technological determinists seriously (and these two approaches are by no means mutually inconsistent), then we are left to observe that the United States' capabilities for global economic leadership are quite likely weakening just at the moment that the international financial architecture is in need of substantial reform in order to cope with the demands of accelerated monetary globalization. The moderate version of the hypothesis of hegemonic stability does not claim that *only* hegemonic leadership can design and maintain effective global economic regimes, but does suggest that multilateral reform and regime maintenance is more difficult, and thus less likely. According to this version of the theory, the relative decline of the United States is ominous for the effectiveness of the international financial regime. At the same time, an unwillingness of the United States to accept hegemonic decline and preemptively strengthen institutions of collective global leadership further prejudices the future of the world's monetary architecture.

Democratic Consistency

A quite different body of contemporary political theory also may have something important to say about the performance of past and future financial architectures. What I term the *hypothesis of democratic consistency* is my more general reformulation of the analysis made by Beth Simmons (1994), Barry Eichengreen

(1996), and others of the domestic political causes of the failures of the interwar attempts to reestablish the gold standard. This hypothesis states that once countries become mass democracies, their leaders inevitably confront strong electoral incentives to minimize national participation in global financial architectures, such as that of the classical gold standard, that periodically deliver violent shocks to the domestic economy. Instead, elected leaders with mass constituencies, assuming that these leaders are rational, will try to create global financial architectures that buffer the domestic economy from such shocks.

The hypothesis rests on three assumptions. First, all national political leaders without exception, including authoritarian rulers and leaders of elite democracies, are responsive to a group of politically relevant constituents, a set whose membership varies from one political system to another.[27] One of the demands any politically relevant group of constituents will make is for reasonably stable and, if possible, improving material outcomes. Those with political voice almost always will condition their support on credible assurances from the leader that he/she has given adequate attention to their material well-being. A second assumption is that where the set of relevant constituents of a national leader is small, it often is possible to skew the economic regulatory framework so that favored groups can protect themselves even though the national economy as a whole endures periodic violent shocks. Thus, for example, financial capital and a small wealthy stratum with access to investment in diversified financial assets may protect themselves or even profit from periodic sharp deflationary shocks, such as those generated by adjustment under the classical gold standard. If political incumbents are responsive only to a small elite, then these leaders face no strong pressure to devote material or international bargaining resources to securing institutions that might buffer the domestic population as a whole from, for example, harsh exogenous shocks created by the adjustment mechanism built into a particular international financial architecture (Armijo 2001).

The third assumption underlying the hypothesis of democratic consistency is simply the converse of the second. When national political leaders instead must respond to a broad mass constituency, it will not be possible to offer everyone a targeted means of escape from overall national macroeconomic conditions. Leaders who do not succeed in providing a reasonably stable national macroeconomic environment will not be able to retain office. Instead they will be replaced by new incumbents who recognize that their tenure largely depends on their solicitude for the material needs of ordinary citizens. Therefore, leaders in mass electoral democracies confront a powerful incentive to provide buffering of global economic and financial shocks for their domestic populations. Under these conditions, political incumbents will face a strong disincentive to participate in an international financial architecture in which adjustment to trade imbalances occurs by means of dramatic fluctuations in either the level of domestic economic activity (as under fixed exchange rates with laissez-faire private capital movements) or the relative domestic prices of tradable and nontradable sectors (as under floating rates with free capital flows). Political incumbents will also be under great pressure to avoid the collapse of the currency and/or the national banking system. If participating in a given global financial architecture is tantamount to committing political suicide, then rational democratic leaders should either try to negotiate cooperative rules of a new international financial architecture that can buffer the domestic economy from the full force of exogenous shocks, or they should try to delink from the global economy at a national level, perhaps via capital controls or trade barriers.[28]

Table 1.5 summarizes the argument in this section. Column one judges each period as hegemonic or multipolar, a point I return to below. Like the

Table 1.5 Politics and International Financial Architectures

International Financial Architecture	*International Balance of Power*	*Prevalence of Mass Democracy*	*Democratic "Sensitivity" of Financial Architecture*	*Financial Regime is Politically . . .*
Classical Gold Standard ~ 1870–1914	• Hegemonic	• Extremely rare	• Very low	• Consistent
Interwar Experimentation 1919–1939	• Multipolar	• Core capitalist states get universal male suffrage (female follows)	• Low	• Inconsistent
Bretton Woods System 1944– ~ 1971	• Hegemonic (among participants in the global trade and payments systems)	• Core capitalist states are mass democracies • Few democracies in periphery	• High for core capitalist states • Moderate for periphery	• Consistent
Post–Bretton Woods System ~ 1973–Present	• Hegemonic, but becoming multipolar	• Core capitalist states are mass democracies • Periphery also has many mass democracies from mid 1980s on	• Moderate for core capitalist states • Low for periphery	• Increasingly inconsistent

theory of hegemonic stability, the hypothesis of democratic consistency also has a plausible explanation of the relative success of the four financial architectures since the mid-nineteenth century, as shown in the third and fourth columns of the table. The classical gold standard operated during an era in which mass democracy was extremely rare. Among the great and middle powers of the time, only the United States instituted near universal suffrage for adult white males in the nineteenth-century (Rueschemeyer, Stephens, and Stephens 1992, 122–126). Although adjustment under the gold standard was harsh, European governments of the time did not have to answer to ordinary workingmen, but only to landed and/or industrial elites, whose interests generally were served by maintaining the value of the currency.[29] Moreover, the links between monetary and exchange rate policies, on the one hand, and employment and the domestic price level, on the other, were not well understood, even by scholars and policymakers, much less the general public. Overall, the democratic "sensitivity" of the international financial architecture, and thus of the national financial architectures of countries that participated in the international regime, was quite low. Yet the prevalence of mass democracy also was very low, so the global financial architecture did not pose a problem for most national leaders. The classical gold standard was politically *consistent* international financial architecture.

After World War I, however, veterans of its horrors demanded and received greater rights, including the rights to vote and to unionize, in most of the core capitalist countries (Rueschemeyer, Stephens, and Stephens 1992, 79–154). Politicians had to reach out to labor constituencies to win elections. Universal male suffrage arrived first; female voting rights usually followed. Gradually national economic policies shifted toward Keynesian macroeconomic management in most countries, though specific national institutions shaped the speed and direction of change (Weir and Skocpol 1985).[30] Thus, while governments were doggedly trying to reestablish the gold standard, its normal operation was becoming less and less politically viable domestically. [31] The interwar attempts at recreating the apparent successes of the prewar era failed because Britain was no longer a credible hegemon and gold standard discipline was politically *inconsistent* with mass democracy in the industrial core countries.

The Bretton Woods regime, negotiated near the end of another terrible war with mass participation, was the international complement of the Keynesian welfare state that had been established domestically in the advanced capitalist democracies. The monetary and financial aspects of the Bretton Woods system, which combined fixed exchange rates with pervasive controls on private capital movements, served to buffer the domestic populations in the core capitalist states from most of the dramatic shocks that could be delivered by the international financial markets of the time. John Gerard Ruggie (1982) has referred to these arrangements as the compromise of "embedded liberalism," in which classically liberal ideas and arrangements for free international trade (and free convertibility on current account, at least in principle) were embedded in domestic regulatory frameworks that kept an uneasy compromise between the international imperative of free trade and capital flows and the national one of maintaining employment. As we have seen, the Bretton Woods financial architecture worked quite well for several decades, despite its evident failure to really deliver the promised adjustment. Although the BW architecture was designed to benefit the core capitalist countries, most developing countries pegged their currencies to those of their major trading partner among the core capitalist states, and thus also were somewhat shielded from exogenous financial shocks. In any case, and this point is crucial, most developing countries were not yet mass democracies.[32] Unlike the situation during the interwar years, most democratically elected national leaders in the postwar decades found their participation in the BW international financial regime politically *consistent* with their domestic obligations.

If we move to the post–Bretton Woods period, however, we notice an emerging serious mismatch of political reality and international financial architecture. As already noted, the PBW financial architecture has not been a product of intentional negotiation among the major state actors in the global political economy. Rather, it resulted from the breakdown of the BW fixed exchange rate regime in 1971–1973. Since then, marginal adjustments in the framework mainly have resulted from the periodic meetings of the G7 financial ministers and central bankers. There has been no intentional, self-conscious, multilateral redesign effort. In the 1970s and 1980s, the ad hoc governance of international monetary affairs did not cause many problems. In the 1990s, however, the acceleration of global financial flows, and their consequent near total divorce from behaviors that plausibly could be called trade balancing, generated increasing worry among the policy elite in the advanced industrial countries. Washington, D.C., policy analysts C. Fred Bergsten and C. Randall Henning (1996) lament a new "consensus for inaction" among the G7 countries, while Harvard economist Dani Rodrik writes that "globalization [of investment and capital flows] . . . results in increased demands on the state to provide social insurance while reducing the ability of the state to perform that role effectively. . . . [T]he ability of the owners of capital to move in and out of the domestic economy with relative ease imposes a negative externality on other groups (such as labor) with more limited mobility" (1997, 53–55). Fears that the advanced capitalist democracies have been engaged in a regulatory "race to the bottom" fueled by heightened global capital mobility have been explored in both in academic and more popular venues (Moses 1994; Schwartz 1994; Solomon 1995; Barber 1996; Greider 1997), although some argue that most of the angst is wrongheaded or at least wildly overblown (Garrett 1998; Drezner 2000).

Thus far, and despite the worries, publics in the core capitalist democracies have felt only relatively mild direct effects from the heightened exchange rate and financial volatility of the 1990s. Developing countries, however, have been in the center of financial market storms. Floating exchange rates, in general, have been disastrous for domestic economic stability in developing countries, even as these countries have increasingly found it impossible to maintain fixed exchange rates, especially with increased financial volatility in the 1990s (see Hausmann et al. 1999). The pressure from global private investors, advanced industrial countries (especially the United States), and the IMF for developing countries to rapidly liberalize their capital accounts clearly increased the vulnerability of many developing countries to financial crises such as the peso and tequila crisis of 1995 and the East Asian crisis of 1997 to 1999.

Does this matter, from the viewpoint of the international financial architecture, taken as a whole? Perhaps. The hypothesis of democratic consistency suggests that the demands imposed by the PBW global financial architecture are increasingly inconsistent with the domestic political systems of many new democracies, particularly those "emerging market" countries whose participation in the world political economy is significant and likely to become more so. The "third wave" of democracy led to the redemocratization of many Latin American polities in the early 1980s, and continued in the late 1980s and early 1990s as many East Asian and most Eastern European countries became democratic, as did several African countries, some more securely than others (Huntington 1991; Diamond 1999). In country after country, newly democratic leaders suddenly had to consider the responses of mass constituencies. Posttransition "honeymoons" often cushioned leaders against their populations' ire for some time, but democratic constituencies have gradually demanded improved economic outcomes. To the extent that the pretransition authoritarian regimes had presided over highly inflationary macroeconomic environments, as was often the case in Latin America, programs of extreme domestic austerity have pleased both international financial markets and domestic voters, at least for awhile. However, mass constituencies eventually demand of their governments both stable prices and economic growth. Heightened financial liberalization has delivered neither for poor countries. Increasingly, there is a conflict between the extreme openness and macroeconomic orthodoxy demanded of developing countries by the post–Bretton Woods financial architecture and the new reality of democratic governance within these countries (Armijo 1999). Even the relatively prosperous and politically stable Asian tigers, long known for their responsible domestic fiscal and monetary policy, were bludgeoned by the late 1990s Asian financial crisis.

If developing countries, singly or as a group, are largely irrelevant to the international political economy, then the economic and political inappropriateness of the contemporary international financial architecture for them has no impact on the functioning of the global financial architecture as a whole. But this calculation changes if emerging-market countries are becoming more important as players—perhaps because of rising multipolarity in the interstate system as a whole, or perhaps simply because of the greater likelihood of financial contagion as financial globalization continues to increase. If they have some global influence, then developing countries' anger with the lack of buffering for their economies built into the current system has negative implications even for the advanced industrial democracies, whose populations have not felt the effects of acute financial crisis since the 1930s. If newly democratic countries possess a useful bargaining chip or two—perhaps a pledge of forbearance from industrializing by means of polluting technologies, or simply an implicit promise not to disintegrate and export their angry citizens and ideologies?—then previously excluded countries may gradually oblige their inclusion in the institutions of global economic and financial management. The hypothesis of democratic consistency predicts that a continued and worsening failure of the international financial architecture to buffer the populations of newly and weakly democratic states from the full brutality of global capital storms will either destabilize democracy in the developing world, and perhaps export financial contagion and political unrest to the core economies into the bargain—or will induce developing country leaders to contemplate policies to delink from the global economy, an option likely to slow economic growth in the periphery and increase pressures for emigration to industrial countries, at a minimum. Democratically elected leaders in developing countries cannot afford to engineer their countries' full participation in open international markets unless the twenty-first-century international financial architecture can find a way to bring their societies, as well as those of the rich countries, under the protective umbrella of something like the Bretton Woods regime's "compromise of embedded liberalism."

In sum, three trends have undermined the overall political viability of the PBW financial architecture. First, the interstate balance of power is becoming less hegemonic, but the international financial architecture as yet has no increased provision for multilateral, representative crisis management. Second, floating exchange rates combined with progressively freer capital movements have undermined the effectiveness of domestic macroeconomic policies, undercutting the "compromise of embedded liberalism" in the industrial world (Andrews 1994). Third, the majority of the states in the global periphery are now mass democracies, whose populations now demand of their leaders protections from imported economic chaos similar to those that the BW regime organized for the core capitalist world. For all of these reasons, the current financial architecture is increasingly politically *inconsistent*.

Interpreting the Historical Record: A Synthesis

This section has examined the plausibility of various alternative interpretations of the reasons for success or failure of previous international financial regimes, as well as the present one. It should be noted that these interpretations are not necessarily rivals, in the sense that the truth of one must imply the falsity of another. What jumps out from the analysis is that *each* of three separate arguments—privileging the importance of, respectively, technological modernization, hegemonic leadership, and democratic consistency—predicts that the current post–Bretton Woods financial architecture, if left alone, in future will become increasingly ineffective. If computerized trading technology truly changes everything, then it follows that the inherited regulatory framework for global finance is becoming ever more obsolete. If the international balance of power is moving toward multipolarity, then a global financial architecture that, de facto, relies upon the U.S. treasury secretary to ride to the rescue is precarious indeed. Finally, if interdependence plus multipolarity suggest that emerging-market countries are today of relatively greater importance to global economic management—even if developing countries can only exercise decisive influence on occasions when the advanced industrial countries disagree—then the deep incompatibility of democratic governance in the periphery with the extreme financial openness demanded by the PBW financial architecture becomes a problem for the health of the system, not simply for emerging market countries themselves.

LAISSEZ-FAIRE, TRANSPARENCY, CAPITAL CONTROLS, AND AUTARKY: THE TERMS OF THE DEBATE THAT IS

Meanwhile, the concerns most frequently expressed in the actual debate over reform of the global financial architecture are rather different. With a few notable exceptions, the centers of discussion most likely to influence actual outcomes are located in the advanced capitalist countries, particularly the United States. The concerns of the industrial world dominate most of the multilateral studies and influential policy papers being produced and widely discussed today (see the chapters by Fernández-Arias and Hausmann, Goyal, Laurence, and Porter and Wood).[33] The final section of this chapter therefore seeks to characterize not the debate that might or should be, but rather the one that is. Combatants might usefully be divided into adherents of four broad, composite positions, which I label "laissez-faire liberalizers," "transparency advocates," "financial stabilizers," and "anti-globalizers" (see table 1.6).

Laissez-Faire Liberalizers

The economic analysis of the laissez-faire liberalizers is that free global capital markets maximize efficiency. Markets are understood as freestanding and autonomous in their workings, needing very little other than reputation and good information flows to restrain criminal or unethical behavior. A central tenet of

Table 1.6 Debating the Global Financial Architecture Today

Preferences	*Adjustment Preferences*	*Liquidity Preferences*	*Stability*
Laissez-Faire Liberalizers	• Automatic, with no room for political discretion	• Gold, gold exchange, or dollar standard	• Many would abolish IMF, World Bank
	• Either a hard fixed rate (as a gold standard) or a pure float	• End all capital controls immediately	• U.S. and other G7 governments should not bail out countries or banks
Transparency Advocates	• Free float or managed float for major currencies	• Dollar standard. • Gradually liberalize capital flows, with interim opt out for developing countries	• Greater transparency; standardization • Great power crisis management, ad hoc and institutionalized (G7, IMF)
Financial Stabilizers	• Managed float for major currencies	• Dollar standard or regional currency blocs • Skeptical of external financial liberalization • Ensure investment in developing countries	• Multilateral, even supranational, crisis prevention and management
Anti-Globalizers	• Fixed exchange rates???	• Preserve national currencies • Oppose free global capital flows, long-term and short-term	• National regulation only • Left: abolish IFIs unless democratic • Right: abolish IFIs

this view is that regulation, including most prudential regulation that limits possibly risky behavior in advance, does more harm than good. Many laissez-faire liberalizers are particularly hostile to the notion that well-functioning financial markets require a lender of last resort in order to protect financial institutions facing temporary liquidity problems from becoming insolvent. Bank runs, capital flight, and speculative attacks on a country's currency are an unfortunate consequence of the high levels of risk inherent in financial markets. The only way to reduce risk, maximal liberalizers would argue, is to eliminate the problem of "moral hazard." Once a lender of last resort exists, even if there is no explicit commitment but merely a perception that debtors (including banks) in trouble will be rescued, then all players, both creditors and debtors, face a deeply deleterious incentive to engage in more risky (but more profitable) behavior than they otherwise might, since no player expects to bear the full cost alone if the risk goes bad. In the aggregate, the safest financial market is one *without* a safety net, because only then will reckless behavior effectively be deterred. A few deaths may be necessary to prove the point, but casualties will be fewer in the long run.

Laissez-faire liberalizers are not in complete agreement over the ideal adjustment mechanism for the world economy. Some, like the editorial page staff of the *Wall Street Journal,* periodically yearn for a revived gold or gold exchange standard as a mechanism for imposing impersonal discipline on spendthrift politicians who otherwise might be tempted to use trade and capital controls to equilibrate their balance of payments. Other laissez-faire advocates prefer floating exchange rates, seeing even the possibility of overshooting and volatility as salutary curbs on domestic policy profligacy. With respect to liquidity, all wholehearted liberalizers would abolish virtually all capital controls. In the interests of international financial stability, they would act boldly to eliminate moral hazard. Many also would close the World Bank and/or the International Monetary Fund, viewing official development assistance, coordination of country debt "bailouts," and even limited and short-term balance of payments support to governments as illegitimate and counterproductive (see Edwards 1998).

Prominent U.S. theorists of radically free capital markets at the international level include Nobel laureate Milton Friedman, former Secretary of State and the Treasury George Shultz, and free market economist Allan Meltzer, head of the expert committee appointed by the Republican-dominated United States Congress to inquire into the Asian financial crisis (see Friedman 1992; Schultz, Simon, and Wriston 1998; Brunner and Meltzer 1993; and C. Fred Bergsten's chapter in this volume). The Institute for International Finance (IIF) is a research institute and advocacy group whose members include most of the world's largest and most influential multinational banks and financial institutions, particularly but not exclusively those headquartered in the United States. Its members, whose earnings depend on international lending, investments, and financial arbitrage, enthusiastically support rapid and thoroughgoing liberalization of existing barriers to cross-border capital flows, but are understandably ambivalent about disestablishing the IMF, whose rescue and structural adjustment packages have enabled many of them to continue to receive payments from countries that otherwise would have been in default (IIF 1999). The Cato Institute, a libertarian think tank and sometime advocacy group, wants to abolish all capital controls and the IMF immediately, and promotes these ideas on its website and in its publications (Dorn 1999).

Through the Cato Institute, and similar conservative U.S. think tanks, the economic ideology that truly free markets can operate largely independently of government oversight and regulation is married to a deep suspicion of liberal internationalism. Many laissez-faire liberalizers in the United States critique their country's involvement in virtually all international institutions—from the United Nations to the World Criminal Court, the 1997 Kyoto Protocol on the environment, and the IMF—on the grounds that such international organizations infringe national sovereignty. The constituency for the "new sovereigntists" (Spiro 2000), especially in the United States, also includes many whom I would term anti-globalizers, and provides a politically salient link between the conservative intellectuals and global financiers who are the core supporters of maximal financial market liberalization and the more numerous conservative populists and nativists who distrust all international organizations, including but not limited to the International Monetary Fund and World Bank.

How influential is this view? The views of wholehearted financial liberalizers are strongest and closest to the centers of power in the United States, especially since the confirmation of George W. Bush as the victor in the U.S. 2000 presidential election, but also find resonance in monetarist and conservative circles in Germany, Britain, Chile, and a limited number of other countries. In practical terms, perhaps the main achievement of the laissez-faire liberalizers has been to convince many policymakers, particularly in the United States and other G7 countries, that it is inappropriate even to consider the existence or consequences of power relationships in the global monetary sphere. This view comes perilously close to declaring that governments should not interfere in markets, and concluding that therefore governments, especially powerful ones, do not interfere. Moreover, financial markets should be decentralized, not oligopolized, and therefore international financial oligopoly does not and cannot exist (for a contrary view, see Haley 1999). In other words, those who disproportionately benefit from the unequal power relations that do exist in the international political economy are rendered cognitively unable to recognize that power enters into the question at all (see Gilpin 1987, chapter 1 and passim). Ideologically consistent laissez-faire liberalizers, therefore, are impatient with and even contemptuous of the theory of hegemonic stability—a subtlety their detractors frequently do not recognize.

Transparency Advocates

A second loose association of participants in the debate over the global financial architecture might be labeled transparency advocates. In general, they support free markets and free trade. They are distressed over the frequency of deep financial crises in developing countries, and also recognize that the advanced industrial world is not immune, only lucky thus far. But transparency advocates recognize few viable options for responding to the problems of financial globalization, because they consider themselves to be realists on one or both of two dimensions. First, they doubt whether national and partial capital controls can work. True, fully liberalized global private capital flows in fact might be dangerous. But there is no going back now. Many transparency advocates, in other words, are technological determinists. Second, most transparency advocates believe that even if strengthened multilateral global financial regulation might be technically feasible, supranational regulation is and will continue to be a political nonstarter. Given this conclusion, publicly admitting the need for strong international supervision and guidance of world financial markets serves only the purpose of undermining confidence, precisely the worst possible outcome. Instead, these would-be responsible realists embrace the solution of greater "transparency" in financial markets, by which is meant fuller and more timely reporting of international financial assets and liabilities by all governments. The core faith of this approach is that better informed market participants will be both less likely to engage in risky behavior and less likely to panic when market indicators suddenly reverse themselves.

With respect to adjustment, most transparency advocates would retain the current system of floating exchange rates, noting that it has worked reasonably well thus far, though several would prefer to see greater cooperation among the United States, Japan, and now the European Monetary Union (as represented by the European Central Bank?) to jointly reduce exchange rate fluctuations. Most of these moderate liberalizers would stick with the dollar standard—they are pragmatists, after all—and endorse further loosening of capital controls worldwide. In contrast to the laissez-faire liberalizers, however, many transparency advocates would allow significant phase-in time for developing countries, recognizing that their relatively shallow financial markets experience much more intense domestic macroeconomic turbulence than the deeper and broader financial markets of the advanced capitalist world. It has not escaped these pragmatists' notice that such countries as Malaysia and Chile employed capital controls in the 1990s, seemingly with reasonably good results (see the chapter by Benjamin J. Cohen).

The views of most transparency advocates on architectural reform to ensure stability are either centrist and pragmatic, or selfish and exclusionary, depending upon one's viewpoint. Most would like to see greater, and more institutionalized, cooperation among the major powers to manage the international financial system. Regularized great power consultation through such bodies as the G7 would not only serve to prevent or ease global monetary crises, but also should serve as a venue for the governments of Japan, Western Europe, and Canada to debate issues of global liquidity growth with the United States, which still holds the predominance of power in this arena. Transparency advocates typically do not concern themselves with issues of representation or equity in global economic management, partly because experienced policymakers understand that collective management by even a few great powers is a difficult task.

As of the very early twenty-first century, the views of transparency advocates undoubtedly dominated the debate over the international financial architecture. The resolutely non-radical views of the transparency advocates are the majority position throughout the U.S. and British foreign policy establishments, on both sides of the partisan aisle in both countries. The recent U.S. Council on Foreign Relations report on international financial reform (see the chapter by Bergsten) reflects them, as also do the three reports of the Group of Twenty-Two (G22), an official multilateral forum with membership of both advanced industrial and developing countries, organized by U.S. policymakers (see Eichengreen 1999 and this volume's chapter by Porter and Wood). Eichengreen's (1999) primer on the international financial architecture debate, and many of the publications of the Institute for International Economics, also belong here. Transparency is now the home, hearth, and apple pie of global financial reform, endorsed by virtually every expert commission across the political spectrum, and thus has some of the characteristics of a lowest common denominator.

The transparency advocates are successful because they propose the least change from the current status quo. The uncomfortable question is whether their consensus and minimalist solutions adequately address either the technical problems of global financial regulation or the less recognized underlying questions of political leadership and representation raised in this book.

Financial Stabilizers

The financial stabilizers include a number of prominent defectors from the transparency advocates, generally individuals who have concluded that a simple shift to greater openness, combined with technical assistance to developing countries around such issues as modernizing their securities markets law and corporate governance statutes, is an insufficient response to the heightened risk of an international financial meltdown in a world of globalized capital markets (see the chapter by Benjamin J. Cohen). Financial stabilizers believe that continuing with the status quo is dangerous, because liberalized financial markets are inherently unstable (see the chapter by David Felix). Members of this group believe that global finance requires global regulation, perhaps including elements of a genuinely supranational authority. Financial stabilizers are much more sensitive to the international distribution of power, both military and economic, than are members of the first two groups, and many make the unequal distribution of costs among the victims of financial crashes or associated economic slowdowns central to their analysis (see the chapters by Eduardo Fernández-Arias and Ricardo Hausmann, and by Ashima Goyal).

Financial stabilizers desire an exchange rate regime that makes national adjustment to trade imbalances effective. However, like the designers of the Bretton Woods monetary regime, they rank exchange rate stability and external equilibration as less compelling objectives than the maintenance of domestic macroeconomic health. Most financial stabilizers put their faith in an actively and collaboratively managed float among the currencies of the great powers, like that of the current post–Bretton Woods international financial regime, only more so. The liquidity preference of those who fear international financial crises and cross-border contagion is generally for the continuation of the present dollar standard for international transactions. Financial stabilizers, as I have defined this term, are not nostalgic for either a gold or a gold exchange standard, per se, although they greatly appreciate the predictability and buffering that the Bretton Woods financial architecture was able to offer domestic economies. Some go so far as to advocate regional currency blocs, arguing that otherwise developing countries will never escape the burden of their national currencies' "original sin" of not being "credible" with footloose global investors (Hausmann et al. 1999; see also Fernández-Arias and Hausmann in this volume). The spread of regional currency blocs would lead most of Latin America to dollarize, and much of the Middle East and some of Africa to adopt the euro, although there is no such straightforward choice for Asia (Cohen 2000, and the chapter by Henry Laurence). The first such large currency bloc that was not a colonial holdover, of course, came into existence in early 1999 as the European Monetary Union (see the chapter by Erik Jones).

Many financial stabilizers are explicitly concerned with the provision of international money and credit, as this is a crucial determinant of future world economic growth. Moreover, many or most financial stabilizers think the global financial architecture should assertively promote medium and long-term investment—private or if necessary public, as through the IFIs—in developing countries as a positive good, for which there is both an efficiency and a fairness rationale. Consequently, many financial stabilizers, whether in Japan, Europe, or developing countries, would strongly prefer more cooperative, and even explicitly representative, management of global money supply growth, as well as more transparent rules for allocating credits from the international financial institutions such as the IMF or World Bank (Mayobre 1999). At the same time, most would prefer to limit very short-term capital flows, arguing that they typically do not reflect underlying economic fundamentals such as a country's trade position or the quality of its investment opportunities. Knowing that countries pay a price for unilaterally imposing capital controls or any other significant new financial regulation, stabilizers would prefer joint regulatory action, presumably with the great powers taking the lead (Ocampo 1999). Similarly, analysts and advocates in this group would like to see the lender of last resort function, and other crisis prevention and management measures, be collective and more representative. Innovations that have been suggested include a global bankruptcy court, making the IMF into a formal lender of last resort, and a global credit rating agency (Blecker 1999, 85–146). Devesh Kapur (2000) recently observed that a good place to start in making the international financial institutions, along with other international organizations, more representative and responsible would be to formalize the present clientelistic and ad hoc selection process for their leaders!

The majority of national governments—excepting those crucial ones in the United States and Britain—lean toward the financial stabilizers' positions, including most of the remaining G7 countries (Kirton 2000; see also this volume's chapters by Laurence and Goyal). The European Monetary Union can be understood as an ambitious policy response to the concerns raised by the financial stabilizers' analysis. Other prominent financial stabilizers include Nobel Laureate James Tobin, proposer of the famous "Tobin tax" on short-term international capital flows; former World Bank chief economist Joseph Stiglitz, who publicly criticized the IMF in 1998 for its handling of the Asian financial crisis; the United Nations Economic Commission on Latin America and the Caribbean (ECLAC); the Division on Transnational Corporations and Investment of the United Nation's Conference on Trade and Development; and recently even financier George Soros (Tobin 1978; Stiglitz 1998, 2000; Ocampo 1999; Soros 1998). In the 1990s, several highly respected, traditional free market economists endorsed a notion that directly contradicts the core intellectual premise of all laissez-faire liberalizers and some transparency advocates. Notable free traders such as Jagdish Bhagwati (1998) concluded that international capital markets are fundamentally *dissimilar* to global markets for goods and services: they are not self-equilibrating, and therefore need careful oversight and regulation. The World Bank in the late 1990s placed itself somewhat cautiously in the camp of financial stabilizers, while several of the regional development banks, very aware of the devastation of financial crises in emerging markets, are more wholehearted in their belief that unchecked financial liberalization is dangerous.

The influence of the financial stabilizers in those international committees that have the capability of affecting actual reforms of the global financial architecture is hard to know. Those who feel most strongly are the governments of developing countries, who have relatively little clout. Advanced industrial countries other than the United States have considerably more potential influence, yet are more united in their opposition to U.S. hegemony than in supporting any concrete alternative proposals. Since the financial crises of the 1990s, however, prominent scholars and policymakers among the transparency advocates have begun to take the analyses of the financial stabilizers more seriously. Unfortunately, the United States' present international bargaining stance of transparency advocacy is under strong pressure from the United States Congress, where both laissez-faire liberalizers and anti-globalizers are prominent, and from the U.S. private financial sector, a strong supporter of laissez-faire liberalism. Under the circumstances, the conversion of a few academics and midlevel policymakers doesn't much matter.

Anti-Globalizers

I term the last broad group of interests and advocates the *anti-globalizers*. Those in this group are deeply skeptical of free trade, and thus much less willing than adherents of the other three positions to evaluate designs for monetary and financial affairs in terms of their ability to promote trade. Similar mistrust of both trade and international financial integration uneasily unites strong partisans of both the political left and right. Many anti-globalizers, especially those on the right, suspect all international initiatives, especially those organized by national governments, although others, almost invariably on the left, are committed internationalists, albeit ones that trust nongovernmental organizations (NGOs) significantly more than national governments. Most distrust corporations, particularly large transnational firms. What unites this group is less an economic analysis per se than a skepticism about established power structures, and a preference for the little guy over the Goliath of big government. In this sense, members of this group, including both those whose overall social, religious, and political orientation is on the left and those identified on most issues with the conservative right, are populists.

Most anti-globalizers don't want to have to think about assuring adjustment, liquidity, and stability in the global financial system. They resent both volatile exchange rates and the adoption of foreign monies. Their preference, if they are forced to articulate one, is for fixed rates and use of their own national currency. They have no desire to return to the gold standard, but, unless Americans, resent the hegemony of the U.S. dollar. They favor both trade and capital controls, including barriers to both short-term flows and long-term foreign direct investment. This group opposes globalization of everything from culture to finance, perceiving it as handing control from real people to faceless giant corporations, and assumes that the remedy for international financial instability is less porous borders and self-reliance. Those on the political right perceive the international financial institutions as threats to national sovereignty, often seeing satanic overtones in the very existence of international organizations. Those on the left fervently support multilateralism and multiculturalism in principle, yet believe most existing international organizations, and almost certainly the IMF and World Bank, to be corrupted and compromised almost beyond redemption. Activists in either camp, however, often can unite on issues such as reducing foreign aid, cutting back or eliminating contributions to and/or cooperation with the international

financial institutions, and opposing novel schemes for heightened international economic cooperation, such as the European Monetary Union, which likely would not
have come into being had not the French public narrowly ratified the Maastricht
Treaty in September 1992, only a few months after the Danes narrowly rejected it.

Anti-globalists include intellectuals, politicians, and members of social
strata discomfited by globalization. Unlike the other three influential currents of
opinion on reform of the international financial architecture, all of which are
overwhelmingly elitist coalitions of technocrats, intellectuals, business leaders,
and responsive politicians, the anti-globalization alliance has significant popular
support in national legislatures and among church and religious groups and
community organizers. Most of the political clout of the position comes from
activists residing in advanced industrial countries, though left anti-globalizers in
the advanced industrial countries have forged important links with groups, often
minorities or the relatively disadvantaged, in developing countries through such
organizations as the Rainforest Alliance, the networks of NGOs opposed to the
North American Free Trade Association (NAFTA) and the World Trade Organization (WTO), and the Jubilee 2000 movement for international debt forgiveness
for highly indebted poor countries. Leaders of the left anti-globalizers in the
United States include Ralph Nader, Green Party candidate for president in 2000;
the American Federation of Labor-Congress of Industrial Organizations (AFL-
CIO), the United States' most influential labor confederation; and the Reverend
Jesse Jackson, African American activist and former Democratic presidential
candidate. The message is spread by activist coalitions such as the International
Forum on Globalization, whose affiliates include the Friends of the Earth, the
Third World Network, the Institute for Policy Studies, and Public Citizen (IFG
1999; see also Armijo 2000).

Right anti-globalizers tend toward nativism and chauvinism, either of which
render international links more difficult. But they have wide popular appeal in
countries experiencing strains from trade and financial opening, from Australia
to Central and Eastern Europe, India, and Indonesia. They frequently elect politicians and control sizeable blocs in national legislatures, including the United
States Congress. In the United States, 1992 Reform Party presidential candidate
Ross Perot, Christian conservative and sometime presidential candidate Pat
Buchanan, and numerous members of Congress, from former House Majority
Leader Dick Armey to Chairman of the Senate Foreign Relations Committee
Jesse Helms, all have opposed inward and/or outward foreign investment, U.S.
contributions to the international financial institutions, the early 1995 financial
rescue package for Mexico, and other core elements of contemporary financial
internationalism. They share a deep, often religiously based, suspicion of "one-
worldism" with the libertarian intellectuals among the laissez-faire liberalizers.
On matters of specific policy, the right anti-globalizers, and sometimes also left
anti-globalizers, often are willing to unite with the radical free marketeers to

bash the established organizations of the post–Bretton Woods international financial architecture, the IMF and World Bank, along with other institutions of incipient global governance, such as the United Nations.

CONCLUSIONS: DEMOCRACY AND INTERNATIONAL FINANCIAL REFORM

This chapter began by defining three core functions that any international financial regime must facilitate: national adjustment to external imbalances, provision of liquidity or credit to the global economy, and a mechanism to manage crises and provide monetary and financial stability. I described four historical financial architectures and ranked them. The classical gold standard performed brilliantly, in terms of its ability to satisfy the needs of the relevant political actors of its time. The Bretton Woods financial architecture, though very different in most of its technical particulars, was nearly as successful. In contrast, the interwar attempts to restore the gold standard were a disaster. Arguably their failure had more to do with their political unsuitability than specific technical flaws. Today's ad hoc post–Bretton Woods financial architecture has performed adequately since the mid-1970s, but since the 1990s has been under obvious—and occasionally frightening—strain. In my view, technical modernization is important, but if the global financial architecture of the twenty-first century is not also *politically consistent,* then it probably will not endure. Unfortunately, the shape of the current debate over reform primarily reflects the distribution of elite opinion within the United States—not that in the larger world.

The financial architecture debate has not yet internalized either of two crucial political transformations around the world: emerging global multipolarity and the spread of mass democracy to developing countries. The unexpected violent attacks on the United States in late 2001 demonstrated the necessity of multilateralism to the hitherto notably unilateralist administration of U.S. President George W. Bush. Moreover, numerous pundits immediately thereafter highlighted the strong empirical association between democratic societies and the inculcation of cultural and religious tolerance in their citizens, suggesting an excellent reason for the advanced industrial world to support democracy in poor countries. Nevertheless, the current minimalist and hegemonic post–Bretton Woods international financial architecture makes it difficult for elected leaders in poor countries to maintain both domestic mass democracy and external economic integration, because the PBW financial architecture requires developing country publics to endure precisely those extremes of economic volatility that citizens in the Western democracies made clear to their leaders in the 1930s that they would no longer tolerate. In the future, questions of participation and political process will be as relevant to the search for a credible and legitimate global financial architecture as are the myriad technical problems of regulating cross-border money and credit flows.

NOTES

I thank Mark Brawley, David Felix, Ashima Goyal, Eric Helleiner, Kaizad Mistry, Eric Wibbels, and an anonymous reviewer for comments, as well as the other contributors to this book, who graciously let me read their chapters before I had to write mine. Special thanks go to my students at Reed College in 1999–2000 for their thoughtful responses to many of these ideas.

1. Old and new classics on "international regimes" include Krasner 1983; Keohane 1988; Hasenclever, Mayer, and Rittberger 1997; and Katzenstein, Keohane, and Krasner 1999.

2. The expansion or contraction due to the injection or withdrawal of reserves from a country's central bank is magnified under the now nearly ubiquitous system of "fractional reserve banking." This means that the central bank only holds reserves adequate to redeem some fraction (often less than 10 percent) of the country's paper currency held by the public. Were the credibility of the currency ever to be challenged, the central bank would shortly run out of reserves.

3. Imagine that a U.S. trade deficit generates a net outflow of dollars from the United States. If foreigners choose to hold or invest those dollars abroad (instead of redeeming them for goods, gold, or foreign currency held by the United States), then the international money supply has increased by that amount.

4. This statement is more true for national governments than for private financial actors, who may be tempted to profit from speculating against one or more currencies, on the assumption that the governments of the core capitalist powers will intervene to prevent system breakdown.

5. In the absence of such a standstill agreement, all creditors have an incentive to get their money out of the troubled firm (or country) rapidly, in order not to be left last in line. Once the process is triggered, even fundamentally solvent (but illiquid) borrowers can quickly be ruined.

6. In several important crises, central banks intervened to help one another through liquidity crises, acting as lenders of last resort (LLRs). For example, during the Barings Crisis of 1890 the Bank of England borrowed from the French central bank, while the Russian monetary authority also pledged further assistance as necessary (Eichengreen 1996, 34). European bankers correctly perceived the governments of peripheral countries, such as those in Latin America, as less deeply committed to domestic price and financial stability, and were reluctant to lend funds to support a given parity of the currency with gold.

7. Britain and France together owed the U.S. government $10 billion for wartime loans, which taxpayers in either Europe or the in the United States would have to absorb.

In 1921 the Reparations Commission found that defeated Germany owed Britain and France the amazing sum of $33 billion in war reparations, although the amount remained under constant negotiation for more than a decade (Lairson and Skidmore 1997, 55). Ultimately, Germany paid around $2 billion during the 1920s to the European Allies, who in turn repaid about $1 billion to the United States (Eichengreen 1996, 69). The United States had a strong currency, an abundance of monetary gold—nearly 45 percent of the world's supply in 1926 (Eichengreen 1996, 67)—and a persistent trade surplus, because its industrial base had not been bombed. Private investment flows from the United States to Europe, including Germany, provided liquidity until the late 1920s, but were not a reliable source of financing. Once private financing from the United States dried up, the system would become illiquid quickly.

8. These were Austria, Germany, Hungary, and Poland.

9. For example, both the French and the Americans had long suspected that the British desire to let central banks hold reserves in foreign exchange, as well as in gold, was a ploy to promote the use of sterling. The Americans, French, and British agreed in 1936 to limit future competitive devaluations.

10. Contrary to much received wisdom, Barry Eichengreen concludes that "currency depreciation in the 1930s was part of the solution to the Depression, not part of the problem," (1996, 89), arguing that the competitive stimulus of increased exports in major economies (even if only temporary, as trading partners responded in kind) was practically the only engine of growth in the world economy.

11. The original BW agreement also contained a clause, for which Keynes had fought hard, empowering the IMF to bless trade retaliation against countries with persistent surpluses by certifying them as "scarce currency" countries, that is, countries whose currencies were much in demand.

12. These were the "special drawing rights" (SDRs), created in 1969. But real countries wanted to hold gold or dollars, sterling, marks, or yen—not SDRs, backed only by an international institution.

13. In the preliminary discussions for the BW conference, the American negotiator, White, shot down the suggestion by Keynes that the proposed world fund have an initial U.S. contribution of $23 billion, countering with the much lower figure of $2 billion. $2.75 billion was the final figure. The World Bank had similarly scant initial resources, despite the fact that both delegations imagined that its initial task would be to give significant aid for the reconstruction of Europe. Within a few years, however, U.S. policymakers realized that the minimum funds needed to influence the economic recovery of Western Europe, and to limit the attractiveness of Communism and Socialism, were much larger. Through the Marshall Plan, the United States transferred $13 billion in reconstruction aid to Western Europe through the early 1950s (Eichengreen 1996, 96–98).

14. As long as the other core capitalist states were willing to run a trade surplus with the United States, the United States could "export inflation." Foreign central banks would either have to expand their domestic money supplies to accommodate the additional dollar reserves they held, or increase the public debt in the course of "sterilizing"

the inflows by additional borrowing from their domestic publics to shrink the money supply.

15. Russia is not a core capitalist economy, but it does have nuclear weapons and the West desperately wants to retain it as a partner in the uncertain post–Cold War world.

16. Kenneth Waltz (1959, 1979) observed that theories of international politics have been pitched at three levels, that of the individual leader (as in psychological or "great man" interpretations of history), the state (as in predictions that authoritarian political systems will generate different foreign policy preferences and actions than demo-cratic ones), or the international system itself (as in theories abstracting from the char-acteristics of both individual leaders and domestic polities and focusing exclusively on the "balance of power" or distribution of capabilities among nation-states in the interna-tional arena).

17. Theorists such as Charles Kindleberger (1981, [1973] 1986) and Robert Gilpin (1987, 2000) suggest that hegemonic management of international economic arrange-ments in an "anarchic world" (that is, a global political economy without an overarching world government) is likely to be more stable and successful than collective management. Others have argued that once a successful international economic regime is established by a dominant state, thereafter cooperative, multilateral management can be almost as effective as continued hegemonic leadership (Keohane 1984; Oye 1986).

18. In asking whether hegemony is "good" for the system, Robert Pahre (1999) defines a hegemon as "benevolent" (in that it pays more for the provision of public goods enjoyed by all than it gets back in terms of special privileges) or "malevolent" (in that it forces other system participants to contribute proportionately more resources to essen-tial regime maintenance than it does). Most hegemonic stability theorists are less focused on the distribution of (the relative) gains from hegemony. They want to know if hege-mony improves the likelihood that a reasonably effective international financial architec-ture (that is, one providing viable, if not always "just," outcomes in terms of adjustment, liquidity, and stability) will be constructed and maintained.

19. A hegemon could, of course, prefer autarkic global economic relations. In such a situation, there also will not be an effective and successful international financial architecture.

20. I admit to theoretical vagaries in this definition. For example, I begin by intimat-ing that I intend to assess "power" on the basis of objective capabilities, but, in the end, state that power will be known by the demonstration of influence, where A has influence over B if A successfully persuades B to make a choice or perform an action that B otherwise would not have. Nor have I specified exactly how I will assess capabilities. Still, my definition works well with our *intuitive* sense of a hegemon, which is a country that is sufficiently prominent, or shall we say dominant, among its fellows as to exercise "leader-ship," *either* in the sense of a) apparently dictating many, or even most, of the rules of international interaction, or in the quite different sense of b) making choices, which it has no ability at all to impose, that others accept for the purpose of solving coordination and/ or collective action problems (Keohane 1984; Hasenclever, Mayer, and Rittberger 1997).

21. My judgments as to which eras were hegemonic and multipolar probably reflects a consensus of scholars, including most of those cited here. However, Pahre (1999, 15) concludes that "there has always been a hegemon during the modern period (1815 to the present)." Waltz (1979), at the other extreme, sees the nineteenth century through the First World War as a time of multipolarity in the interstate system, with five to seven great powers at any given time. In Waltz's view, that is, imperial Britain was considerably less than a hegemon in Europe. It was able to play the role of a balancer, shifting between rival alliance coalitions, largely because its geographic position gave it greater freedom of action than most continental European states. The source of these divergent assessments is the precise definition the researcher gives to the term "hegemon," which can range from merely "first among equals" to the much more demanding "able to *command* the cooperation of all of the other states in the system."

22. It should be clearly noted that the classically liberal character of Britain's relationships with other European and North American states coexisted with distinctly mercantilist policies toward its colonies.

23. "Effective" international leadership does not necessarily mean normatively desirable, in terms of any particular hierarchy of values, or even in terms of an imagined consensus of world leaders. It merely means successful in terms of being a plausible solution to the challenges of global monetary management.

24. Mark Brawley in his chapter below gives slightly different dates to the intellectual debate.

25. Calculated from data available at World Bank website, November, 2000.

26. New research suggests a powerful link between democracy and economic growth, even when controlling for a host of other factors. See Barro 1997; Feng 1997.

27. The set of "relevant political actors" may be as small as a few regionally powerful land barons or the senior military officer corps, or as large as the entire adult population. Political participation may be constituted geographically, by economic class, by ideology, or by ascriptive characteristics such as race, ethnicity, or religion of birth.

28. Some readers may object that leaders of developing countries have no choice but to participate in the reigning international financial architecture, however much it disadvantages them. I assert that all political incumbents make real decisions, even if their best option is to select the lesser evil. The point is that leaders of mass democracies may rank their options differently than rulers who must answer only to a privileged few.

29. Britain was the major industrial power of the time. If its industrialists lost out from maintaining a strong pound vis-à-vis the currencies of Europe and the United States, they could depend upon their government to attend to their exporting needs in setting the values of currencies for the British colonies. The Indian rupee, for example, was deliberately maintained overvalued against sterling in order to aid Manchester cotton exporters.

30. Nazi Germany and fascist Italy also adopted core elements of the welfare state, arguably because their political systems, although not democratic, depended on

mass mobilization and support. In Germany/Prussia, of course, welfare state policies dated from the time of Bismarck.

31. I am suggesting that characteristics of a country's domestic political system can change the type of foreign (economic) policies its leaders adopt. International relations scholars hotly debate the degree to which countries' international policies vary according to domestic politics. Kenneth Waltz (1979) remains the foremost proponent of the "structuralist" (also known as "neorealist," as in Keohane 1986) position that *only* the distribution of capabilities in the international system fundamentally influences international relations; consequently, rational leaders of democratic states, in the aggregate, will make very similar foreign policy choices to those of authoritarian states. Waltz argues that national leaders who do not act to maximize their states' relative power against any and all potential rivals—including states with whom they have special cultural, historical, or ideological affinities—either will cause their countries to be disadvantaged internationally or will themselves be driven from power by their more pragmatic supporters. Andrew Moravcsik (1997) has recently made a persuasive case for the opposing position. Moravcsik and others suggest that states that are liberal democracies possess a somewhat different set of goals for their foreign policies than do dictatorships. These include a strong disinclination to fight other democratic states and a heightened unwillingness to subject their domestic populations to severe economic hardship simply for the sake of honoring international economic commitments, from adherence to the gold standard in the 1920s to membership in the World Trade Organization in the late 1990s.

32. India was the major democratic exception among developing countries. Arguably its decision to pursue near economic autarky, while hurting its prospects for economic growth, enabled Indian politicians to implement a redistributive national economic policy framework that was crucial to securing democracy in the early postindependence decades.

33. An intriguing and hopeful recent initiative, organized outside the G7/G8 but with high level participation from them, has been the study group on global financial issues organized in December, 2000, by United Nations Secretary General Kofi Annan, under the leadership of former Mexican president Ernesto Zedillo. Members included former U.S. Treasury Secretary Robert E. Rubin, former president of the European Commission Jacques Delors, fomer Deputy Director General of the International Labor Organization Mary Chinery-Hesse, and former Indian Finance Minister Manmohan Singh, as well as senior officials or fomer officials from Costa Rica, the Arab Fund for Economic Development, Mozambique, and the British aid organization, Oxfam (Crossette 2000).

REFERENCES

Andrews, David M. 1994. Capital Mobility and State Autonomy: Toward a Structural Theory of International Monetary Relations *International Studies Quarterly* 38, No. 2 (June):193-218.

Armijo, Leslie Elliott. 2000. Skewed Incentives to Liberalize International Trade, Production, and Finance. Unpublished paper, Reed College.

————. 2001. Democratic Inclusion and Macroeconomic Moderation: An Hypothesis and Preliminary Evidence. Unpublished paper, Reed College.

————, ed. 1999. *Financial Globalization and Democracy in Emerging Markets*. London: Palgrave/Macmillan.

(BIS) Bank for International Settlements. 2000. *Annual Report*. Geneva: Bank for International Settlements.

Barber, Benjamin R. 1996. *Jihad vs. McWorld: How Globalism and Tribalism are Reshaping the World*. New York: Ballantine Books.

Barro, Robert J. 1997. *Determinants of Economic Growth: A Cross-Country Empirical Study*. Cambridge, Mass.: MIT Press.

Bergsten, C. Fred. 1998. How to Target Exchange Rates. *Financial Times*, November 20.

Bergsten, C. Fred, and C. Randall Henning. 1996. *Global Economic Leadership and the Group of Seven*. Washington, D.C.: Institute for International Economics.

Bhagwati, Jagdish. 1998. The Capital Myth. *Foreign Affairs* (May/June).

Blecker, Robert A. 1999. *Taming Global Finance: A Better Architecture for Growth and Equity*. Washington, D.C.: Economic Policy Institute.

Brawley, Mark 1993. *Liberal Leadership: Great Powers and Their Challengers in Peace and War*. Ithaca, N.Y.: Cornell University Press.

Brunner, Karl and Allan H. Meltzer. 1993. *Money and the Economy*. Cambridge: Cambridge University Press.

Bryant, Ralph C. 1987. *International Financial Intermediation*. Washington, D.C.: The Brookings Institution.

Coeuré, Benoît and Jean Pisani-Ferry. 1999. The Case Against Benign Neglect of Exchange Rate Stability. *Finance and Development* 36, no. 3 (September):5–8.

Cohen, Benjamin J. 2000. Life at the Top: International Currencies in the 21st Century. *Essays in International Finance*. Princeton, N.J.: Princeton University, International Economics.

————. 2001. Containing Backlash: Foreign Economic Policy in an Age of Globalization. In *Eagle Rules? Foreign Policy and American Primacy in the 21st Century*, ed. Robert J. Lieber. Upper Saddle River, N.J.: Prentice-Hall.

Conybeare, John A. C. 1984. Public Goods, Prisoners' Dilemmas, and the International Political Economy. *International Studies Quarterly* 28 (March):5-22.

Crossette, Barbara. 2000. U.N. Economic Panel to Study Help for World's Have-Nots. *New York Times*, December 16.

Diamond, Larry. 1999. *Developing Democracy: Toward Consolidation*. Baltimore: Johns Hopkins.

Dorn, James A. 1999. Introduction to Special Issue on the Global Financial Architecture. *The Cato Journal* 18, no. 3 (Winter).

Drezner, Daniel W. 2000. Bottom Feeders. *Foreign Policy* 121 (November/December): 64–73.

Edwards, Sebastian. 1998. Abolish the IMF. *Financial Times*, November 13.

Eichengreen, Barry 1996. *Globalizing Capital: A History of the International Monetary System*. Princeton, N.J.: Princeton University Press.

————. 1999. *Toward a New International Financial Architecture*. Washington, D.C.: Institute for International Economics.

————. [1989] 2000. Hegemonic Stability Theories of the International Monetary System. In *International Political Economy: Perspectives on Power and Wealth*, ed. Jeffry A. Frieden and David A. Lake. 4th ed. Boston: Bedford/St. Martin's.

Feng, Yi. 1997. Democracy, Political Stability and Economic Growth. *British Journal of Political Science* 27, no. 3 (July):391–418.

Friedman, Milton. 1992. *Money Mischief: Episodes in Monetary History*. New York: Harcourt, Brace, Jovanovitch.

Garrett, Geoffrey. 1998. Global Markets and National Politics: Collision Course or Virtuous Circle? *International Organization* 52, no. 4 (Autumn):787–824.

Gilpin, Robert. 1987. *The Political Economy of International Relations*. Princeton, N.J.: Princeton University Press.

————. 2000. *The Challenge of Global Capitalism: The World Economy in the 21st Century*. Princeton, N.J.: Princeton University Press.

Greider, William. 1997. *One World, Ready or Not: The Manic Logic of Global Capitalism*. New York: Simon and Schuster.

Haley, Mary Ann. 1999. Emerging Market Makers: The Power of Institutional Investors. In *Financial Globalization and Democracy in Emerging Markets*, ed. Leslie Elliott Armijo. London: Palgrave/Macmillan.

Hall, Peter A., ed. 1989. *The Political Power of Economic Ideas: Keynesianism across Nations*. Princeton, N.J.: Princeton University Press.

Hasenclever, Andreas, Peter Mayer, and Volker Rittberger. 1997. *Theories of International Regimes*. Cambridge: Cambridge University Press.

Hausmann, Ricardo, Michael Gavin, Carmen Pages-Serra, and Ernesto Stein. 1999. Financial Turmoil and the Choice of Exchange Rate Regime. Working Paper #400. Washington, D.C.: Inter-American Development Bank, Office of the Chief Economist.

Hawley, James P. 1987. *Dollars and Borders: U.S. Government Attempts to Restrict Capital Flows, 1960–1980*. Armonk, N.Y.: M. E. Sharpe.

Helleiner, Eric. 1994. *States and the Reemergence of Global Finance: From Bretton Woods to the 1990s*. Ithaca, N.Y.: Cornell University Press.

Henning, C. Randall. 1994. *Currencies and Politics in the United States, Germany, and Japan*. Washington, D.C.: Institute for International Economics.

Huntington, Samuel P. 1991. *The Third Wave: Democratization in the Late Twentieth Century*. Norman: University of Oklahoma Press.

Institute of International Finance (IIF). 1999. Summary Report on the Work of the IIF Steering Committee on Emerging Markets Finance. Washington, D.C.: Institute of International Finance.

International Forum on Globalization (IFG). 1999. The Global Financial Crisis: Information Packet. San Francisco: International Forum on Globalization.

Kapstein, Ethan. 1994. *Governing the Global Economy*. Cambridge, Mass.: Harvard University Press.

Kapstein, Ethan B., and Michael Mastanduno, eds. 1999. *Unipolar Politics*. New York: Columbia University Press.

Kapur, Devesh. 2000. Who Gets to Run the World? *Foreign Policy* 121 (November/December):44–53.

Katzenstein, Peter J., Robert O. Keohane, and Stephen D. Krasner, eds. 1999. *Exploration and Contestation in the Study of World Politics*. Cambridge, Mass.: MIT Press.

Kennedy, Paul M. 1987. *The Rise and Fall of the Great Powers: Economic Change and Military Conflict from 1500 to 2000*. New York: Random House.

Keohane, Robert O. 1984. *After Hegemony: Discord in the World Political Economy*. Princeton, N.J.: Princeton University Press.

———. 1988. International Institutions: Two Approaches. *International Studies Quarterly* 32:379–96.

———, ed. *Neorealism and Its Critics*. New York: Columbia University Press.

Kindleberger, Charles. 1978. *Manias, Panics, and Crashes: A History of Financial Crises*. New York: Basic Books.

———. 1981. Dominance and Leadership in the International Economy. *International Studies Quarterly* 25 (June):242–254.

———. [1973] 1986. *The World in Depression, 1929–1939*. Rev. ed. Berkeley: University of California Press.

Kirton, John. 2000. G7 and Concert Governance in the Global Financial Crisis of 1997–9. Paper presented at the annual meeting of the International Studies Association, Los Angeles, California, March 15–19, 2000.

Krasner, Stephan. 1976. State Power and the Structure of International Trade. *World Politics* 28, no. 3 (April).

———. 1982. Regimes and the Limits of Realism: Regimes as Autonomous Variables. *International Organization* 36.

———, ed. 1983. *International Regimes*. Ithaca, N.Y.: Cornell University Press.

Lairson, Thomas D., and David Skidmore. 1997. *International Political Economy: The Struggle for Power and Wealth*. 2nd ed. Fort Worth, Tex.: Harcourt Brace Jovanovich College Publishers.

Lake, David A. 1993. Leadership, Hegemony, and the International Economy: Naked Emperor or Tattered Monarch with Potential? *International Studies Quarterly* 37 (December):459–89.

Maddison, Angus. 1995. *Monitoring the World Economy, 1820–1992*. Paris: Organisation for Economic Co-operation and Development (OECD).

Mayobre, Eduardo, ed. 1999. *G-24: The Developing Countries in the International Financial System*. Boulder, Colo.: Lynne Rienner.

Moravcsik, Andrew. 1997. Taking Preferences Seriously: A Liberal Theory of International Politics. *International Organization* 51, no. 4 (Autumn).

Moses, Jonathan. 1994. Abdication from National Policy Autonomy: What's Left to Leave? *Politics and Society* 22:125–148.

Mundell, Robert A. 1960. The Monetary Dynamics of International Adjustment under Fixed and Floating Exchange Rates. *Quarterly Journal of Economics* 74, no. 2 (May):227–257.

Nader, Ralph, ed. 1993. *The Case Against Free Trade: GATT, NAFTA, and the Globalization of Corporate Power*. San Francisco: Earth Island Press.

Nye, Joseph S. 1990. *Bound to Lead: The Changing Nature of American Power*. New York: Basic Books.

Ocampo, José Antonio. 1999. Reforming the International Financial Architecture: Consensus and Divergence. *Serie temas de coyuntura 1*. Santiago, Chile: CEPAL/ECLAC, April.

Odell, John S. 1982. *U.S. International Monetary Policy: Markets, Power, and Ideas as Sources of Change*. Princeton, N.J.: Princeton University Press.

Oye, Kenneth A., ed. 1986. *Cooperation Under Anarchy*. Princeton, N.J.: Princeton University Press.

Pahre, Robert. 1999. *Leading Questions: How Hegemony Affects the International Political Economy*. Ann Arbor: University of Michigan Press.

Pollard, Sidney. 1985. Capital Exports, 1870–1914: Harmful or Beneficial? *The Economic History Review* 38, no. 4 (November).

Porter, Tony. 1999. The Transnational Agenda for Financial Regulation in the Developing Countries. In *Financial Globalization and Democracy in Emerging Markets*, ed. Leslie Elliott Armijo. London: Palgrave/Macmillan.

Rodrik, Dani. 1997. *Has Globalization Gone too Far?* Washington, D.C.: Institute for International Economics.

Rosecrance, Richard N., ed. 1976. *America as an Ordinary Country: United States Foreign Policy and the Future*. Ithaca, N.Y.: Cornell University Press.

Rueschemeyer, Dietrich, Evelyne Huber Stephens, and John D. Stephens. 1992. *Capitalist Development and Democracy*. Chicago: University of Chicago Press.

Ruggie, John Gerard. 1982. International Regimes, Transactions and Change: Embedded Liberalism in the Postwar Economic Order. *International Organization* 36, no. 2 (Spring).

Schwartz, Herman M. 1994. Small States in Big Trouble. *World Politics* 46:527–555.

Shultz, George, William E. Simon, and Walter B. Wriston. 1998. Who Needs the IMF? *Wall Street Journal*, February 3:A22.

Simmons, Beth A. 1994. *Who Adjusts?: Domestic Sources of Foreign Economic Policy during the Interwar Years*. Princeton, N.J.: Princeton.

Snidal, Duncan. 1985. The Limits of Hegemonic Stability Theory. *International Organization* 39 (Autumn):579–614.

Solomon, Steven 1995. *The Confidence Game: How Unelected Central Bankers are Governing the Changed World Economy*. New York: Simon and Schuster.

Soros, George. 1998. *The Crisis of Global Capitalism*. New York: Public Affairs Press.

Spiro, Peter J. 2000. The New Sovereigntists. *Foreign Affairs* 76, no. 6:9–15.

Stiglitz, Joseph. 1998. Must Financial Crises Be This Frequent and This Painful? McKay Lecture, Pittsburgh, Pennsylvania, September 23.

———. 2000. The Insider: What I Learned at the World Economic Crisis. *The National Republic*, April 17.

Tobin, James. 1978. A Proposal for International Monetary Reform. *Eastern Economic Journal*, 4.

Volcker, Paul. 1998. Personal Views on the World Economy: Can We Bounce Back? *Financial Times,* October 7 (online). Available from: <www.ft.com>.

Waltz, Kenneth N. 1959. *Man, the State, and War*. New York: Columbia University Press.

———. 1979. *Theory of International Politics*. Reading, Mass.: Addison-Wesley.

Weir, Margaret, and Theda Skocpol. 1985. State Structures and the Possibilities for 'Keynesian' Responses to the Great Depression in Sweden, Britain, and the United States. In *Bringing the State Back In*, ed. P. B. Evans, D. Rueschemeyer, and T. Skocpol. Cambridge: Cambridge University Press.

II. LEADERSHIP AND THE POLITICS OF GLOBAL FINANCE

Chapter 2

GLOBAL FINANCIAL ARCHITECTURE AND HEGEMONIC LEADERSHIP IN THE NEW MILLENNIUM

Mark R. Brawley

In contemplating the unfolding evolution of the global financial architecture, we need to focus attention on the United States. The United States enjoys a predominant position in the international economy, and wields military forces superior to those of any other country. It also commands a special position in the international financial system. How does American policy shape international monetary relations? If we are interested in developing a global financial architecture that will promote stable, noninflationary growth internationally in the future, how should the United States figure in our calculations? What theories or models can we turn to, to guide our predictions or our policy prescriptions?

As in other disciplines, the study of international political economy is subject to fads. Often however, fads fall out of step with reality. This seems to be the case with theories of hegemonic leadership, that is, theories that emphasize the role of a single dominant power in organizing the world's political and economic affairs. These arguments first drew attention in the 1970s, as several prominent scholars asserted that the comparatively prosperous and economically open era of the Classical Gold Standard, lasting from the 1870s until the outbreak of World War I, had only been possible due to the leadership of Britain. British leadership rested on political, economic, and military advantages—each significantly eroded by the First World War. The economic and eventually political disasters of the interwar period were in part attributed to the failure of either Britain or the United States to exercise effective leadership. Learning from these experiences, the United States made more conscious efforts to lead in the creation (and then operation) of rules or standards for behavior in international economic relations (Gilpin 1975; Krasner 1976), including those laid down in the Bretton Woods agreement governing postwar monetary relations (Ikenberry 1993; Mikesell 1994).

Many of these same scholars went on to predict dire consequences from the relative economic decline of the United States. However, in the 1980s, theories relating the stability and efficacy of international institutions, norms, and behavioral conventions to hegemonic distributions of power were roundly savaged. By the early 1990s, theories of hegemonic leadership had fallen from favor, at least among most academic political scientists.[1] Yet a glance at recent events would seem to suggest that in the first decade of the twenty-first century—perhaps more than at any time since the late 1940s—the theory should be relevant. We see displays of hegemonic leadership on the part of the United States, and even more tellingly, examples of failures of global cooperation due to the lack of hegemonic leadership.

The evidence is particularly clear in military affairs. Multilateral humanitarian interventions, performed in the name of the international community, hinge on the participation of the United States. This is especially true of intervention in the face of armed opposition, as in Kosovo in 1999, where the United States provided the vast majority of forces involved in combat. It reflects the degree of technological advantage the American military possesses over friend and foe alike, but it also represents other asymmetries: in intelligence gathered from a variety of sources, lift capability, command structures, a network of bases, and so forth. Being the only power with all these resources in hand, if the United States refuses to support intervention (as in central Africa on several occasions in the 1990s), the international community fails to act. Journals focusing on security matters refer to the current period as "the unipolar moment," and the concept of hegemony can once again be found in policy and academic discussions (for example, Layne and Schwartz 1993; Hoffmann 1995; Huntington 1999)—though less so in discussions of international economic affairs.

In order to argue that theories of hegemonic leadership remain relevant to an understanding of current and future international monetary affairs, I will attempt to clarify and defend three specific claims. First, I will describe the sources of theories of hegemonic leadership in the international political economy, linking the original theories' roots to the criticisms that have done so much to drive our thinking in other directions. My point will be to illustrate that a modified, alternative version of hegemonic leadership exists, one that maintains much of the vision of earlier versions, yet avoids some of their weaknesses. Second, I will show that by using this alternative version of the theory, an understanding of hegemonic leadership can help decipher patterns in recent monetary relations. Finally, I will elaborate some of the expectations we can formulate about monetary relations in the early twenty-first century based on the claims and conclusions reached above.

THEORIES OF HEGEMONIC LEADERSHIP

Theories of hegemonic leadership first emerged in the 1970s. Their rise signified an appreciation of the political underpinnings necessary for the smooth functioning of the international economy—something that had been forgotten, or at least had been ignored. The international economy appeared to be operating serenely in the 1960s under liberal principles and Western-designed institutions such as the International Monetary Fund (IMF), World Bank, and the General Agreement on Trade and Tariffs (GATT) in the apparent absence of interference from politics. The assessment that international politics could largely be ignored delighted professional economists, who were trained in what political scientists would call the "Classical Liberal" perspective (roughly equivalent to what economists themselves refer to as the "laissez-faire" or "classical" tradition).[2] This tradition holds that economics and politics should be kept separate, for the latter would merely distort and disrupt the former. However, in the early 1970s a series of crises challenged these views. First came the breakdown of the Bretton Woods monetary regime (ending the dollar's tie to gold and fixed exchange rates between the major currencies). This was followed by the OPEC oil embargo. The decade culminated with the developing countries demanding radical transformations of the international economy.

These events underscored the political aspects of economic relations. Having the international economy based on Classical Liberal principles such as free trade or open capital markets is a political choice. Such principles do not arise naturally or without political turmoil, as protests in the late 1990s against the World Trade Organization (WTO) remind us. Nor can a true separation of the political and the economic spheres exist, for any separation that is constructed must be maintained through political action. In the 1970s, the impact of the oil embargo, the disputes among the Western countries over exchange rates, and the final acts of the Vietnam drama all raised questions about the global role of the United States as well. If the Bretton Woods regime fell apart because the United States and its Western allies could not reach agreement on how to manage affairs (and neither the exercise of American coercion nor attempts at reaching a consensus worked), then perhaps a new era was dawning. This would be a period when the interests of the Western powers clashed, and the Americans would no longer be able to impose their will on their major allies. The decline of the United States relative to West Germany, France, Japan, and others suggested that political decision making among the industrialized democracies was undergoing some fundamental changes. The political basis of the international economy was now appreciated, but there were questions about how the political situation was evolving.

The 1970s and the Origins of the Theory of Hegemonic Stability

Hegemonic stability theory emerged as one way of understanding the political economic conflicts of the 1970s, as well as explaining the relative order of the international economy in the prior decades. The theory emphasized a close connection between orderly, open economic relations between states and a particular distribution of power in the international system (Gilpin 1975; Krasner 1976). When there was one country larger, more economically advanced, richer and more powerful than the others, it would be in a position to organize political economic relations to liberalize trade and monetary relations between countries. Being economically ahead of its competitors, it would see its own interests advanced by freeing trade and international finance. That one powerful country could use its power—in both positive and negative ways—to get other states to join in open economic affairs and adhere to Liberal principles. While the theory was used to describe American actions in the wake of World War II, it also drew heavily on the experiences of the nineteenth century, when Britain, as the first industrial nation, promoted Liberal economic practices around the globe.

As ably outlined by others elsewhere, there are several strands of theory which share an emphasis on the role of a dominant or hegemonic power in international relations (Lake 1993; Pahre 1999). The best-known variants are rooted in a body of theory dubbed "Realism" (Gilpin 1975; Krasner 1976). They therefore share the core precepts of that paradigm, including assuming that states are the primary actors in international relations, and that states are treated as single unitary actors who pursue a primary goal: power maximization. Since power is a relative concept (you can only tell whether a state is powerful by comparing its abilities and resources against those of another state), Realists assume states focus on *relative* rather than *absolute* gains. States will seek to get more out of any deal than the other parties to the arrangement, rather than seeking to get the most possible.[3] Realist versions of hegemonic stability theory unsurprisingly exhibit the same general traits attributed to all theories in this tradition: they are parsimonious, yet vague, providing superficially accurate, but not very testable propositions; they fail to take into account differences which spring from the domestic sphere; and their explanations and predictions are often inconsistent across issue areas.

Interestingly, Realist theories of hegemonic stability received some of their inspiration from sources best described as Liberal. In contrast to Realists, Liberals assume that actors are interested in accumulating wealth (that is, pursuing absolute gains rather than relative gains). With such assumptions, it is easier to identify instances where two or more actors can engage in mutually beneficial activities, such as trade. In the Liberal perspective, states have compatible interests—they could share in the gains derived from enhancing their market relations (as in liberalizing their trade), or in providing a public good. Charles Kindleberger's description of the Great Depression (1973) provided the most influential Liberal basis for a theory of hegemonic leadership. His analysis built upon economists' understanding of public goods provision, but applied that logic to the international system.[4] Kindleberger concluded that had the United States exercised more decisive leadership in the service of maintaining an open global economy in the early 1930s, both the United States and other countries would have benefited.

It is important to note that Kindleberger's view represents a "Modern Liberal" perspective rather than that of a Classical Liberal. Classical Liberals of the nineteenth century put their faith entirely in markets. This faith was put to the test in the economic downturns of the late nineteenth century, but most especially in the Great Depression of the 1930s. In these instances, markets proved unsteady and precarious as they fell into deflationary spirals. Markets could only be revitalized and restabilized through government interventions. As a result, Modern Liberals accept that the government has a positive role to play in a market-based economy by providing the basic infrastructure necessary for any market to operate with stability and efficiency. This infrastructure would include, among other things, a set of enforced rules concerning ownership, contracts, and so forth; a medium of exchange (that is, a form of money) to enhance transactions; regulation of monopolies, oligopolies, and other situations produced by the market which do not lead to socially optimal outcomes; regulation of externalities; and the provision of public goods, such as defense, which markets fail to produce.

The best way to establish the infrastructure for a market economy, or to deal with market failures, is to have a political actor exercise authority over the economy's participants. To take one example from the list above, markets work much more efficiently if participants share a medium of exchange (money, in other words). Rather than have a professor exchange a series of lectures for her monthly groceries, those who consume the lectures pay in a means which can be used to purchase other items. Domestically, a currency is usually issued by the government, which can use its resources to make the money attractive, and employ its coercive powers to make acceptance of the money obligatory (what we refer to as "legal tender").

One complication for a Modern Liberal when examining these issues in an international setting, however, is that there is no recognized authority above the level of states capable of carrying out this and similar responsibilities. Ideally, Modern Liberals would look to a central political authority to address these shortfalls, even in the international political economy. This would provide the best technical solution for resolving some of the problems mentioned above. Modern Liberals express a preference for vesting authority in a global body when they talk about refashioning the international political economy, including redesigning the global financial system.

Classical Liberals, due to their continued strong faith in the ability of markets to function on their own, often criticize Modern Liberal views. Some go so far as to recommend that the international economy be left free from government interference. There are points to be made in favor of this view when we look to specific aspects of policy. Can governments manage exchange rates more effectively than markets? Can governments manage financial matters in the face of market pressures? Won't the market win in the end? These questions are more than technical matters, however. Politics enters the equation, since society will not accept all market outcomes. States may have decided that the benefits from participating in international markets are too great to forego, but all states temper their participation in the international economy in some ways, just as they limit or offset the impact of domestic markets. Their publics will not let markets set rates of unemployment or inflation without demanding state intervention at some point. While some economic theorists might argue that unfettered markets remain the best tools for allocating societies' resources, political scientists no longer engage in that debate. Having observed societies choosing to restrain or overturn markets, political scientists instead focus their attention on the political struggle surrounding the extent of the limits placed on markets.

At the level of the international economy, this political struggle takes place between states operating in an anarchic environment—as sovereign actors, states recognize no higher political authority. From a Modern Liberal's point of view, the infrastructure or intervention markets needed for stability and efficiency are unlikely to emerge in the absence of a global government. They would define the problem as one of failed collective action. Although all states might be better off with the public good in place, there is a political failure in allocating the costs for providing the good.[5] For Realists, the infrastructure or intervention necessary for smoothly functioning markets is unlikely to appear because states fear that if they choose to provide these actions individually, the benefits might accrue to other states. Yet both Modern Liberals and Realists can identify conditions when, even in an anarchic setting, the public goods associated with a stable, open international economy might be provided.

The Basis for Expecting Hegemonic Leadership

Perhaps surprisingly, the Modern Liberals and Realists point to *similar* conditions regarding the solution of these shortfalls to market operation. Asymmetries in the international system could create a situation where a single state might choose to fulfill these needs in its own interests. For Realists, a concentration of power in the international system would create a situation where a single powerful state could create the necessary infrastructure and then work to maintain this infrastructure over time. The ability to exercise power in the anarchic environment is crucial, for it helps approximate a central overarching political authority. Critical in this assessment, however, is the notion that the hegemonic leader bears these costs as an investment for attaining relative gains versus others. The incentive to provide leadership declines as other participants gain economically and politically. In this portrayal, the hegemonic leader's ability to provide these goods declines in parallel with its interests in doing so.

For Modern Liberals, the key asymmetry was not one state's power versus the others, but rather asymmetry in the consumption of the public good. This can be seen in Kindleberger's arguments (1973) about American policy in the Great Depression. He argued that the United States would have been better off if it had chosen to reflate its own economy without first resorting to protectionism in the early 1930s. Specifically, he argued that if the United States had run a countercyclical monetary policy, and had left its borders open to others' exports, it would have helped others out of the early stages of the depression (see especially, 1973, chapters 5 and 6). Carrying the burdens of recovery—even doing so alone—would have brought an earlier end to the depression, thereby benefiting all (including the United States). If an American-led recovery would have cost less than the gains to be made by the United States from improved trade and international investment, then the United States made a mistake by not providing leadership. The United States was the only state likely to conclude that leadership would pay, because its disproportionate size meant it would benefit so much (in absolute terms) from global economic recovery.[6]

The two versions looked alike, in that they each emphasized how the role of a hegemonic leader could replicate in the international political economy, however imperfectly, the functions of a government in the domestic political economy. They varied, though, in their understandings of the motivation of the hegemonic leader as well as those of other states. Realists saw things in terms of competition for relative gains, whereas Liberals stressed the absolute gains to be made by the hegemonic power when it provided leadership. Would a hegemonic leader seek assistance from others? The Realist version suggested no, unless such cooperation was merely an attempt by the leader to shift costs onto others. The Liberal version suggested that we should expect to see cooperation with the leader, with others willing to pay some of the costs (though they would often "free ride" on the larger state's actions).

The Realist version of the theory had a slightly different spin on it however. On the one hand, Realists argued that international market relations based on liberal principles would only become widespread when a hegemonic power undertook the burdens of leadership, yet this was not quite the same as saying all instances of hegemonic leadership would automatically lead to this outcome. Some Realists argued that a single powerful state might impose its preferred set of rules or practices on others, and sometimes this would mean liberal rules were put in place. (Some went further than others, by arguing that any disproportionately powerful state would also have to be economically and technologically advanced, so that any instance of a hegemonic distribution of power would lead us to expect an example of liberal hegemonic leadership.) Yet within the Realist framework, it was also possible to imagine a single powerful state imposing nonliberal rules on the international economy.

In its basic form, then, the Realists were arguing that the rules, norms of behavior, or principles guiding international behavior (an international "regime," as we call it) would be most stable when a powerful state was enforcing them. And remember that in the Realist view, states are competing for relative gains, so other states should be resisting the hegemonic leader's attempts to impose these rules. A simple test of the basic Realist version of the theory, then, was to see if hegemonic distributions of power matched the stability of international regimes (Keohane 1980), hence the name of the best known proposition to flow from this literature: hegemonic stability theory. Evidence easily illustrated that the stability of international regimes was not necessarily directly related to changes in the distribution of power. The discrediting of hegemonic stability theory led to the disapproval of theories of leadership in international political economy more generally.

While the criticisms of hegemonic stability theory itself were accurate, the implications for other propositions flowing from either the Realist or Liberal version of theories of leadership were less clear. On the one hand, it is easy enough to imagine situations where a hegemonic leader, in the pursuit of relative gains, might denounce existing international regimes, including those rules or norms that the same hegemonic leader had propounded earlier. The hegemonic leader may feel it has a better chance of succeeding when the participants' behavior (most especially its own) is unrestricted. The connection between regime stability and hegemonic leadership is not as simple as some critics of the theory would have us think.[7]

If leaders might play a critical role in the creation of open international economic regimes, yet it was also possible to think of situations which would lead the hegemonic power to seek to alter the regime (that is, destabilize it), then no single simple test existed for evidence of hegemonic leadership. Moreover, given the differences between the Liberal and Realist versions, different propositions could be generated concerning the relations between hegemonic and nonhegemonic states. These differences make it difficult for both those who argue for and those who argue against employing the concept of hegemonic leadership.

Is There Evidence of Hegemonic Leadership in Previous Monetary Regimes?

Over the previous century and a half, has hegemonic leadership been necessary, or perhaps even sufficient, for achieving stable and successful multilateral cooperation on important world monetary and financial matters? Theorists

emphasizing hegemonic leadership, such as Gilpin (1975), have argued that
Britain played a key role in creating international regimes in the nineteenth
century based on Liberal principles. This conclusion has been challenged, most
notably in the area of trade. John Vincent Nye (1991) argued that British tariffs
provided ample protection for those sectors that needed it (especially agricul-
ture). Patrick O'Brien and Geoffrey Pigman (1992) have also highlighted aspects
of British trade policy to stress that it looked similar to that of other states, and
not like that of a leader of an international regime. Earlier, Timothy McKeown
(1983) had argued that Gilpin's version of hegemonic leadership failed to provide the most persuasive account of British trade policies. Gilpin argues that
Britain's victory in the Napoleonic Wars gave that country a hegemonic position
in the international system, enabling it to promote free trade in the middle of the
nineteenth century. Yet as McKeown points out, there is a rather large time gap
between the changes in the international system Gilpin identifies, and the policy
outcomes he wishes to explain.

In international monetary relations, the most serious challenges to the
utility of theories of hegemonic leadership have come from Barry Eichengreen
(1989) and Guilio Gallarotti (1995). In line with other economic historians critical of the theory, Gallarotti challenges the view put forward by Realists that
Britain played the pivotal role in stabilizing or maintaining the gold standard.
His points boil down to several pertinent observations. In monetary affairs in that
period, important policy decisions were handled by a private institution (the
Bank of England) rather than the government (1995, 87). The Bank did not
speak for the state per se. Moreover, market mechanisms were key to the gold
`standard's stability. Gallarotti also argues that we should have seen indications
of Britain coercing or bribing other states to join the gold standard.[8] The implicit
character of the regime, and the unwillingness of Britain to use side payments
to lure members of the Latin Monetary Union onto the gold standard are presented as evidence challenging notions of hegemonic leadership.

I find such criticisms unconvincing. Noting that market mechanisms are
central to a regime is hardly a reason for rejecting claims about hegemonic
leadership. Economic power can be exercised through the market. Similarly,
nothing in the theory requires that leadership be exerted towards making an
international regime more explicit—especially if keeping the regime implicit
also enables the leader to be vague about its own responsibilities. Plenty of
evidence indicates that in both the pre– and post–World War I years, the gold
standard operated through adjustment policies that were neither automatic nor
uncoordinated, though there is disagreement about evidence of leadership in the
process (Simmons 1994; Broz 1997a, 1997b). The question to pose, then, is
whether the performance of the regime (fostering higher volumes of trade and
international investment by lowering uncertainty) was due to British leadership
exerted through the markets.

Britain did enjoy special advantages that suggest it could play a leading role in the gold standard era. One element would most certainly be the preference for the pound in international transactions. As Gallarotti notes, the British pound was the first currency to be used widely in international transactions; its appeal was based on Britain's open markets, where a wide variety of goods could be found, and on the fact that Britain was the primary source of international capital flows. Both these characteristics rested on political decisions, not accidents.[9] Gallarotti also does not dispute the fact that London could attract capital more effectively than any other financial center in this period (1995, 39), or that its ability to export capital gave it an important role in the regime. Thus he winds up arguing that "Great Britain played a central role within the collective core. To the extent that Great Britain was the best at recycling capital, we can say that it was a stabilizing force within the core as well as the international monetary system." He later concludes that "[t]he British functioned efficiently as the hub of global adjustment" (1995, 195). Despite his claims to be refuting theories of hegemonic leadership, in the end Gallarotti concludes that Britain (or at least British institutions) played a central, perhaps even essential, role in maintaining the stable performance of the gold standard.

In another ostensible critique of the theory of hegemonic stability, Barry Eichengreen ([1989] 2000) identifies three specific tasks hegemonic leaders should undertake: facilitating the balance of payments adjustment process, providing (or managing) international liquidity, and acting as a lender of last resort. Yet expecting to find evidence of these three specific tasks in any historical context is a tall order, for one would not find any public authority, except on occasion the Bank of England, accepting the responsibility of being the lender of last resort *in the domestic sphere* until the twentieth century (Goodhart 1988). Eichengreen highlights two sorts of problems with the theory. One has to do with the willingness of the hegemonic power to engage in stabilizing activity. As he ably shows, on several occasions the dominant economic power has destabilized the international monetary regime. This underscores a problem with Realist versions of the theory, already discussed above.

Another problem with the Realist version of hegemonic leadership is that evidence of leadership in monetary affairs is rarely in the form of coercion, though some evidence along these lines does exist (Kirshner 1995). More often, the most important financial centers can provide focal points for coordinating policy actions such as market interventions. Even when each actor wishes to cooperate, leadership may be required. At the other extreme, instances where a state is in such a dominant position that it can dictate norms and practices to other states in the international system are rare and fleeting (Eichengreen 1989).

Eichengreen's conclusions, like Gallarotti's, are mixed. He concludes, "While one cannot simply reject the hypothesis that on more than one occasion the stabilizing capacity of a dominant economic power has contributed to the smooth functioning of the international monetary system, neither can one reconcile much of the evidence, notably on the central role of international negotiations and collaboration even in periods of hegemonic dominance, with simple versions of the theory." ([1989] 2000, 222). Eichengreen therefore favors an approach somewhere between hegemonic stability theory and Robert O. Keohane's alternative: Institutionalism. Unlike Realism, Institutionalism assumes that states pursue other goals (such as wealth) as well as—or even instead of—power. They may partake in international regimes in order to improve their ability to make decisions together. By cooperating, they may be able to pursue mutually beneficial outcomes, in contrast to the largely competitive outcomes usually expected by the Realists.[10] Institutionalism does not preclude a role for leadership, but merely suggests that mutual interests can go a long way towards explaining cooperation, even in the absence of leadership.

As these criticisms make evident, there are serious questions leveled against theories of hegemonic leadership as used in the study of monetary affairs. Most of Eichengreen's criticisms rest on particular expectations about the interests the hegemonic state pursues. As with Gallarotti's reasoning, the arguments are quite potent against the basic Realist version of hegemonic leadership. There are other theories of hegemonic leadership, though, which have evolved away from the simple Realist view. Such refinements offer better rationales for the goals of hegemonic leadership, thus enabling us to understand when a powerful state might act to destabilize an international arrangement, but still be pursuing its own interests, as well as providing a better understanding for why other states might accept hegemonic leadership.

An Alternative View of Hegemonic Leadership

Many of the criticisms of the theory reflect its Realist roots. In particular, the structural accounts suffer from problems in explaining how and when states capable of stabilizing the international economy actually do so, as opposed to acting in ways that fail to provide stability, or worse, actually destabilize the international economy. Yet intuitively and logically, leadership could be an important factor in providing public goods, or in eliciting international cooperation;[11] what is needed is a way to understand the conditions under which leadership would be exercised. By addressing these issues, we might be able to understand whether or not a hegemonic leader helps attain global monetary cooperation, and when it will exert its own resources to help stabilize the international monetary system in times of crisis. In this section, I provide an alternative explanation for the hegemonic leader's motivations, which allows us to understand the inconsistencies in the evidence often cited by critics of hegemonic stability theory.

Elsewhere (Brawley 1993), I have sought to improve our understanding of hegemonic leadership by examining factors previously ignored. Rather than assume that each time power was concentrated in a single state, these hegemonic states had similar preferences about international economic outcomes, I developed a model grounding such states' goals in theories of international trade and domestic politics. I argued that hegemonic states were not pursuing relative gains versus other states, but instead were trying to deliver benefits to their constituents. I employed the Stolper-Samuelson theorem to identify domestic interests in international economic policies. These interests were then filtered through domestic institutions. Using this analysis, I argue that the states most likely to attempt to create and maintain open economic relations with other states would be nonautocracies relatively well endowed with capital.[12] The owners of capital within such states stood to gain the most from integrating national markets.

Saying such states would attempt to lead the integration of national markets does not mean we should conclude they would automatically be successful. Any argument about the results of leadership should also rest on an understanding of the systemic environment confronting the hegemonic leader, including an analysis of the motivations of other states. The degree of a leader's success, in my view, is not only a function of its power, but of the degree of opposition or support it is likely to face when utilizing its power. That requires judging attitudes of other powerful states.

More than one state could have demands from its constituents to pursue similar policies. Leadership in the international political economy comes about if one state can respond to such demands by implementing policies that would alter decisions made by other actors. Several states might desire the integration of national markets or financial systems, but that alone is not enough to ensure such a result. Asymmetries in resources held explain how some of these states could more effectively pursue those policies, though the exact amount of power they would require would depend upon the obstacles or resistance they faced.

This view rests much more closely with a view of hegemonic leadership drawing on the Liberal version of the theory (emphasizing the provision of public goods). It also aims to explain characteristics of international regimes other than stability. *Hegemonic leaders are trying to garner economic benefits for their citizens, but the policies they pursue have the potential for positive-sum interactions with others.* In international monetary affairs, one example would be the use of a national money as an international medium of exchange. When Britain chose to base the pound on gold, and to give the Bank of England power to manage the currency's characteristics, it was modifying the national currency in order to give it greater appeal as an international medium of exchange. This delivered benefits to a certain set of constituents within Britain's borders, but by developing a medium of exchange used by others, also made it easier for international economic exchanges to take place.

In this example, the government of Britain does not locate itself in the international system, discover it is hegemonic, and then act in a certain fashion. Rather, it reacts to demands for action by domestic interests by engaging in cost-benefit calculations about policy. In this instance the public good of an international medium of exchange is produced, but there are private benefits for Britain as well. I would not expect a hegemonic state to put systemic considerations above the interests of its own citizens, and in this formulation of hegemonic leadership such clashes are entirely possible.[13] Hegemonic leaders may decide to alter (that is, destabilize) regimes that no longer serve their citizens' interests, they may prefer not having any regime at all, or they may defend or stabilize an existing regime. My point would be that you must examine whether a hegemonic state has both the interests *and* the capabilities to lead in a given international context. Interests, capabilities, and the international context should all be derived independently from each other, if one is to come to grips with the disparate patterns observed in international affairs.[14]

Using this sort of logic to examine examples of American leadership in international monetary affairs, we see that the United States has exhibited leadership in different ways at different points in time. Ever since World War II, American interests in this issue area have been shaped by the fact that the United States is relatively well endowed with capital compared to other countries. In other words, capital is more readily and cheaply available in the United States than in most other countries. Investments abroad tend to earn higher returns, all other things being equal. Americans who own capital have consistently had an interest in employing some of their capital abroad for the last fifty years. American policies in monetary affairs naturally reflect those interests—though the conditions in which these policies are pursued have changed, including changes in the power of the United States compared to other states, as well as levels of competition in international financial matters. These factors cause policies to be remade.

As the supplier of the currency most widely used internationally, and as the most important creditor (but one that has also come to rely on inflows of capital), the United States remains very interested in defending the status quo. Specifically, this requires keeping national financial systems linked together, international barriers to capital low, and confidence in the dollar high. American financial actors have extensive international exposures, and the U.S. government will use the resources at its disposal to defend the interests of its citizens. Since it can bring to bear more resources than either other states or international financial institutions, and since it has special capabilities associated with the international role of the dollar, it can pursue its interests in this area more effectively than other states as the new millennium opens.

This is not to imply that the United States can dominate or dictate policy to all other states. It cannot. What it can do, and does more effectively than other states, is use side payments or sanctions to influence the policies of other states.

As some examples below will show, this ability remains unmatched. It can provide international public goods such as stability or emergency lending in a crisis more effectively than other actors—*when it chooses*. Stability will be produced by American policy as a by-product of, or as a means to, the pursuit of American private ends.

The best test for evidence of leadership comes in instances of crisis. As Eichengreen made clear in establishing his standards for evidence of hegemonic leadership in international monetary affairs, a leader would be expected to act as a lender of last resort. This then will be the test I set forth in the following cases I briefly sketch out, but tempered with the sort of cost-benefit calculations derived from my alternative model. Does the United States, in order to pursue the international financial interests of its citizens, act to provide stability in international crises through lending to other states (or more precisely, other states and/or their citizens) facing a financial crisis? The lender of last resort acts through a specific logic: it bails out troubled banks before those banks collapse, preventing the difficulties from spreading to other financial actors. The lender of last resort safeguards the financial system's stability and health by intervening to save individual actors within the system.

In a domestic setting, a central bank provides this help, but only in view of an agreement with private financial actors participating in the system. The lender of last resort assists banks in trouble due to liquidity problems (that is, the banks are basically healthy, but unable to meet their immediate obligations because they cannot liquidate their assets quickly). To prevent difficulties from spreading through the network of financial actors bound together through complex contractual obligations, the lender of last resort provides liquidity as quickly as possible to the banks experiencing problems. Speed is of the essence, as is the ability to provide sufficient amounts of funds. If the lender of last resort were to bail out every bank automatically, however, banks would be encouraged to take undue risk.[15] Indeed, domestically, central banks publicly accept the responsibility of being lender of last resort only for those banks they monitor through their regulatory functions. In a crisis, the lender of last resort may bail out creditors who have acted rashly, not because those creditors deserve assistance, but rather because the action will defend the stability or integrity of the financial system itself.

When we transfer these matters to the international level, we once again face the issue of lack of governance. International regulation of banks does not take place per se; banks are only regulated through national agencies. When a banking crisis begins, threatening the integrity of the international financial system, or merely threatening to cause disruptions beyond its point of origins, will an international lender of last resort step in? No actor has accepted that responsibility, due to the moral hazards involved absent regulatory powers. In the case of a crisis in terms of a currency's value, international financial institutions have established some procedures for providing assistance, though this is not the same as saying they have accepted obligations to act.

I am not arguing that the international monetary system could not be stabilized in any other manner than through hegemonic leadership. It is quite possible to visualize international agreements, backed by powerful international institutions, which could potentially ensure the integration of national financial systems, along with stabilizing mechanisms. Such arrangements remain on the drawing board, however. It seems unlikely that states will concede either sufficient decision-making powers or resources for such schemes to come to fruition in the near future.

Cooperative measures (in the absence of asymmetry among the actors) may also be created to achieve similar outcomes, but politically, such arrangements are only likely to yield sustained, positive results under very circumscribed conditions. The historical analogue in the domestic setting would be the development of clearinghouse associations in the nineteenth century. Clearinghouse associations sought to create shared private means to increase efficiencies in the interactions of banks, as well as provide a central coordinating agency in crises. Some worked well, but most were superceded by more effective arrangements centering on a central bank at the apex of a hierarchical structure. The central bank could perform its stabilizing and regulatory functions precisely because of asymmetries in resources, information, and power.

As noted earlier, when we turn to the international arena, there is no world government capable of creating a global central bank backed by sufficient regulatory powers. In some ways, certain regional and multilateral financial institutions resemble clearinghouse style arrangements. When we consider recent examples, however, the evidence will illustrate the continued importance of American leadership during crises. That leadership is inconsistent. The United States has acted to stabilize the international monetary system at times—when it has seen its own interests at stake. The greater those interests, the more decisively it has acted. These actions have benefited others in the international political economy, but the United States puts its own interests first. The United States leads, but only on its own terms.

EVIDENCE OF HEGEMONIC LEADERSHIP IN THE 1980S AND 1990S

In the crises that erupted in international monetary relations in the last two decades of the twentieth century, the United States has often played a decisive role—for better or worse. My goal in this section is not to cover every crisis, or even to describe the ones selected for discussion in great detail. Instead, I will briefly discuss several prominent crises in order to illustrate that the United States can and does exercise leadership in monetary affairs by acting as an international lender of last resort. Crises serve to reveal the extent of that leadership, and its relative effectiveness; these examples also underscore that American leadership is offered unevenly, since it varies with the extent of American interests at stake.

U.S. Leadership in the Debt Crisis of the 1980s

In late 1982, Mexico and then Brazil announced they would soon be unable to meet their international debt obligations, sparking an international crisis. The basic story is well known, and bears repeating in only simple fashion. During the 1970s, borrowers had benefited from relatively low real interest rates; low rates were caused by inflation, but also by the highly competitive, largely unregulated offshore lending of U.S. dollars. Sovereign actors in particular had run up large debts, but as long as inflation raced on and the Eurodollar market remained available, it made sense to continue to borrow. Conditions were only changed once the Federal Reserve began to raise interest rates to restore confidence in the dollar in 1979. The combination of the changing value of the dollar, the higher interest rates on the accumulated debt, plus the contraction of the U.S. economy sparked by the Fed's policies (which lowered debtor countries' export earnings), brought about the international debt crisis of the 1980s.

As many critics have pointed out, the previous inflation, and the Fed's actions to correct that inflation with its tight money policy, clearly destabilized the international monetary system. American officials put American interests before the interests of the international system as a whole. On the one hand, critics of theories of hegemonic leadership point to this period to say the United States was pursuing unilateral goals, even to the point of endangering the international financial system. Yet by claiming that self-interest guides policy, which particular theories of hegemonic leadership were being criticized? The United States acted in defense of its own position and interests, which in this instance did not create positive spillovers for others.

Once problems began to emerge elsewhere, the United States moved to offset some of the repercussions associated with its actions. Other groupings of states or even international institutions were not prepared to act with the same decisiveness or weight as the U.S. government. The United States took the lead in stabilizing the situation, and eventually promoted several solutions for reducing levels of debt. A pattern is discernible that is repeated in other crises: the United States took responsibility only grudgingly (often only after it was apparent others were unable or unwilling to, and after it was clear there would be significant damage if no action was taken). The United States then tried to take the necessary steps to avert widespread disruptions, but at minimal cost to itself. Some read this pattern as a failure to lead; I would rather argue that it is evidence of rational calculation regarding leadership.[16]

To make this case, we can compare the actions of the United States with those of other interested actors. Which actor came closest to acting as lender of last resort in the 1980s? As debtor countries declared their inability to pay back international debts, the two most important international financial institutions, the IMF and the World Bank, were both poorly positioned to be of assistance. The IMF had been created to perform other duties (namely, to provide short-term assistance to countries with a balance of payments problem under a fixed-exchange-rate regime), and lacked the funds or the mechanisms to intervene quickly and with sufficient force to deal with the problems that were emerging. Over time, the IMF would adapt, and would raise additional funds from contributors, but it has been unable to increase its resources at the pace with which international financial flows have grown. The World Bank was also ill prepared to deal with the problems associated with the debt crisis of the 1980s. Its facilities were designed to stimulate long-term growth, not help countries get out from under a burden of debt in the short- to medium-term. In short, these international financial institutions (IFIs) lacked the mandate, resources, and internal capabilities to provide sufficient funds with the rapidity required. Neither could play the role of lender of last resort effectively, even though they each may have tried.

While both these IFIs would play significant parts in the debt crisis of the 1980s, their actions had to be supplemented with funds from other sources. In the really tight spots, the United States moved directly and forcefully. Moreover, the U.S. government could act with speed as well as force, unlike the more bureaucratized IFIs. In the opening years of the crisis, the process for applying to the IMF took too long, and the amounts available (disbursed over a length of time) were not likely to be enough to do much good on their own. The U.S. government directly loaned money to Mexico when the crisis first occurred, and it would move to make direct loans to other debtors at later critical moments.

At other times in the 1980s, the U.S. government played a central role. It could uniquely bring other elements of power to bear on the relevant actors. More than any other actor, it could coerce private lenders to reschedule debt. By threatening changes in the enforcement of domestic regulations, and in accepting to allow banks to continue to hold questionable loans on their books, the government was able to put pressure on banks to accept reschedulings and other arrangements. While the IMF often got the headlines for organizing reschedulings of private credit, it was the Fed that actually influenced the banks, as illustrated by meetings such as those in November, 1982 (Pauly 1997, 119). More effectively than any other state, the United States could offer its own domestic market as a source for the dollars needed by the debtors to repay their loans. In the end it was the only actor able to coerce or cajole *both* the borrowers and lenders.

In trying to get an overall picture of the crisis, we see the first set of responses geared towards short-term solutions. As the crisis continues, the banks reposition themselves as new monetary instruments are developed. Banks began writing down the loans and selling off portions; the secondary market emerged, allowing the debtors themselves to buy back some of their original obligations. The possibilities for resolving the crisis changed as a result. With first the Baker Plan and then the Brady Plan, the U.S. government worked to keep the banks solvent and reduce their exposure over time, but also keep the debtors' relations with the banks positive. The United States consistently worked to find a solution that would maintain the health of its banks, and put that goal ahead of the welfare of the debtors whenever the two interests clashed. Its ultimate goal, however, was to have the banks and the sovereign debtors both healthy once again.

I would argue that both the causes of the 1980s debt crisis, as well as the pattern of responses to that crisis, represent evidence highlighting the importance of American hegemonic leadership. The patterns one discerns can best be understood by viewing how the United States has defined and pursued its own interests, which can have a negative or a positive impact on others. American policy decisions sparked the crisis because the dollar served as the key international currency. Once the crisis broke, American interests were to put the health of private creditors first, though the United States also wanted to rebuild sound relations between debtors and lenders. Throughout, the United States also sought to protect the international role of the dollar. These interests are observable in later financial crises. IFIs and other creditor countries had roles to play, but by and large their positions were defined by how well they could fit into broader American concerns.

The Peso Crisis of 1994

In coming to an understanding of the financial crisis gripping Mexico in 1994, we once again can look to the United States as the source of international monetary instability. This time, however, the instability spilling over from American domestic policy was much more unexpected. The United States had become such a major importer of capital (though it exports capital, too) that domestic policy actions were drawing in substantial funds, causing capital to be inadvertently denied to other possible borrowers.

To be sure, domestic factors inside Mexico played a role, ensuring that America's neighbor to the south suffered rather than some other country. In the wake of the liberalizing and privatizing reforms begun in the 1980s, and in resolving problems with the federal government's budget, Mexico had been able to increase its inflow of foreign capital substantially in the early 1990s. Yet because its inflation rate was higher than that of the United States, but the peso-dollar exchange rate fixed, Mexicans were taking the capital loaned from abroad and spending it. This was to be expected when the peso was overvalued vis-à-vis the dollar, as many economists and analysts recognized. When the foreign reserves used to defend the peso were run down from some $30 billion in the spring of 1994 to only $5 billion by the end of the year, the peso's exchange rate could no longer be maintained. The peso's fall was more dramatic than anticipated, however, as foreign capital shied away from the country—much of it drawn to the United States, exacerbating the exchange rate problem.[17]

Without fresh capital inflows, foreign investors moved to withdraw their funds and place them in more attractive investments elsewhere (often in the United States). No one wanted to be left holding investments in Mexico if the government were to declare a default, or even if the government pushed inflation higher (which it might do to cover its peso-denominated debts). The other option for the government was to jack up interest rates to keep foreign investors in, but this would bring the economy to a grinding halt—an unpopular measure. The country's economic fundamentals were not out of order so much as its exchange rate had been poorly managed, causing capital flows to change unexpectedly. The country faced a liquidity crisis.

However one wishes to distribute the blame for triggering the crisis, it is rather clear that the United States played a positive role in resolving the crisis. The U.S. government and the IMF pulled together a package of $40 billion ($12 billion coming directly from the U.S. government). Mexico was able to use the money to generate a substantial trade surplus in 1995, which enabled it to service its international debts and begin building up its foreign reserves again. Mexico had to undertake serious adjustments (a contraction in the economy combined with the devaluation) and pledge collateral against the funds it received (it used oil revenues), but the money from outside made the adjustment shorter and much more effective.

Unable to gather the congressional (and popular) support for the rapid decisive move the situation called for, the Clinton administration used funds from the Treasury's Exchange Stabilization Fund. (The administration's move was actually urged by Republicans in Congress, though it was a novel use of the funds in this particular account.) The U.S. government could disburse funds much more rapidly than the IMF. Also importantly, the United States pressured the IMF into contributing $18 billion of its own funds—far beyond what should have been allowed under existing regulations. Yet as Devesh Kapur has remarked, the IMF's largest relief package ever "was only possible because Mexico borders on the IMF's largest shareholder" (1998, 120, also see Pauly 1997, 124–5).

There are also those who point out that the U.S. government made a handsome profit on the interest for the money loaned to Mexico (an accounting profit of $1 billion), though that pales when compared to the value of having a more stable economy south of the border. More importantly, it is fairly easy to see that the intervention in this case had positive-sum results: gains for Mexico, for the United States, and for others who might have been hurt in the spread of the "tequila effect." Overall, the handling of this crisis shows that the United States can act decisively (in terms of both speed and power) in the face of a crisis, if that crisis is perceived by the executive branch to be important. It also illustrates that the IMF can be forced to move quickly, but again, only if the U.S. government is pushing it to act and helping it gather the resources required.

U.S. Leadership in the East Asian Financial Crisis of the 1990s

In 1997, the East Asian "economic miracle" turned sour. Countries that had been touted as the paragons of economic development because they embraced liberal international economic principles were suddenly confronting an economic and financial collapse. Once again, however, the United States took the most direct and decisive intervention to stabilize the situation. The United States also got the IMF to act more speedily and with more weight than it otherwise would have in this instance.

In the case of Indonesia's financial troubles in 1997, the United States was one of the first contributors to the stabilization package put together in the name of the international community. As Secretary Robert Rubin stated to the *New York Times* on November 1, 1997, "Financial stability around the world is critical to the national security and economic interest of the United States." The United States pledged $3 billion out of the estimated $15 to $18 billion offered to Indonesia by the international community in November 1997. Indonesia proved to be only one among several countries stricken at that time. Altogether, the IMF would set aside $100 billion for emergency loans to South Korea, Thailand, and Indonesia. (The amounts from various sources were estimated to total $17 billion for Thailand, $43 billion for Indonesia, and $57 billion for Korea.) The Clinton administration proposed to Congress that the United States pump an extra $18 billion into the IMF, too.

Importantly, the crisis was largely a manifestation of a liquidity shortage that spread across the region. For instance, South Korea's problem was not the size of its foreign debts compared to its economy or its trade, but rather the size of those debts compared to its foreign exchange reserves. What it needed most was a rapid and decisive infusion of cash. The IMF could muster sizable sums of foreign exchange, but it could not disburse this money with the requisite speed to stave off problems. Within weeks of the signing of a letter of intent with the IMF, the South Koreans were requesting more immediate assistance. Once again it took the U.S. government's direct assistance (*and* the Fed's pressure on private creditors) to do the "heavy lifting" in the crisis. The United States appears as the real lender of last resort in this instance, not the IMF.

The scope of American activity is more clearly appreciated when one compares it to the inaction of the other potential sources of stability in the region. Japan urged the creation of an Asian stability fund as part of the response to the crises in East Asia, but this was blocked by the United States. While the United States may not always enjoy having to do much of the work in stabilizing crises, it also does not want to lose its commanding voice in these situations. Moreover, Japan was not in a position to offer a wide range of economic policies to aid a regional recovery (such as taking in more imports) because of its own problems. And despite having some of the "deepest pockets" in the world (in terms of reserves of foreign currency), Taiwan too was of little import in the regional financial crisis.

There are those who suggest that the U.S. role in the East Asian crises was less than it should have been. After all, the crisis was allowed to spread through the region precisely because help did not arrive swiftly enough. Masaki Shiroyama, deputy president of Nikko Research Center, believes the United States was concentrating its efforts elsewhere—where its interests were more clearly defined. The position of U.S. financial actors in Russia and Brazil was greater than in the East Asian economies, in Shiroyama's view, and this prompted swifter action on the part of the American government in those other regions (Shiroyama 1999). In purely economic terms Shiroyama does not have that strong a case, but certainly the United States was worried about the political vulnerability of the governments in Russia and Brazil, which may have prompted it to act more quickly in those cases. In the end, the United States played a critical role in stabilizing the financial systems in all three regions. The way in which the United States exerted leadership varied considerably across the three regions however, reflecting its own calculations of its interests, not systemic stability above all else.

Summary: Assessing Evidence of U.S. Leadership

Even on the narrow terms of being an international lender of last resort, there is evidence the United States has played a leading role in international monetary affairs. There are those who have charged that its performance has been uneven, and I have argued that the speed and decisiveness with which it has acted in the past does indeed vary. Rather than seeing this as evidence of a lack of leadership, however, I consider this pattern to illustrate how the United States leads by pursuing its own interests. The greater its stake in the situation, the more swiftly it moves. Mexico's peso crisis is perhaps the most extreme example.

The evidence also highlights how critical the U.S. role typically is in an international financial crisis. Other actors, such as the IMF, the Bank for International Settlements (BIS), or the other G7 countries, have also played a part in the unfolding of crises, but their roles are largely defined by American decisions. Even when the IMF got the headlines (such as during the East Asian crisis in the late 1990s), American action was critical when the IMF could not move quickly enough in the crisis, or when IMF resources were simply too small to be effective. This does not mean that the United States can or even wishes to act separately from other major economic powers, or the international institutions to which it belongs. Burden-sharing with like-minded allies is a sensible strategy, and politically the IMF provides a multilateral endorsement for actions that might be less appreciated if seen as purely American. What these examples bear out is that financial markets generate instabilities, and that international action to regain stability is often sensible for the United States. When American interests are at stake, especially when those interests go beyond the merely financial and touch on broader economic issues (as in the peso crisis) or even security concerns (as in the Russian default), the United States will act.

AMERICAN LEADERSHIP IN THE FUTURE

Thus far, I have presented the argument for utilizing models of hegemonic leadership to understand patterns in international monetary affairs. I began with the rationale behind models of hegemonic leadership, noting the criticisms leveled against such approaches as they are applied in international monetary affairs. I then argued that a more sophisticated model of leadership exists which employs a sounder economic logic for explaining the actions of the hegemonic leader. Moreover, this logic creates the possibility for the hegemonic leader to share interests with other states. The hegemonic state accepts a leading role in order to pursue and defend the interests of its constituents, rather than defining its interests to be entirely equal to systemic stability. Along these lines, I then presented evidence of U.S. leadership. Beyond noting that the United States promoted its national currency for use as an international medium of exchange, I also illustrated how the United States has acted as a lender of last resort in several instances in the last two decades. The United States acted to stabilize the global financial system, perhaps not out of systemic imperatives so much as to limit dangers to the interests of some of its citizens. The United States has not automatically defined any and all dangers to the international financial system as threats to its own citizens' interests; it has, however, at times moved to defend the interests of its citizens in such a way that it did stabilize the international financial system.

The Need for Hegemonic Leadership in the Future

Given the consistency over time of the interests of the United States (or more specifically, the interests of its constituents) in maintaining stable international financial relations across much of the globe, in increasing the integration of national financial systems, and in opening up foreign markets for American financial actors, we can form distinct expectations about the future. The U.S. government will play a leading role in international monetary affairs because it will continue to defend the international role of the dollar and work to stave off local or regional crises that could damage wider financial circles. It will seek cooperation to attain its aims.

Despite an emerging agreement on the hegemonic position of the United States in military affairs, debates remain, but for some surprising reasons. In the decade following the collapse of the Soviet Union, the United States didn't seem to have a global security strategy of any kind. Is it possible to have a hegemonic leader without a system-wide strategy? As the authors of the Strategic Survey of 1999 concluded, "[I]n a unipolar world, the incentives for a truly hegemonic role are low." In other words, in security affairs the threats confronting the United States prior to September, 2001 seemed purely regional, and therefore generated only regional responses. A proactive, global strategy was not needed, absent an overarching threat. This left some analysts wondering whether we could refer to American "leadership."

In international monetary affairs, dangers were more obviously system-wide in character than in the international security realm. Yet these threats are new in character and difficult to discern. Among the most dangerous of the new threats to the international monetary system are contagion effects of the type that brought on Brazil's problems in late 1998 and early 1999. Given the wide use of derivatives to hedge against various types of risk, unseen links between disparate financial activities have been established. When Russia failed to service its debt, derivatives caused repercussions for the value of Brazil's currency. Given the existing difficulties in regulating international financial markets, and in finding these hidden links between domestic financial systems before a problem arises, the ability to respond to a crisis swiftly and forcefully will be needed now more than ever. Existing IFIs seem ill-suited to meet the tasks which lie ahead.

Relying on American leadership entails numerous risks as well. The future exercise of American economic leadership hinges on several factors. Will the United States continue to have large enough stakes in the international monetary system to wish to carry the burdens of leadership? Will it continue to have the resources enabling it to carry out stabilizing interventions? Answers to both questions depend very much on what one expects to happen to the role of the dollar. If people around the world continue to have confidence in the future value of the dollar (which in turn depends on policies of the Fed, performance of the U.S. economy, and the performance of other currencies such as the euro and the yen), the dollar will continue to serve as the most widely used international medium of exchange and reserve asset. The dollar's position helps define American interests in the global financial system as well as give it special powers when executing its monetary policies. As long as the dollar is the key international currency, U.S. private financial actors will continue to have extensive interests prompting the government to lead in international affairs. And as long as the dollar commands confidence, most future interventions to stabilize currency or international banking crises will require infusions of dollars, giving the United States a unique capacity in this sphere.

Certainly for the next decade if not longer, the evidence points to a continuation of American leadership. It is unlikely that another major economic power will emerge with the desire to undercut American leadership, for instance, or that the euro or yen will soon rival the dollar in international use. Cooperation through existing institutions, or even the adaptation of institutions to ensure more effective burden sharing is much more likely. And most important of all, American interests will continue to be tied to the smooth functioning of the international financial system. As Lawrence Summers put it, "[F]inancial liberalization, both domestically and internationally, is a critical part of the U.S. agenda" (Kapur 1998, 121).

As the pace of financial liberalization continues, and as the scale of monetary flows increases, the scale and speed required for successful interventions also grow. How can these challenges best be met, given the unwillingness of states to relinquish decision making to international organizations? Will the United States be able to muster the requisite resources for effective interventions, without the help of allies? Will the U.S. government be capable of acting decisively in instances where the systemic threat is hazy and hard to judge? Would coordinated action be more effective if it were channeled through existing multilateral IFIs? Could a better institutional arrangement be designed, and implemented? Those are the critical questions to be addressed in any attempt to formulate recommendations about rearranging the global financial architecture.

CONCLUDING THOUGHTS

Rather than give highly speculative answers to such questions, I wish to emphasize that my earlier arguments identified a critical starting point for any other discussions about the future. American leadership will be there in the near future; any new international arrangements must take that into account. The interventions of the United States will perhaps be inconsistent, but given that it will have the most widespread, deepest interests in these matters, it will be more likely to intervene earlier and with more resources than other actors. While international institutional arrangements might be improved, issues of burden sharing and control will probably hamper these. The United States is unlikely to relinquish political leadership in exchange for greater commitments by others, and others should be expected to limit their contributions in light of that position. While a new institutional setup could provide a far superior technical solution to the threats facing the international financial system, the political conditions for creating such an institution simply do not currently exist.

Theories of hegemonic leadership may have fallen out of favor in the discipline, but they remain useful for understanding the outcomes we observe in monetary relations. Absent a grasp of the actions of the American government in recent international monetary crises, it would be difficult to reach any understanding of what happened. To understand how the international financial system will evolve in the next few decades, one needs to begin by looking inside the United States. Only by appreciating the domestic forces calling for action, and by understanding how the resulting policies match with or compete against the policies generated elsewhere, can we get a handle on likely outcomes at the international level. At the international level, some things may change—other currencies (such as the euro) may eventually rival the dollar, and unification of Europe's financial system may eventually give it interests and strengths matching those of the United States. Yet, European and Asian interests appear currently to be much more in step with American interests, rather than marching to their own beat. We have, then, the key ingredients for continued American leadership—a single powerful state, supported by its allies, already cognizant of its interests, and prepared to act. The United States can be expected to continue to exercise leadership in future monetary relations—though a good place to start would be in admitting its leadership responsibilities to itself (Garten 1999). The manner in which it achieves its leadership, the terms on which it works with others, and the consequences of its leadership for others will ultimately depend on American policy choices. We need to choose well.

NOTES

I wish to thank Mahdvi Gupta for research assistance, and Hans Kammler for offering insightful advice on an earlier draft. Any errors or omissions are entirely my responsibility. I would also like to thank Leslie Elliott Armijo both for inviting me to participate in this project and for her helpful editing and suggestions.

1. A real indication of the theory's lack of popularity came with the publishing of an article asking how political scientists could ever have regarded this approach seriously (Grunberg 1990). This piece, in a leading international relations journal, was premised on the assertion that not only was there no significant evidence worth refuting, but there was no logic to argue against. The theory's previous popularity was presented as a mystery, best explained by referring to arguments concerning psychology, American propaganda, and the construction of myths.

2. See the chapter by David Felix in this book.

3. To illustrate this point, we often use an example of a hypothetical trade agreement between two countries. Should the United States prefer an agreement with Canada that delivers an extra $5 billion in benefits to each, or should it prefer an arrangement where the United States gains by $4 billion, and Canada by $3 billion? A Realist would

recommend the latter, though the United States would be $1 billion poorer compared to the other option, in order to gain more than the other country.

4. Public goods have characteristics making them less likely to be provided in a market situation, namely non-excludability and non-rival consumption. The first term refers to the ability of the provider to block or discriminate between consumers; the second notes that one consumer's enjoyment of the good does not impair others from partaking of the same good. Many examples of market failures fall into this category, or involve goods with one of these characteristics. For example, goods with non-rival consumption, but where excludability is possible, are referred to as "club goods." They often are not produced via markets, but rather through a set of privileged actors (a "club") who have joined together to provide the good.

5. Some questioned whether actions attributed to hegemonic leadership (such as support for more liberal international trade or monetary relations) should be described as public goods or as club goods, since participation in most international regimes can be excluded (Conybeare 1984; Snidal 1985).

6. Consider the difference between the Realist and Modern Liberal views for this example. For the latter, unilateral action makes sense so long as the leader's own benefits of recovery are greater than the costs of leading recovery. For the former, the hegemonic leader does an additional calculation. The leader figures out its net benefits of recovery (that is, benefits less costs) but then compares this to the net benefits accruing to other states. The benefits (or losses) for itself must be advantageous compared to the benefits (or losses) flowing to others.

7. Even better examples come from the evolution of the law of the sea. In the years after World War II, when U.S. naval forces dominated, the United States had little need to establish any sort of rules; rules would simply bind the United States and provide no significant advantages. Therefore, the United States actively scrapped various aspects of the law of the sea at that time. Only after its relative power in this issue area declined did it make sense for the United States to engage in rule making. Another example might come from the current discussions about missile defenses. The United States may be willing to forfeit existing agreements on ABM systems because it can easily win any arms races that may reignite.

8. In chapter 3 Gallarotti presents the international monetary conferences of the late nineteenth century as examples of Britain's failure to construct a regime, though he recognizes a regime existed. He should have been examining explanations for changes in the characteristics of the regime (such as increases in membership, or the failure to make its rules more explicit). Gallarotti clearly assumes that Britain stood to gain by making the regime more explicit, a point I would question. In his view, however, Britain's refusal to pay to formalize the regime is a sign of a failure of leadership.

9. Eichengreen for one has referred to the gold standard as "one of the great monetary accidents of modern times" (1996, 7). While he was referring to the gold standard's origins in the eighteenth century, there were several other critical junctures in the development of the Bank of England's powers, and the spread of the gold standard internationally. Each involved conscious, political choice (Brawley 1999, chapters 1 and 2; Broz 1997b, chapters 2 and 3).

10. It is worth noting that Realists too have theories about cooperation based on shared benefits, as seen in alliance formation via balancing. This logic can then be applied to leadership in economic affairs, as in interpretations of American actions after World War II. American-led international regimes were for its allies to participate in, while rivals were excluded. Economic cooperation was to ensure success in a broader military competition. For a sophisticated attempt to merge the security and economic logics in play here, see Skalnes (2000).

11. Some models, which place these arguments in a dynamic setting, expect leadership to be counterproductive to the provision of public goods however (see Pahre 1999).

12. Different types of extremely powerful states would pursue policies that other states would be unlikely to find mutually beneficial. Since leadership is an open-ended concept, one can conceive of benevolent or malevolent leaders (see Pahre 1999).

13. In fact, I treat such instances as puzzles to be explained (Brawley 1999). These episodes (when systemic stability and/or openness was pursued even when it was too costly or no longer reflected the interests of the majority of the hegemonic leader's constituents) are typically failures to adjust policies during relative decline. The speed of policy change depends on the interplay of bureaucratic politics, the urgency of systemic threats, and the structure of domestic coalitions.

14. It is interesting to examine how such issues are described in military terms. One would be unlikely to deduce, for example, that the United States did not hold a special place in security affairs by the failure of its intervention in Somalia. The United States had few interests at stake, and when the costs of the operation began to rise, it simply backed out. Nor would one deduce from Operation Allied Force that NATO mattered more than the United States or that the participation of so many allies was proof that theories of hegemonic leadership offer little insight into outcomes. To act, even the hegemonic state must have both interests and capabilities; to succeed, the hegemonic state must have adequate capabilities, depending upon the contributions of allies and the level of opposition to overcome.

15. This is the "moral hazard" problem identified in the study of insurance.

16. The comparison to make is with Gallarotti's characterization of the monetary conferences under the gold standard.

17. Political factors also played on investors' nerves: there were several assassinations in the bitter political campaign that year, violence broke out in Chiapas, and the United States Congress threatened to block or delay NAFTA.

REFERENCES

Brawley, Mark R. 1993. *Liberal Leadership: Great Powers and Their Challengers in Peace and War*. Ithaca, N.Y.: Cornell University Press.
————. 1995. Political Leadership and Liberal Economic Sub-systems: The Constraints of Structural Assumptions. *Canadian Journal of Political Science* 28, no. 1, 85–103.

————. 1999. *Afterglow or Adjustment? Domestic Institutions and the Responses to Overstretch.* New York: Columbia University Press.

Broz, J. Lawrence. 1997a. The Domestic Politics of International Monetary Order: The Gold Standard. In *Contested Social Orders and International Politics,* ed. David Skidmore. Nashville, Tenn.: Vanderbilt University Press.

————. 1997b. *The International Origins of the Federal Reserve System.* Ithaca, N.Y.: Cornell University Press.

Conybeare, John. 1984. Public Goods, Prisoners' Dilemmas and the International Political Economy. *International Studies Quarterly* 28:5–22.

Eichengreen, Barry [1989] 2000. Hegemonic Stability Theories of the International Monetary System. In *International Political Economy: Perspectives on Global Power and Wealth,* ed. Jeffry A. Frieden and David A. Lake.

————. 1996. *Globalizing Capital: A History of the International Monetary System.* Princeton, N.J.: Princeton University Press.

Gallarotti, Guilio. 1995. *The Anatomy of an International Monetary Regime: The Classical Gold Standard, 1880–1914.* New York: Oxford University Press.

Garten, Jeffrey. 1999. Lessons for the Next Financial Crisis. *Foreign Affairs* 78, no. 2:76–92.

Gilpin, Robert. 1975. *U.S. Power and the MNC.* New York: Basic Books.

Goodhart, Charles. 1988. *The Evolution of Central Banks.* Cambridge, Mass.: MIT Press.

Grunberg, Isabelle. 1990. Exploring the "Myth" of Hegemonic Stability. *International Organization* 44, no. 4:431–477.

Hoffmann, Stanley. 1995. The Crisis of Liberal Internationalism. *Foreign Policy* 98:159–177.

Huntington, Samuel. 1999. The Lonely Superpower. *Foreign Affairs* 78, no. 2:35–49.

Ikenberry, G. John. 1993. The Political Origins of Bretton Woods with comments by John Odell. In *A Retrospective on the Bretton Woods System,* ed. Michael D. Bordo and Barry Eichengreen. Chicago: University of Chicago Press.

Kapur, Devesh. 1998. The IMF: A Cure or a Curse? *Foreign Policy* 101:114–129.

Keohane, Robert. 1980. The Theory of Hegemonic Stability and Changes in International Economic Regimes, 1967–1977. In *Changes in the International System,* ed. Ole R. Holsti, R. M. Siverson, and Alexander L. George. Boulder, Colo.: Westview Press.

Kindleberger, Charles. 1973. *The World in Depression.* Berkeley: University of California Press.

Kirshner, Jonathan. 1995. *Currency and Coercion.* Princeton, N.J.: Princeton University Press.

Krasner, Stephen D. 1976. State Power and the Structure of International Trade. *World Politics* 28, no. 3:317–347.

Lake, David. 1993. Leadership, Hegemony, and the International Economy: Naked Emperor or Tattered Monarch with Potential? *International Studies Quarterly* 37:459–489.

Layne, Christopher, and Benjamin Schwarz. 1993. American Hegemony—Without an Enemy. *Foreign Policy* 92.

McKeown, Timothy. 1983. Hegemonic Stability Theory and Nineteenth Century Tariff Levels in Europe. *International Organization* 37, no. 1:73–92.

Mikesell, Raymond F. 1994. The Bretton Woods Debates: A Memoir. *Princeton Essays in International Finance* no. 192. Princeton, N.J.: Princeton University.

New York Times. 1997. Clinton Hopes $3 Billion for Indonesia Will Dull Panic. November 1.

Nye, John Vincent. 1991. Revisionist Tariff History and the Theory of Hegemonic Stability. *Politics and Society* 19:209–232.

O'Brien, Patrick K., and Geoffrey Pigman. 1992. Free Trade, British Hegemony, and the International Economic Order in the Nineteenth Century. *Review of International Studies* 18:89–113.

Pahre, Robert. 1999. *Leading Questions: How Hegemony Affects the International Political Economy*. Ann Arbor: University of Michigan Press.

Pauly, Louis. 1997. *Who Elected the Bankers?* Ithaca, N.Y.: Cornell University Press.

Shiroyama, Masaki. 1999. "Why the U.S. was eager to support Brazil." Retrieved from www.gwjapan.com/ftp/pub/nrca/ctv3n12e.html.

Simmons, Beth. 1994. *Who Adjusts? Domestic Sources of Foreign Economic Policies during the Interwar Years*. Princeton, N.J.: Princeton University Press.

Skalnes, Lars. 2000. *Politics, Markets and Grand Strategy*. Ann Arbor: University of Michigan Press.

Snidal, Duncan. 1985. The Limits of Hegemonic Stability Theory. *International Organization* 39, no. 4:579–614.

Chapter 3

CAPITAL CONTROLS:
WHY DO GOVERNMENTS HESITATE?

Benjamin J. Cohen

Few observers doubt that the financial crisis that struck Asia in 1997 and 1998 was a watershed event for the global monetary system. For years the tide had been running just one way—toward ever closer integration of national financial and currency markets. Politically, governments found themselves increasingly thrown on the defensive by the rapid growth of international capital mobility. As I wrote a few years ago, "Like a phoenix risen from the ashes, global finance [has taken] flight and soared to new heights of power and influence in the affairs of nations" (Cohen 1996, 268). The only question, it seemed, was how much the traditional monetary authority of sovereign states had, as a result, been compromised. As I continued, "The phoenix has risen. Does it also rule the roost?" (Cohen 1996, 270).

But then came the fall of the Thai baht and all the contagion—the "bahtulism"—that followed. For many, these events only served to affirm the new power of markets to constrain policy. The phoenix did indeed rule the roost. Governments had no choice but to live with new limits on their authority. But for others, myself among them, choice was precisely the issue. The crisis posed an opportunity to think again about the priority popularly attached to financial globalization. Why should governments meekly submit to the dictates of market forces? Perhaps the time had come to cage the wilder impulses of the phoenix— to tame it, if not slay it, by imposing limitations of one kind or another on the cross-border mobility of capital.

Has that time, in fact, come? Not long after the crisis broke, I proposed that "when viewed in historical perspective, the decade of the 1990s may eventually be seen as a high-water mark in the empowerment of financial markets. . . . The tide, I suggest, is starting to turn as policymakers, faced with the worst financial calamity since the Great Depression, have sought to reclaim some of their powers that had hitherto been ceded to market forces. Particular attention is being paid to the case for capital controls. Once scorned as a relic

of the past, limits on capital mobility could soon become the wave of the future"
(Cohen 1998b, 2). Looking back, that judgment now seems premature. Capital
controls have not become the wave of the future—at least, not yet. The purpose
of this chapter is to explore why.

At issue is the governance of monetary relations in the global economy. I
begin the first section with a brief look back at the transformation of the global
financial environment that gradually occurred in the decades prior to the recent
crisis—an epoch during which governments found it increasingly difficult to
manage monetary affairs within their own sovereign territories. So long as the
tide was running toward ever greater mobility of capital, states assumed they had
little choice but to learn to live with the consequences. Focusing on the countries
of East Asia, the second section then considers how policy calculations were
recalibrated as a result of the 1997–1998 crisis, bringing new attention to the old
case for capital controls. The pros and cons of capital controls are evaluated in
the third section. Though brief, analysis suggests that the intellectual case for
controls is actually stronger than conventionally supposed.

But if that is so, why then has the tide not turned more decisively? Why
do most governments still hesitate to do more to limit capital mobility directly?
The answer is elusive but undoubtedly has much to do with the prominent role
of the United States, the dominant power in international monetary affairs, in
opposing new controls. The question is addressed in the fourth section, followed
by a brief conclusion.

THE NEW GEOGRAPHY OF MONEY

That the global financial environment has been greatly transformed in
recent decades is undeniable. The full significance of that change for monetary
governance, however, has only lately begun to be widely appreciated. Prior to
the recent crisis, policymakers were only starting to learn how to cope with the
rising challenge to their authority.

The postwar resurrection of global finance was truly phenomenal. A half
century ago, after the ravages of the Great Depression and World War II, financial
markets everywhere—with the notable exception of the United States—were generally weak, insular, and strictly controlled, reduced from their previously central
role in international economic relations to offer little more than a negligible amount
of trade financing. Starting in the 1950s, however, deregulation and liberalization
began to combine with technological and institutional innovation to breach many
of the barriers limiting cross-border activity. In a cumulative process driven by the
pressures of domestic and international competition, the range of commercial
opportunities gradually widened for lenders and borrowers alike. The result was
a remarkable growth of capital mobility, reflected in a scale of financial flows
unequaled since the glory days of the nineteenth-century gold standard.

Even more phenomenal were the implications of these changes for monetary governance and the long-standing convention of national monetary sovereignty. With the deepening integration of financial markets, strict dividing lines between separate national monies became less and less distinct. No longer were economic actors restricted to a single currency—their own home money—as they went about their daily business. Cross-border circulation of currencies, which had once been quite common prior to the emergence of the modern state system, dramatically reemerged, with competition between national monies gradually accelerating. This is what I have referred to elsewhere as the new geography of money—the new configuration of currency space (Cohen 1998a). The functional domain of each money no longer corresponded precisely with the formal jurisdiction of its issuing authority. Currencies instead became increasingly *deterritorialized*, their circulation determined not by law or politics but rather by the dynamics of supply and demand.

Currency deterritorialization posed a new and critical challenge to governments, which had long relied upon the privileges derived from a formal monetary monopoly (in particular, the powers of seigniorage and macroeconomic management) to promote their conception of state interest. No longer able to exert the same degree of control over the use of their monies, either by their own citizens or others, governments felt driven to compete, inside and across borders, for the allegiance of market agents—in effect, to sustain or cultivate market share for their own brand of currency. Monopoly yielded to something more like oligopoly, and monetary governance was reduced to little more than a choice among marketing strategies designed to shape and manage demand.

Broadly speaking, four strategies were possible, depending on two key considerations—first, whether policy was defensive or offensive, aiming either to preserve or promote market share; and second, whether policy was pursued unilaterally or collusively. The four strategies were:

1. *Market leadership*: an aggressive unilateralist policy intended to maximize use of the national currency, analogous to predatory price leadership in an oligopoly.

2. *Market alliance*: a collusive policy of sharing monetary sovereignty in a monetary or exchange-rate union of some kind, analogous to a tacit or explicit cartel.

3. *Market preservation*: a status-quo policy intended to defend, rather than augment, a previously acquired market position.

4. *Market followership*: an acquiescent policy of subordinating monetary sovereignty to a stronger foreign currency via some form of exchange-rate rule, analogous to passive price followership in an oligopoly.

Strategies, in turn, could embody tactics of either *persuasion* or *coercion*. Persuasion involved investing in a money's reputation, acting to enhance confidence in the currency's continued usefulness and reliability—in effect, to establish or sustain a successful brand name. Coercion could be exercised through a wide range of measures designed to regulate or prohibit diverse financial activities (in principle, up to and including the unfashionable option of capital controls). Though neither persuasion nor coercion was foolproof, each type of tactic could be highly effective in influencing a currency's market position. In practice, most governments learned to make use of both in varying combinations, since the two were not mutually exclusive.

Nothing demonstrated the challenge to monetary governance more than the financial crisis that hit Asia in mid-1997. Governments that previously had taken pride in the competitiveness of their currencies suddenly found themselves unable to preserve user loyalty. Strategies that once seemed adequate to sustain market share now had to be reevaluated in the light of a worldwide "flight to quality" by mobile capital. Inevitably, policymakers were drawn to take a new look at the neglected option of capital controls.

SHOCK AND AFTERSHOCK

Initially, as the first shockwaves of crisis swept over the region, the impulse of Asian governments was to go on the defensive, investing expensively in determined efforts to reinforce confidence in their currencies—the "confidence game," as Paul Krugman ironically dubbed it (1998a; 1999b). The aim of the confidence game was market preservation, at almost any cost.[1] But as user preferences proved more resistant to tactics of persuasion than first anticipated, a search for new approaches began. The question was: Could anyone think of an alternative?

Currency Boards?

For a few, the answer seemed obvious: Abandon any pretense of national monetary sovereignty and adopt instead a strategy of strict market followership in the form of a currency board, as already existed in Brunei and Hong Kong. Long promoted by a small coterie of specialists inspired by the writings of American economist Steve Hanke,[2] the currency board idea enjoyed a brief vogue in Indonesia in early 1998 prior to the forced resignation of President Suharto in May. In February, 1998, on Hanke's advice, the government announced its intention to move ahead with plans to establish a currency board system linked to the U.S. dollar. The *Economist* quoted Suharto himself referring to the project as an "IMF-plus" program (March 7, 1998, 43).

In the end, however, the idea was abandoned under pressure from the Fund and other foreign creditors, who—with very good reason—sensed a disaster in the making. Certainly a currency board had not protected Hong Kong from the relentless pressures of destabilizing speculation. Given the extraordinary level of uncertainty in Indonesia at the time, establishment of a currency board might well have led to a rush to buy dollars, generating sky-high interest rates that in turn could have crushed what was left of the country's banking system. The Indonesian government was soon persuaded that it first needed to strengthen financial markets, deal with foreign debts, and bolster central bank reserves before it could even think of embarking on such a risky experiment. Accordingly, the plan was formally abandoned in March, 1998,[3] and no other country in the region has since indicated any interest in moving in the same direction.

Monetary Union?

For others, the answer seemed to lie in a different direction—in abandoning monetary sovereignty not to a currency board but rather to a monetary union of some kind on the model of Europe's new Economic and Monetary Union (EMU). In short, go on the offensive with a forceful strategy of market alliance. Union would offer the benefit of numbers—and thus the hope that the whole might, in effect, be greater than the sum of the parts. Who could doubt, after all, that one joint money might be more attractive than a myriad of separate national currencies? Even before the crisis broke, the idea was already being actively explored by prominent economists (for example, Eichengreen 1997). Once the region's troubles began, interest rapidly spread. Wrote one observer, "Some kind of monetary regionalism in the region is . . . inevitable" (Mundell 1997). Wrote another, "Asia should . . . create an Asian Monetary Union" (Walter 1998). Official responses, however, were for the most part distinctly unenthusiastic.[4] For obvious reasons, political as well as economic, no government was yet prepared to forsake completely its own brand of money.

In fact, it is evident that the political preconditions for monetary union in Asia are not yet in place.[5] As I have written elsewhere, the lessons of history on this issue are clear (Cohen 1993; 1998a, 84–91). To be sustainable, a joint currency among sovereign states requires one or the other of two prerequisites: either a local hegemon to enforce discipline or else a broad network of institutional linkages sufficient to neutralize the risks of free riding or exit by any participant. Neither prerequisite would seem to be in evidence in Asia today.

Certainly it is clear that, as yet, Asian countries lack a broad constellation of commitments of the sort that might make a full surrender of monetary sovereignty immediately acceptable to each partner. The void is not for want of trying. Even before the crisis, regional central banks had begun building institutional linkages in a series of low-profile forums designed to promote dialogue and mutual exchanges of information.[6] Such groupings, many hoped, might help weave precisely the sort of fabric of related ties that could one day support more ambitious strategies of monetary alliance. But despite such efforts there is still little tradition of true financial solidarity—to say nothing of political solidarity—across the region.

A Yen Bloc?

On the other hand, there obviously is a potential hegemon in the neighborhood: Japan. Indeed, it is fair to say that no initiative toward monetary alliance in the region would have much chance at all without the active participation of Asia's dominant financial power. Collusion to promote market share would require determined leadership from Tokyo to create a currency bloc based on an internationalized yen. But are Asians yet prepared to bury historical suspicions of Japanese motivations and interests? Japan might well aspire to a strategy of market leadership, but it is not at all clear that others in the area would voluntarily follow. Nor, in view of the country's own economic travails, is it evident that Tokyo presently has the capacity to sustain an effective campaign to cultivate regional use of its currency. In fact, nothing approximating a formal yen bloc is likely to emerge any time soon.

To be sure, that does not rule out less ambitious forms of joint collaboration with the Japanese, so long as Japan's hegemonic pretensions remain relatively muted and within the limits of its present capabilities. In early 1996, for example, as many as nine neighboring governments were happy to sign up for a series of agreements committing the Bank of Japan to make yen credits available when needed to help stabilize exchange rates (*New York Times*, April 27, 1996, 20). And in 1997, after the first shockwaves hit, they were even more enthusiastic about Tokyo's proposal for a new regional financial facility—what quickly came to be called the Asian Monetary Fund (AMF)—to help protect national currencies against speculative attack.[7] The AMF proposal was by far the most ambitious effort by Japan to implement a strategy of market leadership in Asian finance. Although successfully blocked by the United States, which publicly expressed concern about a possible threat to the central role of the IMF,[8] the idea continues to attract interest (Bergsten 1998).

Moreover, despite economic troubles at home and the steady repatriation of private investments from abroad, Tokyo has persisted in seeking new ways to promote its monetary role in the region (Hughes 2000). In October 1998, Finance Minister Kiichi Miyazawa offered some $30 billion in fresh financial aid for Asia in a plan soon labeled the "New Miyazawa Initiative," and two months later made clear that Japan had every intention to revive its AMF proposal when the time seemed right (*Financial Times*, December 16, 1998). Similarly, in late 1999, Japanese authorities floated a plan to drop two zeros from the yen (which is currently valued at over one hundred yen for either the dollar or the euro) in order to facilitate its use in foreign transactions. Simplifying the currency's denomination, said one official, "might have a positive effect in that the yen would be more internationally easy to understand" (*NYT*, November 19, 1999, C4). And in May 2000 Tokyo engineered agreement among thirteen regional governments on a new network of swap arrangements centered on Japan's yen (*The Economist*, May 13, 2000). Clearly, Japan has no intention of abandoning its hopes for a yen bloc in Asia. The process, however, is apt to be more evolutionary than revolutionary in nature. In the meantime, the question remained: Was there any alternative to deal with the immediate crisis?

Capital Controls?

Gradually, attention began to focus on the option of capital controls—a strategy of market preservation conventionally based more on coercion than persuasion, inspired above all by the obvious example of China. Though hardly without troubles of their own, including a near bankrupt banking system, loss-making state industries, and rising unemployment, the Chinese were spared the worst ravages of the crisis. Where other economies were being pushed into recession, China's growth barely faltered; and where other regional currencies were being depreciated in value by anywhere from 10 to 20 percent in Taiwan and Singapore to as much as (at one time) 80 percent in Indonesia, the yuan held steady. One of the main reasons, observers concurred, was China's vast panoply of exchange and capital restrictions, which made it virtually impossible for users, domestic or foreign, to bet heavily on a devaluation. Might similar limits work for other countries as well?

The most dramatic response came from Malaysia, which in early September 1998 imposed strict controls of its own over the convertibility of the national currency, the ringgit, for both trade and investment uses. Kuala Lumpur's new strategy was adopted quite self-consciously in emulation of the Chinese. Said one government official, "Malaysia's new currency controls are based on China's model" (Wade and Veneroso 1998, 20).[9]

In the first year of the crisis the Malaysian economy had shrunk by close to 7 percent, the ringgit by 40 percent, and the Kuala Lumpur stock market by 75 percent. By the end of August, the country's authoritarian leader, Prime Minister Mahathir Mohamad, was no longer prepared to tolerate the orthodox policies of his finance minister (and then heir apparent) Anwar Ibrahim, who was fired and later jailed. Those policies, the prime minister believed, simply collaborated in a Western conspiracy to ruin the Malaysian economy. The time had come, he asserted, to take back control from international speculators, led by George Soros and "the Jews." Henceforth trading in the ringgit would be carefully controlled, the exchange rate was to be rigidly fixed, and capital invested in the country would have to remain for at least one year before it could be repatriated. The idea was to provide room for more expansionary domestic policies than had otherwise seemed possible. Monetary policy was immediately eased, with interest rates cut sharply, and in October a new budget was brought in combining substantial tax cuts with heavy new public spending programs. "The plan," Dr. Mahathir told legislators, "aims at freeing Malaysia from the grip of the Asian financial crisis and to place Malaysia's economy on a stronger footing" (*NYT*, October 24, 1998, B15).

That the prime minister's radical new controls would prove controversial was hardly surprising. Though easy to ridicule for his conspiratorial views, Dr. Mahathir nonetheless posed a difficult challenge for conventional views on monetary governance, which took the primacy of capital mobility as a given. For decades, emerging nations had been lectured on the virtues of financial-market liberalization—yet here was a government that was doing just the reverse. Dr. Mahathir's audacity, many thought, could turn out to have a powerful demonstration effect. What if Malaysia should indeed recover more quickly as a result of its freshly installed insulation from international speculation? The experiment was carefully watched.

Nor was Malaysia alone. Some countries in the region, including most notably South Korea and Taiwan, had always maintained residual controls to limit the volatility of capital flows. And even before Dr. Mahathir acted, Taiwan and others had already resorted to new restrictions, albeit none so draconian as Malaysia's. One example was the Philippines, which in mid-1998 reintroduced limits on selected transactions involving repatriation of capital or remittance of profits. Another example, rather more startling, was Hong Kong, long considered the region's last bastion of true laissez-faire capitalism, where in late summer a broad program of new regulations was instituted to limit speculation on the local stock and currency exchanges.

By the fall of 1998, therefore, it was clear that capital controls were no longer a forbidden topic.[10] As one source commented, "[C]apital curbs are an idea whose time, in the minds of many Asian government officials, has come back" (Wade and Veneroso 1998, 23). Like it or not, an approach once dismissed as obsolete—a leftover of a more interventionist era—was now back on the policy agenda.

THE CASE FOR CONTROLS

Capital controls are controversial. Critics oppose them as inefficient and unworkable. Advocates justify them as a tonic for stricken economies. For decades the burden of proof was on those who would foolhardily try to block the seemingly irresistible tide of financial globalization. With the crisis in Asia, however, came a new respectability for limits of some kind on the cross-border mobility of capital. Both theory and history suggest that the burden of proof has now shifted to those who would defend the conventional wisdom rather than those who attack it.[11]

Pros and Cons

The traditional case against capital controls is simple. It is the case for free markets, based on an analogy with standard theoretical arguments for free trade in goods and services. Commercial liberalization is assumed to be a mutual-gain phenomenon, so why not financial liberalization too? Like trade based on comparative advantage, capital mobility is assumed to lead to a more productive employment of investment resources, as well as to increased opportunities for effective risk management and welfare-improving intertemporal consumption smoothing. We are all presumably better off as a result.[12] In the words of Federal Reserve Chairman Alan Greenspan, an authoritative representative of the conventional wisdom, "The accelerating expansion of global finance . . . enhances cross-border trade in goods and services, facilitates cross-border portfolio investment strategies, enhances the lower-cost financing of real capital formation on a worldwide basis, and, hence, leads to an expansion of international trade and rising standards of living" (1998, 246).

All these gains, conversely, would be threatened by controls, which it is assumed would almost certainly create economic distortions and inhibit socially desirable risk taking. Worse, given the inexorable advance of financial technology across the globe, restrictions in the end might not even prove to be effective. Again in Alan Greenspan's words, "We cannot turn back the clock on technology—and we should not try to do so" (1998, 249). Any government that still preferred controls was, in effect, simply living in the past

Against these arguments, which have long dominated thinking in policy circles, two broad lines of dissent may be found in the scholarly literature. One approach focuses on the assumptions necessary to support the conventional wisdom, which are as demanding for trade in financial assets as they are for exchanges of goods and services. Strictly speaking, as a matter of theoretical reasoning, we can be certain that free capital movements will optimize welfare only in an idealized world of pure competition and perfect foresight. In reality, economies are rife with distortions (such as asymmetries in the availability of information) that prevent attainment of "first-best" equilibrium. As Richard Cooper has written, "It has long been established that capital mobility in the presence of significant distortions . . . will result in a misallocation of the world's capital and, indeed can even worsen the economic well-being of the capital-importing country" (1999, 105).[13] A plausible case for controls, therefore, may be made on standard "second-best" grounds. Judicious introduction of another distortion in the form of capital restrictions could actually turn out to raise rather than lower economic welfare on a net basis. For every possible form of market failure, there is in principle a corresponding form of optimal intervention.

The logic of this kind of argument is not disputed. An omniscient government dealing with one clear distortion could undoubtedly improve welfare with some form of capital-market restriction. What is disputed is the value of such logic in the real world of multiple distortions and imperfect policymaking. As Michael Dooley (1996) has noted in an oft cited survey of the relevant literature, the issue is not theoretical but empirical. The assumptions necessary to support an argument based on second-best considerations are no less "heroic" than those underlying the more conventional laissez-faire view.

The second line of dissent, much more relevant to today's circumstances, looks not to marginal economic distortions but rather to the very nature of financial markets, which even in the absence of other considerations tend to be especially prone to frequent crisis and flux. At issue here are the interdependencies of expectations inherent in the buying and selling of claims, which unavoidably lead to both herd behavior and multiple equilibria. Financial markets are notoriously vulnerable to self-fulfilling speculative "bubbles" and attacks. They also have a disturbing tendency to react with unpredictable lags to changing fundamentals—and then to overreact, rapidly and often arbitrarily. The resulting flows of funds, which may be massive, can be highly disruptive to national economies owing to their amplified impact on real economic variables. Hence here too a logical case may be made for judicious intervention by state authorities, in this case to limit the excessive instabilities and contagion effects endemic to the everyday operation of financial markets. Representative are the words of a former governor of the Bank of Mexico: "Recent experiences of market instability in the new global, electronically linked markets . . . have made the potential costs of massive speculative flows difficult to ignore or underestimate. . . . The assumed gains from free capital mobility will have to be balanced against the very real risks such mobility poses. Some form of regulation or control . . . seems necessary to protect emerging-market economies from the devastating financial crises caused by massive capital movements" (Buira 1999, 8–10).

Admittedly the value of this sort of argument too may be open to challenge on empirical grounds—but least so in the midst of a global emergency, when the disadvantages of unconstrained mobility are so obvious for everyone to see. In fact, recent research demonstrates that financial liberalization is almost always associated, sooner or later, with serious systemic crisis (Williamson and Mahar 1998). It is precisely the explosion of these costs that has been decisive in shifting the terms of discourse on capital controls. Increasingly the question is posed, Why should freedom of capital movement be given absolute priority over all other considerations of policy? Why, in effect, should governments tie one hand behind their back as they seek to shape and manage demand for their currency?

Perhaps most influential in shifting the discourse was a widely quoted article by the prominent trade economist Jagdish Bhagwati, which first appeared in May, 1998. Although other economists had been making the case for controls for some time,[14] Bhagwati's celebrity succeeded in bringing the issue to a new level of public awareness. After Asia's painful experience, Bhagwati asked, could anyone remain persuaded by the "myth" of capital mobility's benign beneficence? In his words, "It has become apparent that crises attendant on capital mobility cannot be ignored. . . . When a crisis hits, the downside of free capital mobility arises. . . . Thus, any nation contemplating the embrace of free capital mobility must reckon with these costs and also consider the probability of running into a crisis. The gains from economic efficiency that would flow from free capital mobility, in a hypothetical crisis-free world, must be set against this loss if a wise decision is to be made" (1998, 8–9).

In a similar vein, shortly afterward, Krugman decried the failure of the "confidence game"—orthodox strategies of market preservation that he labeled "Plan A." "It is time to think seriously about Plan B," he contended, meaning controls. "There is a virtual consensus among economists that exchange controls work badly. But when you face the kind of disaster now occurring in Asia, the question has to be: badly compared to what?" (1998b; see also 1999, chapter 9). Likewise, within months, George Soros was writing that "some form of capital controls may . . . be preferable to instability even if it would not constitute good policy in an ideal world" (1998, 192–3). By the fall of 1998 the intellectual momentum had clearly shifted toward some manner of reappraisal of the conventional wisdom. As Bhagwati concluded, "Despite the . . . assumption that the ideal world is indeed one of free capital flows . . . the weight of evidence and the force of logic point in the opposite direction, toward restraints on capital flows. It is time to shift the burden of proof from those who oppose to those who favor liberated capital" (1998, 12).

Back to the Future?

Reappraisal of the conventional wisdom could also be justified on historical grounds. Many people fail to remember that the original design of the IMF did not actually call for free capital mobility. Quite the contrary, in fact. Reflecting an abhorrence for the sort of "hot-money" flows that had so destabilized monetary relations in the 1920s and 1930s, the charter drafted at Bretton Woods made explicit allowance for the preservation of capital controls. Virtually everyone involved in the negotiations agreed with the influential League of Nations study, *International Currency Experience*, that some form of protection was needed against the risk of "mass movements of nervous flight capital" (Nurkse 1944, 188). The option of controls, therefore, was explicitly reserved to the discretion of individual states, provided only that such restraints might not be intended to restrict international commerce.[15] The idea was to afford governments sufficient autonomy to promote stability and prosperity at home without endangering the broader structure of multilateral trade and payments that was being laboriously constructed abroad. It was a deliberate compromise between the imperatives of domestic interventionism and international liberalism—the compromise of "embedded liberalism," as political scientist John Ruggie (1983) later called it.

Pivotal in promoting that compromise was none other than John Maynard Keynes, universally respected as the greatest economist of his day and intellectual leader of the British delegation at Bretton Woods. For Keynes, nothing was more damaging than the free movement of speculative capital, which he viewed as "the major cause of instability. . . . [Without] security against a repetition of this . . . the whereabouts of 'the better 'ole' will shift with the speed of the magic carpet. Loose funds may sweep round the world disorganising all steady business. Nothing is more certain than that the movement of capital funds must be regulated" ([1941] 1980, 31).[16] Keynes carefully distinguished between genuinely productive investment flows and footloose "floating funds." The former, he concurred, were vital to "developing the world's resources" and should be encouraged. It was only the latter that should be controlled, preferably as a "permanent feature of the post-war system" ([1942] 1980, 129–130). Following Bretton Woods, Keynes expressed satisfaction that his objectives in this regard had been achieved: "Not merely as a feature of the transition, but as a permanent arrangement, the plan accords to every member Government the explicit right to control all capital movements. What used to be heresy is now endorsed as orthodox" (as quoted in Pauly 1997, 94).[17]

As we know, though, that achievement did not last. Over the course of the next half century, as the phoenix of global finance rose from the ashes, Keynes's strictures were largely forgotten and what had been endorsed as orthodox once again became heresy. More and more, controls came to be regarded as wrongheaded if not downright anachronistic. Less and less were states thought within their rights to resist the preferences of the marketplace. By the 1980s, financial liberalization had become the goal of every self-respecting industrial or middle-income country. By the 1990s, the tide was clearly moving toward the consecration of free capital mobility as a universal norm. Perhaps the high-water mark was reached in April 1997 when the Interim Committee of the IMF approved a plan to begin preparing a new amendment to the Fund's charter to make the promotion of capital-account liberalization a specific IMF objective and responsibility (*IMF Survey,* May 12, 1997).[18] Evidently insensitive to the irony involved, Fund Managing Director Michel Camdessus asserted that the IMF's plan amounted to a mandate to add the "unwritten chapter" of Bretton Woods (*IMF Survey* May 12, 1997, 136).

And then came the fall of the Thai baht. Despite determined resistance from such prominent economists as Sebastian Edwards (1999a, 1999b), the tide has now decisively turned. Even the IMF has changed its tune, dropping active discussion of a new amendment and talking instead of the possible efficacy of selective financial restraints[19]—a tentative step back to the future envisaged by Keynes and others when the Fund was first created. Plainly, the pressure of events has conspired with a reawakened sense of history to cast the case for capital controls in a new light. Limitations on capital mobility, as a result, have gained new legitimacy as an instrument of monetary governance.

EXPLAINING HESITATION

Yet for all their newfound legitimacy, new capital controls have been adopted by remarkably few countries. Can we understand why? Four possible reasons come to mind. Governments may hesitate because of concerns for (1) technical issues; (2) lack of convincing evidence; (3) ideological principle; or (4) the political opposition of the United States. Of these four concerns, the last would appear to be most decisive.

Technical Issues

To begin, governments may hesitate for technical reasons. It is one thing to grant new respectability to capital controls in principle—but quite another to implement effective limits in practice. Shifting the burden of proof is only the start of the story, not the end. Even granting that an intellectual case for some kind of restraint may be made, important operational questions remain to be resolved if monetary governance is to be improved, on balance, rather than disrupted. The two most critical questions are, What kinds of capital flows should be subject to limitation, and what kinds of controls might be most effective? Answers to these questions, as I have suggested elsewhere (Cohen 1998b)[20] are not at all obvious.

In thinking about what kinds of flows to limit, at least three key distinctions are important: differences involving the *direction* of capital movement, the *type* of capital movement, and the *identity* of the actors involved. Should it be outflows of capital that are controlled, for instance, or inflows, or both? Should it be short-term flows only, or longer-term portfolio transactions and perhaps even direct investments as well? Should controls apply to residents or nonresidents? Likewise, in thinking about what kinds of restraints to use, key distinctions must be drawn involving both *duration* and *tactics*. Should barriers be temporary, implemented only during periods of crisis, or permanent? Should they take the form of quantitative restrictions or outright prohibitions or, rather, rely on taxes or instruments with tax-like effects to alter market behavior? After decades of financial liberalization, when the whole thrust of policy was to abandon controls rather than revive them, governments are only beginning to reeducate themselves on such critical issues.

To take just one example, consider the distinction between outflows and inflows of capital. Controls are inherently unworkable, many people argue, because of technological advances that have made evasion ever easier for market actors. That is what Alan Greenspan means when he says that we cannot turn back the clock on technology. One of the more pernicious by-products of financial globalization has been the creation of a vast network of private institutions and intermediaries, backed by the latest in information technology, that can be used— legally if possible, illegally when deemed necessary—to circumvent even the most draconian of public controls. Much as water seeks its own level, restraints will simply encourage a search for new routes of escape from oppressive governmental authority.

But is this equally true for all types of capital movement? Experience suggests that as far as outward movements are concerned, critics like Edwards (1999a, 68–71) have a point. The longer restraints remain in place, it seems, the more they must be expanded if their impact is not to be gradually eroded.[21] The dike will have to be built ever higher and wider to contain turbulent liquidity. But that is not necessarily true for inflows, since it is obviously easier to keep capital out than in. Barriers to outflows drastically reduce the choices available to a currency's users, sowing frustration and creating incentives for evasion. Restraints on inflows, by contrast, limit only one option among many, leaving capital abroad free to continue looking for profitable outlets elsewhere. Technology does not guarantee that control of inflows will be unworkable.

Still, in view of such uncertainties, governments could be forgiven for seeking more time to study available alternatives. Three years, however, appears an unusually lengthy delay in the high pressure arena of public policy, where responses to crisis are more often measured in hours or days. If governments were seriously considering new limitations on capital mobility, there would certainly have been some indication by now. It seems fair to conclude, therefore, that something more fundamental must be involved here than simple concern about complex technical issues.

Evidence

An alternative explanation might be found in a lack of convincing evidence. As we know, only one country—Malaysia—formally abandoned financial-market liberalization after the crisis began; and the results of Mahathir Mohamad's unorthodox experiment are not yet all in. Malaysia, in the eyes of many, was a test case for controls. It could be that other governments are unwilling to follow suit until a more conclusive verdict is possible.

To date, the evidence is mixed. On the one hand, Malaysia's economy did seem to recover reasonably quickly from the worst ravages of the crisis, fulfilling Kuala Lumpur's initial objectives. Within months domestic growth was restored, exports and reserves were up, and the stock market was once again on the rise— all seemingly vindicating Dr. Mahathir's audacious challenge to conventional wisdom. By the spring of 1999, the prime minister was publicly proclaiming victory in his determined war on speculators (*Economist,* May 1, 1999, 73). The program's success seemed confirmed in the summer of 1999 when, Morgan Stanley Capital International decided to readmit Malaysia to its principal portfolio indexes, which many fund managers use a guide for where and how much to invest (*NYT*, August 14, 1999, B2).[22]

On the other hand, most other crisis-hit countries also recovered during the same period—some even more rapidly than Malaysia—leading outside observers to a rather less sanguine conclusion. Typical are the remarks of economist Linda Lim. "My own opinion is that capital controls in Malaysia were neither necessary nor sufficient for recovery. . . . Indeed, given Malaysia's much stronger macroeconomic fundamentals and financial institutions before the crisis, one would have expected its recovery to be faster and stronger than that of other countries. That this has not happened suggests that capital controls . . . may be exerting a drag on recovery" (1999, 2–3).

Most noticeable was an understandable reluctance of international capital to return to Malaysia in substantial amounts even as funds began flowing back to regional neighbors like Thailand and Korea. As early as February 1999, less than half a year after they were imposed, Kuala Lumpur's restrictions on capital repatriation were eased significantly, with further liberalization coming in September, 1999. The aim, quite plainly, was to lure more foreign investors back into the country. Many saw the relaxation of controls as an implicit admission of defeat, not victory. Certainly it could be construed as evidence that the Mahathir experiment had not helped the government's efforts to sustain market share for its currency. But, by equal measure, relaxation could also be understood simply as the next logical step once the worst of the crisis was over. The reality is that as this chapter goes to press, the jury is still out on Malaysia's defensive market preservation strategy. As Paul Krugman has written, "The truth is that while

Malaysia's recovery has proved the hysterical opponents of capital controls wrong, it has not exactly proved the proponents right" (1999a).[23]

Nor is the verdict any more conclusive for other recent experiments with controls, such as Chile's oft discussed program of capital import restraints. Early in the 1990s, surging inflows generated a growing conflict between the Chilean government's internal and external policy objectives. The problem was how to maintain a tight monetary policy without generating an exchange rate appreciation that might hinder export competitiveness. The solution, officials decided, was a program of administrative measures designed to discourage various forms of short-term borrowing or portfolio investment from abroad. Central was the so-called unremunerated reserve requirement (URR) on most forms of external financing other than foreign direct investment. Any investor or lender wishing to enter the Chilean market was required to leave a sum equal to a specified percentage of the transaction on deposit with the government for a period of one year. (The percentage was gradually raised to as high as 30 percent and then reduced to 10 percent in 1998 before being finally phased out.) Since no interest was received on the deposit, the requirement acted in effect like a tax to discourage volatile movements in and out of the country. Although the program was largely dismantled in 1998, economists still debate whether in fact the controls had any lasting effect on the maturity composition of Chile's external debt.[24]

However, even admitting a lack of conclusive evidence to date, enough exists in the way of positive results to provide justification for any other government that might be inclined to go down Malaysia's or Chile's route. That none has done so again suggests that something more fundamental is involved here to explain behavior.

Ideological Principle

A third possible explanation might lie at the level of ideological principle. Governments may hesitate to resort to capital controls because restrictions are seen as violating deeply held values, either economic or political.

In economic terms, controls may be resisted simply because they interfere with private market processes. Academics can talk about distortions or multiple equilibria all they like. For many politicians, with less schooling in the nuances of economic theory, all this is so much double-talk. Markets will always and inherently remain superior to any form of public sector intervention. The resurrection of global finance in recent decades, we must remember, was part and parcel of a much broader ideological shift across the globe from Keynesian-style activism to what has come to be known as the "Washington consensus"—a newly triumphant "neoliberal" economics emphasizing the virtues of privatization, deregulation, and liberalization wherever possible. In this sense the move to consecrate capital mobility as a universal norm was but one strand of a mighty, almost holy, crusade. Crusaders can usually be expected to cling tightly to their convictions.

Likewise, in political terms, controls may be resisted simply because they are considered incompatible with the standard norms of democracy. That is certainly what economist David Hale means when he suggests that "capital controls represent a form of command economy intervention which could have implications for a country's political freedom, not just its economic freedom" (1998, 11). Journalist Samuel Brittan (1998) puts the point even more bluntly: "The most basic argument against exchange control . . . is that it is one of the most potent weapons of tyranny which can be used to imprison citizens in their own country." That capital mobility might exercise its own form of tyranny—as it surely does for countries choosing to play the confidence game—seems, in such thinking, to count for little. The only imperative that matters is the need to protect the property rights of money's users against the overweening power of the state.

Both possibilities are plausible. The power of ideas to condition human action should never be underestimated. But as with all cognitive explanations, there is a problem: How would we know? Ideological principles may indeed be the core motivation for a government's chosen policies. But they might also be nothing more than a public rationale for other, more private interests and objectives. Values do matter, but they are rarely decisive on their own. Once again, it appears that there must be something more fundamental involved.

The Role of the United States

That more fundamental "something" would appear to be the United States, which continues as it has throughout most of the postwar period to set the agenda for international financial affairs. Though somewhat eclipsed in the 1970s and 1980s, America's monetary hegemony was decisively reaffirmed by the long economic expansion of the 1990s—a record of success that stood in sharp contrast to lingering unemployment in Europe, stagnation in Japan, and repeated crises elsewhere. Not for nothing do the French call the United States the world's only hyperpower *(hyperpuissance)*. Few governments today are inclined to overtly defy Washington's wishes on monetary and financial issues.

In fact, Washington has made no secret of its firm opposition to any significant reversal of financial liberalization in emerging markets. Typical was the advice of President Clinton's Council of Economic Advisers. For countries facing the prospect of volatile capital flows, the Council suggested, "the need [is] to strengthen their domestic financial systems and adopt appropriate macroeconomic policies"—not a resort to capital controls (Council of Economic Advisors

2000, 226). On the contrary, the Council warned, "many considerations argue against the use of capital controls" (Council of Economic Advisers 1999, 281).

Governments have been openly pressured to keep on playing the confidence game, both directly and through the policy conditionality imposed on crisis-hit countries by the IMF, which was once described to me by a U.S. Treasury assistant secretary as "a convenient conduit for U.S. influence" (Cohen 1986, 229). Joseph Stiglitz, the World Bank's recently retired chief economist, has vividly described the close collaboration between the Treasury and Fund that was instrumental in enforcing neoliberal orthodoxy after the fall of the baht in 1997 (Stiglitz 2000). We know that countries such as Kim Dae Jung's Korea, which has been willing to play the game by Washington's rules, have been rewarded with generous financial assistance and other forms of support. Conversely, when Indonesia's newly elected president, Abdurrahman Wahid, briefly flirted with the idea of controls during a period of renewed currency pressure in June 2000, he was firmly discouraged by the IMF's managing director, who insisted that Indonesia must adhere strictly to the Fund's policy prescriptions (*NYT*, June 6, 2000, C4). We also know that Mahathir Mohamad's Malaysia came in for a good deal of opprobrium after its rash break with the Washington consensus in 1998. In such circumstances, is it any wonder that most policymakers might hesitate to follow in Kuala Lumpur's footsteps?

Undoubtedly, one reason for Washington's opposition lies in ideological conviction. Most of the officials in charge of U.S. policy after the crisis broke, from Robert Rubin and Lawrence Summers on down, were trained in neoliberal economics and firmly persuaded of its essential merit; and the same can be said of their replacements in the George W. Bush administration as well. But that is hardly the only reason. Intellectual bias can explain only a predisposition toward some set of policies. It is unlikely to dominate hard-nosed political calculation. In practice, two other considerations have clearly taken precedence.

First has been a concern for systemic stability, which obviously seemed jeopardized by the Asian crisis and its subsequent spread to Russia, Brazil, and elsewhere. Not only did lending markets around the world threaten to seize up, risking a global credit crunch. There was also the possibility of crashing stock markets, worldwide depression, and resurgent protectionism in international trade. Nightmare scenarios were a dime a dozen after the fall of the Thai baht. As the dominant architect of the prevailing monetary structure, the United States was presumably also one of its principal beneficiaries. In that context America's leaders have had every reason to seek to suppress any challenge to the status quo.

Second has been domestic politics in the United States, which also favors preservation of the status quo. Few outsiders would be directly benefitted by restraints on capital mobility in emerging markets. Many, however, could see their interests hurt, including especially major financial institutions and investors based in the United States. Such powerful market actors are not the kind to keep their preferences under a bushel; nor are their elected representatives apt to be entirely insensitive to their pleas for support. This is not to suggest that Washington is merely the tool of an exploitative capitalist class. The world is rarely as simple as that. But it does imply a common interest in opposing controls. As one source has commented, in polemical but compelling terms, "The United States has a powerful interest in maintaining and expanding the free worldwide movement of capital. . . . Moreover, Wall Street banks and brokerage firms want to expand their sales by doing business in emerging markets. . . . [Hence] there is a powerful confluence of interests between Wall Street and multinational corporations in favor of open capital accounts worldwide. In response, the U.S. Treasury has been leading a campaign . . . to promote capital liberalization" (Wade 1998–99, 45–47).

Faced by such a formidable confluence of interests, the only surprise is that any country might *not* hesitate to adopt new capital controls.

CONCLUSION

The Asian crisis provided one of those rare watershed moments when conventional wisdom could be seriously challenged. With the apparent failure of more orthodox strategies of market preservation—the confidence game—the time seemed ripe for a revival of capital controls as a legitimate tool of monetary governance. Yet governments still hesitate, despite the persuasiveness of both theoretical argument and historical precedent. That they do still hesitate is testament, ultimately, to the power of the United States. Determined opposition from the financial system's undoubted hegemon is difficult to resist.

Yet resistance is not impossible. In practical terms, the critical issue is one of feasibility: how to fight fire with fire. Against foes of controls, whether in the public sector or private, it is necessary to build an even more forceful coalition of proponents. The aim must be to mobilize political constituencies everywhere with an interest in restoring the compromise of embedded liberalism written into the Fund charter at Bretton Woods—in other words, to free governments to use the hand presently tied behind their back. To be effective, such a coalition could not rely on emerging-market governments alone. Quite obviously, it would also have to draw in sympathetic and influential elements in the United States or elsewhere that until now have maintained a relatively low profile on the issue.

Potential allies are there. One source of support might be found in the World Bank, which has delicately suggested that "[t]he benefits of capital account liberalization and increased capital flows have to be weighed against the likelihood of crisis and its costs" (World Bank 1999, xxi). Stiglitz, while still at the Bank, was certainly well known for his opposition to Treasury views on capital controls. Other support might be found among the leadership of such elite organizations as America's Council on Foreign Relations, which recently published a task force report highly favorable to certain kinds of capital controls (Council on Foreign Relations 1999). If elements like these could be recruited to the cause, governments might finally hesitate no longer.

NOTES

1. In Krugman's words, in the confidence game economic policy "must cater to the perceptions, the prejudices, the whims of the market. Or, rather, one must cater to what one *hopes* will be the perceptions of the market. . . . [Policy becomes] an exercise in amateur psychology" (1999b, 113; emphasis in the original).

2. See for example, Hanke and Schuler 1994. For additional discussion and references, see Cohen 1998a, 52–55.

3. For a bitter postmortem, see Culp, Hanke, and Miller, 1999. These authors dismiss the risk at the time of a rush to buy dollars as a "nightmare scenario," suggesting that opposition to an Indonesian currency board—led by the U.S. Treasury and the IMF— was motivated not by "the fear that it would not have worked but rather that it would have worked *too well—viz.*, saving Indonesia and postponing the end of the Suharto regime" (1999, 61, 64). This seems a bit strong in view of Washington's traditional support of Suharto's rule in Indonesia.

4. A notable exception was the head of the Hong Kong Monetary Authority, Joseph Yam, who in early 1999 made a spirited plea for "our own Asian currency" to reduce the region's vulnerability to speculative attack (*Financial Times,* January 6, 1999)— though even he later admitted that in current circumstances the idea was a "political nonstarter" (*Financial Times*, December 7, 1999).

5. See for example, Eichengreen and Bayoumi 1999.

6. Perhaps most ambitious was EMEAP (Executive Meeting of East Asia and Pacific Central Banks), a self-described "vehicle for regional cooperation among central banks" encompassing Australia, China, Hong Kong, Indonesia, Japan, Malaysia, New Zealand, the Philippines, Singapore, South Korea, and Thailand. Other examples include SEACEN (South East Asian Central Banks) and SEANZA (South East Asia, New Zealand, Australia), both of which provide for regular meetings of central bank officials as well as a variety of training programs.

7. For details, see Altbach 1997 and Rowley 1997.

8. Privately, of course, Washington also feared a loss of political influence in the region, since the AMF, if implemented, would obviously have been dominated by Tokyo. In economic terms, Washington's response to the AMF proposal was remarkably reminiscent of a similar episode a quarter of a century earlier, when an agreement to create a Financial Support Fund in the OECD (Organization of Economic Cooperation and

Development, based in Paris) was torpedoed by the U.S. Government on almost identical grounds (Cohen 1998c).

9. The official was Special Functions Minister Diam Zainuddin.

10. For a snapshot of the policy debate at the end of 1998, compare and contrast Hale 1998 and Wade and Veneroso 1998.

11. The earliest example I can find of this change of tone was a column by *Financial Times* commentator Martin Wolf in early March, 1998. Ordinarily a firm champion of free markets, Wolf reluctantly concluded, "After the crisis, the question can no longer be whether these flows should be regulated in some way. It can only be how" (Wolf 1998). Ten months later, at the annual World Economic Forum in Davos, Switzerland—always a useful source for tracking authoritative public- and private-sector opinion—it was clear from most remarks that absolutely unrestricted capital mobility was no longer much in favor. See for example, *New York Times*, January 29, 1999, C1.

12. See for example, Obstfeld and Rogoff (1996), who provide elegant theoretical arguments to demonstrate the potential for gains from intertemporal trade through a free international market for securities.

13. See also Eichengreen *et al.* 1998 and López-Mejía 1999.

14. See for example, Grabel 1996a, 1996b.

15. Article VI, sections 1 and 3 of the Articles of Agreement of the International Monetary Fund.

16. For " 'ole," read "hole"—a handy place to hide one's money.

17. For more on Keynes's views and how they relate to the contemporary scene, see Cassidy 1998 and Kirshner 1999.

18. Under the plan, two articles were to be amended: Article I, where "orderly liberalization of capital" would be added to the list of the Fund's formal purposes; and Article VIII, which would give the Fund the same jurisdiction over the capital account of its members as it already enjoys over the current account. The language would also *require* countries to commit themselves to capital liberalization as a goal.

19. See for example, Adams *et al.* 1998, 79, 150; Eichengreen *et al.* 1998, 2–3, 29; Adams, Mathieson, and Schinasi 1999, 92, 101; and Ariyoshi *et al.* 2000. The Fund's annual report for 1999 reports that its board of executive directors took up the issue of capital controls at a meeting in March 1999, where several directors were said to argue that, in a crisis, limitations on capital flows "could play a useful role" (IMF 1999, 47).

20. Other recent discussions of key technical issues relating to capital controls include Ries and Sweeney 1997 and Kahler 1998.

21. For a statement of the same point, see Cohen 1965. In my bolder and more dogmatic youth, I was even willing to raise this observation to the status of an economic

law—what I ambitiously labeled the "Iron Law of Economic Controls." To wit, "[T]o be effective, controls must reproduce at a rate faster than that at which means are found for avoiding them" (Cohen 1965, 174). Today I find myself less inclined to be quite so categorical.

22. Malaysia's readmission was initially scheduled for February 29, 2000. Later, under pressure from some reluctant investors, Morgan Stanley agreed to delay implementation until May 31 (*New York Times*, December 4, 1999, B2).

23. For balanced discussions, see Adams, Matheison, and Schinasi, 1999, 97–101 and Haggard 2000, 73–85.

24. See for example, Adams et al. 1998, 176–179; Cooper 1999, 116–118; and especially the exchange between Edwards (1999b) and Cline (1999). Inflow control measures similar to Chile's have also been implemented in a number of other countries, with varying degrees of success (Reinhart and Reinhart 1998, 117–119).

REFERENCES

Adams, Charles, Donald J. Mathieson, Garry Schinasi, and Bankim Chadha. 1998. *International Capital Markets: Developments, Prospects, and Key Policy Issues.* Washington, D.C.: International Monetary Fund.

Adams, Charles, Donald J. Mathieson, and Garry Schinasi. 1999. *International Capital Markets: Developments, Prospects, and Key Policy Issues.* Washington, D.C.: International Monetary Fund.

Altbach, Eric. 1997. The Asian Monetary Fund Proposal: A Case Study of Japanese Regional Leadership. *JEI Report* 47A.

Ariyoshi, Akira, Karl Habermeier, Bernard Laurens, Inci Otker-Robe, Jorge Iván Canales-Kriljenko, and Andrei Kirilenko. 2000. *Country Experiences with the Use and Liberalization of Capital Controls.* Washington, D.C.: International Monetary Fund.

Bergsten, C. Fred. 1998. Missed Opportunity. *The International Economy* 12, no. 6:26–27.

Bhagwati, Jagdish. 1998. The Capital Myth. *Foreign Affairs* 77, no. 3:7–12.

Brittan, Samuel. 1998. Exchange Controls: The Economic Trap. *Financial Times*, October 1.

Buira, Ariel. 1999. *An Alternative Approach to Financial Crises.* Princeton, N.J.: International Finance Section.

Cassidy, John. 1998. The New World Disorder. *The New Yorker*, October 26, 198–207.

Cline, William R. 1999. International Capital Flows and Emerging Markets: Discussion. In *Rethinking the International Monetary System*, ed. Jane Sneddon Little and Giovanni P. Olivei. Boston: Federal Reserve Bank of Boston.

Cohen, Benjamin J. 1965. Capital Controls and the U.S. Balance of Payments. *American Economic Review* 55, no. 1:172–176.

———. 1986. *In Whose Interest? International Banking and American Foreign Policy.* New Haven, Conn.: Yale University Press.

———. 1993. Beyond EMU: The Problem of Sustainability. *Economics and Politics* 5, no. 2:187–203.

———. 1996. Phoenix Risen: The Resurrection of Global Finance. *World Politics*, 48, no. 2:268–296.

———. 1998a. *The Geography of Money.* Ithaca, N.Y.: Cornell University Press.

———. 1998b. "Taming the Phoenix: Monetary Governance after the Crisis," Paper presented at conference on The Asian Financial Crisis and the Architecture of Global Finance, Melbourne, December.

———. 1998c. When Giants Clash: The OECD Financial Support Fund and the IMF. Chapter 5 in *Institutional Designs for a Complex World: Bargaining, Linkages, and Nesting,* ed. Vinod K. Aggarwal. Ithaca, N.Y.: Cornell University Press.

Cooper, Richard N. 1999. Should Capital Controls be Banished? *Brookings Papers on Economic Activity* 1, 89–141.

Council of Economic Advisers. 1999. *Annual Report.* Washington, D.C.: U.S. Government Printing Office.

———. 2000. *Annual Report.* Washington, D.C.: U.S. Government Printing Office.

Council on Foreign Relations. 1999. *Safeguarding Prosperity in a Global Financial System: The Future International Financial Architecture.* Report of an Independent Task Force. New York: Council on Foreign Relations.

Culp, Christopher L., Steve H. Hanke, and Merton H. Miller. 1999. The Case for an Indonesian Currency Board. *Journal of Applied Corporate Finance* 11, no. 4:57–65.

Dooley, Michael P. 1996. A Survey of Literature on Controls over International Capital Transactions. *International Monetary Fund Staff Papers* 43, no. 4:639–687.

Edwards, Sebastian. 1999a. How Effective are Capital Controls? *Journal of Economic Perspectives.* 13, no. 4:65–84.

———. 1999b. International Capital Flows and Emerging Markets: Amending the Rules of the Game? In *Rethinking the International Monetary System,* ed Jane Sneddon Little and Giovanni P. Olivei. Boston: Federal Reserve Bank of Boston.

Eichengreen, Barry. 1997. International Monetary Arrangements: Is there a Monetary Union in Asia's Future? *The Brookings Review* 15, no. 2:33–35.

Eichengreen, Barry, and Tamim Bayoumi. 1999. Is Asia an Optimum Currency Area? Can It Become One? Regional, Global, and Historical Perspectives on Asian Monetary Relations." Chapter 21 in *Exchange Rate Policies in Emerging Asian Countries,* ed. Stefan Collignon, Jean Pisani-Ferry, and Yung Chul Park. London: Routledge.

Eichengreen, Barry, Michael Mussa, and a Staff Team. 1998. *Capital Account Liberalization: Theoretical and Practical Aspects.* Washington, D.C.: International Monetary Fund.

Grabel, Ilene. 1996a. Financial Markets, the State, and Economic Development: Controversies within Theory and Policy. *International Papers in Political Economy* (University of East London) 3, no. 1.

———. 1996b. Marketing the Third World: The Contradictions of Portfolio Investment in the Global Economy. *World Development,* 24, 1761–1776.

Greenspan, Alan. 1998. "The Globalization of Finance." *Cato Journal* 17, no. 3:243–250.

Haggard, Stephan. 2000. *The Political Economy of the Asian Financial Crisis.* Washington, D.C.: Institute for International Economics.

Hale, David D. 1998. The Hot Money Debate. *The International Economy* 12, no. 6:8–12, 66–69.

Hanke, Steve H., and Kurt Schuler. 1994. *Currency Boards for Developing Countries: A Handbook*. San Francisco: Institute for Contemporary Studies.

Hughes, Christopher W. 2000. Japanese Policy and the East Asian Currency Crisis: Abject Defeat or Quiet Victory? *Review of International Political Economy* 7, no. 2:219–253.

International Monetary Fund. 1999. *Annual Report*, Washington, D.C.: International Monetary Fund.

Kahler, Miles, ed. 1998. *Capital Flows and Financial Crises,* Ithaca, N.Y.: Cornell University Press.

Keyes, John Maynard. 1941. Post-War Currency Policy. British Treasury memorandum, September. In *The Collected Writings of John Maynard Keynes,* ed. Donald Moggridge, vol. 25 (Cambridge: Cambridge University Press, 1980), 31.

———. 1942. Plan for an International Currency (or Clearing) Union. In *The Collected Writings of John Maynard Keynes,* ed. Donald Moggridge, vol. 25 (Cambridge: Cambridge University Press, 1980), 129–130.

———. 1980. *The Collected Writings of John Maynard Keynes,* ed. Donald Moggridge. Vol. 25. Cambridge: Cambridge University Press.

Kirshner, Jonathan. 1999. Keynes, Capital Mobility and the Crisis of Embedded Liberalism. *Review of International Political Economy* 6, no. 3:313–337.

Krugman, Paul. 1998a. The Confidence Game. *The New Republic*, October 5, 23–25.

———. Saving Asia: It's Time to Get Radical. *Fortune Magazine* 138, no. 5:74–80.

———. 1999a. Capital Control Freaks: How Malaysia Got Away with Economic Heresy. *Slate*. Retrieved from September 27, http://slate.msn.com.

———. 1999b. *The Return of Depression Economics*. New York: Norton.

Lim, Linda. 1999. Malaysia's Response to the Asian Financial Crisis. Testimony prepared for hearings before the House Committee on International Relations, Subcommittee on Asia and the Pacific, June 16.

López-Mejía, Alejandro. 1999. Large Capital Flows: A Survey of the Causes, Consequences, and Policy Responses. Working Paper WP/99/17. Washington, D.C.: International Monetary Fund.

Moggridge, Donald, ed. 1980. *The Collected Writings of John Maynard Keynes*, Volume XXV, Cambridge: Cambridge University Press.

Mundell, Robert A. 1997. Forum on Asian Fund. *Capital Trends* 2:13.

Nurkse, Ragnar. 1944. *International Currency Experience: Lessons from the Inter-War Period*. Geneva: League of Nations.

Obstfeld, Maurice, and Kenneth Rogoff. 1996. *Foundations of International Finance*. Cambridge, Mass.: MIT Press.

Pauly, Louis W. 1997. *Who Elected the Bankers? Surveillance and Control in the World Economy.* Ithaca, N.Y.: Cornell University Press.

Reinhart, Carmen M., and Vincent Raymond Reinhart. 1998. Some Lessons for Policy Makers who Deal with the Mixed Blessing of Capital Inflows. Chapter 4 in *Capital Flows and Financial Crises*, ed. Miles Kahler. Ithaca, N.Y.: Cornell University Press.

Ries, Christine P. and Richard J. Sweeney, eds. 1997. *Capital Controls in Emerging Economies*. Boulder, Colo.: Westview Press.

Rowley, Anthony. 1997. International Finance: Asian Fund, R.I.P. *Capital Trends* 2, no. 14.

Ruggie, John G. 1983. International Regimes, Transactions, and Change: Embedded Liberalism in the Postwar Economic Order." In *International Regimes*, ed. Stephen D. Krasner. Ithaca, N.Y.: Cornell University Press.

Soros, George. 1998. *The Crisis of Global Capitalism*. New York: PublicAffairs.

Stiglitz, Joseph. 2000. The Insider: What I Learned at the World Economic Crisis. *The New Republic,* April 17 and 24:56–60.

Wade, Robert. 1998–99. The Coming Fight Over Capital Controls. *Foreign Policy* 113:41–54.

Wade, Robert, and Frank Veneroso. 1998. The Gathering Support for Capital Controls. *Challenge* 41:6, 14–26.

Walter, Norbert. 1998. An Asian Prediction. *The International Economy* 12, no. 3:49.

Williamson, John, and Molly Mahar. 1998. *A Survey of Financial Liberalization*. Princeton, N.J.: International Finance Section.

Wolf, Martin. 1998. Flows and Blows. *Financial Times*, March 3.

World Bank. 1999. *Global Economic Prospects and the Developing Countries, 1998/99: Beyond Financial Crisis*. Washington, D.C.: International Bank for Reconstruction and Development.

Chapter 4

REFORMING THE INTERNATIONAL FINANCIAL INSTITUTIONS: DUELING EXPERTS IN THE UNITED STATES

C. Fred Bergsten

T he international financial crises of the 1980s and 1990s have spawned widespread calls for reform of the international financial architecture. In fact, a good deal of reform is already taking place. As of early 2000, most emerging-market economies have floated their exchange rates, reducing the risk of disruptions due to doomed efforts to preserve unsustainable parities. Moreover, and in response to accusations that large institutional investors got off too lightly in the 1994–1995 Mexican peso crisis, private lenders are increasingly "bailed in" to country workout situations, spreading the burden of international rescue packages and dampening the prospects for excessive future flows to emerging markets. Within the private investor community, as well as in the multilateral financial institutions, there is growing acceptance of host-country restraints on short-term capital inflows—as deployed in different forms by Chile, China, and Malaysia—to avoid excessive buildups of liquid foreign debt. Progress is being made to reduce imperfections in the private capital markets through improved data statistics, expanded disclosure of country data and International Monetary Fund (IMF) analyses of its members' economies, and implementation of international best-practice benchmarks for the reform of national banking systems. Finally, modest but politically important institutional innovations have taken place with the creation of the G20 and the Financial Stability Forum (see Porter and Wood in this volume).

As of this writing in late 2000, however, little reform had occurred in the functioning of the main international financial institutions (IFIs)—the International Monetary Fund and the World Bank. Two reports have recently been published on this set of issues. The first, from an Independent Task Force sponsored by the Council on Foreign Relations (CFR), was unanimously agreed upon by its members and released in September 1999 (CFR 1999). The group included a number of notable Americans such as Paul Volcker, George Soros, several corporate CEOs, former cabinet members Ray Marshall and Jim Schlesinger, top economists including Martin Feldstein and Paul Krugman, former members of Congress Lee Hamilton and Vin Weber, and political experts Ken Duberstein and Norman Ornstein. It was cochaired by former cabinet members Peter G. Peterson and Carla Hills, and directed by my colleague at the Institute for International Finance, Morris Goldstein.

The second report, released in March 2000, is from the International Financial Institutions Advisory Committee (IFIAC), created by Congress in 1998, and popularly known as the "Meltzer Committee," after its chairman, Princeton economist Allan Meltzer (IFIAC 2000). According to the *Dallas Morning News* of March 13, 1998, its "majority was handpicked by (House Majority Leader Richard) Armey." The IFIAC split by a vote of $7^1/_2$–$3^1/_2$ (with the halves reflecting the fact that one member signed both the majority and the dissenting statements). I and three colleagues submitted a joint dissent, which is included in the published report.

As the only person who was a member of both commissions, I believe it is valuable to compare the two reports in considering the proper path for international financial reform. There was significant agreement between them on several key issues. Both emphasized the need for a clearer delineation of the future responsibilities of the IMF and the World Bank. There was a consensus that the Fund should be responsible for macroeconomic, exchange rate and financial sector problems, while the Bank should offer assistance to countries pursuing solutions to long-term, microeconomic, and largely structural difficulties. There was no argument over the need for much stronger banking systems in emerging market economies or that the international financial institutions should devote priority attention to promoting such improvements. Both commissions agreed that the IMF should urge countries to avoid adjustable peg currency regimes, because they frequently become unsustainable and lead to crises. It was also easy to endorse today's frequently heard calls for greater transparency and accountability in the member countries of both the Fund and the Bank and in the functioning of the IFIs themselves, including through full publication of the IMF's annual appraisals of its members' economies. Formally, both groups of experts rejected the idea of abolishing the IMF—although two members of the IFIAC majority indicated a preference for such a radical step in their separate statements and the chairman of that group, Professor Allan Meltzer, has proposed abolishing the Fund in numerous presentations over the years.

The differences between the two reports, however, are much more significant than their similarities. Some of the central proposals of the IFIAC majority are radical. They would almost certainly increase rather than decrease global monetary instability, and thus would be deeply injurious to the national interests of the United States. The differences between the CFR and IFIAC reports can be grouped under three main headings.

First, *the IFIAC report paints a very misleading picture of the impact of the IFIs over the past fifty years.* The economic record of that period is a success unparalleled in human history, both for the advanced industrial countries and for most of the developing nations (see Felix in this volume). Hundreds of millions of the poorest people on earth have been lifted out of poverty. The severe monetary crises of recent years have been overcome quickly with little lasting impact on the world economy. The IFIs have contributed substantially to this record. In his March 8, 2000, article on the IFIAC report, *Financial Times* columnist Martin Wolf, seldom characterized as a fuzzy idealist, concluded that "on most measures, the IFIs have been a staggering success." The bottom line on the work of the Bank and the Fund, and their contributions to sane, multilateral management of the global economy, is unambiguously positive, but the IFIAC majority portrays a negative picture that badly distorts reality. By contrast, the CFR (1999:3) report emphasizes that "[a]s costly as the Asian crisis has been, no doubt we would have seen even deeper recessions, more competitive devaluations, more defaults and more resort to trade restrictions if no financial support had been provided by the IMF to the crisis countries (1993, 3)."

Second, the *recommendations of the IFIAC majority would severely undermine the ability of the IMF to deal with financial crises and hence would promote global instability.* As Paul Krugman put it in his *New York Times* op-ed on the report on March 8, 2000, the majority "suggested restrictions that would in effect make even emergency lending impossible." The problem is that the majority would authorize the Fund to lend only to countries that had prequalified for its assistance by meeting a series of criteria related to the stability of their domestic financial systems. This approach has two fatal flaws. On the one hand, *it would permit Fund support for countries with runaway budget deficits and profligate monetary policies.* This oddity results from the fact that the IFIAC majority believes that IMF conditionality does not work, and, apparently, that national financial systems can be "sound" and "credible" even when the underlying macroeconomic environment is not. If adopted, this rule would enable the countries to perpetuate the very policies that triggered the crisis in the first place, squandering public resources and eliminating any prospect of resolving the crisis.

On the other hand, and in my view equally irresponsibly, the recommendation that the Fund offer emergency aid only to a set of predetermined model countries *would prohibit IMF support for countries that were of systemic importance but had not prequalified, again running a severe risk of bringing on global economic disorder.* For example, the IFIAC model would have prohibited the Fund from lending to *any* of the East Asian crisis countries in 1997 and 1998, not to mention countries of such obvious systemic importance as Russia or China.

Interestingly, the majority on the IFIAC was not entirely insensitive to these criticisms. The final version of the report added a sentence including a "proper fiscal requirement" to the list of requirements for prequalification. No rationale for that addition is stated, however, and the term is not even defined. If the "fiscal requirement" were intended to be a quantified level of permissible budget deficits, it would represent an international equivalent of the Maastricht criteria for membership in the European Monetary Union, which mandate that a country's debt/GDP ratio not be above 60 percent, nor its fiscal deficit exceed 3 percent. These inflexible and specific criteria have been extremely difficult to implement even in relatively homogenous Europe; they would be impossible globally. If fiscal health instead were simply a qualitative notion, then the International Monetary Fund would be back in the business of conditionality—a grant from member governments and to the IMF itself of bureaucratic discretion which the report explicitly and strongly rejects. Moreover, the IMF then would be obliged to confront the prospect of dequalifying and requalifying countries as their policy stance shifted, adding an important new element of destabilization to the picture.

The final IFIAC report made a second last-minute addition in response to the criticism that the prequalification scheme would make it impossible for the IMF to respond to crises originating in, or threatening to spread to, countries that for one reason or another had not qualified for the inner circle. The revised version signed by the commission's majority suggested a takeout from its own prequalification requirements "in unusual circumstances, where the crisis poses a threat to the global economy." But the concept was mentioned only in the executive summary and not even in the chapter of the report dealing with the IMF. It was never explained or defended, and hence cannot be taken seriously.

In contrast, the report of the widely representative commission brought together by the Council on Foreign Relations would retain the IMF's current authority to exercise fiscal and monetary policy conditionality in order to underpin improvements in the balance of payments in crisis countries. The CFR report also would avoid the "all or nothing" flaw of the IFIAC proposals by permitting IMF financial support to countries of systemic importance. At the same time, committee members were concerned to address the issue of "moral hazard," or the tendency of both private financial institutions and countries to engage in risky but profitable behavior, so long as they expected that the IMF or rich-country taxpayers would bail them out in case of a crisis. The IMF could promote the proper incentives, the CFR report observed, by allowing countries who did more to prevent crises to pay less for their IMF borrowing, and by permitting very large loans—such as those extended to Mexico, Korea, Indonesia, Russia, and Brazil in the 1990s—only after a super-majority of creditor countries had determined that the situation did indeed represent a systemic crisis.

The radical proposal of the IFIAC is based on the view that "moral hazard" is the dominant problem facing the global financial system (see the chapters by Armijo and Fernández-Arias and Hausmann). The problem with this view is that there is no empirical support for it. The majority's argument that the Mexican support package caused the East Asia crisis is pure theory and, indeed, theology. The CFR report recognizes that some degree of moral hazard exists whenever insurance contracts are written but places that concern in proper perspective relative to other risks and addresses it through a series of much more constructive steps, including smaller IMF lending packages, greater flexibility of exchange rates, greater private-sector sharing of debt workout costs, and so on.

The third major flaw in the IFIAC report is that *the recommendations of the majority might well undercut the fight against global poverty* despite their avowed intent to have the opposite effects. The report's principal suggestion with respect to the World Bank is that it cease lending to all countries whose governments or businesses have successfully accessed private global capital markets, transforming itself exclusively into a grant-giving institution extending multilateral aid only to the poorest countries. The majority on the Meltzer Committee *would shut down two major sources of funding for the poor*, the regular lending program of the World Bank, which transfers about $20-25 billion per year from the developed to the developing world, and the Poverty Reduction and Growth Facility at the IMF, responsible for loans of an additional $1-2 billion per year. The IFIAC majority in fact proposes a program of "reverse aid" to the world's richest countries, returning as much as $50 billion of capital to them from the World Bank and its affiliates. The International Finance Corporation, a World Bank affiliate created in 1956 to extend loans to promising *private* entrepreneurs in developing countries, would be closed.

It is important to examine the incentives inherent in these recommendations in order to understand how perverse they are. The suggestion that the World Bank *terminate lending to even the poorest countries if they had obtained access to the private capital markets* is the clearest possible disincentive for developing countries to undertake the institutional and policy reforms necessary for their projects, entrepreneurs, and government securities to become credible with private investors. It is worth recalling that even countries with extremely low per capita incomes, such as India, have successfully obtained some private funds in global capital markets. Moreover, the IFIAC majority wants *the more advanced developing countries*, even those which still include tens of millions of the world's poorest people, such as Brazil and Mexico, *to rely wholly on the very volatile private capital markets.*

Most importantly, the Meltzer Committee majority wants the poorest countries to *rely in future primarily on grant aid appropriated by rich-country govern-*

ments. Yet we know that the United States Congress, and parliaments in many other advanced industrial countries, are highly unlikely to support sharp increases in such funding, even if the majority's reforms were to produce much more efficient aid programs. If we need evidence of this, we need only recall the extremely difficult progress in Congress of appropriations for previously negotiated U.S. contributions to the World Bank, particularly to its soft loan affiliate for the poorest countries, the International Development Agency (IDA), through the years.

Harvard economist Jeffrey Sachs, a member of the majority, presented its views on these development issues to the Executive Board of the IMF in March 2000 (see also Sachs 2000). Directors from the poorest countries—the countries that Sachs purports to help—responded that his recommendations "would be a disaster for Africa" and that "no one in Africa would buy them." His arguments were labeled "superficial," "careless," and "baseless" in their claims. The majority's proposal to effectively abolish conditionality was verbally characterized as "endangering the future of the Fund" and "*increasing* moral hazard."

The CFR report does not address these development assistance issues directly. And, as noted above, there clearly *is* a need to reform the Fund and the Bank to avoid duplication and overlap in the conduct of their respective responsibilities. But the CFR Task Force properly envisages continuation of the World Bank's current lending programs, including an "expansion of its work on social safety nets."

I believe that *neither* the CFR nor the IFIAC reports address some of the key problems still facing the international monetary system, as indicated in the additional views that I and several other participants appended to the CFR report. Of greatest importance, crisis prevention needs to be augmented by much more serious "early warning" and "early action" systems, through which the IMF—and perhaps new regional institutions—could use the sophisticated new early warning indicators now being developed to anticipate crises and head them off (see Goldstein, Kaminsky, and Reinhardt 2000).

The IMF also needs to accept the challenge of guiding emerging market economies on *how* to manage their flexible exchange rates, since very few will (or should) float freely despite the advice of most academics (and the IFIAC report) that they do so. In addition, and before crises strike, clear guidelines need to be developed for private sector involvement in debt workout situations, to replace the ad hoc approach now being pursued to "bail in" the private creditors. Finally, I would argue that we need new arrangements among the major industrial countries—especially the G3 of the United States, the Economic and Monetary Union in Europe, and Japan—to limit the frequently prolonged misalignments in their own exchange rates which are so destabilizing to the rest of the world as well as to their own economies (see Bergsten 1998).

Further reform of the international financial architecture thus remains essential. The CFR and IFIAC reports point the way toward a number of constructive steps. The IFIAC report also suggests a number of destructive ideas, however, that must be rejected. Secretary of the Treasury Lawrence Summers did so in his testimony to the House Banking Committee on March 23, 2000, echoing much of our joint dissent from the recommendations of the IFIAC majority. I believe that renewed attention to the CFR Report, in whose direction then U.S. Treasury Secretary Lawrence Summers made several initial proposals in early and mid-2000, would be a fruitful step toward further desirable reform.

REFERENCES

Bergsten, C. Fred. 1998. How to Target Exchange Rates. *Financial Times*, November 20.

Council on Foreign Relations (CFR). 1999. *Safeguarding Prosperity in a Global Financial System: The Future International Financial Architecture*. Report of an Independent Task Force sponsored by the Council on Foreign Relations. Washington, D.C.: Institute for International Economics (September).

International Financial Institutions Advisory Committee (IFIAC). 2000. *Report of the International Financial Institutions Advisory Committee*. Submitted to the U.S. Congress and U.S. Department of Treasury, March 8.

Goldstein, Morris, Graciela L. Kaminsky, and Carmen M. Reinhart. 2000. *Assessing Financial Vulnerability: An Early Warning System for Emerging Markets*. Washington, D.C.: Institute for International Economics.

Sachs, Jeffrey. 2000. The Charade of Debt Sustainability. *Financial Times*, September 26.

III. STABILITY, EQUITY, AND THE ECONOMICS OF GLOBAL FINANCE

Chapter 5

THE ECONOMIC CASE AGAINST
FREE CAPITAL MOBILITY

David Felix

In the debate on reforming the global financial architecture, a central issue
is whether globalizing free capital mobility and free trade are compatible
objectives. The United States (and thus the International Monetary Fund)
contends that these two goals are mutually reinforcing. Until the 1997–1998
financial crises, this was also the position of the other G7 governments and of
most mainstream economists. But the crises have generated a shift among economists, a growing number of whom are returning to the Bretton Woods view that
financial markets are too prone to instability to be given free rein. And the
United States is now encountering increasing difficulty in keeping its G7 partners and the World Bank from forcing capital controls onto the official reform
agenda, preventing developing countries from unilaterally adopting them, and
dissuading financially squeezed economies from turning to open or disguised
protectionist remedies.

Other chapters in this book deal with the political dimensions of this
debate. This essay concentrates on the economic dimensions. It assesses criti-
cally the theoretical and empirical claims that globalizing free capital mobility
necessarily brings net economic benefits to humankind, and that this is already
manifest from the drive of the past quarter century to decontrol financial markets
around the world.

The theoretical claim is grounded in two key conjectures: the efficient
market hypothesis (hereafter EMH) and its cousin, the rational expectations
hypothesis (or Ratex). Combined, they are used to support the twin assertions
that liberated financial markets consistently price capital assets correctly in line
with future supply and demand trends (that is, the "fundamentals"), and that the
correct asset pricing of liberated capital markets will, in turn, provide a continually reliable guide to saving and investment decisions in decentralized market
economies, and hence to the efficient allocation of their economic resources.
Section one of this essay demonstrates that neither the EMH nor the Ratex

hypothesis has general backing from more basic theorizing about the stability of competitive market economies. Rather, the theorizing indicates that liberated financial markets are inherently prone to destabilizing dynamics that can also destabilize aggregate production, trade, and employment in such economies.

The next component of the argument for free capital mobility is empirical. Section two of this essay summarizes post–World War II evidence to date on free capital mobility and its consequences. It shows that the postwar global economy grew faster and more steadily and equitably when the Bretton Woods pegged exchange rate regime assisted by capital controls prevailed, than it has since the regime was replaced in the early 1970s by floating exchange rates and the lifting of capital controls. The comparison falsifies the prediction of economists who promote the lifting of controls, which was that it would elevate the performance of the international economy. It is not sufficient, however, to assign primary causal responsibility for the slowdown to the freeing of capital mobility, since other factors also may have been at work. That is, it can be shown that volatile financial flows impede the growth of trade and production (McKenzie 1999), but not that continuing with capital controls would have fully prevented the global slowdown.

If both the theoretical and the empirical support for free capital mobility are weak, what are the appropriate policy lessons from the past? Section three compares the structural and political conditions that curbed the internationalizing of domestic financial disorders in the presence of open capital markets prior to World War I with the changed conditions that made open capital markets untenable after World War I and led to the post–World War II Bretton Woods restrictions on global capital mobility. It concludes that the structural conditions and welfare considerations that led the architects of the original Bretton Woods Accords to that conclusion still prevail. The U.S. project of globalizing free capital mobility *and* free trade is thus embarked in uncharted waters, with neither valid theory nor history to guide it. My fourth section highlights two current policy problems: high G7 interest rates and the unsustainability of U. S. capital exports.

FLAWS IN THE EFFICIENT MARKET AND RATIONAL EXPECTATIONS HYPOTHESES

The expansion of aggregate output and its distribution depends not merely on the growth of productive inputs and improvements in techniques, but also on how well the institutions coordinating inputs and outputs perform their tasks. As the division of labor expands to exploit new technologies, so do intertemporal and interspatial coordination requirements. The characteristic response of capitalist economies has been to centralize borrowing and lending in banks and the trading of ownership claims in formal securities markets. By the latter half of the nineteenth-century these institutions and their appendages, crucially aided by

risk-shifting legal changes such as the limited liability corporation, had become
the central coordinators of aggregate production and capital accumulation. Banks
rolled over their short-term liabilities—deposits and banknotes—into loans of
varying duration to firms and households. Investment banks marketed new issues
of bonds and shares to insurance companies and wealthy families. Securities
markets facilitated the funding of long-term projects by offering equity and
bondholders the opportunity to unload ownership claims more easily in order to
slough off risks of illiquidity and insolvency.

These developments, however, have remained risk laden. Banks, with their
main liabilities of shorter duration than their loans, risk liquidity crises from
sudden runs on their demand deposits and, in the nineteenth-century, on their
banknotes. They risk insolvency should a sizeable proportion of their borrowers
default. Holding down the ratio of loans to bank capital reduces both types of
risk, but at the cost of lowering expected returns from the bank capital. And
waves of depositor panic and cascading interfirm payment delinquency could
topple even conservatively run banks and firms. Time inconsistency problems
also afflict borrowing firms, since the outlay to expand capacity precedes the
expected cash flow from the completed project. Debt leveraging augments expected returns on equity, but also increases liquidity and insolvency risks. Striking an optimal balance is chancy, since the difficulty of accurately assessing
future cash flows is compounded by the need to assess the effects of future
actions of competitors, as well as the likelihood that economy-wide crises might
abruptly depress cash flows and access to credit. Security markets also have
innate risks. To be useful for transferring risk, the markets have to provide ready
buyers on demand, which requires a large presence of buyers pursuing quick
turnover trading strategies focused on profiting from asset price movements.
These speculative activities can generate large swings in asset prices that augment market risk—especially the risk that the prices might swing too low to
protect the seller's liquidity or solvency.

Thus by the latter half of the nineteenth-century it had become evident that
output expansion was being periodically interrupted by major breakdowns accompanied by collapsing asset prices, widespread bankruptcies and bank failures. The response in leading capitalist countries was to introduce controls to
dampen financial instability and its impact on the real economy. Fiduciary regulations of banks were strengthened and the issuance of banknotes centralized in
a single private bank. In return for the monopoly, that bank, dubbed the central
bank, had to assume the task of regulating domestic money market rates, and to
serve as lender of last resort to banks undergoing liquidity crises. Control over
currency expansion was tightened by demonetizing silver, and fixing an official
price at which the domestic currency was convertible on demand into gold. As
holder of official gold reserves, the central bank was obligated to manage its
banknote and credit emissions so as to protect the reserves. Other interventions

included agricultural and industrial tariff increases to alleviate downward pressure on prices, so that in contrast to the recent era, international capital mobility of the latter nineteenth-century was accompanied by rising protectionism in most of the leading capitalist countries, with Great Britain the chief exception. The period also saw incipient labor market and welfare regulations: laws limiting work hours and child labor, old age pensions in Germany and so on. Post–World War II interventionism dwarfs that before World War I, but it's a stretch to label the prewar period an era of laissez-faire.

Because the pre–World War I interventions failed to eliminate the intermittent breakdowns with their financial disorders, mainstream economists soon divided between those pushing for stronger interventions and those blaming the existing interventions for intensifying instability by hampering the self-adjusting properties of the markets. This division persists to the present, with the shifting balance probably responding more to recent events than to intellectual progress in economics. But the inconclusiveness of the intellectual debate has been also in part because it has been conducted largely within the confines of neoclassical economics, which is singularly ill equipped taxonomically for analyzing financial market dynamics.

Neoclassical economics came to dominate mainstream economics in the latter nineteenth-century, displacing the classical economics of Smith and Ricardo. Classical economics had focused on the determinants of capital accumulation and aggregate economic growth. It assumed a background of decentralized, interacting markets, but built its formal analysis around the interaction of broad socioeconomic classes with enduring differences in their modes of economic behavior and types of asset ownership. Neoclassical economics, by contrast, focused on individual market structure and adjustment mechanisms, which it linked to the behavior of individuals instead of classes, while putting capital accumulation and aggregate growth issues in the background.

Neoclassical analysis takes as operating premise that the behavior of economic agents in all situations can be modeled as maximizing the attainment of their desired objective within externally given constraints. Its analysis of economic dynamics focuses on how maximizing agents respond to changes in the constraints. Consumers spend to maximize utility from consumption, given their income and prices; firms maximize profits, subject to selling price and cost constraints, and so forth. Buying and selling of consumption goods and the inputs required to produce these goods creates markets that establish exchange ratios or prices at which the aggregate quantity demanded equals the quantity supplied. Markets adjust to changing incomes and production requirements by establishing new equilibrating prices. A market economy consists of a set of interacting markets, whose relative prices coordinate production and distribution of goods and the incomes of the economic agents involved in these activities through labor or ownership of productive assets. A static societal welfare optimum requires that all agents maximize correctly and that markets be free of monopoly; that is, no single agent or group of agents is able to alter the quantity supplied or demanded sufficiently to move the market clearing price. Smooth economic expansion requires also that the agents be farsighted, not myopic maximizers. They must incorporate correct expectations about future supply and demand trends in their current decisions to buy and sell, which means that today's prices will embody accurate information about tomorrow. The efficient market hypothesis (EMH) is merely an application of this condition to the market for capital assets and intertemporal borrowing and lending.

The optimum for neoclassical economists is an efficiency optimum. It serves as their normative guide for assessing the adjustment efficiency of real markets and market economies, and biases them toward policies that remove monopoly and promote the wider dissemination of economic information, and against government policies that fix prices and restrict entry. The bias is tempered, however, by awareness that the efficiency optimum falls short as a social welfare norm, since it provides no guidance on distributive justice. Thus many of the policy disagreements among neoclassical economists have to do with whether interventionist policies are giving up efficiency for more equity, and if so, whether the tradeoffs are socially desirable. The debate over free capital mobility has such a tradeoff component. Proponents favor it in part because it enables the capital markets to "discipline" national policies by rewarding "sound" policies with capital inflows, and punishing "unsound" ones with outflows. Opponents contend that to the capital markets "sound" policies are those that reduce taxes on capital, weaken unions, roll back social welfare programs, and generally tilt toward an increased concentration of income and wealth.

But while the equity case for free capital mobility remains debatable, the efficiency case is simply wrong. This is because the EMH on which it is grounded turns out to have no support from the neoclassical efficiency optimum. Proof comes from the general equilibrium branch of the neoclassical school. Pre–World War I neoclassical economists had tended to hand-wave away some dicey problems: how a market reaches an equilibrium; how an economy of interacting markets produces a set of equilibrium prices that fully utilizes the available labor supply; and how such an economy adjusts, as input supplies and technologies change, so as to remain on a full employment expansion path. In the interwar period, sparked by the debate over whether socialist economies relying on physical central planning could allocate resources more efficiently than capitalist economies, the general equilibrium branch emerged to explore mathematically the necessary and sufficient conditions for such optima to be reached and to persist.[1] The models took as axiomatic that consumers were fully informed utility maximizers, producers were fully informed profit maximizers and all markets were purely competitive, and asked what additional conditions were required for an economy-wide vector of prices that simultaneously equalized supply and demand in all markets to form, and for the economy to return to equilibrium when disturbed by shifts in supply and demand. The effort produced alternative sets of additional constraints on technology and behavior required to produce locally stable equilibria (that is, ones that would return to balance when subjected to small disturbances) and a set of conditions that sufficed for global stability.

However, a troublesome feature of the proofs of local stability is that money enters only as a unit of account. The real-life functions of money as a basic source of liquidity and store of value, and the financial markets that evolve around these functions, have had to be excluded.[2] More devastatingly, the globally stable case, produced by the Arrow-Debreu model, requires that a complete set of futures markets must exist, or emerge as needed, to enable economic agents to insure against all possible risks. Could such a condition be met, it would transform entrepreneurs, who in neoclassical theory are bearers of uninsurable risk, into accountants able to profit endlessly from riskless portfolios. And since an appropriate timing of payments and receipts would eliminate the need to hold assets for their liquidity, wealth maximizing economic agents would not hold money, a zero earning asset. Nor would entrepreneurs turned accountants need to protect their wealth by overseeing production and disciplining the work force. Hence as self-interested consumers valuing leisure over work, they would head for the golf course instead of the office. In sum, realization of the complete futures market requirement is prevented by a gigantic and insoluble moral hazard problem. *C'est magnifique mais ce n'est ne pas le capitalisme.*[3]

Whether capital markets are capable of pricing assets accurately in accordance with changing supply and technology conditions as the EMH claims, cannot, therefore, be derived from the idealized neoclassical models of competitive market economies. This has moved the debate over the validity of the EMH and the desirability of free capital mobility to a less extreme level of abstraction, in which all parties accept the ubiquity of uninsurable risk, and proponents of the EMH assert it as a looser, more or less valid hypothesis.

Following the Great Depression "less" became the mainstream position. In his magnum opus, Keynes (1936, chapter 12), included an all-out critique of the logic and realism of the EMH notion that investors can and do base their investment decisions on accurate valuation of long-term payoffs. The first generation Chicago School—Milton Friedman's mentors—proposed 100 percent reserves against deposits as a solution to bank crises; a bank's capacity to lend should be no greater than its equity capital (Simons 1948; Mints 1950). Ragnar Nurkse expressed the dominant view on floating exchange rates and free capital mobility when he wrote, "If there is anything the inter-war experience has clearly demonstrated, it is that paper currency exchanges cannot be left to fluctuate from day to day under the influence of market supply and demand. . . . If currencies are left free to fluctuate, speculation in the widest sense is likely to play havoc with exchange rates—speculation not only in foreign exchanges, but also, as a result, in commodities entering into foreign trade." (1944, 137–138).

The 1944 Bretton Woods Articles of Agreement, which reflected the mainstream views of U.S. and British economists, also restricted capital mobility on equity grounds. As explained by Harry Dexter White (1945), head of the U.S. delegation to the Bretton Woods Conference, "Englishmen have not forgotten that in the sterling crisis of 1931 social services were cut in the attempt to maintain the fixed sterling parity. To use international monetary arrangements as a cloak for the enforcement of unpopular policies whose merits or demerits rest not on international monetary considerations as such but on the whole economic program and philosophy of the country concerned, would poison the atmosphere of international financial stability" (1944/45, 200).

The Articles thus represented a collective attempt to restore convertible currencies, stable exchange rates and multilateral trade and foreign investment, while providing ample autonomy for member countries to pursue employment and social welfare policies independently. The Bretton Woods framework accomplished this by allowing members to alter their exchange rates when they severely impeded output and employment stability, and to restrict capital account transactions as needed. The IMF, created to monitor compliance and to provide short-term credit to members in balance of payments difficulty, was also obligated under Article VI to cut off credits when they were used to fund capital flight.

The neoclassical counterattack on the Bretton Woods regime began soon after it went into operation. In a polemical essay that took aim at both Nurkse and Keynes, Milton Friedman (1953) contended that floating exchange rates plus free capital mobility had the following advantages over the regnant Bretton Woods regime:

1. Floating rates would insulate each economy from external monetary shocks, giving it more autonomy over its macroeconomic policies.

2. The nominal exchange rate would move in close step with the domestic price level, thereby minimizing the volatility of the real exchange and interest rates.

3. Arbitraging speculators, free to operate, would hasten the adjustment of the nominal exchange rate to its new equilibrium, forestalling the development of massive hot money flows.

4. Long-term capital flows would bring about a global convergence of real interest rates, optimizing the global allocation of productive capital.

Friedman relied on a weak form of the EMH to support his contention that speculation was stabilizing. He extended to the foreign exchange market the general neoclassical stability requirement, that out-of-equilibrium price movements induce negative feedback from well-informed agents. Negative feedback traders would come to dominate, he claimed, because they would profit consistently from arbitraging away differences between the actual and the equilibrium price at the expense of losses to positive feedback speculators who bet that price movements away from equilibrium would persist. The experience would either lead the latter to adjust their perspective, or accumulating losses would drive them from the market. This is, of course, merely stating a necessary condition for exchange rate speculation to be stabilizing.

When the floating rates that had replaced the Bretton Woods fixed but adjustable system in the 1970s became increasingly volatile, economists sympathetic to the Friedman position sought, by invoking the postulate of rational expectations (Ratex), to show that the volatility embodied rational maximizing trading behavior. Ratex is a modification of the self-contradictory postulate of perfect foresight, which earlier neoclassical economists had invoked to explain away uncertainty. Under Ratex, economic agents lack complete information about future prices, but process all available current information optimally and thus know the means and variances of these prices as implied by the current information set. This information is embodied in current asset prices, which change significantly only as new information appears that requires agents to assess its likely effect on future prices. Ratex also "solved" the problem of how individual assessments aggregated into a unique market price by asserting that information processing led all agents to know the "true model" describing the laws of motion of the aggregate economy. Hence macroeconomic analysis could be linked to individual behavior by the simplifying device of the "representative agent," whose reactions to opportunities and constraints mimicked the entire set of economic agents.

Ratex is a central component of the New Classical Macroeconomics school that emerged in the 1960s to reject the Keynesian contention that countercyclical monetary-fiscal policies could stabilize capitalist economies. To the New Classical school, the true model was Friedman's version of the quantity theory of money, which was anchored in the presumed existence of a stable demand for money function, and whose policy inference was that a slow, stable growth of the money supply sufficed to stabilize aggregate output, employment, and the price level. Ratex strengthened that inference by asserting that countercyclical policies introduce "policy surprises" that roil the asset markets. But unless policymakers have better economic information than do the asset markets, a possibility that is ruled out by Ratex, they will be unable to move the economy to a superior output path.

The rising volatility of post–Bretton Woods exchange rates and short-term capital movements led neoclassical explanations of this volatility to shift from focusing on flow adjustments that eliminated trade imbalances, to portfolio adjustments that eliminated discrepancies between cross-currency exchange and interest rates. The Ratex postulate embedded in the theorizing meant that the financial stock adjustments were efficient; they eliminated the discrepancies, unless blocked by controls and transaction costs. Easing capital controls, and improvements in electronic data processing, were therefore viewed as hastening the adjustments.

This produced a succession of "news models" of exchange rate determination. In these models, foreign exchange rates reflected an efficient processing of all relevant information about future rates available to the markets, with the relevancy determined by the "true model," to which all agents adhered. As new relevant information, "news," was absorbed in the information set, financial flows moved the exchange rates to a new equilibrium, and so on. When the initial true model—open economy Friedman monetarism—proved to be a poor predictor of exchange rate movements, Ratex-embedded true models with different structural features were proposed. The coup de grace to this general line of neoclassical research came when it was shown that the out-of-sample predictions of all these models were worse than those of a naïve random walk model. In the latter, today's exchange rate is always equal to yesterday's, plus or minus a stochastic deviation of constant variance and zero mean. That this minimal information model predicted better than models purporting to provide more structural information on exchange rate dynamics was devastating. The shock was compounded by subsequent econometric explorations that showed that the random walk model was itself dominated by a martingale model, in which today's rate is equal to yesterday's plus or minus deviations of varying size, whose variance was neither stable over time nor with zero mean. Such a model provides exchange market traders with even less positive information than the random walk model.[4]

Reinforcing these adverse empirical findings has been the mathematical demolition of the Ratex postulate. One facet has been to show that the solution of the linear difference equations used to depict the rational expectation of future exchange rates contains an explosive constant which can move expected exchange rates to anywhere between plus and minus infinity. The constant, dubbed the "rational speculative bubble," is arbitrarily set to zero in Ratex-embedded modeling on the premise that rational speculators, aware that in reality such bubbles burst sooner or later, would be able to forecast the timing of this future explosion and make huge profits by cashing in before the explosion. But since all speculators are, by assumption, equally rational, they would all do likewise. Collectively, the accurate market timing would move the explosion closer and closer to the present, leading to the conclusion that a rational expectations bubble can never get started. However, this implies that the speculators draw on information that is not contained in the underlying Ratex model, which predicts everlasting bubbles. De Grauwe, Dewachter, and Embrechts conclude that "this problem is a very general one and appears in all rational expectations models. In all these models there is an infinity of solutions, most of which are unstable. The need then arises to select one particular solution. This selection will necessarily be based on information not contained in the model. Thus even in rational expectations models, *ad hoc* assumptions will be necessary. Fully consistent expectations appear to be impossible" (1993, 69).

A second significant criticism comes from nonlinear or chaos mathematics. For some initial values, low dimensional nonlinear difference or differential equation systems exist that bound the time path of variables and lead to stable solutions. But chaos mathematics also demonstrates that the time paths and solutions can be very sensitive to minute differences in initial values, and that for some values no stable solution exists. Thus, the logistic equation, $X_{t+1} = kX_t (1-X_t)$, has different solutions, depending on the value of k.

1. For k < 1, X reaches a stable asymptotic value of 0.

2. For 1 > k < 3, the asymptotic value is $1-1/k$.

3. For 3 < k < 3.57, the trajectory produces limit cycles, with periodicity increasing as k approaches 3.57, called the "Feigenbaum bifurcation."

4. For k > 3.57, the trajectories become irregular and extremely sensitive to minute differences in the initial value of X.

What this means is that a completely deterministic model (with no stochastic elements reflecting the random impact of unspecified exogenous forces) can endogenously generate seemingly random time paths. The phase diagram of the logistic equation indicates, however, that even for the unstable cases 3 and 4, the time paths for different initial values k and X begin to diverge substantially from one another only after around five thousand iterations. In high-frequency financial markets, where prices change within seconds, this means that the accuracy of price forecasts of two days or less is relatively insensitive to small data or computational errors, but beyond that, sensitivity to error shoots up dramatically.

The logical demolition of Ratex allows more reality to enter the modeling of financial markets. For example, chartists and other technical traders, who try to time asset price movements by searching past price and volume data for hidden behavioral patterns that indicate to them how the market is likely to react to current price and volume momentum as well as to news about fundamentals, are a permanent and sizeable component of financial markets.[5] Yet they cannot last long in Friedman type models, and can never exist in Ratex-embedded models. Freed of these blinkered spectacles, modeling efforts now try to explain financial market dynamics as generated by interactions between momentum and fundamentals traders, with the relative weights of the two groups shifting in response to recent outcomes.

The demolition also requires replacing its "representative agent" simplification with analysis of how prices are formed in markets made up of heterogeneous traders. When these markets consist of agents with differing trading strategies, whose views on what information is relevant are shaped by their strategies, rationality as maximization goes out the window. This is because the relevant information for rational trading on news about fundamentals should include an assessment of how other traders with differing strategies are likely to react, plus the awareness that those reactions will also be influenced by assessments of how others are likely to react. Since a priori deductions of each others' expectations involve an infinite regress into subjectivity, rational traders have no choice but to resort to inductive reasoning. They have no way to validate their expectational hypotheses other than by applying them and observing the results. Inductive reasoning is a rational decision process that precludes maximizing decision making. Heterogeneous traders arriving at a common set of expectations would be a highly special case, based not on reaching consensus on the true model, but on a confluence of judgments about the likely reaction of traders to news.[6] Such equilibria are likely to be unstable, producing the price bubbles and crashes that Ratex modeling cannot explain. What this comes to is a general validation of Keynes's perspective on investor behavior under uncertainty, as put forth in chapter 12 of his magnum opus (1936).

The policy implication is that capital market decontrol, which unleashes financial markets with their innately unstable dynamics on the global economy, lacks justification from economic theory, whether neoclassical or Keynesian. Since neither Ratex, nor its corollary the EMH, is valid, the contention that free capital mobility will improve the performance of the global economy through a more effective use of global resources, and through disciplining national governments to pursue "sound" economic policies, has to be validated inductively, that is, empirically, rather than by a priori theorizing.

POST-BRETTON WOODS BEHAVIOR OF THE GLOBAL ECONOMY

The Bretton Woods system of exchange rates pegged to the gold-convertible dollar faded out in the early 1970s when the United States abrogated its gold convertibility commitment. Replacing it has been a changing assortment of floating rates, managed and unmanaged, as well as various forms of pegged rates. Among developing countries the trend has been toward floating; those with some type of pegged regime declined from 87 percent in 1975 to 40 percent in 1997 (IMF 1999, 23). Among the industrialized countries "dirty floating" predominated. There were intermittent central bank interventions in otherwise market-determined rates, with the European Community countries using a collective currency band system en route to its single currency, the euro.[7] Meanwhile, this confusing evolution of exchange rate arrangements has been paralleled by sustained movements toward trade and capital market liberalization in both the industrialized and the developing countries: "Indeed, the integration of global financial markets has proceeded much more rapidly than that of the goods markets—in part because the latter has been inhibited by protectionism" (IMF 1991, 7).

Nevertheless, the globalizing of capital decontrol has not been complete. Among the industrial countries, Bretton Woods restrictions on cross-currency financial flows imposed for macroeconomic stabilization objectives had been abolished by the mid-1980s. But among developing countries the liberalization drive was then just gaining speed. And despite prodding by the IMF and World Bank, the majority of developing countries still retain some stabilization-motivated controls.[8] But the earlier Bretton Woods financial architecture also had been incompletely implemented. The comparative performances of the post–World War II economies under each of the policy regimes cannot, therefore, be invalidated merely because the liberalization is not yet complete.

Bretton Woods and Post–Bretton Woods Output, Exports, and Productivity Growth Rates

It is useful to compare the empirical results of the Bretton Woods and post–Bretton Woods years (see also the chapter by Armijo). Table 5.1 compares the post-1971 GDP growth of industrialized and developing countries with that of the Bretton Woods years for which good data are available, 1960–1971. The sample consists of the fifty-three World Bank members whose GDP in 1983 was at least $10 billion, and for which continuous GDP data have been available since 1960. GDP growth declined in the first decade after the demise of Bretton Woods in over two-thirds of these countries, with retardation spreading to 90 percent of the countries in the following decade. There was a small pickup from 1992 to 1998, but a much more powerful rebounding of GDP growth would be needed to bring the world economy back to its 1960s pace.

The slowdown encompassed all the industrialized countries as well as most of the developing countries of the capitalist world.[9] GDP per capita data for the same sample of countries indicates the depth of the retardation. In fully half the developing country group, the growth of GDP per capita per decade fell monotonically after 1960–1971, becoming negative in 1982–1991. The share of developing countries with falling income per capita had been only 9

Table 5.1 Global GDP Growth:
Floating Exchange Rate Decades Compared to 1960–1971

	Total Sample(N = 53)		Excluding Oil Exporters*	
	Percent** with Growth above 1960–1971	Percent with Growth below 1960–1971	Percent with Growth above 1960–1971	Percent with Growth below 1960–1971
1972–1981	32.1	67.9	25.0	75.0
1982–1991	9.4	90.6	9.1	90.9
1992–1998	18.9	81.1	22.7	77.3

* Oil Exporters : Algeria, Ecuador, Egypt, Indonesia, Mexico, Nigeria, Norway, United Kingdom, Venezuela
** Percent is unweighted average of all countries in sample.
Source: World Bank, *World Tables*.

percent in 1960–1971, rising to 15 percent in 1972–1981 (Felix 1996a, tables 2 and 5).

The growth retardation after 1971 also is associated with a slower rate of expansion of gross fixed investment. Table 5.2 reports this for the advanced industrial countries, while Schmidt-Hebbel and Serven (1999, 18–19) report a similar drop in the growth of world investment. The second and third components of table 5.2 throw a cold dash of reality on the vaunted acceleration of global economic integration in the post–Bretton Woods period. The export/GDP ratios of the industrialized countries did rise further after Bretton Woods, but only because their export growth rates *declined* less than their GDP growth rates after the 1960s.

As for productivity growth, table 5.3 reproduces OECD data showing a dramatic and sustained drop in the growth of both labor and total factor productivity after 1973 in both the G7 and the rest of the OECD countries. Supporters of financial liberalization can still claim that matters would have been even worse had liberalization not replaced the Bretton Woods system. But appealing to an untestable counterfactual cannot gainsay the fact that to date liberalization has failed to produce the efficiency gains claimed for it.

Post–Bretton Woods Financial Trends

Further evidence that the post–Bretton Woods financial architecture was not an improvement comes from an examination of financial market trends. The removal of restrictions on the cross-border movement of funds reached critical

Table 5.2 Growth of Investment and Exports
(Constant Prices, Percent)

	G7	OECD	World
Growth of Gross Fixed Investment			
1959–1971	6.1	6.0	
1972–1984	2.5	2.3	
1985–1997	3.6	3.7	
Average Annual Export Growth*			
1959–1971	7.8	8.5	8.2
1971–1984	6.2	6.3	7.6
1985–1997	6.6	6.7	5.9
Export Growth/ GDP Growth*			
1959–1971	1.7	1.8	
1971–1984	2.1	2.3	
1985–1997	2.5	2.5	

*G7 and OECD exports are weighted averages, using relative GDP as weights. World Exports for 1959–1974 are deflated by the average of U.S. import and export price indices, and for 1975–1997 by the IMF unit export value index.

Sources: OECD, *Economic Outlook*, various years, and IMF, *International Financial Statistics*, various years.

Table 5.3 Productivity Growth in the OECD
(Percent, Annual Averages)

	G7	Other OECD	All OECD
Labor Productivity			
1960–1973	4.5	5.0	4.6
1973–1979	1.6	3.1	1.8
1979–1997	1.4	2.6	1.6
Total Factor Productivity			
1960–1973	3.1	2.9	3.0
1973–1979	0.7	1.2	0.8
1979–1997	0.8	1.4	0.9

Source: OECD, *Economic Outlook*, June 1999

David Felix

mass by the early 1980s. Funds could now move freely between banks and security markets domiciled in the industrial countries and offshore tax havens. By the early 1990s the integrating of national financial sectors encompassed also a sizeable share of the developing countries. An explosive growth of cross-currency transactions ensued. Table 5.4 summarizes this growth. It also highlights consequences that contradict the efficiency claims of proponents of floating exchange rates and the lifting of capital controls.

The first consequence is that financial globalization has knocked the props from under a central component of the allocative efficiency case for floating exchange rates. The claim was that free-market-determined exchange rates would bring about a more rapid and smoother adjustment of trade imbalances than under the Bretton Woods fixed exchange rate system. Through the 1970s the claimants could still blame the rising exchange rate volatility on OPEC and other supply shocks to the global market for goods rather than on disruptive financial behavior. The low ratio of global foreign exchange turnover to global exports—3.5 in 1977, according to table 5.4—lent plausibility to the inference that forex transactions were largely related to the financing of trade. But as forex turnover kept rising, reaching 34 times the value of global exports in 1986, plausibility vanished. It was now obvious that exchange rate movements among the industrialized countries, which had become even more volatile in the 1980s, were driven primarily by financial dynamics.[10] And it also became evident that the payoff expectations motivating financial movements between currencies were pushing exchange rates well out of line with the rates required to equilibrate

Table 5.4 Foreign Exchange Turnover, Exports, and Official Reserves

	Foreign Exchange Turnover (Annual US$ trillions)	Forex Turnover/ Exports	Global Reserves/ Exports
1977	4.6	3.5	0.23
1986	67.5	33.9	0.28
1998	380.2	67.8	0.29
Memo:			
1961–1965			0.43
1966–1970			0.32

Sources:
Bank for International Settlements, *Central Bank Survey of Foreign Exchange Activities*, triannual surveys, 1986–1998. Daily turnover data multiplied by 250 trading days.
U.S. Federal Reserve Bank of New York, *Summary of Results of the U.S. Foreign Exchange Market Turnover* (New York: September, 1992). U.S. 1977 estimate divided by 0.17, the average U.S. share of global turnover computed from the BIS surveys.
International Monetary Fund, *International Financial Statistics*, various issues.

exports with imports. Thus despite an expanding U.S. trade deficit, the nominal and real dollar exchange rates kept rising through the first half of the 1980s, and it took collective intervention in fall 1985 by the central banks of the five major financial powers to knock down the two rates.

Also refuted by table 5.4 and related data is the claim that countries which had been holding sizeable official reserves to protect their fixed exchange rates under the Bretton Woods system would by turning to floating rates release much of their reserves for additional importing. The table shows that the initial decline of the global reserve/export ratio in the 1970s was short lived. Indeed, to defend against exchange volatility and frequent currency attacks, developing countries have been raising their reserve/export ratios far above the global average. Currently, developing countries hold over half the global official reserves, while accounting for merely one-fourth of global exports.[11]

A third claim refuted by table 5.4 is that floating exchange rates would minimize short-term speculative capital flows, so-called "hot money flows." The table shows that by 1998, annual global forex turnover had risen to 234 times global official reserves (67.8/0.29 = 234). Moreover, over 80 percent of the turnover related to round trip operations of a week or less (Felix 1996b, table A5). The chief motives have been hedging operations against exchange rate risks, speculation on exchange rate movements, and arbitraging of cross-currency interest rate differentials. Instead of reducing hot money flows, floating exchange rates and capital decontrol set off a recursive dynamic that has magnified hot money flows. The increased risks and speculative opportunities created by the volatile exchange rates have induced more hot money flows, which increase exchange rate volatility, which induces more hot money, and so on.

Table 5.5 refutes yet another efficiency claim: that floating exchange rates and free capital mobility would enable movements of the nominal exchange rate and the price level to absorb shocks to the economy, while protecting the stability of the real exchange rate. Stable real rates would, in turn, lower producer risk and investment misallocation. But as table 5.5 shows, since 1970 the real exchange rates of both the developed and the developing countries have also become highly volatile. The rates in the table are decade averages of annual data. The table also shows that developing countries were beset with higher real exchange rate volatility than developed countries. Among the latter, the declining volatility of the Euroland countries has been pulling down the developed country average since 1980.

This reflects the concerted move of Europe to monetary union and the euro, which offset more undular trends in the other developed countries. For the key reserve currencies—the dollar, deutschmark, and yen—volatility in the 1990s was lower than in the1980s, but higher than in the1970s. This is also true for the Latin American and Middle East-Africa groups, reflecting the increased complexity of exchange rate arrangements in the 1990s that was in part a reaction

Table 5.5 Exchange Rate Variability and Volatility*
(Mean Real Exchange Rates for 1970–1979 = 100)
(Trade-weighted Indices)

	1970–79			1980–89			1990–99		
	Mean	Range	Coef. of Var.	Mean	Range	Coef. of Var.	Mean	Range	Coef. of Var.
All Indust. Countries	100	0.1975	0.0671	102.15	0.2436	0.0859	103.24	0.1745	0.0564
U.S.	100	0.2153	0.0742	107.66	0.3478	0.1205	100.47	0.1836	0.0628
G3	100	0.1716	0.0577	102.76	0.2659	0.0930	105.32	0.1844	0.0635
Euro 11	100	0.2184	0.0738	93.91	0.1794	0.0719	96.64	0.1487	0.0486
Other OECD	100	0.1845	0.0628	104.28	0.1811	0.0559	110.55	0.1814	0.0506
Developing Countries	100	0.4284	0.1500	105.90	0.4982	0.2673	94.38	0.3791	0.1882
Asian 10	100	0.3375	0.1178	94.13	0.3515	0.1785	78.59	0.2876	0.1123
Lat. Am. 8	100	0.2424	0.0789	97.91	0.6043	0.2888	94.93	0.3325	0.1329
Mideast/ African 6	100	0.7053	0.2535	125.67	0.5389	0.3171	109.62	0.5173	0.2904

* The range is the difference between the highest and lowest annual values in the decade, divided by the mean. The coefficient of variation is the standard deviation divided by the mean. In each case, higher numbers represent greater volatility.—Ed.

G3 = U.S., Japan, Germany
Euro 11 = Austria, Belgium, Finland, France, Germany, Greece, Ireland, Italy, Netherlands, Portugal, Spain
Other OECD = Australia, Canada, Denmark, New Zealand, Norway, Sweden, Switzerland, U.K.
Asian 10 = Hong Kong, India, Indonesia, Korea, Malaysia, Pakistan, Philippines, Singapore, Taiwan, Thailand
Latin American 8 = Argentina, Brazil, Chile, Colombia, Ecuador, Mexico, Peru, Venezuela
Mideast/Africa 6 = Kuwait, Morocco, Nigeria, Saudi Arabia, South Africa, Turkey

Source: Morgan Guarantee Trust, *World Financial Markets*, various issues

to the upsurge of volatility in the 1980s. Nevertheless, the overall volatility of real exchange rates remains disruptively high.

Paralleling the post-1970s explosive growth of international capital flows has been a sharp rise of long-term real interest rates.[12] By 1995 the real interest rates of ten-year treasury bonds of the G7 were double their 1960s average, with a similar doubling reported for the average global real interest rate (Felix 1997, table 7; Schmidt-Hebbel and Serven 1999, 8).

The "hurdle rate" model helps delineate causal links from the higher real interest rates and real exchange rate volatility to the growth retardation shown in tables 5.1 to 5.3. The hurdle rate is the minimum expected rate of return required to induce risk-averse investors to invest in projects involving front-end outlays, which are fixed costs, and delayed net revenue flows. Formally, it's the cost of capital multiplied by a coefficient ranging upward from unity that represents the investor's premium from "waiting," that is, from postponing the project. The underlying premise is that since information about future costs and returns is unavoidably incomplete, delaying a project can reduce risk by allowing more information to be gathered about prospective costs and revenues. Since this also delays the start of the revenue flow, the waiting premium is the difference between the expected present values of starting the project today or delaying it (Dixit 1992). A higher interest rate, as a component of both the cost of capital and the discount factor, raises the hurdle rates for all projects, but does so unevenly. It tilts the investment choice toward lower fixed-cost and quicker-payoff projects. Similarly, increased volatility of real exchange rates raises the hurdle rates of exporting, importing, or foreign investing projects, but penalizes more those whose forex intensity and duration are relatively higher.

The dramatic rise of real interest rates and exchange volatility has therefore tilted both domestic and foreign private investment toward financial asset plays. Strategies to "grow" the corporation have turned from building new capacity to acquiring it through mergers and acquisitions (M & A). The successful political and ideological push to privatize state assets has further enlarged domestic and international opportunities to acquire existing capacity. Yet the drop of productivity growth (see table 5.3) suggests that the net contribution to aggregate productivity from more efficient use of existing capacity under the new management has been modest at best. The tilt toward M & A, however, helps account for the slower growth of global investment in new capacity.

Financial market liberalization and the lifting of restrictions on capital movements also induced the transformation of financial divisions of large corporations into major profit centers pursuing intricate international liability and portfolio management strategies. According to a postmortem by the Bank for International Settlements, multinational corporations were more important than hedge funds in mounting the speculative attacks that set off the September, 1992, European currency crisis. Liability management largely accounts for why the increasing shares of domestic production in both the developed and developing countries controlled by foreign corporations since the demise of Bretton Woods have hardly lowered the high correlation between gross domestic investment and national savings that had prevailed in both groups of countries in the 1960s.[13] Through borrowing in local currency, and by forex option strategies, multinational corporations have offset exchange rate and political risks by effectively remaining in their home currencies. Feldstein concludes, "The vast majority of the capital stock of the foreign subsidiaries of U.S. multinational corporations does not come from the United States but is accumulated or raised locally by the subsidiary. . . . Informal inquiry with corporations and banks suggests that the obligations incurred by subsidiaries are generally kept in local currency, while the obligations incurred when the parent borrows abroad for use at home is generally hedged back to the home currency. . . . Since the subsidiary's borrowed funds are used locally, there is no cross-border transfer of capital" (1994, 690).

Similarly, foreign portfolio investments of pension and mutual funds, which have expanded rapidly since the 1980s, have also been almost completely hedged against these risks by operations with forex options (Feldstein 1994, 685). For the recipient countries, on the other hand, these varied hedging operations have minimized their net receipt of real resources from foreign direct and portfolio investments.

Globalized Capital Markets as Policy Discipliners and Crisis Producers

The ballooning of short-term capital flows stemming from these operations has significantly increased the power of the financial markets to "discipline" national policy making around the globe. With global official reserves down to one day of global forex turnover, the ability of central banks to intervene effectively in the exchange markets to contain volatility has greatly diminished. The success of the 1985 Plaza Agreement in knocking down an overvalued dollar was short lived. Follow-up efforts to stabilize the dollar-yen and dollar-mark exchange rates were soon overridden by the exchange markets. Short of ammunition for effectively counterspeculating in the exchange markets, central banks have turned to appeasing the markets. Raising interest rates has become the weapon of choice against runs on the currency, which is essentially rewarding financial capital for not fleeing. Broader economic and social policies are also being reshaped under pressure from the capital markets. Egged on by the IMF and World Bank, developing countries try to deter capital flight by adopting "sound" macroeconomic policies, notably by measures to stabilize the price level and balance the fiscal budget. They compete for foreign investment by reducing tax progressiveness, deregulating their financial and goods markets, privatizing and "leveling the playing field" between foreign and domestic capital. Economic policy making in the industrialized countries has, despite thicker financial markets and greater production prowess, also been giving way to these pressures.

Nevertheless, this procapital trend of economic and social policy has been paralleled by a rising frequency of national banking and currency crises around the globe, some setting off international financial crises, others sandbagged by such crises. Of the 181 members of the IMF, nearly three-fourths, including a substantial percent of developed countries, suffered one or more bouts of banking crises or significant banking problems from 1980 to 1995. Banking crises, defined as "cases where there were runs or other substantial portfolio shifts, collapses of financial firms or massive government intervention," afflicted 36 countries. Significant banking problems, defined as "extensive unsoundness short of a crisis," afflicted another 108 (Lindgren, Garcia, and Saal 1996, annex 1). The 1997 Asian crisis and its ramifications have since raised these numbers significantly.

An analysis of 26 developing and industrialized countries undergoing banking and currency crises from 1980 to 1995, found that financial sector liberalization within five years of the crisis accurately predicted 67 percent of the banking crises and 71 percent of the currency crises. Evidently, domestic liberalization, easier access to foreign funds by banks and corporations, and the resulting increase of banking competition promoted liability leveraging and lowered bank credit standards. The M2 money multiplier rose to crisis peaks that averaged 20 percent higher, while the ratio of domestic credit to nominal GDP rose to crisis peaks averaging 15 percent higher than their respective pre-liberalization ratios (Kaminsky and Reinhart 1996).[14]

The macroeconomic costs of the frequent crises has been substantial. A World Bank study of fourteen banking crises estimated that lost output growth averaged 5.2 percent of GDP, while an IMF study obtained an average 14.6 percent decline below trend growth in its sample of developing country banking crises. Banking crises, however, have become closely intertwined with currency crises due to "surges in international capital inflows—especially private-to-private flows—to developing countries and the growing integration of these economies with world financial markets" (World Bank 1998/99, 125–126). The costs of these twin crises have averaged much higher than for each occurring in isolation: 18 percent of GDP for developing countries and 17.6 percent for industrialized countries. The average recovery to trend growth has also been longer: 2.6 years for twin crises compared to 1.9 years for banking crises (World Bank 1998/99, box 3-1).

With events demolishing the aggregate welfare claims for financial liberalization, mainstream economists have been returning to the Bretton Woods view that capital market liberalization is simply incompatible with macroeconomic stability. Economist Dani Rodrik observes,

> A sad commentary on our understanding of what drives capital flows is that every crisis spawns a new generation of economic models. When a new crisis hits, it turns out that the previous generation of models was hardly adequate. . . . The earliest models were based on the incompatibility of monetary and fiscal policies with fixed exchange rates. These seemed to account well for the myriad balance of payment crises experienced through the 1970s. The debt crisis of 1982 unleashed an entire literature on over-borrowing in developing countries, placing the blame squarely on expansionary fiscal policies (and in some countries on inappropriate sequencing of liberalization). But crises did not go away when governments became better behaved on the fiscal and monetary front. The exchange rate mechanism (ERM) crisis in 1992 could not be

blamed on lax monetary and fiscal policies in Europe, and therefore led to a new set of models with multiple equilibria. The peso crisis of 1994–95 did not fit well either, so economists came up with yet other explanations—this time focusing on real exchange rate overvaluations and the need for more timely and accurate information on government policies. In the Asian crisis neither real exchange rate nor inadequate information seems to have played a major role, so attention has shifted to moral hazard and crony capitalism in these countries. (1998, 58–59)

The IMF still bases its "sound policy" demands from its crisis-ridden clients on the first generation of models, which puts full blame on the clients. But events have forced the IMF to muddy its soundness accolade. Overvaluing the exchange rate to lower inflation and/or to pacify the financial markets, and devaluing to balance trade accounts now each qualify as sound," with no clarification on how to square the contradiction. The IMF now acknowledges that crises may involve investor miscalculations, but blames crony capitalism and inadequate information from client governments for misleading investors. And it clings to the view that more timely and "transparent" information from governments and improved risk evaluation procedures by foreign exchange dealing banks are the keys to enabling free capital mobility to function smoothly.

This tenacious faith in the EMH and in the virtues of policy disciplining by the financial markets brushes aside the accumulation of microeconometric findings that the actual behavior of foreign exchange markets belies that predicted by Ratex and the EMH. The "forward discount anomaly," that is, the failure of the forward exchange rate to predict correctly even the direction of movement of the future spot rate, is now a generally accepted finding (Engel 1995). The forecasting errors of foreign exchange dealers, according to various surveys, are serially correlated rather than mean reverting, which implies trend-following behavior (Ito 1990; Takagi 1991). And the cumulative short-term forecasts over a three-, six-, or twelve-month interval usually badly over- or undershoot the direct forecasts made at the beginning of the interval on what the end of interval spot rate will be (Froot and Ito 1989). The practical inference is that in the absence of liquid long-term hedging instruments, long-term international investors cannot fully hedge against the exchange rate risks by rolling over liquid short-term hedging instruments. Knowing this, investors in a volatile exchange rate environment can be expected to raise the risk premium and the hurdle rate of return for undertaking long-term investments.

The faith also disregards the likelihood that neither transparency nor improved risk procedures will stabilize hot money flows. Providing faster and more "transparent" information of impending difficulties to portfolio investors could merely hasten the onset of currency crises by triggering faster capital flight. The value-at-risk (VAR) mathematical models used by banks to control their proprietary foreign exchange dealing, financing of hedge funds, and customized derivative mongering, are charged with encouraging excessive risk-taking and intensifying contagion during the 1997–1998 global financial crisis (Folkerts-Landau and Garber 1998). The charge is that by relying on backward-looking variance-covariance matrices and assuming normal risk distribution, they tended to underestimate the likelihood of large losses from taking long asset positions with short-term leveraged liabilities (the flaw that bankrupted the Long Term Capital Asset Management hedge fund in 1998). Contagion was intensified because a volatility event in one country automatically generated an upward reestimate of credit and market risk in a correlated country, which triggered margin calls and tightening of credit lines in both countries. Such risk control methods help explain why Malaysia's imposition of capital controls and Russia's default produced a widespread cutoff of lending to developing countries. Tightening the VAR methodology to improve risk assessing by banks would likely reinforce such contagious reactions.

Reacting to the "tequila" crisis, the IMF's managing director, Michel Camdessus sketched the task of the IMF as follows: "In today's globalized markets, we must ensure that our ability to react approaches the instant decision making of investors if we want to have the ability to give confidence to markets and our members" (1995, 185). The message from both economic theory and the array of financial disasters is quite the opposite. The task should be to slow the reactions of the globalized financial markets in order to allow the more measured speed of production and policy adjustments to take hold.

The political and ideological forces that still keep the IMF and G7 on Camdessus's road to further disasters are the focus of other papers of this volume. I conclude instead with a brief assay at longer historical comparison.

THE GOLD STANDARD AND FREE CAPITAL MOBILITY: WHAT ARE THE POLICY LESSONS?

A final argument used in favor of free capital mobility is that it worked well during the pre–World War I era of the classical gold standard. This logic, too, disintegrates under careful examination (see also the contributions by Brawley and Armijo). Legal restrictions on the cross-border movement of currency were virtually nonexistent from 1879 to 1914, yet most of Europe and its colonial appendages, the United States and the autonomous British dominions, were able to maintain fixed gold-convertible currencies throughout the period. They endured frequent domestic financial crises, but speculative attacks on their currencies were rare and unsuccessful.[15] Instead capital flows from London and, to a lesser extent from Paris and Berlin, not only financed foreign trade and overseas infrastructure and mining investments on a grand scale, but also played a generally beneficent role in stabilizing gold-convertible fixed exchange rates. In contrast, the efforts of the Europeans to restore the gold standard after World War I were plagued by disruptive capital flows, and the short-lived restoration—from 1925 to 1931—terminated in a massive international banking and currency crisis. Why?

Explanations of why the beneficent role of capital flows turned maleficent in the interwar decades broadly divide, as expected, into those that emphasize governments' *policy flaws* that roiled the post–World War I financial markets, and those that emphasize *post-war changes in the international economic structure and socio-political environment* which precluded the successful implementing of pre-war policies. As with other large-scale historical events, a definitive resolution is not possible, but in this case plausibility is strongly against mere policy flaw explanations.

Some have argued that the interwar gold standard failed because major countries' central banks in the 1920s did not adhere to the gold standard "rules of the game" they had allegedly followed faithfully in the prewar era. The rules, according to this view, required that the major central banks abstain from sterilizing external capital flows. Instead, prewar central banks tightened domestic credit when capital was flowing out and the exchange rate was moving to the gold export point, and eased it when capital inflows were moving the exchange rate to the gold import point. Higher interest rates and depressed demand for imports induced a reversal of capital outflows, while easing credit discouraged capital inflows when they were pushing the exchange rate to the gold import point. Respect for the rules accounted for why gold flows were minimal under the pre–World War I gold standard: short-term capital flows handled most of the adjustment task. Confidence that the rules were being faithfully followed gave the fixed exchange rate policy high credibility in the financial markets, so that attacking the exchange rate was viewed as a losing game. This changed after the war, when central banks, motivated by other priorities, abandoned close adherence to the rules. The domestic and foreign assets of the major central banks in the 1920s tended to move inversely: sterilizing capital flows had displaced adherence to the rules (Nurkse 1944). The fixed exchange rate policy became less credible to the financial markets, making them more prone to destabilizing exchange rate speculation.

The trouble with this explanation is that the alleged "rules" are little more than an ex post facto construct. In reality, sterilization was also widespread under the prewar gold standard, as Arthur Bloomfield (1959), applying Nurkse's test to data from 1880 to 1914, demonstrated. Central banks even then had multiple objectives, notably easing domestic credit crises and providing orderly markets for government debt. Moreover, as profit-seeking private institutions, lesser central banks took to keeping interest-earning deposits with the Bank of England, the Reichsbank, or the Bank of France, as foreign reserves in lieu of gold. Such central bank interflows, Eichengreen (1996, chapter 2) points out, were also central to the stabilizing adjustments under the prewar gold standard. Constrained by their semi-public responsibilities, the European central banks tended to be supportive rather than destabilizing of one another. Eichengreen's overall assessment is that the rules of the game concept is much too simplistic: "Central banks had some discretion over their policies. They were well shielded from political pressures, but insulation was never complete. . . . Among those in a position to influence policy, there was a broad-based consensus that the maintenance of convertibility was a priority . . . and the stronger that consensus and the policy credibility it provided, the more scope central banks possessed to deviate from the 'rules' without threatening the stability of the gold standard" (1996, 30).

That scope diminished after World War I. The interwar gold standard was even more a gold-exchange standard, with the dollar and sterling as the dominant reserve currencies. But cooperative management of inter–central bank deposits was often swamped by destabilizing speculative flows. The tribulations of France and Belgium in returning to the gold standard in the 1920s fit Obstfeld's multiple equilibrium exchange rate model, in which speculators profit by forcing a welfare-reducing exchange rate on the authorities (Obstfeld 1986). The attempt to make the French franc convertible again, with a reduced gold content that reflected a plausible purchasing power parity adjustment from the prewar franc, was overridden by massive capital flight. Only after a right-wing government took office could the franc be stabilized, but with a gold content representing an 80 percent drop from prewar parity (Sicsic 1992). Concurrently, the exchange markets depreciated the Belgian franc to the same extent as the French franc, although Belgian "fundamentals" called for a substantially higher exchange rate (Aliber 1962). Both currencies stabilized at substantially undervalued exchange rates, whereas the British pound, made convertible again at prewar par, was significantly overvalued. The imbalances contributed to the fragility of the interwar gold standard, but neither represented mere policy mistakes. The francs were driven to undervaluation by the markets, which, motivated by redistributive policy fears, overpowered the effort of the authorities to set higher rates. The return of the pound at prewar par was the outcome of an overt political struggle in which the City outpowered the industrialists.

One is pulled, therefore, to explanations that focus on differences between the pre– and post–World War I structural and political contexts that shaped the expectations and behavior of the financial markets. Eichengreen stresses that during the prewar gold standard "those in a position to influence policy" did not yet include the working classes: "The worker susceptible to unemployment when the central bank raised the discount rate had little opportunity to voice his objections, much less expel from office the government and central bankers responsible for the policy" (1996, 31). Reduced aggregate demand could be readily accommodated by falling wages and prices. But by the eve of World War I, "the extension of the franchise and the emergence of political parties representing the working classes raised the possibility of challenges to the single-minded priority the monetary authorities attached to convertibility. Rising consciousness of unemployment and of trade-offs between internal and external balance politicized monetary policy" (Eichengreen 1996, 43). Hence he doubts the gold standard could have long survived had World War I not occurred. In the event, "the interwar gold standard resurrected in the second half of the 1920s shared few of the merits of its prewar predecessor. With labor and commodity markets lacking their traditional flexibility, the new system could not easily accommodate shocks. With governments lacking insulation from pressure to stimulate growth and employment, the new regime lacked credibility. When the system was disturbed, financial capital that had once flowed in stabilizing directions took flight, transforming a limited disturbance into an economic and political crisis" (Eichengreen 1996, 46).

The lesson drawn by the architects of Bretton Woods was that since the enhanced egalitarian pressures of the post–World War I political environment would, and should, persist, restoring stable exchange rates and a more open trading system required restricting international capital mobility. On the other hand, the lesson drawn by post–Bretton Woods neoliberalism is that the prewar compatibility of free capital mobility with stable exchange rates and free trade can be restored by globalizing free market policies. But that misreads the prewar experience. Its stability depended on conditions absent from, or at odds with, the neoliberal policy agenda.

The first is that because "those in a position to influence policy" before World War I included farmers and industrialists, protecting the gold standard required most countries to accommodate the demands from the two groups for protection against competing imports. West and Central European farmers were given tariff protection against grain and meat imports from Russia and the Western Hemisphere, and industrial tariffs were increased on the European continent and in the United States, Canada, and Australia. Except in Britain, the prewar gold standard era was one of rising protectionism. This is, of course, completely contrary to the current neoliberal agenda, which seeks to institutionalize trade liberalizing through binding international compacts.

A second prewar safety net, free migration, is absent from the neoliberal agenda. For the politically weak European working classes, emigration was an important escape from falling wages and rising unemployment. Between 1871 and 1914 about forty million Europeans emigrated, mostly to Western Hemisphere countries with liberal immigration policies. The migrants represented about 25 percent of the 1871–1914 population increase, and, since they were mainly young males, a much higher percent of the increase of the European labor force. The relative size of the inflows to receiving countries—62 percent went to the United States, around 10 percent each to Canada and Argentina, and 7 percent each to Brazil and Australasia—approximates the relative size of the inflows of European capital to the same countries. Brinley Thomas exploited the evidence that prewar European emigration and capital flowed in nearly parallel long waves to test persuasively a push-pull economic model linking the two. The model, in which capital outflows to and investment rates in the United States surged when labor outflows from rural Europe and overseas emigration surged, eased European social tensions from its rural-urban transformations. The pattern ended with the war and the imposition by the United States of severe restrictions on immigration (Thomas 1954, 1972). Restoration of the gold standard in Europe was thus faced, among other problems, with a tattered migration safety net and a much reduced capacity of European countries to finance investment in the receiving countries that had maintained open immigration policies.

By pushing free market and free capital mobility policies on developing countries, but not free immigration on the higher wage developed countries, the neoliberal agenda is implying that the developing countries don't need a migration safety net to handle successfully the socioeconomic and political tensions of their demographic transition and massive exodus of "surplus" rural labor. Such an implication cannot be derived from historical experience. Neither can it be derived from Heckscher-Ohlin trade theory, which provides the neoliberal agenda with its theoretical rationale for globalizing free trade. Pre–World War I European labor and capital migrated in the same direction, indicating that, contrary to the canonical two-sector Heckscher-Ohlin model, the returns to labor and capital were both higher in the recipient countries. Currently the two factors may be moving in opposite directions, but the "factor price equalization theorem" of the two-sector H-O model provides little solace to developing countries. For the theorem to hold, a central condition is that all factor units be of homogeneous quality. This means that developing country labor must embody the human capital levels of their developed trading partners *al principio*, that is, that the developing countries must already be developed.

A third significant contrast between the classical gold standard era and our own is slow speed of international financial transacting then and the almost instantaneous electronic transacting now. Higher transaction costs and information lags impeded international interest rate arbitraging then, so that despite stable exchange rates between the main currencies, covered interest rate parity was not a feature of the pre–World War I gold standard, as it is today. Computing pair-wise correlations between the money market rates of London-Paris-Berlin and New York from 1876 to 1914, Morgenstern obtained an overall average correlation coefficient of 0.54, with the pairings between New York and the three European money centers averaging merely 0.40. (Morgenstern 1959).[16] By raising its bank rate, the Bank of England might have been able to draw funds from the moon, but slowly. The "sand in the gears" of the prewar international financial mechanism allowed more scope for monetary-fiscal policies and production decisions to take effect without being overwhelmed by adverse capital flight than is available today to, say, the directors of the European Central Bank struggling to stabilize the euro.

CURRENT ISSUES

The neoliberal globalization project is thus launched on uncharted seas, with neither prior history nor adequate theory to guide the navigation. Moreover, two barely submerged rocks lie on the near horizon. Table 5.6 illustrates one of them. It shows that since 1985 the "riskless" real interest rate, that is, the real rate on ten-year government bonds, has averaged much higher than the real GDP growth rate in all the G7 except Japan. During the Bretton Woods era, by contrast, the real interest rate averaged considerably lower than the real GDP growth rate, and during the pre-World War I gold standard it merely equaled the real growth rate. Only during the interwar period did the interest rate/GDP growth ratio, elevated by the collapse of GDP during the Great Depression, reach that of 1985 to 1997. Indeed a more detailed breakdown of the current era shows the real interest rate outpacing the growth rate of the G7 by an increasing degree after 1982, overtaking the interwar ratio in the 1990s (Felix 1997/98, table 9).

G7 inflation, and presumably the inflation risk premium, has been diminishing since the early 1980s, as have GDP growth and fiscal deficits. This leaves the removal of capital controls in the early 1980s as the most likely instigator of the rising real interest rates. Opening channels for the rapid global transfer of funds increased the power of financial markets to exact higher premiums for keeping funds at home. Higher real interest rates raise the cost of capital to borrowers, which should depress equity values. Yet while the growth of physical investment did slacken, bond financing and equity market capitalization have boomed. Since 1982 the nominal value of bonds listed on the organized bond markets globally has been expanding at an annual rate that is two-thirds higher, and the capitalization of the global equity markets has been growing at double the global rate of growth of nominal GDP. Together with the rising real interest/GDP ratios, this implies that the share of global income accruing to owners of financial assets as well as debt leveraging and asset inflation have been increasing at rates that cannot persist indefinitely. The sixty-four trillion dollar question is, therefore, whether the liberated financial markets can bring the rates to within sustainable limits smoothly, or whether that will require global financial crises and collapsing asset values. Stay tuned.

A second, less submerged, rock on the horizon relates to the fragility of the post-1970s arrangements by which the United States has sustained its dominance of capital exporting. It's an arrangement without historic precedent. Britain under the prewar gold standard had dominated long-term capital exporting by reexporting part of its sizeable current account surpluses. It also facilitated debt servicing by running chronic trade deficits while not restricting imports. After the war it was impelled by its shrunken current account surpluses to restrict the access to its capital market by nonimperial borrowers, exposing another critical flaw that brought down the interwar gold standard. Unlike Brit-

Table 5.6 Real Long-Term Interest Rates Less
Real GDP Growth Rates in the G7*

	G7	Canada	France	Germany	Italy	Japan	UK	US
1881–1913	0.97							
1919–1939	2.40							
1946–1958	0.36							
1959–1971	0.55	0.65	0.22	0.88	0.49	n.a.	0.71	0.59
1972–1984	0.47	0.63	0.80	1.42	−0.24	0.29	−0.11	0.52
1985–1997	2.34	3.26	2.86	2.35	3.75	0.90	1.63	1.67

* Real long-term interest rates minus real GDP growth. Real long-term interest rates are annual interest rates on ten-year government bonds deflated by national CPI.

Sources: Interest rates and CPIs from IMF, *International Financial Statistics*. Real GDP growth rates from OECD, *Economic Outlook*. Pre-1959 data from Bordo (1993). Real per capita growth rates were multiplied by population growth rates.

ain, the United States, which filled the international lending gap in the 1920s, sustained trade surpluses that were reinforced by protective tariffs. The rest of the world's ability to service existing dollar bonds thus came to depend on being able to sell new bonds. When the more pessimistic investment climate after the 1929 stock market crash curbed the U.S. appetite for foreign issues, the pyramid-like lending pattern also crashed in a wave of defaults of dollar loans that deepened the post-1929 international financial crisis.

Currently, a far less protectionist United States has been running large deficits in its commodity and service trade, and financing its capital exporting by borrowing abroad. Its growing current account deficits reached nearly 4.5 percent of GDP in 2000. The U.S. net international asset position has thus moved from surplus at the end of the 1970s to a $1.8 trillion deficit in 2000, or about 21 percent of GDP. To be sure, most of these external liabilities are payable in dollars, and until recently the net outflow of profits has been merely around $10 billion per annum. But times are changing. The nominal rate of interest on U.S. external debt has begun exceeding the rate of growth of nominal GDP, which in Godley's (2000) recent assessment, makes imminent a "debt trap" dynamic. He projects that rising U.S. interest rates soon will begin raising debt servicing costs enough to require yet more intense borrowing to finance the current account deficit. And while direct foreign investment in the United States still makes up the larger share of U.S. foreign liabilities, the low returns on these assets because of past Japanese misinvestment are being corrected, while a high proportion of foreign acquisitions are being obtained through the exchange of shares, which adds nothing to the financing of the current account deficit. In all, Godley fears that attracting foreign inflows to fund the expanding U.S. current account deficits might soon require such high interest rates and fiscal austerity as to impart a deflationary bias to the U. S. and the world economy.

Godley's projections are meant primarily to highlight his warning that the current U.S. pattern of financing its capital exports by borrowing abroad is not sustainable. His policy assessment is that, while correcting it with preemptive policy adjustments would be difficult and costly, leaving the correction to the markets will be even more costly. It's an assessment more redolent of the 1930s than of the golden age of the gold standard.

CONCLUSIONS

Combining capital market liberalization with free trade to attain a more efficient and faster growing global economy has neither valid theoretical nor empirical justification. The theoretical case for free capital mobility—that it improves the efficient allocation of resources and, through rewards and punishments, improves global policy making—is grounded in the efficient market and rational expectations hypotheses, both of which are discredited by their flawed logic and falsified predictions. They are failed efforts to get around the ineluctable fact of life that financial instability—with its asset price bubbles, destabilizing speculation, overleveraging and bankruptcy crises—is inherent in competitive financial markets, because heterogeneous market agents must unavoidably form their expectations on uncertain knowledge about the future and about each other's reactions to information.

Because capitalist expansion has been halted periodically by financial crises with adverse repercussions on output and employment, twentieth-century governments had sought with varying degrees of success to dampen the crises with financial controls and countercyclical monetary-fiscal policies. The BrettonWoods Agreement was an attempt to coordinate these efforts. The recent abandoning of its capital controls has been destabilizing. It has freed financial markets to interact globally, without providing adequate global substitutes for the domestic stabilizing mechanisms that financial markets are now able to evade more easily. Free capital mobility has thus become a powerful force for elevating local financial crises into international ones and for slowing global output growth.

NOTES

1. The explorations with more powerful mathematics built on the pioneering work of the French economist Leon Walras (1954).

2. Yet "in a world with a past as well as a future and in which contracts are made in terms of money, no equilibrium may exist" (Arrow and Hahn 1991, 361).

3. This is clearly the assessment of Arrow and Hahn 1991, chapter 14.

4. I'm summarizing a more detailed survey of the literature in De Grauwe, Dewachter, and Embrechts 1993, chapter 2.

5. Survey data on the trading strategies of dealers in the London foreign exchange market, the world's largest, indicates the following: 90 percent used charting for short-period trading because, they said, it produced more accurate short-period forecasts than econometric models based on fundamentals. For longer forecasts, information about fundamentals helps shape their position taking (Macdonald and Taylor 1992). The latter is, however, small beer, since over 80 percent of foreign exchange trading involves round-trips of a week or less.

6. A promising approach to modeling stock market behavior along these lines is described in Arthur et al. 1997. The approach consists of varying the parameters of a nonlinear model that allows feedbacks to modify trading strategies of heterogeneous traders. The model is applied to the Santa Fe Institute's computerized Artificial Stock Market to generate alternative numerical runs. Embedded in the nonlinear model is an expectation equilibrium, but whether the traders converge on it depends on the nature and speed of their reactions to the changing prices, volumes, and yields produced by the computer runs. The general finding is that the more quickly traders adjust their strategies to market results, the more the market self-organizes into a complex regime. "A rich market psychology—a rich set of expectations—becomes observable. Technical trading emerges as a profitable activity, and temporary bubbles and crashes occur from time to time. Trading volume is high, with times of quiescence alternating with intense market activity. The price time series shows persistence in volatility . . . and in trading volume. . . . [I]ndividual behavior evolves continually and does not settle down" (Arthur et al. 1997, 301).

7. A recent IMF inventory of the evolution of exchange rate arrangements found it necessary to place member country arrangements in two different classification systems; one, based on officially announced arrangements, has nine classes of exchange rate arrangements; the other, based on IMF judgments of the de facto regimes actually in operation, has thirty-three classes (IMF 1999, tables 8 and 10).

8. The same IMF study also surveys the incidence of capital account controls, using forty-four types of controls on capital transactions. It reports that as of 1997 industrial countries had on average only four such types of controls still on the books, compared to an average of sixteen for "non-industrial countries." The forty-four types, however, included controls directed at sectoral protectionism and national security objectives having little to do with macroeconomic stabilization. Also by 1996 a few developing contries had reached a level of capital account liberalization comparable to the industrial countries (IMF 1999, chapters 3 and 6, tables 5 and 35).

9. Growth retardation also afflicted the Soviet Bloc both before and after its breakup. However, the causal dynamics prior to the 1990s had little to do with market liberalization.

10. The average monthly volatility of the dollar exchange rate with the deutschmark, franc, sterling, and yen was 22 percent higher from 1980 to 1984, and 35 percent higher from 1985 to 1989 than in the volatile 1970s (Blundell-Wignall and Browne 1991, table 7).

11. Computed from the global export and official reserves tables of the IMF, *International Financial Statistics*. In 1996, prior to the Asian crisis, LDCs held 50 percent of all official reserves; in 1998, the peak crisis year, the LDC share rose to 54 percent.

12. A recent OECD econometric study calculated that half the rise of real long-term interest rates in the 1980s was due to financial market liberalization (Orr, Edey, and Hviding 1995).

13. Feldstein and associates have found the correlations between gross domestic investment and national savings remained around 0.9 for developed countries during the 1960s, 1970s, and 1980s (Feldstein and Horioka 1980; Feldstein and Baccheta 1991). For developing countries, Professor Michael Dooley and associates found a slightly lower but persistent correlation (Dooley, Frankel, and Mathisson 1987).

14. A summary of other studies elaborating on the channels by which financial liberalization has encouraged risky bank behavior is provided in World Bank 1998/99, 135–141.

15. Latin American and Asian countries with independent currencies were much less successful in maintaining fixed convertible exchange rates. The Baring Crisis of 1890, during which Argentina was forced off the gold standard, also came close to toppling the pound sterling. That was prevented by emergency French and Russian reinforcement of the Bank of England's threatened gold reserves.

16. Morgenstern used monthly time series that were not deseasonalized. This meant, as he recognized, that the coefficient values were probably biased upward by similar seasonal variations in money demand and supply in the four countries.

REFERENCES

Aliber, Robert. 1962. Speculation in the Foreign Exchanges: the European Experience, 1919–26. *Yale Economic Essays*, spring.

Arrow, Kenneth J., and Frank L. Hahn. 1991. *General Competitive Equilibrium*. Amsterdam: North-Holland Press.

Arthur, W. Brian, John H. Holland, Blake Le Baron, Richard Palmer, and Paul Taylor. 1997. Asset Pricing Under Endogenous Expectations in an Artificial Stock Market. *Economic Notes* (Siena: Banca Monte dei Paschi di Siena) 26, no. 2: 297–330.

Bloomfield, Arthur. 1959. *Monetary Policy Under the International Gold Standard, 1880–1914*. New York: Federal Reserve Bank of New York.

Blundell-Wignall, Adrian, and Frank Browne. 1991. Macroeconomic Consequences of Financial Liberalization: A Summary Report. OECD Working Paper no. 98 (February). Paris: OECD Department of Economics and Statistics.

Bordo, Michael. 1993. The Bretton Woods International Monetary System: An Historical Overview. In *A Retrospective on the Bretton Woods System*, ed. Michael Bordo and Barry Eichengreen. Chicago: University of Chicago Press.

Camdessus, Michel. 1995. The IMF in the Globalized World Economy. *IMF Survey*, June 19.

De Grauwe, Paul, Hans Dewachter, and Mark Embrechts. 1993. *Exchange Rate Theory: Chaotic Models of Foreign Exchange Markets.* Oxford and Cambridge: Blackwell.

Dixit, Avinash. 1992. Investment and Hysterisis. *Journal of Economic Perspectives* 6.

Dooley, Michael, Jeffrey Frankel, and Donald Mathisson. 1987. International Capital: What do the Saving-Investment Correlations Tell Us? *IMF Staff Papers* 34:503–530.

Eichengreen, Barry. 1996. *Globalizing Capital: A History of the International Monetary System.* Princeton, N.J.: Princeton University Press.

Engel, Charles. 1995. The Forward Discount Anomaly and the Risk Premium: A Survey of Recent Evidence. NBER Working Paper no. 5312. Cambridge, Mass.: National Bureau of Economic Research, October.

Feldstein, Martin 1994. Tax Policy and International Capital Flows. *Weltwirtschaftliches Archiv* 180, no. 4:675–97.

Feldstein, Martin, and P. Baccheta. 1991. National Saving and International Investment. In *National Saving and Economic Performance,* ed. B. Douglas Bernheim and John Shoven. Chicago: University of Chicago Press.

Feldstein, Martin, and Charles Horioka. 1980. Domestic Saving and International Capital Flows. *The Economic Journal* 90:314–29.

Felix, David. 1996a. Financial Globalization versus Free Trade: The Case for the Tobin Tax. *UNCTAD Review 1996,* Geneva: United Nations Conference on Trade and Development, 63–104.

———. 1996b. Statistical Appendix. In *The Tobin Tax: Coping with Financial Volatility,* ed. Mahbub Ul Haque, Inge Kaul, and Isabelle Grunberg. New York: Oxford University Press.

———. 1997. Asia and the Crisis of Financial Globalization. Chap. 7 in *Globalization and Progressive Economic Policy,* ed. Dean Baker, Gerald Epstein, and Robert Pollin. Cambridge: Cambridge University Press.

———. 1997/98. On Drawing General Policy Lessons from Recent Latin American Currency Crises. *Journal of Post-Keynesian Economics* 20, no. 2:191–221.

Folkerts-Landau, David, and Peter Garber. 1998. Capital Flows from Emerging Markets in a Closing Environment. *Global Emerging Markets* (London: Deutsche Bank Research) no.3:69–83.

Friedman, Milton. 1953. The Case for Flexible Exchange Rates. In *Essays in Positive Economics,* ed. Milton Friedman, Chicago: University of Chicago Press.

Froot, Kenneth, and Takatoshi Ito. 1989. On the Consistency of Short-Run and Long-Run Exchange Rate Expectations. *Journal of International Money and Finance* 8 (December).

Godley, Wynne. 2000. Interim Report: Notes on the U.S. Trade and Balance of Payments Deficits. *Levy Institute Report* (March). Bard College: The Jerome Levy Economics Institute.

International Monetary Fund (IMF). 1991. Determinants and Systemic Consequences of International Capital Flows. Occasional Paper no. 77. Washington, D.C.: International Monetary Fund.

———. 1999. *Exchange Rate Arrangements and Currency Convertibility: Development and Issues.* IMF World Economic and Financial Surveys. Washington, D.C.: International Monetary Fund.

Ito, Takatoshi. 1990. Foreign Exchange Expectations: Micro Survey Data. *American Economic Review* 80 (June).

Kaminsky, Graciela and Carmen Reinhart. 1996. The Twin Crises: The Causes of Banking and Balance of Payments Crises. *International Finance Discussion Paper,* no. 544. Washington, D.C.: Board of Governors of the Federal Reserve System.

Keynes, John Maynard. 1936. *The General Theory of Employment, Interest and Money.* New York: Harcourt, Brace & Co.

Lindgren, Carl-Johan, Gillian Garcia, and Mathew Saal. 1996. *Bank Soundness and Macroeconomic Policy.* Washington, D.C.: International Monetary Fund, June.

Macdonald, Ronald and Mark P. Taylor. 1992. Exchange Rate Economics: A Survey. *IMF Staff Papers* 39 (March).

McKenzie, Michael. 1999. The Impact of Exchange Rate Volatility on International Trade Flows. *Journal of Economic Surveys* 13.

Mints, Lloyd. 1950. *Monetary Policy for a Competitive Economy.* New York: McGraw-Hill.

Morgenstern, Oskar. 1959. *International Financial Transactions and Business Cycles.* National Bureau of Economic Research Studies in Business Cycles no. 8. Princeton, N.J.: Princeton University Press.

Nurkse, Ragnar. 1944. *International Currency Experience.* Geneva: League of Nations.

Obstfeld, Maurice. 1986. Rational and Self-Fulfilling Balance of Payments Crises. *American Economic Review* 76.

Orr, Adrian, Malcolm Edey, and Ketil Hviding. 1995. Real Long-Term Interest Rates: The Evidence from Pooled Time-Series. *OECD Economic Studies* no. 25.

Rodrik, Dani. 1998. Who Needs Capital Account Convertibility? In *Should the IMF Pursue Capital-Account Convertibility?* ed. Stanley Fischer. *Essays in International Finance,* no. 207 (May), Princeton, N.J.: Princeton University, Department of Economics.

Schmidt-Hebbel, Klaus, and Luis Serven. 1999. *The Economics of Savings and Growth: Theory, Evidence, and Implications for Policy.* Cambridge: Cambridge University Press.

Sicsic, Pierre. 1992. Was the Franc Poincaré Deliberately Undervalued? *Explorations in Economic History* 29:69–92.

Simons, Henry C. 1948. *Economic Policy for a Free Society.* Chicago: University of Chicago Press.

Takagi, Sinji. 1991. Exchange Rate Expectations: A Survey of Survey Studies. *IMF Staff Papers* 38 (March).

Thomas, Brinley. 1954. *Migration and Economic Growth: A Study of Great Britain and the Atlantic Economy.* Cambridge: Cambridge University Press.

———. 1972. *Migration and Urban Development: A Reappraisal of British and American Long Cycles.* London: Methuen & Co.

Walras, León, [1890] 1954. *Elements of Pure Economics,* translated by William Jaffé. Homewood, IL: R. D. Irwin.

White, Harry D. 1944/45. The Monetary Fund: Some Criticism Examined. *Foreign Affairs* 23 (January):195–210.

World Bank. 1998/99. *Global Economic Prospects and the Developing Countries.* Washington, D.C.: World Bank.

Chapter 6

THE REDESIGN OF THE INTERNATIONAL FINANCIAL ARCHITECTURE FROM A LATIN AMERICAN PERSPECTIVE: WHO PAYS THE BILL?

Eduardo Fernández-Arias and Ricardo Hausmann

I nternational financial liberalization and financial integration have not worked out as advertised. In the recent past, emerging markets have been rattled by financial turmoil. The degree of financial volatility and the frequency of panics, crises, and contagion have made the current state of affairs socially costly and politically disappointing in emerging economies. Political support for liberalizing policies in emerging countries is now harder to achieve. The prospect of faster long-run growth has not compensated for these new headaches. All this is especially true in Latin America, which after a decade of solid structural reforms fell prey to international financial turmoil at the time it most needed external finance and unexpectedly suffered a deep recession in 1998 and 1999.

By contrast, industrial countries, and especially the G7, face a different problem. They view with concern the increasing volume of official financial rescue packages that have been dished out in recent years starting with Mexico in 1995, which as of late 2000 totalled almost $200 billion. Fearing that the current strategy to deal with financial turmoil in emerging economies might involve a self-fulfilling explosion of their quasi-fiscal liabilities, both bilateral and to the international financial institutions, industrial country governments have reacted with an agenda to scale back the magnitude of official support and force private lenders to share the burden. In turn, the private transnational financial sector claims that the burden-sharing push can easily lead to the arbitrary disregard of contracts and demands clear and fair rules of the game to engage in development financing in the future. There is consensus that the international financial architecture needs reform, but there is little clarity and agreement as to how to fix it, or even what to fix.

What's wrong with world financial markets? Diagnoses abound. An overview suggests that views can be classified into three groups. First, some see the main problem as one of excessive capital flows to emerging markets, beyond what these economies can productively use. A second diagnosis paints the main problem as just the opposite: world financial markets fail because they fall short of delivering enough financing for productive projects. And finally, a third group sees the volatility and unpredictability of terms and availability of development financing as the main drawback of current financial markets.

There is no shortage of proposed solutions. Numerous reports have been, are being, and will be produced by multilateral organizations, think tanks, academics, and task forces. But the connection between proposed solutions and the problems that need to be resolved is not clear. If the new architectural design does not address the key structural problems and lay new foundations, it will be no more than interior decoration.

All views on problems are complementary and own a portion of the truth. Initiatives to reform the international financial architecture will likely impact differently on the various distortions in international financial markets. From a policy point of view, it is key to pose the issue of reforming the international financial architecture as a second-best proposition, one in which reforms will have to endure the existence of unavoidable distortions. In the context of multiple distortions, the reduction of one of the distortions is not necessarily welfare improving. For example, the objective of eliminating excessive and volatile capital flows could be achieved by impeding the international financial integration of emerging markets, in an extreme case by closing these markets altogether, but at a potentially enormous cost in terms of economic growth. How do we sort through the trade-offs in this multifaceted issue?

Problems and solutions involve three main players: emerging countries, industrial countries (the official sector), and foreign investors with interests in emerging economies (the private sector). Unfortunately, the costs and benefits of addressing the problems of international financial architecture are very unevenly distributed among the players. This unequal distribution may underlie the wide range of diagnoses and initiatives, and help explain the alignments in the debate around the redesign of the international financial architecture. The need for positive net benefits for all players to ensure their voluntary participation in any change of the status quo severely restricts the set of feasible reform proposals and may leave out the most efficient new arrangements. In fact, our own set of proposals (see Fernández-Arias and Hausmann 2000a), which we derive from efficiency principles, are likely to be more costly to industrial countries than the proposals encouraging official disengagement that are the core of the new doctrine currently being advanced by the official sector.

This article discusses this political economy side of redesigning the international financial architecture. It draws heavily from our previous work (Fernández-

Arias and Hausmann 2000a, 2000b). The next section reviews the problems of international financial markets. We subsequently assess their importance in light of the evidence and discuss for whom they are crucial. The last section reviews the solutions that are being proposed and discusses the distribution of their costs and benefits. Concluding remarks follow.

PROBLEMS OF INTERNATIONAL FINANCIAL MARKETS

The problems in international financial markets faced by emerging markets can be grouped under the headings of "Too Much," "Too Little," and "Too Volatile," depending upon which characteristic of capital flows to emerging markets is emphasized.

Theories of Too Much

Theories of Too Much usually assume that moral hazard encourages excessive lending.[1] Resources are also misallocated because they are apportioned to risky projects without internalizing the costs involved.[2] Somebody is providing an implicit guarantee so that the parties to the transaction are not internalizing all the risks. Too much lending and too much risk taking occur. Eventually, the guarantee is called and a crisis emerges. The various scenarios differ in the source of the implicit guarantee.

The most traditional scenario involves government guarantees of the banking system. The same logic will apply to a corporation perceived as being "too big to fail," but banks remain the prime example because they play a critical role in the payments system. Governments cannot afford to let banks simply go broke, because that would trigger a catastrophic sequence of defaults in which otherwise solvent, efficient firms go bust when their clients are unable to make payments from deposits frozen in problematic banking institutions. Counting on the protection provided by an inevitable government bailout, bankers may assume too much risk. A variation of the theory of moral hazard views pegged exchange rates as an implicit guarantee (Mishkin 1996; Obstfeld 1998; Buiter and Sibert 1999). This form of moral hazard would reduce incentives for hedging exposure to exchange rate risk and would favor short-term foreign debt, which falls due in the period in which the guarantee would be more credible.

Another Theory of Too Much follows similar lines but blames the International Monetary Fund (IMF), bilateral creditors, and multilateral development banks for providing rescue packages that shield either foreign investors or governments from the fallout of excessive risk taking. This kind of moral hazard is thought to lead to excessive lending by foreign investors who expect to be repaid from resources provided through future rescue packages if real returns on investment do not materialize. Even if it is true that official rescue packages are quickly repaid, as it is the experience so far, and do not provide a subsidy directly responsible for creating moral hazard, they would still make it possible for the government to extend a moral hazard inducing bailout (an "enabler" of moral hazard, in DeLong 1999 terms). This theory has received much currency, especially among economists (see Sachs 1998a; Burnside, Eichenbaum, and Rebelo 1999).

Theories of Too Little

For all the impressive growth in capital flows to emerging markets, they are surprisingly low relative to what one would expect given the dominant trade theories and the way open economies are usually modeled. In fact, current capital flows are low compared to those observed prior to World War I and, more recently, to those in some particularly telling countries. In this section, we review explanations of this anomaly based on commitment problems at the international level.

It is useful to start by focusing on problems of willingness to pay when the enforcement of financial contacts is limited. Loans are not self-enforcing contracts. After receiving a loan, only coercion or the promise of future loans makes debtors want to fulfill their obligations. In order to compensate for the risk, higher charges are made. But higher interest rates further increase repayment problems by eroding the borrower's ability and willingness to repay in full and by worsening risk through adverse selection in the pool of borrowers and moral hazard in the choice of projects (see Stiglitz and Weiss 1981).

In order to address willingness-to-pay problems, loans are often secured by collateral, and courts adjudicate problems that arise during the life of the contract. When nonpayment occurs or is possible, bankruptcy procedures are set in motion. These allow ability-to-pay problems to be separated from willingness-to-pay problems. They also provide a mechanism to secure the cooperation of the different creditors, to remove management if creditors find it necessary, and to transfer the ownership of assets to creditors.[3] Absence of an adequate bankruptcy law and court system can have deleterious effects on the financial system. It makes coercion less credible, worsening the willingness-to-pay problem. It also increases the cost of crises because it precludes concerted action to provide additional financing needed for the company's survival.

In cross-border finance, the willingness-to-pay problem is severely aggravated by the involvement of a sovereign government. Since sovereigns do not need to abide by the rulings of any foreign court, the problem may be serious and difficult to resolve. Sovereign risk may explain why cross-border lending is so small. In the standard model (Bulow and Rogoff 1989) sovereigns will pay so long as it is not in their interest not to do so, given the "punishment" they may receive for nonpayment. However, the incentive not to pay goes up with the volume of debt owed. This theory, originally developed for public debt, can be extended to apply to private sector borrowing under the "protection" of the sovereign, which may suspend convertibility, nationalize assets, or otherwise interfere in the payment process if such action is perceived as increasing national welfare (Fernández-Arias and Lombardo 1998a, 1998b). As a result, sovereign risk augments overall risk beyond the traditional commercial risk, and therefore, in the absence of financial enhancements, represents a floor for private risk. Sovereign risk will cause markets to impose a credit ceiling on countries so as to keep the volume of aggregate debt below the level that would create incentives for nonrepayment. The lighter the punishment the world can impose on the country, the lower the credit ceiling will be. Economies that are more integrated into the world are more easily punished, and hence should get a higher credit ceiling.

Another aspect of sovereign risk concerns the so-called "original sin" affecting almost all emerging market currencies (Eichengreen and Hausmann 1999): they cannot be used to borrow abroad and cannot be used even domestically to borrow long term. Original sin may be caused in part by sovereign risk. If a capital importing country could borrow in its own currency it would be able to improve its net worth by letting the currency depreciate. This fundamental incompleteness of the financial market has important implications for financial fragility: it causes investments to be financed either in dollars or short term. If the funding is done in dollars, many projects, and the country as a whole, will have a currency mismatch, as cash flows would be denominated in a different currency from that of the debt. If companies try to avoid this problem by borrowing in pesos, they will have a maturity mismatch as only short-term loans are available in the domestic market. Hence, maturity and currency mismatches are endemic in countries with original sin.

Notice that sovereign risk is a commitment problem. If the sovereign could somehow tie its hands and mandate future payments with no tricks irrespective of future conditions (including a change in ruling faction), the problem would disappear. Lending would be more ample and stable. Yet even when the sovereign might well be better off making such a commitment, the binding technology to make the pledge credible once indebtedness is high may be difficult to find. As a result, thus far, private markets have tried to insulate themselves from sovereign risk with relatively rigid contracts lacking clauses that could be exploited to justify nonpayment in legalistic ways. Yet a scheme like this tailored to a pure willingness-to-pay problem may make crises triggered by a reduction in ability-to-pay more difficult to manage and more costly. It usually makes debt workouts quite messy.

Theories of Too Volatile

Recent financial turmoil and unpredicted crises, frequently described as market panics, herd behavior, and financial contagion, have reinforced the idea that this is a new phenomenon in international financial markets. In what follows we discuss liquidity crises and financial contagion, the two main factors underlying recent market volatility and unpredictability.

The traditional example of liquidity crises is a bank run. Banks typically have a term mismatch: they receive short-term deposits, even sight deposits, and lend them at longer maturities. Assume all borrowers are doing just fine. If there is no attack, the bank will do just great. But if suddenly depositors all want their money at the same time, the bank will go bust. In fact, in the bank's attempts to collect loans too quickly, even solvent borrowers may get into trouble due to the credit crunch. Hence, expectations may be self-fulfilling: both optimism and pessimism can be justified ex post.

More generally, capital account imbalances, especially in the presence of high levels of debt, raise the specter of bank-run-like payments crises if market financing dries up, whether or not an actual banking crisis develops. This market reaction may be based on a loss of confidence in a particular country or simply reflect global financial contagion. In fact, a temporary disruption in financial flows, due for example to a prolonged bout of contagion, may cause enough real damage to generate a full-blown crisis. Thus, countries may experience to situations in which the rollover of public debt is subject to multiple equilibria where, in the bad outcome, creditors will refuse to refinance debts, provoking a grave short-term liquidity problem. The ensuing credit crunch can cause a serious contraction, high real interest rates, and payments problems in the corporate sector, thereby deteriorating the health of the financial system and justifying the attack. Furthermore, the pressure on the exchange rate caused by the capital account shock may lead to depreciation, further contributing to the deterioration of the economic segments with net foreign currency exposure. In fact, currency devaluation alone may generate multiple equilibriums and a liquidity-like crisis (Chang and Velasco 1998; Krugman 1999). This occurs even in economies in good fiscal health, irrespective of the exchange rate regime and whether or not the currency was previously overvalued.

Aside from full-blown liquidity crises in specific instances, recent widespread financial turmoil has meant enormous volatility in terms and volumes of financing, and unreliable access to external financing, for most emerging markets. The explanation is the so-called "financial contagion." The main intercountry linkages underlying the high degree of correlation among international financial prices in emerging markets do not appear related to world market conditions, trade relations among them, or other traditional transmission mechanisms.

Instead, the linkage is that they share a common set of investment institutions making joint investment decisions (Fernández-Arias and Rigobón 1998). The most notable example is the collapse of bond prices in Latin America following the Russian default of August 1998; Russia is a country with whom the region has very few economic ties of any kind.

One important explanation to account for the evidence is that investment institutions were hit by big losses in crisis countries, for example Russia, and became capital deficient to back their obligations (fulfill margin calls) and not creditworthy themselves, which forced them to shrink their portfolio and reduce risk bearing. The result was the kind of portfolio reallocation observed in practice. Because of the illiquidity of this market, perhaps because nonspecialized buyers are less informed than specialized sellers (see Calvo 1998), this reallocation requires fire sale prices. The strong contagion in our region would be due to the fact that most of our investors are within a narrow field of institutions specializing in non-investment-grade paper. In this sense, financial regulations in industrial countries prohibit very large institutional investors from holding non-investment-grade assets, and may therefore have caused the inefficient segmenting of the market and drastically reduced its liquidity.

A key implication is that bond spreads under contagion do not reflect country risk. Prices are misaligned but arbitrage opportunities are not exploited because the specialized, informed investors are capital constrained. Over time, the pricing gap would be arbitraged as the constraints over our specialized investors ease and new financial intermediaries are established. Therefore, lack of liquidity resulting from contagion would be temporary, a prediction that also meshes well with the evidence. To a large extent, financial contagion is akin to a liquidity crisis in slow motion, whose ultimate outcome depends on whether the speed of recovery is enough to pull out the economy. It is clear that the possibility of financial contagion makes financial integration unreliable.

ASSESSING THE PROBLEMS

Different types of problems affect different players in different ways. For example, problems associated with Theories of Too Much hurt both emerging countries, which end up in crisis, and industrial countries, which may be required to come to the rescue. Industrial countries may have to provide financial help either bilaterally or through multilateral organizations such as the IMF. Other problems of international financial markets, however, have a lower potential for generating full-blown crises that may directly hurt industrial countries. Problems associated with Theories of Too Little are for the most part suffered exclusively by emerging countries, which cannot enjoy the wealth they could appropriate if they had access to more financing. Similarly, the problems associated with the excessive volatility of flows, unless in extreme cases ending up in crisis, are also suffered mainly by emerging countries.

The assessment of the problems in international financial markets, that is, the analysis of their relative relevance, is therefore important to draw an accurate map of how the status quo is differentially appreciated by emerging and industrial countries and the possibly contradictory implications that changes to the status quo may have. In principle, these asymmetries should not produce any disagreement about the objective assessment of the problems, but only in policy preferences. In practice, however, different subjective perspectives lead to different assessments of objective reality. In this case, discrepancies in the diagnosis of what is wrong in international financial markets can be interpreted as a reflection of discrepancies in interest. We now turn to the analysis of these discrepancies.

Confronting the Historical Evidence

It is well known that capital flows to developing countries are smaller than desirable under any reasonable standard. Taking into account the existing differences in capital/labor ratios, international flows across nations are way too small relative to flows within nations (Bayoumi and Rose 1993; Bayoumi 1997), which underlies the strong correlation between domestic savings and investment first uncovered by Feldstein and Horioka (1980). This evidence implies that Theories of Too Much do not address some of the most important distortions present in the world. Hence, policy recommendations predicated on them, without reference to their impact on other important distortions, cannot be presumed to improve efficiency. At the same time, this evidence supports the Theories of Too Little and, indirectly, the Theories of Too Volatile.

The magnitude of capital flows under the prewar classical gold standard clearly shows that international flows can be much larger than today. As De Long (1999) points out, the historical record of large flows in the gold standard period can also be interpreted as direct evidence against the moral hazard view. First, in that period there was no IMF or functional equivalent to create international moral hazard in developing countries, and yet flows were larger. And second, financial crises then were even more frequent and deep; the IMF is certainly not a requisite for crises!

Theories of Too Much imply that capital flows should be skewed in favor of the type of flows most likely to be covered by guarantees, as Eichengreen and Hausmann (1999) point out. Borrowing by banks and government borrowings would appear at the top of the list. Also, the moral hazard involved in currency risk would suggest that these flows would be skewed toward the short term. But the evidence from international banks that report to the Bank for International

Settlements (BIS) is that their cross-border lending to developing countries shows no evidence of these distortions relative to developed countries. Moreover, portfolio flows, rather than lending by international commercial banks, have been the key players in the 1990s. The massive losses stock-and bondholders have been subject to and the enormous political costs paid by governments in crisis countries make it hard to imagine that moral hazard alone could create such widespread financial havoc.

This is strong evidence that moral hazard is not the dominant distortion in international finance to developing countries. The same holds true in the context of impediments to economic development. Even if moral hazard is a piece of the explanation of the East Asian crises, the fact that these countries have the most successful sustained growth record in known history is countervailing evidence that should make us pause. Radical institutional reform of a financial system recently regarded as a development model in the name of moral hazard appears premature given the current state of knowledge (see Feldstein 1998). Concerning Latin America, our region has made very significant progress in improving banking supervision and regulation, especially since the Tequila crisis in 1995. However, financial turmoil has been at a peak and access to world capital markets has been closed for long stretches.

What Went Wrong in Recent Experiences?

To unearth the causes of financial turmoil, it is important to review the salient features of recent crises. Starting with the Mexican crisis of 1994 to 1995, financial turmoil in emerging countries has surprised analysts. A graphic way to view this is presented in Calvo and Fernández-Arias (1998). There, the six crisis countries of 1997 to 1998 (Indonesia, Korea, Malaysia, the Philippines, Russia, and Thailand) are compared with the six largest countries in our region (Argentina, Brazil, Colombia, Mexico, Peru, and Venezuela). If we classify these countries into low and high risk according to market risk spreads and ratings in mid-1997, right before the crises, we find that, except for Russia, crises occurred in the low-risk countries.

We believe that this lack of predictability of crises is largely rooted in problems of multiple equilibria, rather than in a misunderstanding of the workings of economies. This means that the existence of a potentially "bad" equilibrium may trigger a self-fulfilling financial panic, in which the collapse validates the state of panic that causes it. These problems resemble bank runs and are associated with liquidity problems. In some of the recent crises, fundamentals were consistent with the required capacity to service the debt load, but a sudden lack of liquidity severely damaged the economy, leading to an unexpected change in sentiment. The unnecessary nature of the run that provoked the liquidity crunch can account for the failure of the market to anticipate the crisis.

Most surprising of all—and this is very important—the strong financial contagion associated with these crises infected countries enjoying strong fundamentals that had essentially no economic linkages with crisis countries. This was most notable in Latin America during the Russian crisis. Most emerging markets in the world have lost much of their access to external financing, even though their economies do not present any great inherent weaknesses. Recent experience with financial contagion points to the importance of addressing distortions in the international financial system that lie beyond policy reform in emerging countries.

Finally, we should also keep in mind the severe limitations of policy instruments in stopping a crisis once it has started, which puts a premium on prevention strategies. Once a crisis breaks out, experience shows that it quickly develops into a meltdown with enormous output losses, even if rescue packages are quickly dished out (see Calvo and Fernández-Arias, 1998).

What Is Wrong?

The previous analysis suggests that serious distortions are present in international financial markets. They are behind the fact that flows are on average small, relative to the difference in capital-labor ratios and demographic trends in the world. Distortions are also behind the unusually high volatility and comovement of capital flows. However, the dominant view in industrial countries, as expressed among others in the Report of the Council on Foreign Relations and the G7 Cologne communiqué (see the chapters by Bergsten and Porter and Wood) is centered around concerns of moral hazard, that is, the problems that might cost some industrial country taxpayers money (see also the chapter by Armijo). While much of the policy debate has assumed that the dominant distortion is moral hazard, the preponderance of the evidence suggests that other distortions are more binding.

PROPOSED SOLUTIONS: WINNERS AND LOSERS

In this section we attempt to identify the winners and losers of various proposals for the redesign of the international financial architecture. To do that requires us to a) establish which are the problems of international financial markets that the proposals will solve or aggravate; and b) assess the corresponding implications for each player according to its specific perspective. If all perspectives were compatible, all parties would be either winners or losers and ranking proposals would be a purely technical, objective matter. If not, as we suspect, then the evaluation of proposals depends on the perspective, and there may be winners and losers preventing consensus. In that case, agreement from losers would require a compensation mechanism, which may be difficult to find.

It is probably not feasible to change the status quo in a way that entirely satisfies all parties involved; if it were, solutions to the problems of the international financial architecture, which have been debated for some time now, would have been agreed upon already. Lack of consensus on some key issues probably arises because it is not feasible to make progress uniformly on all fronts of the problem. Rather, as in any interesting issue in economics, proposed solutions involve trading off different problems in international financial markets, which as analyzed in the previous section may produce winners and losers among blocks of countries. Emerging and industrial countries have sharply different perspectives on this matter.

Concerning private creditors, how are problems in international financial markets experienced by the private sector? In a first approximation, the private sector is not affected by problems in international financial markets because the market risk premium would incorporate whatever risks there are of not recovering investments. Ex-post private gains may be positive or negative, and the private sector naturally has a vested interest in actions that maximize recovery after a crisis event. But unless the private sector is systematically misled, which is an assumption difficult to justify either theoretically or empirically, problems should have no ex-ante or long-run consequences for private net returns. This argument also holds for "positive" risks such as public guarantees inducing moral hazard, whose beneficial impact on private returns would also be offset by the corresponding reduction of the competitive risk premium.

It is helpful to think of emerging countries as residual claimants, directly benefiting or suffering from the consequences that international financial markets have on their real economies. Under this interpretation, emerging countries with productive investment opportunities benefit from having access to foreign finance and suffer from access restrictions, and their attendant inefficiencies of underinvestment or crises. These inefficiencies directly accrue to emerging countries.[4] From the perspective of emerging countries, the evaluation of changes to the status quo needs to balance their impact on the level of financial integration and investment outside crisis episodes with their impact on the crisis scenario, that is, the trade-off between the two sources of inefficiency.

In principle, the perspective of industrial countries could be expected to coincide with that reflecting the direct interest of emerging countries for reasons of altruism, and perhaps self-interest. However, the likelihood of transfers from industrial countries in the form of crisis aid, especially if specific programs are designed to this effect, would tilt the balance in favor of reducing the risk and depth of crisis. In other words, industrial countries can be expected to accept a lower level of productive financial integration as the price to pay for any given crisis tolerance. This gap in perspectives holds irrespective of whether industrial country crisis aid causes moral hazard or not. Even if all parties shared the view that moral hazard is highly relevant, the extent to which it is adequate to control moral hazard would be subject to the perspective gap. In the remainder of the section we will explore the implications of this gap for the subjective assessment of proposals to redesign the international financial architecture.

So far we have neglected the perspective of the private sector. As explained above, with competitive risk premiums, private investment and repayment can be viewed as a zero-sum game in expected terms, since any guarantees will have been reflected in the cost of credit. The incentives to private lenders and borrowers can therefore be neglected in a simple model.[5] In practice, private sector agents may be subject to agency distortions, large sunk costs in emerging countries, or other distortions that make them prefer proposed solutions leading to bigger and more stable markets. Interestingly, these "second order" effects could tend to align the private sector with emerging countries more than with industrial countries, a prediction that is at odds with the more usual assumption of a close alliance between private multinational lenders and their home country governments. In this piece we choose not to explore this ramification and neglect the private sector perspective.

Current Proposals under Consideration

We are concerned with the possibility that current proposals under consideration may have a negative developmental impact, because nearly all of them entail smaller capital flows to support development in emerging markets. This outcome comes as a result of fighting moral hazard or as an expedient to reduce financial instability. In what follows we show that this is the case in both initiatives under review and those under actual experimentation.

In our view, the single most important problem with the way the debate on reforming international financial architecture is being conducted is its partial, even unilateral, approach to the problems to be solved. We must remember that reducing any single identified distortion (such as moral hazard) is not necessarily good policy and that successfully alleviating a specific undesirable symptom (such as financial volatility) is not necessarily the manifestation of a welfare improvement. In the context of multiple distortions, policies need to be evaluated in a second-best framework, taking into account their interaction with remaining distortions. For example, the objective of reducing the moral hazard induced by implicit official guarantees to international private capital flows would be served by curtailing official financial support to countries in distress. However, such financial support would be extremely beneficial in the event of a liquidity crisis and financial contagion. The overemphasis on moral hazard would lead to counterproductive policies if the latter distortions are preponderant. Similarly, reducing the incidence of crises by impeding capital flows may be a counterproductive policy once the deleterious growth effects of lower capital integration are factored in.

There is a good chance that most of our reservations with the initiatives currently being advanced in international fora owe to our Latin American perspective. Our assessment is based on the efficiency losses that will occur if external capital does not flow to high return investment opportunities in Latin America. It is clear, however, that an efficient international financial architecture entails financial support from developed countries when things go wrong, which will happen from time to time. From the alternative perspective of developed country taxpayers, it may make sense to prefer reforms that limit financial risks even at the cost of efficiency. The current bias in favor of reforms that limit capital flows may be better interpreted in this way rather than on efficiency grounds.

In what follows we concentrate on a number of core initiatives under active consideration that characterize the main angles of the debate. We omit other initiatives, not because they are without use or importance but because they are either uncontroversial or propose changes that are more decorative than foundational, that is, they take too many walls and windows for granted. For example, we do not discuss standards on transparency, because we see them as uncontroversial but also of limited impact.

We group the initiatives examined in this paper into three sets and review them in turn. The first two sets of initiatives involve the provision of financial support triggered after an emergency arises. First, we consider initiatives concerning the unilateral provision of financial support by the official sector. Second, we consider initiatives in which the private sector is also given a role in providing financial support. Finally, the third set of initiatives refers to reforms to the institutional framework within which international capital flows to emerging markets take place. They encompass standards and regulations applicable to financial systems, both national and international, as well as monetary and currency arrangements in emerging markets.

Official Financial Support

The main idea behind initiatives concerning official financial support relates to its function of lending of last resort at the international level. The basic argument for international versions of a lender of last resort is the same argument used in a domestic context: by promising in advance to provide financial support in case of unexpected need in which fundamentals are right or will be right, (liquidity) crises are prevented. In fact, financial panic rationalized by the damage in fundamentals that a massive financial withdrawal (a "run") would generate cannot exist when there is a commitment of ample support that would avoid such damage. (Alternatively, in the case of insolvency, a lender of last resort could also intervene to facilitate the debt workout of reorganized entities at minimum cost.)

However, current official initiatives attempt to scale back the level of official intervention relative to the volumes involved in rescue packages in recent years. Not only are volumes expected to be much lower, but in the new doctrine the conditions under which such support would be forthcoming will be more discretionary and less transparent, making use of the so-called case-by-case approach and "constructive ambiguity." Furthermore, the extent of official support would be linked to the comparable treatment of private creditors, further limiting the scope of official support. The reason given for this official retrenchment is that large, unconditional, and unilateral support finances the bailout of private creditors, which promotes substantial moral hazard leading to overborrowing and crisis. As we will see, whether this is a good reason for retrenchment depends on the prevalence of liquidity or solvency crises. In the case of liquidity crises, lending of last resort prevents crises at no cost, and is therefore beneficial all around. Successful lending of last resort reduces private default risk, but this is not a source of moral hazard. This is a legitimate reduction in risk obtained from removing an inefficient risk factor, that is, the panic equilibrium. This does not open a gap between social and private risks. In fact, lower expected risks will give rise to more capital flows that will be applied efficiently. Liquidity crises call for large, unconditional, and unilateral official financial support. The drawbacks of generous official financial support are associated with insolvency cases. In these cases unilateral official support is costly and relatively ineffective in terms of helping the real economy, because official financial support "leaks" to private creditors. It is precisely the anticipation of this leakage that leads to moral hazard.

In our view, the balance of crisis cases justifies a rather automatic lending of last resort facility for eligible countries. First, our diagnosis indicates that in this era liquidity crises are prevalent and, therefore, the risk of wrong application of the lending facility and moral hazard would be correspondingly small. Therefore expected benefits would prevail. Second, there are ways to discriminate between liquidity and solvency crises in order to reduce the risk of wrong application. The better the fundamentals before the crisis, the more likely it is that the crisis is of liquidity. Eligibility preconditions to qualify for membership to the facility based on sound economic fundamentals would play the role of screening out cases of insolvency. (In fact, the incentive to attain the required standards would induce "moral safety," the opposite of moral hazard.)

An important case in which the above principles are fully applicable is international financial contagion. This case is similar to the case of liquidity crises in key dimensions. First, recent experience shows that, like liquidity crises, international financial contagion appears to be prevalent in this new era of international finance, and is in fact another distortion underlying the Theories of Too Volatile. Second, from the point of view of the country, the basic problem is not weak fundamentals but lack of financing, that is, distorted risk spreads and lack of access to market. And third, it can be treated with a purely financial solution: the provision of financing is efficient and prevents the crisis. In the case of contagion it works not because it removes the panic equilibrium but because it relaxes a temporary constraint distorting the normal equilibrium.

The above parallels justify a facility similar to a lender of last resort but geared towards enabling countries that are victims of international financial contagion to counteract the cumulative effect of the credit crunch and prevent a full-blown crisis.[6] Once again, the risk is of financing a country with weak fundamentals that will fall into crisis even after contagion ceases. However, the scope for accurately discriminating which countries should be supported is large. First, the widespread nature of contagion makes it quite apparent when countries are victims of this phenomenon; nonsystemic effects should not be attributed to contagion. Second, even when distorted by contagion, relative market indicators across countries, for example, spreads, continue to reflect relative fundamentals and are reliable pieces of information (see Fernández-Arias and Rigobón 1998). An official contagion facility should stand ready to support countries meeting the eligibility conditions.

Our diagnosis of the relative lack of importance of moral hazard in causing recent crises, which is probably the majority view in the profession, can of course be challenged on technical grounds. The scope for implementing a set of eligibility preconditions to weed out most insolvency cases from benefiting from the facility is also debatable. However, there is a good likelihood that the official retrenchment being proposed is not mainly driven by technical discrepancies on these issues but by the asymmetric implications that such a facility has for crisis countries and industrial countries. Despite all of the efficiency gains that, in our view, such a facility would attain, clearly it will sometimes be a costly failure. The problem is that the gains obtained in most cases accrue to crisis countries but the losses when there is failure are paid for by taxpayers in industrial countries. This asymmetry can explain the announced official retrenchment. The same asymmetry can explain the timidity of the attempts to implement official mechanisms to prevent future crises, despite the fact that one of the main lessons from recent experiences of crisis resolution is that an ounce of prevention is worth a pound of cure.

The Contingent Credit Line (CCL) facility approved by the IMF in early 1999 is the main innovation in the provision of official support. In this facility, countries pursuing sound policy that also meet a number of financial and reporting standards would enjoy financial support in the form of a credit line that can be drawn on if they fall victim to panic or contagion. The CCL can be seen as a variant or substitute for a lender of last resort for countries in which good collateral (which is difficult for a sovereign to produce) is replaced by the requirement of a healthy economy. Unfortunately, a hesitant, and perhaps reluctant, approach to the problem has rendered ineffective this well-inspired idea (see Fernández-Arias, Gavin, and Hausmann 1998 for an early CCL proposal). At the time of writing, the CCL facility currently includes too many obstacles to make it attractive to benefiting countries.

Key problems with the IMF version of the CCL facility, from the point of view of a country, are that the committed support may be too small and is not certain, and its delivery may take time, any of which may render the mechanism ineffective against panic. The reason is that, as it stands, delivery is mostly not automatic at the country's choice but requires final approval depending on the Fund's assessment of the situation. A better design would be to set country eligibility criteria on the basis of preconditions and then allow automatic withdrawal. Uncertainty about effective protection defeats prevention, and makes this facility somewhat similar to the traditional rescue package strategy. Once again, additional assurances about the financial safety of official support conspire against effectiveness in preventing crises.

Another problem with the CCL facility is that no individual country wants to be the first to apply and somehow signal the need for special protection. It is important to implement this facility in a way that eligible countries are regarded as the strongest and most prudent of the pack, rather than those seeking potential help for some dubious reason unknown to the market. Whether expectations are positive or negative depends to a large extent on the rules of the eligibility game. For example, if countries need to apply individually and run the risk of not being accepted expeditiously, interest will tend to be low. If, on the contrary, the IMF produced a list of eligible countries and allowed them to join as a bloc (that is, automatically extending the facility privilege as a matter of course), chances are that belonging to the club would be regarded as a prize.

The analysis will not be complete if we do not consider the case of solvency crises. Contrary to a liquidity crisis, in this case the solution does not involve only the provision of finance. Instead, reforms to strengthen fundamentals, including conditionality, are essential. In the absence of these changes, additional financial support would not reestablish confidence and would postpone needed reforms, deepening the inevitable crisis and diluting the market discipline that would otherwise be exerted when fundamentals turn riskier. For countries with solvency problems, it is clear that a lender of last resort is not the best answer and a different approach to official support ought to be applied.[7] Furthermore, it is important to consider the involvement of the private sector in order to arrive at an efficient plan of financial support, because otherwise official support may end up being a bailout of private creditors with little benefit to the country.

Private Sector Involvement

The new doctrine on private sector involvement (PSI) appears to feature nonvoluntary, forced involvement. Forced participation is needed in extreme cases in which domestic adjustment and official international support are deemed insufficient to reestablish confidence. In that case, if confidence is not reestablished then the official money will be quite unproductive since the private sector would exploit the opportunity to bail out of the country. But it is important to keep in mind that forced PSI is likely to be very costly in terms of future access to private capital unless it follows clearly agreed upon rules of the game set beforehand. Therefore, forced PSI in general, and official discretion in particular, ought to be minimized.

It is important to notice that the number of cases that would qualify for PSI is not independent of the supply of official funding. Forced PSI may be required if official support is small, but such a situation ought to be avoided if sufficient official support can do the trick of reestablishing confidence. Unnecessarily forcing PSI to reduce official exposure, especially if it is discretionary and opportunistic, is likely to be counterproductive from a development viewpoint. Another implication of the previous principles is that PSI should not be used as a way to teach a lesson to the private sector with the purpose of reducing moral hazard, because such a strategy is likely to have very large social costs. In general, the traditional approach of domestic adjustment and official support with the private sector coming back on its own is superior and should not be limited by a stingier approach to official international involvement.

As explained above, the gap in the perspectives of industrial and emerging countries leads to excessive official preoccupation with moral hazard and excessive caution in putting official funds at risk. In this context, both biases imply excessive reliance on forced PSI. Our concern is that this approach to the coordination of official and private involvement may lead to eroding private capital markets for development. In deep crisis, the country is unable to sustain its current debt level and, hence, additional official money per se is unlikely to reestablish confidence. Here, debt reduction may need to form part of the solution. Mechanisms to address these cases are now under experimentation. These include renegotiation with private bondholders as a prior condition for Paris Club rescheduling (for example, the "comparable treatment" requirement in Pakistan) or IMF support (for example, default of Brady bonds in Ecuador). However, the experience in Ecuador clearly signals the dangers of a new doctrine of official retrenchment and forced PSI.

First, the official international sector should not lose sight of its fundamental coordinating role during crises. To request private sector involvement as a prior action before the official sector commits itself puts the cart before the horse. It demands that the private sector participate in a still nonexistent program, thus reducing the informational content of the situation. Secondly, the delay involved in waiting for a private sector response may involve a dramatic deterioration of domestic economic conditions as economic activity collapses, aggravating fiscal and financial imbalances and further undermining confidence. Finally, the whole notion of comparative treatment may be the wrong paradigm. After all, during the last "orderly workout" that Latin America went through, that is, the Brady plan, the roles of public and private sector were quite different, with the former putting in additional resources to generate the enhancements that allowed for debt reduction of the latter.

If forced burden sharing becomes part of the implicit contract, it will have a negative effect on the cost of capital and market stability. A case-by-case, secretive approach with weak coordination makes the worst of this approach to PSI. Furthermore, if forced PSI is used for anything other than extreme cases, it runs the risk of becoming a major destabilizing factor. In fact, up to now, if an economy got into trouble, the willingness of the government to call for an IMF agreement was seen as a way to signal its disposition to adjust and thus was a means to reestablish confidence. Under forced PSI, the private sector would interpret such an announcement as a reason to try to get out of the country before a stay or a debt reduction is forced upon them, making governments less willing to call on the IMF for assistance in a timely fashion.

By contrast, we favor the alternative, in which official support is ample and PSI is demanded only when necessary, and then in a way in which the burden is shared according to clear rules not subject to abuse. This mechanism would define a standard of excusable default that would ensure flexibility when needed. An international bankruptcy court, for example, would fit this characterization. In that case, under insolvency conditions PSI would kick in according to international law, coordinated and supplemented by official support.[8] The efficiency of this workout mechanism is likely to lead to lower, rather than higher, ex-ante financial costs and be highly beneficial from an emerging country perspective. At the same time, it will likely be more costly in terms of official financial risk exposure, and therefore less attractive from an industrial country financial perspective.

An international bankruptcy court could be modeled after the corresponding domestic institution. This court would authorize domestic borrowers not to repay when the country is deemed unable, rather than simply unwilling, to pay. This determination would stop legal action against borrowers, thus creating a real difference with respect to an equivalent unilateral sovereign action. By transferring the power to authorize nonpayment to an independent court that does not have a willingness-to-pay problem, this arrangement provides more flexibility while keeping sovereign risk under control. Obviously the sovereign could still decide to violate the decisions of the international court, but in doing so it would forgo the protection against suit provided by the court. More importantly, it would allow those willing but possibly unable to repay to precommit to a more credible arrangement. Since an independent body will have declared the default to be excusable on the merits rather than a unilateral decision by a sovereign, trustworthiness in future dealings would be enhanced.

Finally, there is also scope for voluntary PSI leading to substantial efficiency gains if the official sector is willing to take more risks. For example, PSI in an official international financial contagion facility would also be quite useful in arriving at the kind of sums needed to effectively support countries. It is clear that financial enhancements are needed for the private sector to be willing to lend to countries during the period of contagion. The idea is therefore to provide official enhancements sufficient to spark private interest to resume lending in such a way that leverage is maximized. For example, official enhancements may take the form of partial guarantees of private credits, in such a way that the risk mix becomes acceptable for private lending.

It is worth noting that the use of official enhancements to spark private lending is a way of relaxing the sovereign risk constraint that private creditors face. In fact, official multilateral lenders face a much lower sovereign risk and may be able to leverage their lending by transferring that lower risk to private parties. The reason for their risk advantage is that their policy requires them to suspend operations in countries that run into arrears. Since they are a cheap source of future credit and are committed to stopping lending in case of arrears, sovereigns repay, giving these multilateral institutions their preferred creditor status. In a world where such binding devices are scarce, questions have been raised about whether these institutions are making adequate use of their commitment technology. In the context of countries lacking access to private financial markets, there is no question that the official sector can be very effective in alleviating this distortion. But once again, efficiency gains come at the cost of additional official exposure to financial losses.

Financial Standards and Regulations

Recent crises have uncovered widespread weaknesses in financial systems and have prompted the elaboration of financial standards and regulations to strengthen them. Interestingly, the emphasis on the kind of fixing that needs to be done directly depends on which class of distortions is deemed more substantial. Those who think that moral hazard is the main problem emphasize the strengthening of the solvency of financial institutions to make sure that they do not play with other people's money. The main initiative in this field has to do with capital adequacy requirements for banks in the domestic system and strong supervision to ensure that they are enforced. Basle risk weights for bank lending are also being reformed along the same lines, ensuring that lending to higher risk countries faces a higher regulatory cost.

This agenda has moved forward very quickly in Latin America, especially since the 1995 Tequila crisis, and is behind the resilience of the banking systems in the region and their demonstrated ability to withstand the consequences of the recent financial turmoil and the deep 1998-1999 recession. In fact, most Latin American countries now have capital adequacy requirements that are above the Basle standards, and supervisory systems have been thoroughly reformed. While this has made banks stronger, it has not translated into more stable flows of international capital. Hence, while these policies are quite uncontroversial in the region, it is unclear that they do much to limit international financial turmoil.

Other initiatives are designed to limit financial volatility. One class of initiatives is aimed at strengthening the liquidity of the banking system by setting high liquidity requirements. More generally, there is an emphasis on large international reserves, especially in relation to short-term obligations. To the extent that liquidity concerns are prevalent in recent experience, policies aimed at delivering high reserves and discouraging short-term debt make sense. At the same time, these policies have the drawback of imposing higher cost of capital and reducing the domestic absorption of foreign savings.

Latin America is already doing much of what is being recommended. It is interesting to note that the most prudent Latin American governments have found it useful to have a liquidity policy while the OECD has explicitly eliminated liquidity requirements from its regulatory scheme. At present, international reserve levels relative to M2 are about ten times larger in Latin America than in the typical industrial country. This radical difference must also reflect the presence of a fundamental difference in economic structure. Holding reserves makes sense if there are states of the world in which a country cannot access the international capital markets. For example, by being sufficiently liquid a country can avoid falling into the kind of self-fulfilling liquidity crisis that is associated with rolling over the foreign debt. This is the consequence of distortions other than moral hazard and is unlikely to be addressed by any of the initiatives to curb moral hazard that are on the table.

But it is important to recognize that these kinds of prudential policies are second best. They achieve higher stability by impeding capital flows, rather than by solving or compensating for the fundamental problems. The concern is that they are costly in terms of development. In this sense, the mechanisms of international last resort lending or a contagion facility can be viewed as another, superior way of addressing issues of liquidity since they involve actual insurance, rather than self-insurance. The problem, of course, is that these more efficient solutions pose a financial risk to industrial countries.

Finally, there is the important issue of how to reform financial regulations in developed countries in order to prevent problems that may affect emerging markets. A case in point is international financial contagion, whose main transmission mechanism, if not root cause, resides in how financial intermediation to emerging markets operates. Two interrelated problems have been identified in recent experience: first, the likelihood that financial intermediaries become overleveraged as a result of market losses and are forced to sell off their positions, and second, the dependency of emerging markets on a select group of specialist financial institutions, which makes the market for paper quite illiquid. These problems lead to fire sale prices in times of trouble and the collapse of the market.

The main initiative on the table to address these concerns is the tightening of regulation to discourage high leverage, which would therefore make overleverage less likely. We are concerned that, as in the case of other initiatives on the table, this one seeks financial stability by simply reducing capital flows to emerging markets, thus aggravating one of the important distortions to be fixed. This initiative may be beneficial from an industrial country perspective in relation to its own financial stability, but may be quite costly for development. In fact, from an emerging country perspective, it would be preferable to focus reforms in other directions that offer high efficiency gains at some minimal cost to industrial country taxpayers.

For example, regulatory forbearance in financial centers to be activated in the case of a systemic shock would help to diffuse the sudden jolt that overleverage causes. In this sense, marking to market makes illiquid markets even more unstable when the asset price collapse is not based on fundamentals. Regulatory flexibility under these contingencies in order to impede the cascading collapse would be an effective circuit breaker under peak times, preferable to reducing the flow levels on a permanent basis. Potentially more promising would be a small relaxation of the regulations that prohibit important institutional investors from buying non-investment-grade paper. This may represent a radical change in the structure of emerging markets, which have become overly dependent on a small group of specialized investors. This would permit higher flows and reduce the collapse during contagion episodes. Unfortunately, this efficiency gain comes with an additional risk of the regulated institutions. However small this cost may be, this is again an industrial country cost necessary to produce the emerging country benefit.

CONCLUDING REMARKS

Most current initiatives for reforming the international financial architecture are guided by two principles: a) constrain official financial support in order to avoid bailing out the private sector and creating moral hazard; and b) increase stability in financial markets by limiting capital flows to emerging markets. We find these principles unsatisfactory as a basis for a solution to the problems of international finance for development and propose alternative ones. Even more, we fear that current initiatives may be developmentally counterproductive once their negative effects on the level of capital flows and growth are factored in.

Ours is a Latin American assessment of the initiatives, and therefore not a neutral viewpoint. In order to clarify the debate it is important to recognize that reforms to the international financial architecture have asymmetric effects for the parties involved. In particular, reforms that support deeper financial integration and faster growth in the region may also be more costly to industrial countries in terms of financial risks when disruptions occur. The above principles minimize the financial costs of international cooperation, which may reflect the fact that the efficient integration of emerging markets may be too costly for industrial countries to accept.

We have argued in favor of new institutions to address liquidity and contagion problems. We have expressed support for the idea of an international bankruptcy court. We find value in improving financial regulation and supervision but think that the greater additional payoff in Latin America is related to the improvement of institutions that solve commitment problems and manage liquidity risks. We also find that many of the origins of liquidity crises and problems of financial fragility are caused by original sin, that is, by the fact that the national currency cannot be used to borrow abroad or even domestically to borrow long term. This creates the mismatches that can easily come home to roost at the first sign of trouble. It also limits the ability of central banks to backstop the market unless they hold enormous amounts of international reserves. This calls into question the monetary architecture of the world.

Debate about the new financial architecture is spurred by dissatisfaction with the world as we find it. Financial turmoil is exacting enormous social costs in all emerging-market countries. Contagion has made the problem more difficult and costly to address through the exercise of national virtue. It has transformed localized infections into an international disease that needs an international cure.

How much of current social suffering is attributable to an inadequate international financial architecture is an open question. But it is clear that the costs of this inadequacy are borne mostly by emerging countries, while any decisions on how to change international institutions and their financial backing inevitably involve the industrial countries. One is reminded of Ortega y Gasset's remark that the pain of others is so much easier to bear than one's own.

NOTES

The views and interpretations in this document are those of the authors and should not be attributed to the Inter-American Development Bank, or to any individual acting on its behalf.

1. Excessive lending to the public sector may also be caused by political economy distortions, which may have contributed to the debt crisis of the 1980s. Here we focus on lending to the private sector, and therefore assume that returns pass the market test.

2. Dooley (1997), Krugman (1998), and Corsetti, Pesenti, and Roubini (1998) provide formal models of this intuition.

3. La Porta and López-de-Silanes (1998) provide an empirical analysis of creditor and shareholder rights for a large set of countries and establish their importance as determinants of the level of development of financial systems.

4. In the absence of good investment opportunities, access to foreign finance would be irrelevant, or even counterproductive if, due to distortions, it leads to overinvestment. This inefficiency would also accrue to emerging countries as residual claimants.

5. Nevertheless, it may be relevant for sectoral welfare, that is the internal distribution within the country. For example, a public guarantee in favor of the private sector in an emerging country leads to a gain of the domestic private sector offset by a loss of the domestic official sector, which may alter the sectoral distribution.

6. This kind of initiative has been put in practice under the misleading name of "emergency financing," for example, in the 1998 more than $40 billion Brazil package.

7. Still, many of the lessons derived from recent experiences with liquidity crises are applicable. In particular, it would be desirable for a new generation of financial support programs to be put in place and be activated before crises erupt. Contrary to liquidity problems, presumably, fundamental solvency problems can be detected in advance and are amenable to early action. Otherwise there should be a strong presumption that liquidity is the key issue.

8. At the same time, the country ought to adjust and reform. Ideally, the balance between private and official support would depend on how prudent the country's policies are.

REFERENCES

Bayoumi, T. 1997. *Financial Integration and Economic Activity*. Manchester, U.K.: Manchester University Press.

Bayoumi, T., and A. Rose. 1993. Domestic Saving and Intra-National Capital. *European Economic Review* 37.

Buiter, W., and A. Sibert. 1999. UDROP: A Contribution to the New International Financial Architecture. Unpublished manuscript, University of Cambridge and Birkbeck College, University of London.

Bulow, J., and K. Rogoff. 1989. Sovereign Debt: Is to Forgive to Forget? *American Economic Review* 79.

Burnside, Craig, Martin Eichenbaum, and Sergio Rebelo. 1999. Hedging and Financial Fragility in Fixed Exchange Rate Regimes. NBER Working Paper no. 7143 (May).

Calvo, G. 1998. Capital Market Contagion and Recession: An Explanation of the Russian Virus. University of Maryland, Department of Economics. Unpublished paper.

Calvo, G., and E. Fernández-Arias. 1998. The New Features of Financial Crisis in Emerging Markets. Paper presented at conference, Crisis and Contagion in Emerging Financial Markets: The New Policy Agenda. Inter-American Development Bank, Washington, D.C, October.

Chang, R., and A. Velasco. 1998. The Asian Liquidity Crisis. *NBER Working Paper*, no. 6796. Cambridge, Mass.: National Bureau for Economic Research.

Corsetti, G., P. Pesenti., and N. Roubini. 1998. Paper Tigers? A Preliminary Assessment of the Asian Crisis. Yale University, Princeton University, and New York University. Unpublished paper.

De Long, J. B. 1999. Financial Crises in the 1890s and 1990s: We Remember History: Why Are We Still Condemned to Repeat it? University of California, Berkeley, Department of Economics. Mimeographed.

Dooley, M. 1997. A Model of Crisis in Emerging Markets. *NBER Working Paper* no. 6300. Cambridge, Mass.: National Bureau for Economic Research.

Eichengreen, B., and. R. Hausmann. 1999. Exchange Rates and Financial Fragility. Paper presented at the Federal Reserve Bank of Kansas City, September.

Feldstein, M. 1998. Refocusing the IMF. *Foreign Affairs* (March).

Feldstein, M., and C. Horioka. 1980. Domestic Savings and International Capital Flows. *Economic Journal* 90 (June): 314–29.

Fernández-Arias, E. 1996. Balance of Payments Rescue Packages: Can They Work? *Working Paper* no. 333. Washington, D.C.: Inter-American Development Bank.

Fernández-Arias, E., M. Gavin, and R. Hausmann. 1998. Preventing Crises and Contagion: The International Financial Institutions. Paper presented at conference, Crisis and Contagion in Emerging Financial Markets: The New Policy Agenda, Inter-American Development Bank, Washington, D.C., October 7.

Fernández-Arias, E. and R. Hausmann. 1999. International Initiatives to Bring Stability to Financial Integration. Working Paper no. 402, Washington, D.C.: Inter-American Development Bank.

————. 2000a. Getting it Right: What to Reform in International Financial Markets. OECD Development Centre Seminars, Global Finance from a Latin American Viewpoint. Paris: Inter-American Development Bank/OECD.

————. 2000b. What's Wrong with International Financial Markets? OECD Development Centre Seminars, Global Finance from a Latin American Viewpoint. Paris: Inter-American Development Bank/OECD.

Fernández-Arias E. and D. Lombardo. 1998a. Private Overborrowing in Undistorted Markets. Working Paper no. 369. Washington, D.C.: Inter-American Development Bank.

————. 1998b. Market Discipline and Exuberant Foreign Borrowing. Paper presented at symposium, Banking, Financial Integration, and Macroeconomic Stability, Second Annual Conference of the Central Bank of Chile, Santiago, September.

Fernández-Arias, E., and R. Rigobón 1998. Financial Contagion in Emerging Markets. Working Paper, Washington, D.C.: Inter-American Development Bank.

Krugman P. 1998. What Happened in Asia? Department of Economics, Massachusetts Institute of Technology. Unpublished paper.

————. 1999. Balance Sheet, the Transfer Problem, and Financial Crises. Paper presented at IMF Conference, In Celebration of the Contribution of Robert Flood, International Monetary Fund, Washington, D.C., January.

La Porta, R., and F. Lopez-de-Silanes. 1998. Creditor Rights. Department of Economics, Harvard University. Unpublished paper.

Mishkin, F. 1996. Understanding Financial Crises: A Developing Country Perspective. In *Annual World Bank Conference on Development Economics 1996*, ed. Michael Bruno and Boris Pleskovic. Washington, D.C.: International Monetary Fund.

Obstfeld, M. 1998. The Global Capital Market: Benefactor or Menace? *Journal of Economic Perspectives* 12.

Sachs, J. 1998a. Global Capitalism: Making it Work. *The Economist* (September 12): 23–26.

————. 1998b. The IMF and the Asian Flu. *The American Prospect* 37 (April/May): 16–21.

Stiglitz, J. 1998. The Role of International Financial Institutions in the Current Global Economy. Washington, D.C.: The World Bank. Unpublished paper.

Stiglitz, J., and Weiss. 1981. Credit Rationing in Markets with Imperfect Information. *American Economic Review* 71, no. 3:393–410.

Chapter 7

REFORM PROPOSALS FROM DEVELOPING ASIA: FINDING A WIN-WIN STRATEGY

Ashima Goyal

The repeated financial crises of the 1990s have driven home the point that the structure of the international financial system is not satisfactory. An ideal new international financial architecture should reduce the frequency of crises, or eliminate them totally. If they occur, they should be resolved quickly, and without contagion. The new international financial architecture also has to be feasible.

As East Asia recovers rapidly from the 1997–1999 crisis, it remains deeply committed to globalization. Governments are serious about restructuring, improving regulations, corporate governance, and keeping a balance in macroeconomic policies so as to discourage bubbles, but stimulate recovery. They want to reform, not merely to prevent future crises, but because they think that will help them to perform well in the future.

Even so, proposals for reform of the international financial architecture can be divided into those favored by creditors and those favored by recipients. The former set is valid if the crises of the 1990s were due to inappropriate policies of borrowing countries. But incorrect post-crisis monetary policy advice, contagion, and herd behavior by investors also magnified the crises. Another set of reforms is required to minimize these in the future. These are also on the Asian agenda. Asians are conservative and therefore largely follow the emerging global consensus, which reflects the creditor view, on the causes of the Asian crisis and the best preventive measures. The additional items on the Asian agenda also can affect outcomes if a critical coalition of supporters is formed and pragmatic domestic and international policies give united Asian leaders international bargaining strength.

Private financial interests resist input from emerging market countries in a well-organized coalition. Yet most of the proposals on the Asian financial reform agenda would benefit creditor as well as borrower interests. The disputed items on the Asian agenda are transparency requirements for transnational private investors; debt workouts that bail in private capital; steps for faster and easier international debt restructuring; freedom to use market-based controls on short-term capital flows if necessary; regional initiatives for liquidity support; managed exchange rates; and recognizing that good macroeconomic policy has to be context sensitive. Asian countries are willing to adopt the legal and financial reforms in banks, bonds, and equity markets that creditors are keen on. If some of the items on the Asian agenda are included, it will make for a more balanced set of reforms, and therefore a more stable financial system. This would allow an expansion of capital flows, and offer more opportunities for both creditors and nations.

TWO VIEWS OF INTERNATIONAL FINANCIAL REFORM: THE CREDITOR VIEW AND THE EVOLVING ASIAN POSITION

At the risk of oversimplification, there are two broad views on necessary reforms of the global financial architecture. The first would attribute the crisis to actions or weak institutions of capital-importing countries, and implies that penal provisions are necessary to prevent such mistakes in the future. Moreover, "sound" macroeconomic policies will ensure the safety of international capital and minimize the contagion risk for neighbors. Countries should not try to pursue unsustainably high growth. Lending organizations, home governments of the major private transnational financial institutions, and defenders of the interests of foreign capital hold views that fit in the first group. Academics who are convinced that the free movement of global capital improves the allocation of resources and imposes beneficial discipline on borrowing countries also adhere to this view (Meltzer 1998; Parikh and Shah 1999).[1] Most advanced industrial country governments, international organizations such as the International Monetary Fund (IMF), and interest-group-associated think tanks such as the private sector Institute for International Finance (IIF) also espouse the creditor consensus (IIF 1999; IMF 2000c). The U.S. Treasury Department strongly advocates the free movement of capital (Summers 2000). Although the G7 usually endorses the creditor consensus, Japan, because of crosscutting regional affiliations, sometimes does not.

A second view would blame international financial crises primarily on contagion or the herd mentality of foreign investors. If funds make losses in one country, then they are forced to make good by pulling out from others; since dedicated funds service developing countries, contagion occurs. Creditors, following one another out in a rush to escape a crisis, make it worse. Then currency and banking crises reinforce each other. This alternative view suggests that support for borrowing countries is required for them to be able to brave the turbulence of international financial waters. Policymakers in developing countries that are large net borrowers and in countries that have been afflicted by currency or debt crises take the second view (Kim 2000; Hayami 2000; Hussin 1999; Reddy 2000; Sakakibara 1999). There are, of course, differences among developing countries. Academics located in both advanced industrial and developing countries who believe that some measures are required to prevent ill effects from high short-term capital mobility share some aspects of the developing country position (Eichengreen 1999; Bergsten 2000; Rose 1999; Stiglitz 1999). Extremists argue that the only alternatives left are either free capital flows—with or without an international lender of last resort—or complete controls on capital movements, but the majority believe that only something in between is feasible. Thus while the creditor position is closest to the "laissez-faire liberalizers" (see the chapter by Leslie Elliott Armijo) developing countries are both "financial stabilizers" and "transparency advocates," with the emphasis on the first. "Anti-globalizers" are a minority with very little influence in Asia.

Support for specific proposals on the new international financial architecture can largely be predicted by membership in one of our two groups. There is agreement on the potential benefits of foreign inflows, but there are differences over the domestic policies and new international norms required to make inflows safer and to raise their productivity. Sometimes the differences lie only in the specifics and the emphasis. In general, the reforms creditors favor are acceptance and implementation of international standards of good practice in financial sectors and macroeconomic policy. A report prepared after intensive discussions among fourteen Asian countries (APF 2000) reflects the Asian viewpoint. Among the items listed for countries with capital account convertibility are a managed exchange rate and market-based capital controls to deal with massive capital inflows; strengthening prudential regulation and supervision of financial institutions and developing domestic capital markets to prevent crises; and measures to effectively manage a sudden reversal of capital flows. The first proposed measure is "bailing in" the private sector to ensure that private creditors are involved in the resolution of crises. Second, the report recommends options such as debt-equity swaps, or standstills, collective representation of creditors, and majority action to alter payment terms of contracts to allow quick, orderly debt restructuring. Third, special borrowing facilities such as contingency credit lines should be made available in times of crises; these can be complemented by regional financial arrangements with effective surveillance and conditionality. Fourth, the report proposes restricting holdings of local currency by nonresidents to discourage offshore markets that lower the effectiveness of monetary policy. For countries with relatively closed capital accounts the authors suggest a careful sequencing of reform.

Crucial suggested reforms of the world's financial architecture can be classified into a) new rules and procedures with better risk-management and incentive properties (including transparency and reporting requirements, provision of a bankruptcy option, and capital controls); b) reform of the IMF; and c) changing the conduct of domestic monetary policy in capital-importing countries. I discuss these options in turn, emphasizing the differences between the dominant creditor view and the emerging Asian position.

Transparency and Reporting Requirements

There is general agreement that banks, bond, equity, and foreign exchange markets should be strengthened through deepening, modernization, and prudential regulation. This would reduce incentives for unhedged foreign short-term borrowing. Both private firms and financial institutions should implement adequate risk management systems. If capital flows were based on easily available and up-to-date information, then risk assessment would improve, and the chances of a panic would be reduced. There is broad international support for measures currently being taken to increase detail in the public and private collection of data, reduce lags, and make data more accessible and interpretable (G22 1998). A number of proposals have been made for setting up new international bureaucracies for regulation and supervision (see Eichengreen 1999), but the consensus seems to be that none of these are feasible at present because of conflicts of interest between countries or with existing institutions. Disagreements about transparency and reporting requirements are only over the degree of inclusiveness.

Private financial institutions want even more stringent transparency and accounting standards for developing countries than the IMF has imposed. For example, the Institute of International Finance (IIF), an association of 315 private multinational banks and institutional investors, is not satisfied with the transparency standards set by the IMF, especially in the area of external debt and reserves. The IIF's emerging-market benchmark standards require weekly, rather than monthly, data on official reserves, as well as data on the disposition of and drains on reserves. It is not satisfied with simple data provision; but wants the data put in the context of the evolution of policy and economic performance through active Investor Relations Programs, and also wants the data used to strengthen risk management (IIF 1999).

Recipient countries, however, would like similar requirements imposed on hedge funds, and stricter surveillance not only for emerging markets, but also for developed countries and offshore financial centers.[2] Large investors should make their movements public. Korean President Kim Dae Jung (2000) proposed that a hedge fund monitoring channel be established at an appropriate multilateral institution, since ready exchange of information on the investment activities of highly leveraged financial institutions (including investment banks) would contribute to the stability of international financial markets. Current scrutiny and surveillance are not adequate because regulatory structures have lagged behind the increasing sophistication of financial instruments. Regulators have to find innovative ways to make institutions and markets reveal more information. Y. Venugopal Reddy (2000), deputy governor of the Indian Reserve Bank, points out that surveillance is more frequent and intense for developing countries, yet in recent experience sources of instability have arisen in developed countries as well. Indian Finance Minister Yashwant Sinha (2000) recommends that codes not be so demanding that they degenerate into an exercise in labeling countries as performers and nonperformers, and notes that such codes should be applied equally to all member countries. Regulation has to be tailored to the circumstances and supervisory capabilities in developing countries (Stiglitz and Bhattacharya 1999). In some cases a lot of institution building is required; in others it is possible to jump to best practices.

Events and announcements confirm these attitudes. As the affected Asian countries have made a good recovery from the crisis, they want to resume their earlier rapid gains from globalization, which they regard as inevitable. The economies of the members of the Association of Southeast Asian Nations (ASEAN) grew 4.4 percent in 1999, compared to a contraction of 4.6 percent in 1998 (ASEAN 2000). They want to develop the human resources required to make full use of the information technology boom,[3] participate in the new global order, and to acquire modern institutions, standards, and regulations that will lower their risk in doing so. At their meeting in March, 2000, ASEAN finance ministers decided to take active measures to restore private foreign investment, strengthen corporate governance practices, and deepen and develop ASEAN's capital and bond markets in order to improve risk management (ASEAN 2000). Korea, which traditionally had not encouraged foreign direct investment, now welcomes it. The point is that countries want to reform, not only because of the crisis, but in order to grow rapidly. The aftermath of the crisis has left a stronger determination to remove all poverty in Asia.

Chinese policymakers believe that China escaped the crisis because of its controls over capital flows, foreign exchange and financial markets administrative reform, and steps taken to control inflation, overheating and bubbles since mid-1993.[4] These measures resulted in a successful soft landing in 1997. After that domestic interest rates were aligned to international rates. Keeping the renminbi stable contributed to the resolution of the Asian crisis. But China also wants to move towards more market-determined rather than government-determined systems as the way to modernize. Chinese analysts worry about the low efficiency of state-owned enterprises and their extensive funding from public sector banks.

India is also all for the adoption of transparency practices, core principles, and codes, but policymakers point out that there must be flexibility to allow for differences in economic structure across countries, and the development of the appropriate institutional, technological, and legal infrastructure. In as much as both financial market infrastructure and the overall level of development are higher in East than South Asia, Indian policymakers argue that the latter has to be brought to the required level of sophistication before fuller opening out to capital flows is possible (Reddy 2000).

Still the creditor view has dominated, since the general consensus seems to be that the hard-hit countries themselves were to blame. The allegations of crony capitalism and underregulation of the financial sectors in these countries have some truth to them, but undervalue the steady financial sector reforms and modernization that had been undertaken since the eighties (White 1994). In Malaysia, for example, the first rating agency was incorporated in 1990, the Securities Commission was set up as regulator in 1993, and the Kuala Lumpur Options and Financial Futures Exchange, which provides hedging services, became operational in 1995. The Philippines has also significantly reformed its financial sector in the 1990s. Moreover, it is not clear that conventional practices were entirely a symptom of corruption. Even Cole and Slade (1998), who take the creditor view, argue that the Indonesian crisis was as bad as it was primarily because of the collapse of the implicit guarantee the Suharto connection gave businesses associated with the ruling family. Snowden (1999), however, points out that family and other extralegal connections historically have been a way of moderating special risks in developing countries. They lower problems of asymmetric information that are pervasive in financial transactions.

Liquidity Support, Bankruptcy Procedures, and Bailing In Creditors

Analysts associated with what I have termed the "creditor view" argue that bankruptcy procedures would merely raise the spread and cost of borrowing for developing countries, and private capital would exit even faster. For example, Stanley Fischer writes, "The more certain it is that the private sector will be bailed in, in a compulsory way, the greater the incentive creditors will have to run—and this change will tend to produce more rather than fewer crises" (1999, 575). The report of the G7 finance ministers to the Cologne Economic Summit of 1999, which was accepted by the IMF, suggested that compulsory private sector involvement be avoided. The balance of initiative is to lie with the country concerned, with the IMF to play its traditional catalytic role in cases of moderate indebtedness. Operational procedures for other cases are left unclear (IMF 2000a).

The recipient country response is that such reforms lower the probability of crisis. Rewriting loan contracts to include bankruptcy clauses, as well as adding majority voting and sharing clauses, would prevent a few isolated creditors from holding up settlements that enhance the welfare of the majority. Collective representation clauses that appoint a trustee to represent and coordinate sovereign debt holders and creation of standing committees of creditors would encourage faster negotiations. The IMF could lend into arrears to indebted countries as long as they were involved in such good-faith negotiations, thus keeping the economy running even in a crisis. It could also declare a standstill, to protect a country from its creditors, while restructuring of debt takes place (Eichengreen 1999).

Modern crises have struck currency and debt markets together. If a major cause of crises is traders and creditors following each other's actions, or competing to grab assets when countries default, then reforms can actually protect creditors from each other. Simple game-theoretic models, with two currency traders (Obstfeld 1996) or two creditors (Miller and Zhang 2000) illustrate this. First, consider currency traders. When reserves are low, traders will certainly attack a currency peg, since by selling the currency they will make money from the devaluation that follows. When reserves are high, they lose their transaction cost if they attack, since the government successfully defends the currency. Each game therefore has a unique *Nash equilibrium*[5] in which the payoff of each trader is maximized, no matter what the other does. In intermediate regimes, only if both attack together can they run down the government's reserves. The payoffs for this regime are shown in table 7.1. If any one attacks alone the transaction cost is lost, for a payoff of (–1), while whoever holds gets zero. If both attack together *(sell, sell)* they get a positive payoff from sharing the government's currency reserves, and profit from the currency depreciation. The game changes to a coordination game with two Nash equilibria, which the arrows show. Now either both will hold the domestic currency or both will sell it. Herd behavior leads to self-fulfilling crises, where trader 1 attacks thinking that trader 2 is going to do so. In such a model higher availability of international reserves will allow the government to defeat the attack. Then *hold, hold* in the northwest corner is again the Nash equilibrium. The policy conclusion is that a ready availability of international liquidity can prevent the category of crises that occur due to herd behavior, even when country fundamentals are good.

I turn next to the analysis of international debt. The holders of private or sovereign country debt face a Prisoner's Dilemma if a country becomes illiquid

Table 7.1 Currency Speculation Leading to a Coordination Game

		Trader 2	
		Hold	Sell
Trader 1	Hold	0, 0 ←	0, –1
		↑	↓
	Sell	–1, 0 →	1, 1

even though it is solvent. If both hang on *(hold, hold)* they maximize total welfare. If either one is able to grab assets she does the best for herself and the other is left with nothing. So both will try to grab assets. The firm is forced into premature liquidation or the country forced to devalue, assets fall in value, and both creditors are worse off. Bankruptcy procedures which give equal treatment to creditors of the same seniority can make holding on the unique Nash equilibria since the first to grab no longer gains. Hence both would play *hold.*

But in the presence of short-term debt, those who agree to roll it over would lose out compared to those who refuse, as liquid assets are equally divided on bankruptcy. Then instead of a Prisoner's Dilemma, with a unique equilibrium, we have a *coordination game* as in table 7.1, with two Nash equilibria, since the payoffs are now different for the asymmetric strategies. Inefficient equilibria where both creditors grab, the country goes bankrupt, and all are worse off, can still occur. In such a case, a standstill, which gives protection against creditors, is required. Domestic bankruptcy laws in the United States have a provision for this. Even though such bankruptcy laws lower the legal rights of individual creditors, they protect them because intercreditor conflict poses the greatest risk to asset values (see Miller and Zhang 2000).

Now consider the role of the IMF. It can be forced to bail out creditors, because of the great damage that a creditor grab can do. Table 7.2 depicts the actions, equilibria, and payoffs. The first number is the payoff to the creditor, the second to the debtor—that is, the country. Note that the payoffs are to the country, but the IMF takes the action. The face value of the debt is ten units, and the payoffs to the creditor are the fraction of the face value received. The payoffs to the country consist of earnings from the loan taken. Considering the first two columns of payoffs, the actions available to the creditor are to rollover the debt or to grab assets; the IMF either can do nothing or make emergency funds available under a bailout. As the arrows show, there are two Nash equilibria, the first where there is debt rollover and the IMF does not have to take any action, and the second if there is grab and bailout. But the unique Subgame Perfect Nash Equilibrium is (10,3) if the creditor has first mover advantage.

If the creditor moves first to grab, the IMF is forced to bail out, because the outcome with no action (4,0) is so bad for both the creditor and the country. However, since the bailout involves a full guarantee for the creditor, the creditor in future will push loans without proper investigation or monitoring. Hence the probability of default will rise. To undertake no action is not credible for the IMF, and therefore the creditor will always grab whenever the debtor is unable to service debt, though the creditor may still be solvent. But if the rules of the game are changed so that if the creditor grabs the IMF can impose a standstill, then the creditor will prefer to rollover the debt. Forced to accept a debt reduction under a standstill, the creditor's payoff is relatively higher under a rollover. Now the unique Nash equilibrium is (8, 5), with the creditor rolling over the debt

Table 7.2 Sovereign Debt, Bailouts, and Standstills

		IMF/Debtor		
		No action	Bailout	Standstill
Creditor	Rollover	(8,5) ↔	(8,5)	
		↑	↓	
	Grab	(4,0) →	(10,3)	(6,7)
			—————————→	

and the IMF doing nothing. As the country has basically sound fundamentals, the lengthening of debt service under the rollover will give it time to recover; both country and creditor are better off.

Therefore, if reforms that bail in creditors are adopted, the herd behavior that brings on self-fulfilling crises should be discouraged. Otherwise, since protection from crises can never be complete, there will be a loss of profit-making opportunities for capital and a lower inflow to developing countries. Even with bailout packages and other protective devices all parties involved in a crisis make large losses. Moreover, if a standstill kicks in as soon as a critical mass of creditors are leaving, they will not be able to escape by leaving first, and therefore their incentives to leave will fall, not rise. Such reforms will also not raise the cost of borrowing for developing countries, or make it more difficult for them to get loans, if better monitoring and debtor selection lower the probability of default.

The last implies that cost of borrowing will rise only for countries with a poor record or prospects. Although creditors have not always in the past distinguished between "well-behaved" and "foolish" emerging market countries,[6] this should change when they have to bear some penalty for not doing so. There is evidence that creditors push loans with inadequate analysis or monitoring. Incentive will rise both for recipients to follow good policies, and for creditors to do more careful selection and monitoring. The voluntary choice of policies creates "ownership" which makes them easier to implement. Externally imposed policy conditionalities lead to resistance, and have a poor record of success. Fernández-Arias and Hausmann (1999), argue that bailing-in the private sector won't work unless "willingness to pay," which is the major issue in developing countries, is addressed. But Asian countries have a very good record of repaying debt. Reforms do not have to reinforce willingness to pay or enforcement, so much as the ability to pay or liquidity.

If these arguments are correct, and creditors will gain from bankruptcy procedures, rational creditors should be willing to adopt them. Why is there so much reluctance? There are two potential reasons. First, the probability of a future crisis is still discounted, despite the experience of the 1990s. Second, creditor psychology is such that instead of minimizing the expected value of crisis losses, creditors are more concerned about the loss itself than the reduction in its probability. Therefore the higher bargaining clout of investing nations leads policymakers to give higher weight to creditors' losses in the case of crisis, compared to their gains from a strongly reduced probability of crises. They push to protect taxpayers in investing nations by ensuring they do not suffer a loss in case a crisis occurs. If this analysis is correct, then a loss in bargaining power could actually turn out to be beneficial to creditors.

Capital Controls

Creditors argue that with today's technology capital controls of any kind are impossible to enforce. They have a high cost in terms of foregone capital, and few countries are willing to impose them. Proponents of these views note that many who have used capital controls, including both Chile and Malaysia, eventually have removed them voluntarily.

These conclusions can be challenged. Many developing-country economists have concluded that a tax on short-term capital inflows can discourage the type of capital that is subject to herd behavior and decrease harmful excess volatility of these inflows (see also Cohen in this volume). Since technological change makes it difficult for regulators to keep up with financial institutions, a market-based tax on short-term capital inflows can actually outperform discretionary prudential regulation (Ocampo 1999). Developing countries have few policy instruments that they can use to restrain cycles; therefore countercyclical short-term taxes serve a useful double purpose. More drastic controls on outflows may be required in times of crisis.

In Chile in the 1990s all non-equity foreign capital had to make a one-year, non-interest-bearing deposit. The implicit tax therefore declined with the duration of the investment. This measure succeeded in lengthening the maturity structure of foreign debt, after it was made sufficiently comprehensive so as to plug major loopholes (Agosin and Ffrench-Davis 1999). The ability of private agents to design loopholes, and the costly and invasive monitoring sometimes required to close them, are the weakness of such taxes. Therefore they need to be used along with improvements in regulation and banks' own risk-management practices, and can be discontinued when the regulatory framework is strong enough, or if more capital is needed. Chile lifted its capital taxes in 1998, partly for these reasons. Malaysia introduced exchange controls and other measures in September, 1998, partly to eliminate trading of the ringgit in offshore markets (APF 2000). It controlled the transfer of funds in the external accounts, fixed the nominal exchange rate, and introduced a twelve-month rule to discourage short-term capital flows. These policies allowed it to lower interest rates and revive economic activity. The measures were gradually relaxed as conditions improved.

International, or failing that, regional, agreements make capital taxes easier to use. There are higher costs for one country to do it alone. It is difficult to tax a mobile factor of production, and capital mobility is now higher than that of labor. This is eroding the postwar liberal compromise whereby expenditures on social welfare were paid by taxes on capital in return for industrial peace (Armijo 2000). In postcrisis countries the demands for such expenditures are rising. Coordinated taxes on short-term capital provide one answer to this dilemma. To some extent, the old conflict between labor and capital becomes less acute if the tax funds human resource and skill development, which improve returns to capital.

Although all countries accepted the possibility of using capital controls, at least temporarily, just after the East Asian crisis, nations in which creditor interests dominate are more doubtful about the measure. The Group of Seven includes Western developed nations and Japan. According to Eisuke Sakakibara, Japanese vice-minister of finance during the Asian crisis, the G7 advocated a middle-of-the-road position, with which Japan agreed fully. Sakakibara observes, "It has sometimes been suggested by the press and others that Japan is advocating more controls on capital flows while other G7 countries are arguing for free capital movements. This is simply not true. . . . Japan's position from the outset was that maintaining market-friendly controls that would prevent turbulent capital inflows should be justified when a country wants to keep capital inflows at a manageable level according to the stage of development of its financial sector, and that there might be some cases that would justify the reintroduction of controls on capital outflows as an exception, for example, in order to avoid a bail-out by IMF loans. . . . [T]his stance . . . is shared by all G7 countries" (1999, n.p.). But Sakakibara also feels the need to emphasize the costs of capital controls, a point the collective G7 report emphasizes. He continues, "Such steps may carry costs and should not in any case be used as a substitute for reform. . . . [C]ontrols on capital flows can carry even greater long-term costs . . . although they may be necessary in certain exceptional circumstances" (1999, n.p.).

The argument that technological changes make controls on short-term capital at best infeasible and at worst inefficient is not borne out by the experiences of Chile, Columbia, Malaysia, India, and China, all countries that have successfully used partial (prudential) or more complete controls, either as a short- or long-term measure. There is a consensus that market-based and need-based controls work better, and they do impose a cost.

Reform of the IMF

The so-called Bretton Woods institutions were set up in the aftermath of the Great Depression, with the mandate to safeguard global economic interactions.[7] One of the objectives of the International Monetary Fund, as laid down in Article I of its Articles of Agreement, is "To give confidence to members by making the general resources of the Fund temporarily available to them under adequate safeguards, thus providing them with opportunity to correct maladjustment in their balance of payments without resorting to measures destructive of national or international prosperity" (Article I (v), see Fischer 1999, F571). Thus special help is mandated for countries in times of crisis. The functioning has been criticized but the need for such aid and the validity of the objective remain. All agree that the IMF will continue to be necessary, but will require serious reform to reflect the changes in the regime of global capital flows. The severity, frequency, and contagion effects of recent financial crises have exposed the inadequacy of the IMF's resources. In both the Mexican and East Asian crises it had to draw upon other bilateral and multilateral sources. Although it is not a world central bank, since it does not have the ability to create money, it is often called upon to serve as an international lender of last resort (LLR), but with funds that are puny compared to private capital flows.

The perspective of one influential group among the creditors is not that the IMF does too little too late, but that it does too much. The main problem for this group is the moral hazard for countries induced by indiscriminate bailout packages. If countries know that they will be rescued from a crisis, then they will not take adequate preventive measures. The Meltzer Committee's recommendations to the United States Congress in early 1999 (see Bergsten in this volume) include narrowly focusing the IMF on international lender of last resort functions, and the abolition of its developmental functions as well as the special funds made available to developing countries. Many of these activities, it is argued, should devolve to the private sector. Moreover, lender of last resort funds should be made available only to countries that prequalify with a strict set of capital markets and fiscal-policy-based criteria. Conditionality thus would be *ex-ante* rather than *ex-post*.

Developing countries have a radically different viewpoint. They want faster response time and greater availability of funds. For example, developing countries have long demanded that the Fund be allowed to issue Special Drawing Rights (SDRs), the IMF's own "currency," to itself (Ocampo 1999; Sinha 2000). This option would make funds available faster, as required, without a permanent increase in unconditional liquidity. The consensus is that some competition, more transparency, help from the private sector, and more focused developmental activities will improve the functioning of the IMF. Recently, the Japanese government and many Asian policymakers suggested a competing Asian Monetary

Fund (see Laurence in this volume). In any event, many Asian scholars and policymakers argue that prescribing medication effective in old-style crisis of the current account will not do when today's crises originate in the capital account (Sakakibara 1999). Conditionality should be more context sensitive.

Unsurprisingly, the reforms that have been carried out so far at the IMF reflect the dominance of the main creditor countries. The Supplementary Reserve Facility (SRF) was introduced at the end of 1997 and the Contingency Credit Line (CCL) in April 1999. Both make large short-term loans, at penalty rates, to crisis-struck countries satisfying policy conditionality. The CCL can be used in a preventive mode, to reward good policies. These new facilities push the IMF towards the international lender of last resort role, thus preventing loss to global capital, but still ignore the other cardinal rule suggested by efficiency criteria: unstinting liquidity support. Bagehot argued in his classic that central banks worsen crises when they lend "hesitatingly, reluctantly and with misgiving. . . . In fact, to make large advances in this faltering way is to incur the evil of making them without obtaining the advantage" (Bagehot 1873, quoted in Mayer 1999, 6). Advances instead should be made freely but at a penal interest rate. When it is known that liquidity is available, the panic subsides. The new facilities made available do not meet these criteria. As Sinha (2000) points out, no country has availed itself of the CCL since its inception in 1999, implying that it does not meet the needs of borrowers. If no one uses it, how will it fulfill its role of crisis prevention? Special programs had been created for developing countries, which need longer-term structural adjustment. One such program, the Extended Structural Adjustment Facility (ESAF), was replaced in 1999 by the Poverty Reduction and Growth Facility (PRGF), which seeks to make recipient country governments more accountable and improve targeting.

The IMF reports to ministries of finance and central banks, and therefore reflects their views more than those of its shareholder countries as a whole (Stiglitz 1999). Central bankers focus narrowly on stabilization and controlling inflation, yet the impact of such policies falls disproportionately on the poor. Within a country, democratic processes bring about a consensus among conflicting views and interests, so that national interests have a chance to dominate special or group interests (Stiglitz 1999). But in the IMF the views of the different groups in its member countries do not get a full hearing, and democratic processes are skewed. Voting rights are proportional to the GDP of member countries, since these define contributions. The United States gets the largest vote, with near veto power in the Executive Board (Jha and Saggar 2000; Porter and Wood in this volume). With this structure it is difficult for the IMF to fulfill its objectives of representing a diverse set of national interests; these do not always coincide with those of the United States. Reforms that improve transparency and public accountability, and competition from regional funds that would check its natural monopoly would therefore help the IMF to truly promote global interests. The other alternative is expanding liquidity available with the IMF and adjusting voting rights. One suggestion is to rebalance quota formulas, giving more weight to the size of the domestic economy measured in purchasing power parity terms (Tobin 1998; Jha and Saggar 2000). The quota formula could then determine country contributions, drawing power, and voting rights.

Even in the absence of harsh and one-size-fits-all external conditionalities, the developing country desire to leverage capital inflows is sufficient to force the countries to adopt conservative macropolicies and global standards. Recent empirical studies have shown the ineffectiveness of World Bank *ex ante* policy conditionality (Gilbert, Powell, and Vines 1999). Bank conditionality frequently created a conflict-based relationship with client governments that made reforms less successful than they might otherwise have been. An alternative approach being promoted is for the Bank to lend more to countries which follow good policies, and limit itself to spreading knowledge of what these good policies are in others. This is defined as *ex post* conditionality. Countries in charge of their own reform program would be better motivated to make it successful. They might form clubs that stimulate reforms of reciprocal benefit; there could be demonstration effects and regional spillovers. Low or less rigid conditionality facilities must be available when the imbalance is due to an international shock, or to contagion. Conditionality should be relaxed more automatically if conditions worsen (Ocampo 1999).

Many policymakers in recipient countries prefer this idea of participation by groups of countries, leading to greater policy "ownership."[8] As private sector participation rises, and if there is effective bailing-in of the private sector, the market will charge lower rates to countries with better policies. Given the diversity among borrowers in macroeconomic conditions, which we discuss below, it is better that international lender of last resort conditions are partially conditioned on results, rather than on arbitrary or uniform preconditionalities. Another alternative, which lowers disincentives and was successfully used in Scandinavia, is to save the banks but not the owners. In order to minimize wealth transfers to original shareholders, in one case, the central government guaranteed all of a bank's obligations except its equity (Mayer 1999).

Perhaps a competing Asian Monetary Fund would have a better understanding of the Asian context. Since the contagion that accompanies a crisis is often regional, a regional fund would be more active and involved. In effect the AMF would just replace the current ad hoc country groups that support IMF packages with bilateral aid; therefore there should be no conflict with the IMF (Rose 1999).[9] It would also save U.S. taxpayers money. A task force organized by the United Nations Economic Commission on Latin America and the Caribbean (ECLAC) sees the future IMF as the apex of a network of regional funds

(Ocampo 1999). Since in any case the IMF can no longer raise the kind of money required in current crises, its major role should be that of an honest broker in bringing debtors and creditors together and in the use of moral suasion, backed by its loans, to ensure the adoption of common standards. Surveillance by the AMF would be good because of its focused mandate and regional expertise, and as long as lending is with tough but context-sensitive conditionality, it would not lead to moral hazard (APF 2000).

In 1998 Argentina purchased liquidity insurance as a contingent repo option involving fourteen international banks. Such deals become more feasible if the IMF offers partial insurance cover for the collateral required. An IMF or World Bank guarantee reassures private creditors. It helps ensure repayment since debtors have a long-term relationship with these institutions. Private sector monitoring and funds then complement the IMF's efforts, and enhance liquidity available sufficiently to forestall crises. An AMF could complement such efforts for Asia. Because there is a first-mover disadvantage in, for example, redesigning debt contracts, the IMF has a major role in coordinating the simultaneous adoption of such measures. It is difficult for a country to adopt private sector bail-in policies unilaterally, since capital would then easily boycott it.

While the suggested reforms of the IMF can ensure fast action and appropriate conditionality, financial sector restructuring, tighter regulations, and the bailing-in of creditors can lower the moral hazard associated with crisis loans. Fast response is the key to effective liquidity support. Faster postcrisis program loans helped Korea and Thailand; Malaysia did not get this (perhaps because it was more independent in the reforms it chose) and private capital flows also did not resume. Therefore it had a deeper contraction although its precrisis situation was better than that of the others (Cho and Rhee 1999).

Macroeconomic and Exchange Rate Policies

Creditors advocate conservative fiscal and monetary policies to maintain the value of developing country currencies and allow integration with the global economy (Fischer 1999). With respect to designing a crisis-free exchange rate policy, many suggest that the only two viable alternatives, given the extreme fluidity of global markets, are a completely free float or a fixed peg validated by a currency board or monetary union. Otherwise a fixed peg is not credible and invites attack (Eichengreen 1999, 105). Mussa (IMF 2000b) maintains that a free float is not possible in developing economies because they do not have the deep foreign exchange markets that are required for a free float to be operational.

Capital recipient countries in contrast argue for balanced and pragmatic policies suited to local circumstances. As goals and conditions change, dynamic adjustments are required. With respect to exchange rate policy, many

Asian economists and policymakers argue that only a managed float is both politically feasible and desirable (Bergsten 1998; Tobin 1998; RBI 1997), and would help to prevent crises (APF 2000). The main theme of a recent international conference organized by the Asian Development Bank Institute was to identify exchange rate regimes for developing economies that would fall between the two corner solutions (ADBI 2000).[10] Managed exchange rates with sufficient two-way movement force all parties to hedge exposures, so that losses from sudden shocks do not become cumulative and intensify crises (Goyal 1999). This also frees monetary policy to adjust to the domestic cycle, to some extent.

There is an argument that since domestic banks cannot borrow long domestically or abroad in their own currency, they have to borrow long in foreign currency. Therefore they cannot hedge, and a floating exchange rate will expose their maturity mismatch.[11] This reasoning is more valid for Latin America, but in Asia domestic savings are relatively high, so that long-term funds are available internally for domestic banks. As Stiglitz and Bhattacharya (1999, 117) write, "[W]ith its high savings rate, East Asia does not need a foreign supply of capital." Reform currently seeks to develop bond markets and pension funds. This will also make more long-term funds available. Moreover, even if natural hedges (by holding liabilities of similar maturities in multiple currencies) are not available, derivatives are, at a cost. If controlled two-way movements occur in exchange rates, open positions cancel out over time. Unhedged losses made on a net positive foreign currency balance when the nominal exchange rate appreciates will be neutralized when it depreciates.

There is less agreement within Asia on interest rate policy, although it is recognized that this has to be very different in a regime of fast and free global capital movements. If exchange rates are kept fixed interest rates become more volatile; but interest rates have a larger macroeconomic impact, and it is easier to hedge against exchange rate volatility (Furman and Stiglitz 1999). It is important to distinguish between macro policies followed before and during crisis. The usefulness of raising interest rates in the course of a crisis is a separate analytical question from that of following systematic tight monetary policies so that domestic interest rates exceed international rates prior to a crisis. Currency crises in the 1990s were associated with financial or banking crises. The interest rate crisis defense was specially damaging in Asia because of high gearing and weak banks.[12] High domestic interest rates can defend the exchange rate only if country risk stays unchanged; but high interest rates can raise the latter and therefore lead to higher expected depreciation (Furman and Stiglitz 1999).

With respect to longer-term policies, it is argued that relatively higher interest rate regimes are required in developing countries, because capital is scarce and returns to investment projects are higher (Eichengreen 1999). But increased global capital mobility in the 1990s has modified this constraint. Long-term flows of private capital to emerging markets that were below $50 billion in 1990 were at $290 billion in 1997 (World Bank 1998). Short-term flows and foreign exchange transactions are many magnitudes higher.

Under perfect capital mobility, monetary policy is not independent if exchange rates are fixed. With floating exchange rates, it is, but fiscal policy loses its effect. If there is a demand stimulus, interest rates rise above world interest rates and induce a capital inflow that appreciates the exchange rate until export demand is cut equivalently. But the problem is that the latter mechanism cannot be allowed to work in a developing country. Since high potential growth draws in net inflows, a floating exchange rate would appreciate and therefore harm exports, when stimulating them is a major objective for such countries. Although developing countries may be small in world export markets, they do compete intensively with each other. The capital account, influenced by expected future growth, now dominates the current account. Therefore current account adjustments can no longer ensure equilibrium.

There is a growing consensus that the exchange rate has to be managed, and monetary policy operational procedures in developing countries also have to focus on interest rates. Most major central banks worldwide now target a short-term interest rate as the best operating procedure of monetary control (Goyal 1997, 1999). Since the float cannot be total, monetary policy cannot be fully independent. Inflation can serve as a target to fix nominal expectations in lieu of a fixed exchange rate, but inflation is best lowered, in such countries, by policies that improve productivity and boost cost-effective supply. There are many administered prices, and with more openness the nominal exchange rate will also affect inflation.

If developing countries keep their domestic real interest rates as close to international rates as possible, it will stimulate their real economy. Capital will be attracted by higher profits rather than by high interest rates (Goyal 1999).[13] As long as revenue deficits are contained, and productivity is rising on the supply side, inflationary pressures will be contained. Smooth interest rates should discourage asset price volatility and deepen financial markets (Goyal and Dash 2000). China is an example of the successful use of this strategy. From 1997 to 1999, while countries around it raised interest rates sharply, interest rates on yuan-denominated assets in China were close to those on dollar-denominated assets in the United States, showing a negligible country risk premium. And there was no shortage of foreign investment flows.

Ideally a flexible exchange rate should give a country the freedom to vary the domestic interest rate procyclically, and smooth the business cycle. But in practice most countries seek to manage the exchange rate, when it fluctuates beyond acceptable limits, by raising domestic interest rates when the exchange rate is depreciating. But since this normally occurs in a business slump, it aggravates the depression. Therefore market-based cyclical capital controls offer a tool to manage fluctuations in exchange rates, and free the domestic interest rate for procyclical movements (Ocampo 1999), or alignment to lower international real interest rates (Goyal 1997). A well-designed exchange rate policy can achieve this purpose even without the use of controls.

The argument can be extended to developed countries also. Raising interest rates in order to attract or keep foreign capital is a "beggar-my-neighbor" policy and invites retaliation. Moreover, it is not always successful since raising interest rates can create expectation of rising inflation or currency depreciation even where these do not yet exist. The contributions of rising U.S. interest rates to the Latin American debt crisis of the eighties, and of U.S. Federal Reserve Bank rate cuts to nipping contagion from the Asian crisis in 1998, are well known. Short-term capital flows respond to changes in relative nominal interest rates. Since inflation rates are low worldwide, interest rates should show little variation in response to domestic needs, and not in order to defend exchange rates. This will discourage the less desirable volatile debt creating short-term capital flows. Real interest rates are converging internationally again. Obstfeld and Taylor (1997) show that interest rate arbitrage is working well in developed countries since the 1970s; interest rate differentials are down to what they were in 1910. Global capital flows are forcing convergence of interest rates as capital flows to areas where interest rates are relatively higher, but emerging market countries still need to use policy to achieve this convergence.

Precrisis tight monetary policy was partly responsible for the East Asian crisis. Since nominal exchange rates were largely fixed, in a regime of capital inflows and tight monetary policies, domestic interest rates exceeded international so that domestic financial institutions had an incentive to overborrow abroad (Goyal and Dash 1998; Furman and Stiglitz 1999). It cannot simultaneously be argued that the overborrowing by domestic institutions was due to weak regulations and crony capitalism, while overlending by foreign banks was due to higher interest rates—that is, to price incentives. If the tight regulations under which foreign banks operate did not prevent them from overlending, why will tighter regulations prevent developing country banks from overborrowing, if interest rate differentials induce them to do so? It follows that, in addition to lax regulations, responsibility for the crisis lay with the higher domestic, compared to foreign, interest rates in a regime of fixed exchange rates.

Turning to the crisis itself, most Asian policymakers agree that the macro conditionality imposed by the IMF after the crises was incorrect. Austerity measures, designed for countries where crises were caused by large fiscal deficits, were routinely applied to countries where government budgets were in surplus and conservative macroeconomic policies were being followed (Chang and Velasco 1999). The effect of the steep rise in interest rates in deepening the bankruptcies of highly geared private banks and firms was not foreseen. Most Asian countries later implemented lower interest rate regimes to stimulate demand and lower financial intermediation costs. In Korea, Thailand, and Malaysia interest rates were lower than precrisis levels by the end of 1998, as monetary policy was relaxed in the second half of the year. Malaysia introduced capital controls to allow it to lower interest rates when tight monetary policy failed to stabilize its exchange rate. China and India (Goyal and Dash 1998) lowered interest rates in the crisis period, which, together with capital controls, helped them escape the East Asian crisis.

Cho and Rhee, after reviewing postcrisis adjustments in the crisis-hit economies, argue that "policy packages to be imposed on the crisis-hit countries will need to be better tuned to individual market circumstances. In economies such as Korea and Thailand, which are quite open, private sector oriented, and have a very high leverage ratio in the corporate sector, the sensitivity to a stabilization package could be higher than in other economies" (1993, 387). In other words, such countries will suffer more from a steep rise in interest rates. Meanwhile, Reddy (2000) articulates the Indian position: with respect to capital account convertibility and exchange rate regimes, one size cannot fit all—context and institutional sensitivity is required. Along with financial reforms, sustainable macrobalances need to be defined in the context of maintaining some national monetary and exchange rate policy autonomy under an open capital account. Proper sequencing of reform is another concern of policymakers. Financial liberalization too early can lead to harmful sharp peaks in interest rates. This has been documented for Africa (Collier and Gunning 1999) and Latin America in the 1980s.

The East Asian crisis has led to the realization that although in accounting and regulation uniform standards should be accepted, in macroeconomics there may be a case for acknowledging that good fundamentals are context sensitive. If financial capital comes to believe that some variation in good macroeconomic policies is justified, it will not panic at a slight deviation from a rigid norm. Capital flows are so large today that they can force obedience to expected norms, even if they are not optimal. This problem can be mitigated if countries are judged by results, not acontextual preconceptions of good policy. Better data availability needs to be supplemented with more country-specific analysis. Monetary policies have to find a fine balance between being too tight and too lax (Goyal 1997).

Asian countries are conservative and want to follow international best practices. Part of their problems arose from this Casablanca-style obedience. What is the best monetary and exchange rate policy is no longer so clear in the new global regime of capital mobility. Academics, the IMF, and policy makers have to debate this and arrive at a consensus; this is a major current research area. Central banks need guidance.

With the exception of Europe, all the currency crises of the 1990s involved developing economies. There is a tendency for capital to fly from what are regarded as "soft" currencies, at the least provocation, to "hard" currencies such as the dollar. Special features could be designed to make global capital markets safer for these countries.[14] Donor countries also suffer from the disruption, but if the NIFA only protects donor countries, developing countries will be forced to take other less efficient measures. Full Asian engagement with the global economy awaits reforms in the global financial architecture. Countries will be less inclined to adopt unilateral or group-based defensive measures if the new international financial architecture takes care of their concerns and provides stability, so that they have confidence in globalization.

The recovery in East Asia is largely following the V-shape observed after the Mexican crisis of 1994. The V-shape was not observed in the Latin American crisis in the 1980s, partly because it took much longer to negotiate rescue packages. The international community apparently has learned from the crises, since recovery was faster in the 1990s compared to what it was in the1980s. But attention has to turn to measures of prevention in the light of experience. Although recovery is faster, the frequency of crises has also become greater— so reforming the global financial architecture is of high priority. I now turn to the prospects for the Asian view influencing the global dialogue on financial reform.

NEGOTIATIONS: GIVING A LITTLE AND GAINING A LOT

The two positions explored above define the likely dialectics of the debate. Developing countries are willing to reform their financial sectors and adapt their monetary policies to international best practices. But many reforms they would like to see are stalled. Lender countries and interests dominate the international financial institutions. As a tightly organized interest group, they can better push their agenda compared to the more diffused group that is harmed by a financial crisis. Armijo (2000) argues that the political elites of industrial countries are easily persuaded by transnational financial capital to push its agenda, while individuals who lose are dispersed. But there are reasons why a more representative consensus may emerge.

First, academic discussion continues to clarify many technical issues and to make clear the win-win nature of more complete reform for most if not all participants. Nonetheless, several conclusions that seem clear when these debates are modeled as strategic games are not yet widely appreciated. This chapter has suggested that some forms of bailing-in the private sector could protect creditors from each other, yet private multinational financial institutions thus far have mainly employed their superior bargaining clout to prevent any restrictions from being placed on them. Still, learning may influence future behavior.

A second reason for optimism has to do with the dynamics of the bargaining process. The basic negotiator's dilemma (Kremenyuk, Sjostedt, and Zartman 2000) can be paraphrased as follows. If a party to a negotiation is too soft, the contract will come through but that party will get very little out of it. If a negotiator is too hard, the contract might fall through. Asian countries are attempting to meet many of the creditors' requirements. If the latter do not make concessions to Asian sensitivities, then the countries will be pushed to adopt measures that in the long run will improve their bargaining position and leave creditors with a smaller share in any mutual contract than they would have otherwise got. Bargaining theory says that as the disagreement utility associated with the outside option rises for one party, so does its share in the bargain (Muthoo 1999). It is never wise to push too hard. Asian countries in the past have made a strategic use of globalization to develop rapidly; in the future, they will be able to adjust their policies pragmatically to do so again.

An example of the consequences of pushing hard is Asian countries' greater willingness since the financial crisis to adopt some measures that creditors dislike. Thus, the assistant governor of the Malaysian Central Bank, in defending his country's capital controls introduced in September 1998, remarked, "There is no other choice for us, as we cannot continue to wait forever, hoping for the international community to set the framework for regulating short-term capital flows and controlling currency trading" (Hussin 1999, n.p.). Given that the Asian crisis has pointed to the existence of failures in the private sector of both borrowing and lending countries, one of the preconditions for full capital account convertibility is a reformed and well-functioning international financial architecture (Reddy 2000).

Third, if there are no substantial reforms to the global financial architecture at the international level, then the likelihood of regional action rises. At the 1999 meeting in Manila of the ten ASEAN members plus Korea, China, and Japan, crucial Asian players began to hammer out a consensus (*Korea Herald*, September 29, 1999). The ASEAN finance ministers took up the theme at their meeting, pledging among other goals to examine "a possible mechanism to monitor capital flows with a view to establishing a regional monitoring system of capital flows in ASEAN," as well as regional protection measures in the event of "a sudden shift in capital flows" (ASEAN 2000, n.p.).

Although strong regional groups such as the North American Free Trade Area (NAFTA) and the European Union have emerged, there has been a relative vacuum in the Asian region—arising partly due to the weakness of Japan in the 1990s. Links between South and East Asia are weak at present. Asian nations are diverse with varying levels of development. But it is beginning to be recognized that if the three big nations come closer, the others will also. Commercial links between these three have improved in the 1990s. Japan's Sakakibara (2000), in a lecture given in India, remarked that greater Asian regional cooperation—including the South Asian Association for Regional Cooperation (SAARC), ASEAN, and the remaining East Asian countries—would be desirable, despite past border and regional conflicts. He went on to say that the strengthening of the Indo-Japanese relationship also could serve as a catalyst in inducing China to cooperate with the rest of Asia. Analysts have recognized the usefulness of regional groupings in negotiations in the World Trade Organization (Drysdale 2000) and on the environment. When there are so many issues whose solutions pose collective action problems, the possibility of cooperation rises. Asian countries are also strengthening their think tanks, which generate advice that is independent of governments yet understands the local context. These institutions have the potential of bringing countries together. The new information technology has made such activities much more feasible. The Asian Policy Forum (APF 2000) is a good example of such initiatives.

Regionalism is not incompatible with globalization. It can even raise the probability of optimal globalization by improving the balance of global power and stability (Ocampo 1999). A consensus may more easily be hammered out at the regional level and then taken to the international forums. The governor of the Bank of Japan emphasized this point when he talked of the necessity of sending a coherent message from Asia to the various international forums, but at the same time he said, "[W]e should never forget the importance of maintaining the basic philosophy of 'open regionalism' as a major underlying premise to contribute to the stability and development of the world economy" (Hayami 2000, 3). Regionalism also will improve Asia's bargaining power.

Those who feel they are not getting a fair hearing in global groups have more incentive to form their own. There is a perception that aid was arranged much faster for Mexico in 1995 than it was for Asia in 1997. Better regional groupings of Asian nations stimulated by the crisis have several advantages. They can help in the dissemination of standards and information sharing, improve bargaining position, and lead, if not to an Asian Monetary Fund, to its informal analogue. If central banks are willing to lend to each other, it greatly enhances reserves available. At the Chang Mai Asian Development Bank (ADB) meeting in March, 2000, it was agreed to do this in times of crisis. Given the speed and complexity of modern financial transactions, no country can ensure stability on its own. Regionalism will develop faster in the future, but without the NIFA it might become "closed" instead of open regionalism.

A fourth reason for optimism assumes rational actors on all sides, perhaps an heroic initial postulate. Being "hard" can lead to the breakdown of a negotiation, yet if the more powerful party in a negotiation is strategically "soft," this tactic can sometimes give huge payoffs. There is a tradition of enlightened policymaking as exemplified by the Marshall Plan in the 1950s, or more recently the Brady Plan, which resolved the 1980s debt crisis. In each case, instead of pushing the weaker party to the wall, the stronger party initially yielded a little but ended up gaining a lot. Hirschman (1998, 41–42), evaluating the negotiations that led to the Marshall Plan, showed that personalities made a big difference. American policymakers accepted disadvantages for the dollar and U.S. exports to Europe, but successfully pushed European countries into a union that served long-term American strategic and economic goals. Hirschman quotes Marjolin, one of the architects of the policy: "This way of acting unselfishly, while apparently absurd, would bear its fruits. In the course of the fifties, Europe's payments to the rest of the world could increasingly be paid without recourse to American aid. . . . Progressively, the discriminatory measures against American foreign trade would be abolished. . . . The sort of wager the Americans had made in the last ten years has therefore been won. In the course of history, it is rare to see long-term and highly uncertain benefits accrue so neatly" (Hirschman 1998, 41–42). Hirschman explicitly notes that the policy attracted unremitting hostility from parts of the U.S. Government and from the IMF because the temporary discrimination against the imports from the United States was seen as going against the principles of multilateralism. Still the policy was pushed through by a section of the American administration, and it ended up benefiting everybody. Softness in some areas could make hardness in others, such as regulations and standards, more acceptable.

If there are such personalities and processes this time also, then ten years from now we may have a thriving global economy and not one divided by "narrow [regional] walls."[15] Such policies also require a sense of community among nations, at present somewhat lacking between advanced industrial and Asian developing countries. But as more contacts, facilitated by new technology, occur, and as commercial interests rise, this fellow feeling could increase. Strategic softening in this context would mean implementing more of the reform proposals that recipient countries are keen on.

The repeated financial crises of the 1990s have already caused setbacks to reforms that creditor countries were keen on, and which were on the verge of being pushed through. Examples are full convertibility on the capital account, and a consensual agreement on norms for foreign direct investment through the G7 proposed Multilateral Agreement on Investment (MAI). Capital and countries will lose more opportunities if there is not adequate reform of the international financial architecture, the crises continue, and walls come up as a consequence.

CONCLUSIONS

Private financial institutions have been lobbying hard to prevent any measures that restrict their freedoms. Although what I have termed the "creditor view" thus far has dominated most of the influential discussions of global monetary and financial reform, this could—and should—change in the future. The rapid recurrence and severity of financial crises has the potential to hurt private finance as well as developing countries. Developing countries do have to restructure and adopt efficient financial practices, but international norms that make capital inflows safer are also necessary to ensure that the new mobility of global capital provides more funds for development, and profits for itself, and ensures a prosperous new century.

Ideas for reform fly thick and fast after each crisis, but most die without implementation. Many of the ideas being discussed now were in the air after the Mexican crisis of 1994 to 1995. If reforms are not implemented, Asian countries will be forced to go it alone, to experiment with varieties of capital controls, and improve regional cooperation. There will be some loss for capital as well, if the best feasible financial architecture is not built. Debate can keep the sense of urgency alive. We cannot predict when the next crisis will occur, but with each one, our understanding of the causes should deepen. If institutions are reformed accordingly, the probability of future crises can be lowered.

NOTES

I thank Leslie Elliott Armijo, Kovid Goyal, Raghabendra Jha, Manas Paul, and Bibhas Saha for very useful comments, and T. S. Ananthi for secretarial assistance.

1. A committee of the Reserve Bank of India (RBI 1997) argued for a phased introduction of capital account convertibility in India. The report was submitted before the Asian crisis; as of late 2001, its recommendations had not been acted upon.

2. OECD (2000) is an initiative to regulate offshore centers and eliminate tax havens by implementing a common approach to restrain harmful tax practices.

3. This paragraph summarizes news reports and analysis on the East Asian crisis appearing in the Korea Herald from 1998 to 2000. Available at www.koreaherald.co.kr.

4. See analysis and news reports in *China Daily*, a Chinese newspaper available at its website, http:/www.chinadaily.com.cn.

5. Formal definitions of the equilibrium concepts used, and of game types such as prisoner's dilemma and coordination games can be found in Binmore (1991).

6. I thank Leslie Elliott Armijo for raising this point. There is evidence that foreign institutional investors do not allocate funds efficiently, and tend to follow each other (Haley 2000; see also Fernández-Arias and Hausmann in this volume). But on the whole, foreign capital has preferred countries which have bigger markets, more stable regimes, and higher growth (World Bank 1998).

7. The Bretton Woods institutions have done a difficult job well in that there has been no repeat of the Great Depression, and many countries have had rapid development in this period. See the first and second chapters of this volume for a review of this history.

8. Asia Pacific Economic Cooperation (APEC) worked as such a club in the nineties (see Gilbert, Powell, and Vines 1999).

9. Of the $112 billion required in the East Asian crisis, bilateral sources provided $52.5 billion; the IMF itself only $34.7 billion (Jha and Saggar 2000, 597). If a region

were to run out of money in a crisis, the IMF and other multilateral sources could in turn support it.

10. ADBI (2000) quotes John Williamson as identifying three less vulnerable intermediate regimes in his keynote speech. One of them is a crawling peg with soft margins. The relative effectiveness of alternative exchange rate regimes depends on their ability to focus the market expectations that help in limiting exchange rate misalignments. The conference had representatives from thirty-four institutions worldwide.

11. See the contribution by Fernández-Arias and Hausmann, who call this "original sin." Eichengreen raised a similar point at a seminar at IGIDR in 1999.

12. Aghion, Bachetta, and Banerjee (2000) show theoretically that it might not be desirable to implement a tight money policy when investment and production are highly interest sensitive. Stiglitz (1998) collects theoretical and empirical arguments against the interest defense in a currency crisis.

13. East Asia, which has higher expected growth, opportunities, and profitability, received 44 percent of foreign direct investment and 34 percent of aggregate net resources flowing to developing countries in 1997. The comparative figures for South Asia plus Sub-Saharan Africa were only 6 percent of direct investment and 12 percent of aggregate net resource flows (World Bank 1998).

14. Similarly, the United Nations Conference on Trade and Development (UNCTAD) has long pushed the view that special trade concessions are justified for developing countries because of the secular decline in terms of trade in products exported by them.

15. Rabindranath Tagore (1913 [1994]) used the phrase "narrow domestic walls" in his poem the *Gitanjali*, verse 35.

REFERENCES

Aghion, Philippe, Philippe Bacchetta, and Abhijit Banerjee. 2000. A Simple Model of Monetary Policy and Currency Crises. *European Economic Review* 44:728–738.

Agosin, M. R., and R. Ffrench-Davis. 1999. Managing Capital Inflows in Chile. In *Global Financial Turmoil and Reform: A United Nations Perspective*, ed. Barry Herman. Tokyo: United Nations University Press.

Armijo, Leslie Elliott. 2000. Skewed Incentives to Liberalize: Trade, Production and the Capital Account. Revision of paper presented at the annual meeting of the International Studies Association, Los Angeles, California, March 15–18.

Asian Development Bank Institute (ABDI). 2000. New Exchange Rate Regimes for Emerging Economies (online). *ADBI Newsletter* (Tokyo) 2, no. 1. Available from <www.adbi.org/news/news3lhtm>.

Asian Policy Forum (APF). 2000. Policy Recommendations for Preventing Another Capital Account Crisis. Tokyo: ADBI (Forum Secretariat).

Association of Southeast Asian Nations (ASEAN). 2000. The Joint Ministerial Statement of the Fourth ASEAN Finance Ministers Meeting. Bandar Seri Begawan, Brunei Darussalam, March 15–26.

Bagehot, W. 1873. *Lombard Street: A description of the Money Market*. London: William Clowes and Sons. Quoted in Colin Mayer, The Assessment: Financial Instability, *Oxford Review of Economic Policy* 15, no. 3:6.

Binmore, Ken. 1991. *Fun and Games*. San Francisco: D. C. Heath.

Bergsten, C. Fred. 1998. How to Target Exchange Rates. *Financial Times*, November 20.

———. 2000. Reforming the International Financial Architecture (online). Testimony before the Committee on Banking and Financial Services, U.S. House of Representatives, March 23. Available from: (http://www.iie.com).

Chang, Roberto, and Andres Velasco. 1999. Liquidity Crises in Emerging Markets: Theory and Policy. *NBER Macroeconomics Annual 1999*. Cambridge, Mass.: MIT Press.

Cho, Yoon Je, and Changyong Rhee. 1999. Macroeconomic Adjustments of the East Asian Economies after the Crisis: A Comparative Study. *Seoul Journal of Economics* 12, no. 4:347–390.

Cole, David C., and Betty F. Slade. 1998. Why Has Indonesia's Financial Crisis Been so Bad? *Bulletin of Indonesian Economic Studies* 34, no. 2:61–66.

Collier, Paul, and Jan Willem Gunning. 1999. The IMF's Role in Structural Adjustment. *The Economic Journal* 109, no. 459:634–651.

Drysdale, Peter. 2000. APEC Offering Asian-Pacific Economies a Fresh Solution to Current WTO Impasse (online). Presentation delivered during APEC Forum on Shared Prosperity and Harmony, reported in *The Korea Herald*, April 1. Available from: <www.koreaherald.co.kr>.

Eichengreen, Barry. 1999. *Towards a New International Financial Architecture: A Practical Post-Asia Agenda*. Washington, D.C: Institute for International Economics.

Fernández-Arias, Eduardo, and Ricardo Hausmann. 1999. What's Wrong with International Financial Markets? Paper presented at the Tenth International Forum on Latin American Perspectives, Inter-American Development Bank and OECD Development Center, Paris, November 25–26.

Fischer, Stanley. 1999. Reforming the International Financial System. *Economic Journal* 109, no. 459:F557–F576.

Furman, Jason, and Joseph E. Stiglitz. 1999. Economic Crises: Evidence and Insights from East Asia. *Brookings Papers on Economic Activity* 2:1–114.

Gilbert, Christopher, Andrew Powell and David Vines. 1999. Positioning the World Bank. *Economic Journal* 109, no. 459:F598–F633.

Goyal, Ashima. 1997. Inflation, Exchange and Interest Rates: A Macroeconomic 'Rashomon.' In *India Development Report 1997*, ed. Kirit S. Parikh. Mumbai: Indira Gandhi Institute of Development Research and Oxford University Press.

——— 1999. The Impact of Structure and Openness on the Causal Ordering of Inflation, Exchange and Interest Rates in India. Discussion Paper no. 156. Mumbai: Indira Gandhi Institute of Development Research.

Goyal, Ashima, and Shridhar K. Dash. 1998. Arbitrage: An Explanation for Southeast Asian Crisis and Indian Immunity. *Economic and Political Weekly* (August 1):33, 31, 2098–2104.

————. 2000. Real and Financial Sector Interaction under Liberalisation in an Open Developing Economy. *Meteroeconomica* 15, no. 3:257–283.

Group of Twenty-Two (G22). 1998. Report of the Working Group on Transparency and Accountability (online). Available from: <http://www.imf.org/external/np/g22>.

Haley, Mary Ann. 2000. Emerging Market Makers: The Power of Institutional Investors. In *Financial Globalization and Democracy in Emerging Markets*, ed. Leslie Elliott Armijo. London: Palgrave/Macmillan.

Hayami, Masaru. 2000. Globalization and Regional Cooperation in Asia (online). Presentation to Asian Pacific Bankers Club, March 17, 2000. Available from: <www.boj.or.jp/en/index.htm>.

Hirschman, Albert O. 1998. *Crossing Boundaries*. New York: Zone Books.

Hussin, Awang Adek. 1999. The Recent Exchange Control Policy and Its Impact (online). MCA Seminar, Currency Stabilization: An Assessment after Six Months, Bank Negara Malaysia, Kuala Lumpur, February 4. Available from: <http://www.bnm.gov.my>.

Institute of International Finance (IIF). 1999. Data Release Practices of Emerging Market Economies: 1999 Assessment (online). Available from: <www. iif.com>.

International Monetary Fund (IMF). 1999. Involving the Private Sector in Forestalling and Resolving Financial Crises (online). Available from: <www.imf.org/external/pubs/ft/series/01/index.htm>.

————. 2000a. Statement by the Acting Managing Director to the International Monetary and Financial Committee on Progress in Reforming the IMF and Strengthening the Architecture of the International Financial System (online). April 12. Available from: <www.imf.org/external/ex/np/omd/2000/state.htm>.

————. 2000b. Press Conference on Exchange Rate Regimes in an Increasingly Integrated World Economy (online). April 14. Available from: <www.imf.org/external/np/tr/2000/TR000414.htm>.

————. 2000c. US and the IMF (online). July 28. Available from: <www.imf.org/external/ex/country/USA/index.htm>.

Jha, Raghbendra, and Mridul K. Saggar. 2000. Towards a More Rational Quota Structure: Suggestions for the Creation of a New International Financial Architecture. *Development and Change* 31:579–604.

Kim, Dae Jung. 2000. Opening Address to the APEC Forum on Shared Prosperity and Harmony at the Onset of the New Millenium, Hilton Hotel, Seoul, April 1.

Korea Herald. 1999. Joint Statement on East Asia Cooperation (online). Available from: www.koreaherald.co.kr.

Kremenyuk, Victor, Gunnar Sjostedt, and I. William Zartman. 2000. International Economic Negotiation: Research Tasks and Approaches. In *International Economic Negotiation: Models versus Reality*, ed. Victor Kremenyuk and Gunnar Sjostedt. Cheltenham, U.K.: Edward Elgar.

Marjolin, Robert. 1986. *Le Travail d'une Vie*. Paris: Robert Laffont. Quoted in Albert Hirschman, *Crossing Boundaries* (New York: Zone Books, 1998), 217–218.

Mayer, Colin. 1999. The Assessment: Financial Instability. *Oxford Review of Economic Policy* 15, no. 3:1–8.

Meltzer, A. 1998. Asian Problems and the IMF. Testimony prepared for the Joint Economic Committee, U.S. Congress, Washington, D.C., February 4.

Miller, Marcus, and Lei Zhang. 2000. Sovereign Liquidity Crises: The Strategic Case for a Payments Standstill. *Economic Journal* 110 (January):335–362.

Muthoo, Abhinay. 1999. *Bargaining Theory with Applications*. Cambridge, U.K.: Cambridge University Press.

Obstfeld, Maurice. 1996. Models of Currency Crises with Self-fulfilling Features. *European Economic Review* 40:1037–1047.

Obstfeld, Maurice, and Alan M. Taylor. 1997. The Great Depression as a Watershed: International Capital Mobility over the Long Run. NBER Working Paper no. 5690. Cambridge, Mass.: National Bureau of Economic Research.

Ocampo, José António 1999. Reforming the International Financial Architecture: Consensus and Divergence (online). Santiago, Chile: United Nations Economic Commission for Latin America and the Caribbean (ECLAC). Available from: <www.eclac.cl>.

Organization for Economic Co-operation and Development (OECD). 2000. Towards Global Tax Co-operation (online). Report to the 2000 Ministerial Council Meeting and Recommendations by the Committee on Fiscal Affairs. Available from: <www.oecd.org/daf/fa/harm_tax/Report_En.pdf>.

Parikh, Kirit S. and Ajay Shah 1999. "Second Generation Reforms." In *India Development Report 1999–2000*, ed. Kirit S. Parikh. Mumbai: IGIDR (Indira Gandhi Institute of Development Research) and Oxford University Press.

Reddy, Y. Venugopal. 2000. Bretton Woods Institutions in 2000 (online). Dr. V. S. Krishna Memorial Lecture, March 18, Reserve Bank of India, Mumbai. Available from: <www.rbi.org>.

Reserve Bank of India (RBI). 1997. Report of the Committee on Capital Account Convertibility. Mumbai: Reserve Bank of India.

Rose, Andrew. 1999. Is There a Case for an Asian Monetary Fund? *FRBSF Economic Letter* (December 17):99–37.

Sakakibara, Eisuke. 1999. Post-Crisis Financial Architecture. Speech at conference on the 2nd anniversary of the Asian Development Bank Institute, Tokyo, December 10.

———. 2000. Asia in the 21st Century: The Role of India and Japan (online). Exim Bank Commencement Day Annual Lecture, Mumbai, March 29. Available from: <www.eximbankindia.com>.

Sinha, Yashwant. 2000. Statement by the Honorable Mr. Yashwant Sinha, Finance Minister of India, to the International Monetary and Financial Committee (online). April 16. Available from: <www.imf.org/external/spring/2000/imfc/ind.htm>.

Snowden, Nicholas. 1999. The New International Financial Architecture and National Development: Uplifting or Oppressive? *Journal of International Development* 11, no. 6:837–842.

Stiglitz, Joseph E. 1998. Knowledge for Development: Economic Science, Economic Policy, and Economic Advice. In *Annual World Bank Conference on Development Economics 1998*, 9–58. Washington, D.C.: World Bank.

———. 1999. The World Bank at the Millenium. *Economic Journal* 109, no. 459:F577–F597.

Stiglitz, Joseph E., and Amar Bhattacharya. 1999. The Underpinnings of a Stable and Equitable Global Financial System. In *Annual World Bank Conference on Development Economics 1999*, 91–130. Washington, D.C.: World Bank.

Summers, Lawrence H. 2000. Statement by U.S. Treasury Secretary, Lawrence H. Summers, to the International Monetary and Financial Committee (online). April 16. Available from: <www.imf.org/external/spring/2000/imfc/usa.htm>.

Tagore, Rabindranath. [1913] 1944. *The English Writings of Rabindranath Tagore*. Vol. 1, *Poems*. Edited by Sisir Kumar Das. New Delhi: Sahitya Academi.

Tobin, James. 1998. Financial Globalization: Can National Currencies Survive? In *Annual Bank Conference on Development Economics 1998*, 9–58. Washington, D.C.: World Bank.

White, L. 1994. A Summary and Overview of the Financial Sector in Developing Countries: The Experiences of Seven Asian Countries. Asian Development Bank. Tokyo. Unpublished paper.

World Bank. 1998. *Global Development Finance 1998*. Washington, D.C.: World Bank.

IV. THE CONUNDRUM
OF MULTILATERAL REFORM

Chapter 8

JAPAN AND THE NEW FINANCIAL ORDER IN EAST ASIA: FROM COMPETITION TO COOPERATION

Henry Laurence

In the 1970s we were told there were two ways of doing things: the right way and the wrong way. In the 1980s we were told there were three ways: the right way, the wrong way, and the Japanese way. Now, we are told there are just two again: the American way and the wrong way.

—Japanese delegate to the Symposium on Building the
Financial System of the 21st Century, Kyoto, Japan, June 25, 1999

D iscussion of the international financial architecture has been an almost exclusively post 1997–1999 financial crisis phenomenon in East Asia. For most of the postwar period, Japan and the countries of East Asia maintained tight capital controls. They neither needed nor wanted much to do with the increasing levels of international capital mobility that were becoming an important part of the political economy in other regions. In many countries, including Japan, South Korea, and Indonesia, high degrees of government intervention in the economy were facilitated by relatively closed and easily controlled financial systems. High rates of domestic savings meant that Asian governments were far less reliant on foreign investment capital for growth. Their governments enjoyed the luxury of relative independence from the vagaries of speculative international capital. Exchange rates were fixed or pegged to the dollar.

The mid-1990s saw rapid liberalization of capital markets throughout Asia, much of it at the prompting of the International Monetary Fund (IMF) and the United States. But liberalization was soon followed by the shock of the "Asian Crisis" of currency and stock market crashes which began in Thailand in July 1997 and spread like wildfire to Indonesia, the Philippines, South Korea, and elsewhere. In the aftermath of the crisis, Asian countries began to reassess their attitude toward the so-called "Washington Consensus" which stresses the desirability of free-flowing capital and floating exchange rates, with international organizations including the IMF and World Bank as crisis managers. However, although there is widespread agreement among the countries of East Asia that the crisis highlighted the inadequacies of this Washington model, they have so far had only limited success in rewriting the rules.

I suggest four reasons for this lack of success. First, East Asia faces historic obstacles to cooperation that can be overcome only slowly and gradually. Second, there has been considerable disagreement among key Asian countries about possible solutions to the problem of "hot money." Third, Japan, the only country economically powerful enough to act as regional hegemon in securing cooperation, has been hamstrung by internal economic problems and by its reluctance to abandon the central tenet of its postwar foreign policy of maintaining good relations with the United States at all costs. Finally, Western interests, particularly the United States and the IMF, have been active in combating Asian challenges to the status quo. Nonetheless, the years since the crisis have seen a significant improvement in the articulation of a distinct Asian voice in debates on reform of international finance. This has been a result partly of a marked increase in Japan's willingness to lead regional initiatives to challenge the Washington model, and partly of a growing degree of regional cooperation.

In the section that follows I discuss the nature of international financial diplomacy in Asia before the 1997 crisis. Section two examines Japan's initial effort to create an Asian Monetary Fund independent of the IMF in 1997. This was the first attempt to solve the currency crisis by reform of the international financial architecture, and represents a major shift in Japan's economic diplomacy from passive to active. Japan's failure to win approval for the project in the face of opposition from the West and parts of Asia is an instructive lesson in the difficulties of achieving reform. Section three looks at the evolving Asian debate over reform in the aftermath of the crisis. Section four charts the series of initiatives undertaken by Japan and others both to make Asian voices heard in the debate on the new financial architecture, and to establish self-reliant regional arrangements to provide financial stability.

FINANCIAL POLITICS IN ASIA BEFORE THE 1997 CRISIS

The pan-Asian economy has been marked until very recently by the striking failure of any formal regional economic institutions to take root. Forums such as the Association of South East Asian Nations (ASEAN) and the Asia-Pacific Economic Community (APEC) have been little more than talking shops, seemingly unable and unwilling to take significant steps toward regional economic integration. Regional financial institutions include the Asian Development Bank (ADB), established in 1966, and an ASEAN regional currency swap arrangement established in 1977. Neither made much impact on regional economic development. The fact that the ADB was perceived as dominated by Japan—a Japanese has served as head since inception—undoubtedly hindered it as a regional institution (Tang 2000). A swap-and-repurchase arrangement among eleven Asian central banks, organized in 1995 by Hong Kong, was deemed to be so ineffective that it was not even tapped during the currency crisis two years later (Crampton 2000).

Scholars have attributed the lack of regional economic institutions in Asia to a number of factors (Katzenstein and Shiraishi 1997, especially 1–47). There is a wide variety of political and economic regimes. There are massive disparities in the size of Asian economies and their levels of development, from postindustrial Japan to developing Cambodia and bankrupt North Korea, and from vast China to tiny Laos. Diversity of political regime types is equally striking: the region hosts democratic Japan; Communist-turned "market socialist" China; authoritarian-turned-democratic Taiwan and South Korea; "soft-authoritarian" Malaysia and Singapore; colonial Hong Kong, and so on. The painful history of Japanese colonialism, and the widespread perception that Japan has still not come to terms with this past, is another obstacle to cooperation. Attempts at regional cooperation were bedeviled by long-standing hostilities among some of the major economies, most notably between China and Taiwan, and South and North Korea, and therefore among their sponsors, the United States, Japan, and China. Since the 1980s, growing prosperity has brought an increasing assertiveness by China as it attempts to wrest what it regards as its usurped regional hegemony from Japan. Finally, regional cooperation in Asia has been hindered by the fact that the United States, the greatest presence economically and military, is an outsider to the region culturally, politically, historically, and geographically.

Japan should have been the central player in Asia's financial history over the past two decades or so, but it never achieved influence over Asian capital markets anywhere near commensurate with its primacy in regional trade. Issues of international financial management first arose in the early 1980s when the United States, concerned about its rising trade deficit with Japan, pushed for the internationalization of the yen. The first such moves came in 1984 with the yen-dollar talks (Frankel 1984). However, although Japan took some tentative steps to promote greater yen use, it never established a "yen bloc" in the way that, say, the deutsche mark was to dominate Europe or the dollar dominates the Americas. There were two reasons why the yen bloc never materialized. First, Japanese policymakers were unconvinced of the desirability of liberalizing Japan's capital markets in the ways which would have been necessary to encourage the use of the yen as a reserve currency. Japanese economic policymakers within the Ministry of Finance (MOF), and the Ministry for International Trade and Industry (MITI) have historically been highly interventionist, instinctively preferring stability to liberalization. As Ronald Dore famously put it, "The Japanese, despite what their political leaders say at summit conferences about the glories of free enterprise . . . have never really caught up with Adam Smith (1998, 95)."

Second, the interests of key financial players were for a continuation of the old system of a protected financial market. The Japanese financial system was closed, cartelistic, and highly fragmented. This served the interests of both policymakers and bankers (Rosenbluth 1989). The high degree of government control was well suited to informal "administrative guidance" by the Ministry of Finance (Zysman 1983). Cartelization and protection also served the interests of major sections of the financial community. Large "City" banks and the big securities houses were key financial supporters of the ruling Liberal Democratic Party (LDP), while thousands of small credit unions, local banks, and particularly the agricultural cooperatives in the Nokyo system provided grass-roots support for LDP politicians' local support groups. These groups were therefore key political constituencies and had little interest in financial liberalization either at home or abroad. This situation began to change over the late 1980s and 1990s, as pressures to deregulate finance grew from both internal and external sources.[1] But even as Japan's domestic market liberalized, there was little pressure from the financial community to press for reform of the international marketplace.

But even if Japan had wanted to redraft the region's financial architecture, its traditional diplomatic weakness would have been a problem. Many scholars have pointed to the shortcomings of Japan's foreign economic policy apparatus, and the country's extreme reluctance to undertake diplomatic initiatives independently of the United States, on whom it relies for both military security and export markets. Kent Calder (1988) describes Japan as a "reactive state" for whom foreign economic policy is almost entirely a matter of reacting to U.S. pressure. He ascribes this partly to the structurally subordinate relation of Japan to the United States, and partly to Japan's domestic political fragmentation, which hinders strong leadership. Some analysts are more critical. Michael Blaker argues that even in situations where Japan has both a strong interest in regime building and the ability and opportunity to do so, "[t]he gap between Japan's diplomatic wind-up and its diplomatic delivery is huge" (1993, 27). He cites a political system which punishes those who stray from the prevailing consensus as a key reason for Japan's "minimalist" diplomatic strategy. An alternative view is offered by Susan Pharr (1993), who notes the difference between being low-key and being ineffective. She reinterprets Japan's "reactive" diplomatic style as being pragmatically defensive: Japan pursues its interests and secures its goals, but does so without diplomatic fanfare. Yet she notes that this economic diplomacy is possible only within the framework of a close relationship with the United States.

Until the late 1980s, therefore, there was little pressure from within Asia for regional financial cooperation. On the contrary, competition was more prevalent as regional capital markets vied for international business. Prompted by the United States at the yen-dollar talks in 1984, Japan tried to make Tokyo a more attractive center for international financial transactions, but without real conviction. In 1986, for example, the MOF established an offshore banking facility in Tokyo, but with so many tax and regulatory disadvantages that it failed to take off (Rosenbluth 1989, 84–89). Meanwhile, other Asian exchanges made deep inroads into Tokyo's international investment business. The highly competitive Singapore and Hong Kong stock exchanges both introduced financial products such as futures and derivatives based on Japanese assets (*Economist,* July 19, 1986). This provoked the ire of Japanese financial officials who wished to keep all aspects of the Japanese financial system under domestic regulatory control. In 1984, for example, the Singapore Stock Exchange introduced trading of futures contracts on Japanese Government Bonds. The head of the Tokyo Stock Exchange failed to persuade his counterpart to desist, and the Japanese grudgingly introduced similar instruments one year later (*Japan Economic Journal,* Summer 1989:6). Japanese financial diplomacy in this era consisted mostly of aggressive but usually unsuccessful attempts to persuade the foreign authorities to follow Japanese restrictions on new products (Millman 1995). With many key neighbors, including South Korea and China, operating strict capital controls, even this was a limited undertaking.

The boom in Japanese stock prices during the "Bubble Economy" period of the late 1980s altered the financial landscape somewhat. As Tokyo share prices inflated to the point where the Tokyo Stock Exchange became the most valuable stock market in history, Japanese officials became less concerned with the threat of competition from their Asian neighbors, and more concerned with their perceived status as the regional financial hegemon. Many observers, not just in Japan, saw Tokyo as the vital third leg in a twenty-hour, global financial marketplace with London and New York as the other corners (see for example, Hayes and Hubbard 1989). In 1992, hubris in Tokyo had reached the point that a leading Ministry of Finance official openly advocated an explicitly hierarchical division of labor among the Asian financial centers. Ezawa Yuichi, director general of the international finance bureau of the MOF, urged Hong Kong to concentrate on financing China and Singapore to finance ASEAN while leaving the big global investment business to Japan. His counterparts were reportedly less than impressed, and nothing came of the initiative (Rowley 1992).

The 1990s saw a marked increase in intraregion trade and investment, stimulated by a significant shift in Japanese trading and investment patterns toward Asia rather than the United States or Europe (Hatch and Yamamura 1996). But the astronomical rise in Japanese asset prices during the late 1980s proved unsustainable. Rising interest rates in 1990 brought about a stock market crash, soon followed by a collapse in land prices and a debt crisis among Japan's highly leveraged banks. The bad loan problem, and the attendant recession, diverted the attention of Japanese financial policymakers from international financial diplomacy to more pressing domestic concerns. Meanwhile, the healthier Japanese banks, facing stagnant demand for domestic loans, turned to Southeast Asia for new markets. Yet elsewhere in Asia the early and mid-1990s saw a growing sense of regional identity. Leaders such as Lee Kuan Yew of Singapore and Mahathir Mohammed of Malaysia articulated a view of Asian exceptionalism in both the political and the economic realms under the rubric of "Asian values" (Mahathir 1998).

In 1993, the electoral defeat of Japan's conservative Liberal Democratic Party after almost four decades in power led to a thawing of relations with neighbors including South Korea and China. An early manifestation of this was Japan's support for a South Korean candidate to be head of the World Trade Organization (WTO).

But the dominant voices in international financial matters during this time were those of the United States and the IMF and World Bank, all insisting on rapid capital account liberalization as a precondition for trade and assistance privileges (Kristof and WuDunn 1999a). Many Asian countries followed the Washington line in the mid-1990s, only to find themselves at the wrong end of a reversal of investor sentiment beginning in Thailand in 1997. Currency and asset prices collapsed across the region. It is beyond the scope of this paper to detail the events of the currency crisis. Instead, we focus on the first attempts to contain the crisis by means of institutional reform.

THE ASIAN MONETARY FUND

By the early summer of 1997 the Thai baht was under sustained speculative attack. In May, Thai authorities had tried to tap the ASEAN currency swap arrangement, but only Singapore and Hong Kong lent reserves to them. In any case, the miniscule funds set aside (maximum $200 million) proved useless against the enormous volume of selling (Khanthong 2000). In July, the baht was allowed to float. The authorities approached Japan directly for financial assistance. Japan had a tremendous economic interest in Thailand, stemming in part from massive foreign direct investment (FDI) undertaken by Japanese manufacturers in the mid-1980s under the shock of yen appreciation, and in part from massive Japanese bank lending in the 1990s. In 1996, Japanese banks held about half of Thailand's foreign debt of around $90 billion, and Japan accounted for 35 percent of total FDI in the country (Saito 1997). Yet, ironically, the currency basket to which the baht was pegged was comprised of an 80 percent dollar and only a 10 percent yen component. Japanese officials were concerned that since most Thai trade was not in dollars, this peg resulted in an overvalued baht which damaged Thai competitiveness. They had long urged Thailand to delink from the dollar, to no avail (Ishizuka 1997).

The Japanese considered a unilateral loan but quickly decided not to make one, under pressure from the United States. Instead, at U.S. prompting, Japan insisted that Thailand apply for help through the IMF and accept with the conditionality that such a course entailed (Kristof and WuDunn 1999b). Under prevailing quota rules, the IMF was technically allowed to pledge less than $1 billion to Thailand, but the Fund adjusted this figure up to $4 billion. Even so, this fell far short of Thailand's needs. A rescue package of $17 billion was organized, with contributions from most Southeast Asian countries in addition to China, and with Japan making the largest contribution of $4 billion. The United States declined to take part in this rescue, a sign misinterpreted by many that the United States wanted to see greater Japanese leadership in the region (Fujii 1997).

However, the assistance package did not stop the crisis in Thailand or elsewhere. Asian leaders began to debate a broader and more institutional solution. The idea of a regional fund to battle financial speculation had already been aired by Japan's chief financial bureaucrat, Vice Minister for Finance Sakakibara Eisuke. President Suharto of Indonesia had made a similar call in August, 1997, although Suharto's proposal was for an ASEAN-only scheme (Lingga 1997). By early September Thailand, the Philippines, and other Asian countries had taken up the idea, but approached Japan to act as a major contributor (*Agence France Presse,* September 18, 1997). Sakakibara and Japanese finance minister Mitsuzuka Hiroshi immediately took the initiative, stressing that they were acting at the request of the ASEAN nations. "Japan's basic position is that we would like to respond to the initiative from Asean countries. Japan does not have the intention of going ahead and then asking Asean countries to follow us," claimed the ambassador to Thailand, Ota Hiroshi (*Nation,* Bangkok, October 7, 1997). Mitsuzuka and the ASEAN finance minister agreed on the plan at a meeting just prior to the IMF/World Bank annual meeting in Hong Kong in September and unveiled it at a concurrent meeting of G7 finance ministers.

The original proposal was vague on specifics, but a central component was an approximately $100 billion standby facility to which Japan would contribute half and China, Hong Kong, Taiwan, and Singapore the other half. The goal was to provide liquidity to allow central banks in East and Southeast Asia to protect themselves against further speculative attacks on their currencies. It was not clear, under the original proposal, whether the levels of conditionality attached to these loans would be as strict as those of the IMF. One interpretation was that there might be few, if any, conditions attached to some loans since part of the rationale for the fund had been dissatisfaction with the scope, nature, and appropriateness of IMF conditionality in Asia. Mitsuzuka noted, in presenting the proposal, that many East Asian countries were deeply unhappy with the demands for U.S.-style financial market liberalization that the IMF demanded (Ishizuka 1997). The possible lack of conditionality, though, greatly disturbed the United States (Agnote 2000b). Japanese officials reacted to U.S. concerns, stressing that conditionality would be as tough with the Asian Monetary Fund (AMF) as the IMF. AMF supporters were also at pains to state publicly that the fund was envisioned as a complementary organization that would work closely with the IMF, although some Japanese officials stated that it would retain at least some autonomy (Kynge and Tett 1997).

The AMF plan received only mixed support even within Asia. Thailand, South Korea, Cambodia, and the Philippines were vocal supporters, with Philippine president Fidel Ramos promising to campaign for it personally (Mehta 1997). Malaysia's two key leaders were both supportive, although Prime Minister Mahathir Mohammed favored a much more radical approach, arguing that any AMF should be completely independent of the IMF. Deputy Prime Minister Anwar Ibrahim was more conciliatory to the IMF, referring to the plan as "the ASEAN Standby Facility" rather than using the more controversial term "Fund," which implied rivalry to the existing institutions (Fauziah 1997).

However, the proposal did not receive the support of either China or Singapore. Officially, China supported attempts at regional cooperation, with one senior official stating that "Chinese and East Asian economies are like lip and teeth" (*Nation*, Bangkok, October 7, 1997). Unofficially, the Chinese were reported to have been worried that such a fund would bolster the yen as a reserve currency, to the detriment of China's regional economic status (*Nation*, Bangkok, November 18, 1998). Prime Minister Li Peng announced that the proposal was premature in the absence of further study (*Agence France Presse*, November 18, 1997). Senior Minister Lee Kuan Yew of Singapore preferred to let the management of financial crises in Asia remain the prerogative of the IMF since this would prevent either Japan or China from gaining overwhelming regional influence (Montagon and McNulty 1998). Moreover, he noted that it was politically easier for the IMF to impose painful austerity packages on Asian countries than for friendly neighboring countries to have to do so. "Bitter medicine" is best administered by an outsider than a home doctor, he remarked (Rowley 2000).

Many Asian commentators noted problems with the plan. Some voiced doubts about whether recession-struck Japan could afford it (Fujii 1997). This objection prompted Japan to propose that contributions could take the form of pledges rather than paid in capital (Rowley 2000). Another worry was the imposition of conditional structural reform. If the AMF did not demand financial system reform for recipient countries, the moral hazard problem would be huge. On the other hand, some noted that the Japanese authorities were themselves stalling on precisely the sort of financial system liberalization that they would be demanding of other countries, which would surely undermine the legitimacy of their demands.

Predictably, the plan encountered immediate and implacable opposition from the IMF, the United States, and the rest of the G7 nations. Michel Camdessus, managing director of the IMF, was diplomatic in tone but stated that he opposed any plan set up outside the IMF (Kynge and Tett 1997). He did agree, however, that a regularly scheduled surveillance group of regional finance ministers would be a desirable improvement on the current architecture (Richardson 1997). Stanley Fischer, deputy managing director, was more blunt, describing the moral hazard problems threatened by the AMF as "a mistake" (Saito 1997). U.S. Treasury Secretary Robert Rubin was reportedly furious that he had not been consulted and was also very concerned about the possible loss of U.S. influence the AMF represented. The Clinton administration's view at this time was that the cause of the crisis was "crony capitalism" and that nothing less than IMF-administered structural reform was necessary to solve the immediate crisis and prevent recurrence. Furthermore, U.S. officials doubted that Japan—itself in the depths of a banking crisis with spiraling budget deficits—had the money to underwrite such an initiative (Kristof and WuDunn 1999b). Rubin and Deputy Secretary Lawrence Summers set about to squash the plan, later described by a U.S. staffer as "Vapor. . . . It was ill thought out"(Kristof and WuDunn 1999a).

The European countries in the G7 were also "stunned" at the AMF proposal (Segall 1997). They shared U.S. concerns that a bailout fund without conditions would create an unacceptable degree of moral hazard. Some worried that a regional fund would be more susceptible to local political influences than a global one. Moreover the Europeans were, if anything, more troubled than the United States by the threat to IMF dominance by Japan's initiative. Many European officials were reportedly worried about the implications of a shift in financial crisis management from the global and multilateral style of the IMF to a more regional and unilateral style. Officials, mindful of the possibility of a European currency crisis stemming perhaps from East Europe or the Balkans, feared that no single European country could play a hegemonic role in the way that Japan could in Asia or the United States could in the Americas (Segall 1997). Indeed, the Europeans were so hostile to the idea when it was first proposed in Hong Kong in September that Robert Rubin had to act as peacemaker, suggesting prompt further discussions by all interested parties (Rowley 1997). On the other hand, some Europeans voiced sympathy for Japan's obvious sense of frustration at the United States' domination of the IMF, and the disparity between Japan's large financial contribution to the organization and small degree of influence within it (Coyle 1997).

Faced with overwhelming hostility to the idea of any form of autonomous regional financial organization, Japan backtracked. In October Sakakibara toured Asia and the United States trying to secure more support for the proposal, but without success. Less than a month after the original announcement, Japanese officials, including Mitsuzuka and Sakakibara, were making it clear that the proposed AMF was not intended to supplant the IMF (Saito 1997). Faced with continuing opposition from the United States, the IMF, Europe, and China, the MOF withdrew the proposal in early November. At the APEC meeting of finance ministers in Manila in November, 1997, despite lingering support in some quarters and approval among some Asians for the general idea, participants rejected the plan (Sawatsawang 1997). Thus, the first AMF proposal was "stillborn," in the words of Japanese finance minister Miyazawa Kiichi (*Kyodo News Service*, May 17, 2000). But its failure did not by any means imply that Asian countries were satisfied with either the existing financial regime or the IMF's role in handling the crisis.

THE IMF DEBATE IN ASIA

Most East Asian economies soon returned to relative stability and positive or high growth rates after the series of massive IMF bailouts in late 1997 and early 1998. But as the immediate crisis passed, criticisms of capital liberalization and the role of the IMF began to grow. At the heart of the debate was the question of what had caused the crisis. Had it been, as the IMF, the Clinton administration, and many economists such as Paul Krugman argued, essentially a crisis of inadequate domestic financial regulation and other manifestations of "crony capitalism" (IMF Staff 1998; Krugman 1998)? Or was it, as Sakakibara and others argued, caused by too much short-term speculative capital – a "crisis of global capitalism" (Sakakibara 1999)?

Asian observers tended to incline strongly to the latter view (see the chapter by Goyal). Much of the criticism focused on specific policy errors by the IMF. In particular, many argued that the policies applied by the IMF—tight fiscal policy and high interest rates – had been designed during the Latin American crisis for countries with high inflation and public-sector budget deficits. They were inappropriate and counterproductive for countries suffering from liquidity problems and private-sector debt problems (Kohr 1998). IMF conditionality had thus made the crisis worse, a point the IMF eventually conceded (*Business Week*, May 29, 2000). Economist Ito Takatoshi faulted the United States for having used its influence with the IMF to insist on strict economic reforms for Asian countries while taking a much softer approach with both Russia and Brazil (Takokoro 1999).

More significantly, many Asian countries voiced broad concerns about the structural dangers of international capital mobility. The Japanese president of the Asian Development Bank, Chino Tadao, argued, "High volatility of capital flows has been devastating" (Tadao 1999). He also noted that international investment in Asia had flocked overwhelmingly to just a few Asian economies, and had thus failed to alleviate much of the poverty in a region which was home to most of the world's poor. Japanese finance minister Miyazawa claimed that "a herd mentality prevailed over otherwise rational, detailed calculation of emerging market risk" and called for "a new global infrastructure . . . to stem speculation" (Miyazawa 1999). Sakakibara echoed the phrase "herd mentality" and cast doubt on the rationality of investors by invoking Long Term Capital Management

(LTCM), the U.S. hedge fund that employed two Nobel-prize-winning economists and had crashed in 1998 (Sakakibara 1999). Deputy prime minister of
Singapore Lee Hsien Loong argued, "We cannot afford to assume that the existing system is too flawless to need improvement and that the Asian crisis was
simply an unavoidable mishap" (*Xinhua News Agency*, March 3, 2000). Philippine president Estrada noted that a key lesson of the crisis was that liberalization
redefined but did not reduce the need for government. Specifically, he called for
"a new global financial architecture" which would improve supervision and
surveillance of capital flows (*XNA*, October 21, 1999). In May 1999 the APEC
meeting ended with a call to reform the international financial architecture designed "to control the threat of volatile capital flows" (Ahmad 1999). This call
was echoed in September 1999 when the ASEAN Interparliamentary Organization (AIPO) announced the need to "strengthen and review its financial architecture" (*XNA*, September 21, 1999).

Overt criticism of the IMF was muted in some quarters because the countries in question were still in receipt of IMF assistance. By 1998 both Thailand and
South Korea had new administrations which happened to be more sympathetic to
the Washington consensus on financial reform. South Korean President Kim Dae
Jung, elected in late 1997, had long been a friend of the United States and a critic
of South Korea's traditional economic infrastructure. Thailand's incoming administration also included many Western-educated reformers (Chang 1998). Both
governments blamed the crisis on the outgoing administrations and also used the
IMF as the "bad cop" to take the political blame for unpopular structural reforms
such as bank closures or changes in employment law (Kim 1998).

But even if official government pronouncements publicly supported the
IMF, the crisis spawned anti-Americanism throughout the region. There was,
and still is, a palpable sense that the currency crisis was used by the West in
general and the United States in specific to advance a particular economic agenda
designed to serve selfish interests (J. C. Y. 1998). A common joke in Japan runs,
"First Admiral Perry . . . then Douglas MacArthur . . . now Secretary Summers,"
referring to the series of American leaders who have, not disinterestedly, imposed radical change on Japan. For unemployed South Korean workers, IMF
stood for "I'M Fired." South Korean newspapers refer to the "IMF occupation"
(Kawachi 1998) and the Chairman of the Thai Star conglomerate referred to
IMF Letters of Intent as "Letters of Surrender" (Kim 1998). According to a
western observer "The IMF's main role in Asia is increasingly seen as chief debt
collector for international banks" (Kohr 1998).

The unashamedly triumphal reaction to the crisis in much of the western
media undoubtedly helped fuel these negative feelings (Wade 1998). A fairly
typical comment can be found in *Newsweek*, a major U.S. weekly, where the
author describes the Asian crisis as "the historic confrontation taking place between
open, Western-style financial markets and Asia's closed, crony-friendly eco-

nomic systems" (Hirsh 1998). Such comments do not go unnoticed in Asia. Indeed, reporting on anti-Asian sentiments in the U.S. press has become something of a boomlet in Japan. One commentator wrote, "Edward Lincoln's 'Japan's Financial Mess' in the May/June 1998 issue of 'Foreign Affairs' is so consistently and unrelentingly critical in tone that one is almost inclined to imagine it was written with the objective of fanning anti-American sentiment in Japan" (Saeki 1998). In 1998, an entire book was published devoted to charting the anti-Japanese bias of a single newspaper, the *New York Times* (Zipangu Group 1998).

The hectoring tone of U.S. financial officials urging reform also clearly grates on their Japanese counterparts, even on those who agree in principle with the points being made. One mild but exasperated MOF bureaucrat put the point as politely as possible to a roomful of American financiers and government officials: "If you're fat, you don't mind being told to lose weight. But after the hundredth person has yelled at you to diet, you start to think more positively about the virtues of overeating." (Japanese delegate to the Symposium on Building the Financial System of the 21st Century, Kyoto, Japan, June 25, 1999).

There was, therefore, considerable political capital to be made from proposing an alternative to the U.S.-dominated financial structure. But while many East Asian leaders agreed that the present financial system was unsatisfactory, there was far less consensus on its replacement. Reform proposals for Asia lay across a wide spectrum of possibilities. At one extreme were China and Malaysia, neither of which had been IMF "patients" and both of which openly favored capital controls and, for sound domestic political reasons, wanted little to do with the IMF. Other groups favored the introduction of a common currency. At the other end of the spectrum were those who were, at least in public, content with the status quo. This group included Singapore, which had escaped the crisis, and whose leader dismissed ASEAN's efforts at regional financial cooperation as "the solidarity of fellow chicken-flu sufferers" (*Economist,* February 28, 1998). In between were IMF wards such as Thailand, South Korea, Indonesia, and the Philippines. These countries have been relatively silent on the issue of global financial reform. In part, this reluctance to speak out reflects the conflicting influences they are under. On one hand, these are the countries which have suffered most from international capital volatility and IMF reform programs. On the other hand, as noted earlier, they are understandably reluctant to criticize their doctor while undergoing treatment. Thus, while plenty of virulent criticism of the IMF and the "Washington consensus" may be found among their populations, their governments have not generally been as radical in formulating reform proposals (*Business Asia,* May 31, 1999).

The deep divisions within those countries in receipt of IMF assistance was dramatically illustrated in South Korea. Official government policy, strongly endorsed by President Kim Dae Jung, was to support the IMF. In 1998, however, South Korean prime minister Kim Jong Pil broke ranks to endorse the "Asian development model," praise Japanese leadership during the crisis, and call for an independent Asian Monetary Fund (Shin 1998). This call was prompted in part by the troubled politics of the ruling coalition, but it underscores the ambivalence toward the IMF felt throughout the region. Finally, in the middle of the spectrum and trying to find a consensus, was Japan.

Malaysia, China, and Capital Controls

The most outspoken and notorious critic of "hot money" was Malaysian prime minister Mahathir Mohammed. He has referred to currency speculators as "terrorists," the IMF as "colonialists," and hedge fund manager George Soros as a "moron," and described the so-called discipline of the financial markets thus: "If you don't behave, you get whacked on the ringgit, not on your buttocks" (Mahathir 1998).[2] In 1997, when he proposed capital controls, he was regarded as wildly radical by the western investment community. Two years later, at the Davos World Economic Forum, the same proposals were greeted warmly, although Mahathir lost considerable sympathy for his attacks on a "Jewish conspiracy" in international finance, and for his treatment of Deputy Prime Minister Anwar Ibrahim, an economist widely respected by the international financial community, who was arrested on sodomy charges and beaten in 1998 (*Time International*, February 15, 1999). But beneath the bombast and the viciousness lay sound politics. As Shiraishi Takeshi (1998) argues, Malaysia is a multiracial country, with approximately 56 percent Malays, 34 percent ethnic Chinese, and 9 percent Indians. Racial harmony is delicately balanced, and submission to indiscriminate IMF austerity measures could destroy that harmony in short order. Thus, Mahathir was prepared to go to great lengths to avoid the IMF (Shiraishi 1998).

In September 1998 Malaysia introduced selective currency controls. They were designed to keep out short-term capital flows by greatly restricting the circumstances under which portfolio capital could be withdrawn from the country. Authorities were also reportedly impressed by the success that Chile had enjoyed pursuing similar policies. According to Mahathir, "We . . . are not disloyal to the free market if we disallow currency trading. Our real trade should not be affected nor should foreign investment in productive capacities suffer" (*Xinhua News Agency*, September 2, 1999). A year later, the decision appeared to have been vindicated as high growth returned without the social upheavals experienced in South Korea or Indonesia.

Chinese influence was very clear in Malaysia's decision to impose capital controls. Malaysian officials made no secret of their admiration for China's success in simultaneously attracting trade and foreign direct investment while avoiding the excesses of hot money and the currency crisis. According to one official "Malaysia's new currency controls are based on China's model" (Wade and Veneroso, 1998b, 19).[3] Indeed, the crisis led to growing bilateral cooperation between the two countries. Relations had been cool in the past, due to a territorial dispute over the Spratley Islands. But the shared desire for autonomy from international capital markets drew the countries together. In 1999 Chinese prime minister Zhu Rongji publicly endorsed Mahathir's latest proposal for an East Asian Monetary Fund (Ng 1999).

Indeed, China has successfully used the currency crisis not only to bolster its regional leadership, but also to win favor with the United States. The collapse of neighboring currencies put great pressure on Chinese exporters, but China's determination not to devalue the renimbi earned valuable political points in the United States as well as with its crisis-stricken neighbors. President Clinton's warm praise during his 1998 visit to Beijing stands in stark contrast to the criticisms his administration regularly levels at Japan. Even massive government intervention in the Hong Kong stock market at the height of the crisis did not draw criticism from a U.S. administration supposedly committed to free-market ideology. A vital lesson China drew from the crisis was that financial market reform was essential, but that capital liberalization should be deferred until after the serious problems in the banking sector are addressed (Steinfeld 1998; *Economist*, May 2, 1998).

A Common Asian Currency

Many Japanese organizations recommended some form of fixed exchange rate system as an alternative to both the national capital controls advocated by Malaysia and China and the fully liberalized system preferred by the West. Manufacturing industries, which had undertaken extensive foreign direct investment in Southeast Asia, were particularly anxious to promote regional currency stability. For some this entailed supporting Sakakibara's plans to promote greater use of the yen in Asia. Keidanren (the Federation of Economic Organizations, Japan's largest industrial organization) favored such an approach. Some went further, advocating a common Asian currency as a long-term solution to regional financial instability. Group 21, a well-respected private-sector think tank representing primarily financial and business interests, made such a proposal in 1999. The group argued that regional overdependence on the dollar had been a large component of the financial crisis. Moreover, they pointed out that most of Japan's trade was denominated in dollars, with only 40 percent of Japanese exports and 20 percent of imports denominated in yen. For both reasons, they recommended the adoption of an "Asian euro," to be called the "yan," borrowing from the Chinese character upon which the Chinese yuan, Japanese yen, and Korean won are all derived (Group 21 1999). A similar idea had been recommended by, the Japan External Trade Organization (JETRO), the previous year (*Nikkei Weekly*,

June 22, 1998). Both proposals, however, acknowledged that Japan's persistent failure to promote the internationalization of the yen bore much of the responsibility for the dollar's primacy in the region. Although the idea of a common currency found sympathy across Asia, support was more emotional than practical: it was viewed at the level of long-term goal rather than realistic policy. President Estrada, for example, referred to a common currency as a "dream," to aspire to "if we persevere and work harder" (Teresa 1999).

JAPAN AND THE REFORM OF THE GLOBAL FINANCIAL ARCHITECTURE

Meanwhile, Japan found itself caught between Malaysia's calls for capital controls and the U.S. call for complete capital liberalization, and between Asian demands for regional leadership and U.S. and IMF insistence that Japan take a back seat. Following the failure of the first Asian Monetary Fund initiative, Japanese policymakers abandoned the attempt to challenge the Washington consensus head-on. But resentment at the way the United States had handled that episode was palpable. The *Financial Times* (November 19, 1998, 29) reported that one high-ranking member of the long dominant Liberal Democratic Party (LDP) described the American action as "outrageous impudence." The same source quoted a Ministry of Finance official observing that Japan had given fourteen times as much aid to crisis-affected Asian countries as the United States and concluding, "If the U.S. has ideas, it should put up the money too." Thus, the MOF opted for a strategy which, while it explicitly accepted capital market liberalization and the primacy of the IMF as the global financial regulator, nevertheless sought to impose Japanese views more forcefully within the existing framework.

There were two broad components to this strategy. The first was to articulate reform recommendations—to challenge the orthodoxy at the intellectual level rather than the political level, as one MOF staffer put it. Much of what the MOF recommended from 1998 to 2000 echoed mainstream Western calls for reform—the need for financial sector reform in developing countries, greater transparency, closer coordination of central banks, and so on. But there were four key differences. First, Japan favored closer attention to the sequencing of capital account liberalization, arguing that liberalization should be delayed if domestic economic and structural conditions were not ripe. Second, Japan was more forceful in demanding greater monitoring, in particular of highly leveraged institutions such as hedge funds. Third, Japan recommended the use of currency pegs under certain circumstances. The MOF certainly had misgivings about the virtues of completely floating exchange rates, but was equally unenthusiastic about the idea of a common currency, or any other form of completely fixed rates. Finance Minister Miyazawa (1999) argued that "the diversity of cultures, races, histories and developmental stages of the Asian economies" made European-style unification impossible. Miyazawa's proposal to allow a currency basket, whereby the currencies of emerging economies would be pegged to a basket of yen, dollars and euro, was an attempt to find a middle ground between free-floating and fixed rates. Finally, Japan called for greater use of regional organizations and governments to allow the IMF a better understanding of the real conditions of local economies than it had shown hitherto (Sakakibara 1999).

The second broad component of Japan's postcrisis strategy was a carefully planned campaign to put these ideas into action with a series of diplomatic and economic initiatives. The first practical manifestation came in November 1998 in the form of the "New Miyazawa Initiative." In October 1998 Finance Minister Miyazawa announced a $30 billion fund to assist crisis countries to recapitalise banks and write down bad debts. The money, to be provided entirely by Japan, was to invest in government bonds and trade finance. At the APEC meeting in Kuala Lumpur in November, he announced a joint initiative with the United States to provide $5 billion each in aid to crisis countries. Finally, at the ASEAN meeting in December, Prime Minister Obuchi Keizo announced a $5 billion aid package for infrastructure projects. He used the occasion to stress the importance of "human security" and contributed a further $4 billion to a United Nations fund for this purpose (*Straits Times,* Singapore, December 24, 1998).

The Miyazawa initiative was well received in both Asia and Washington, with President Clinton calling it an "important contribution to regional stability" (Kristof and WuDunn 1999b). This success showed that, one year after the failure of the first AMF, the terms of the debate had shifted in three critical areas. First, officials at the MOF were convinced that the fund would have helped the crisis, and were prepared to be openly critical of the IMF and the United States (Suzuki 1998). Second, there was growing academic support for the idea of an Asian financial institution among Western observers (Matthews and Weiss 1999; Wade and Veneroso 1998a). Finally, the views of the Clinton administration had softened considerably. While they stood by their decision to block the 1997 proposal, they were much more supportive of the new Japanese initiative (Janviroj 1998).

The positive reception in Washington, coupled with continuing demand among Asian countries for better safeguards against international capital, emboldened Japan to revive the AMF. In December 1998 Miyazawa raised the plan again, arguing that greater financial stability was desirable and that an Asian fund was still needed "to forestall speculative attacks" (Tett 1998). Again, this proposal was dismissed by the IMF, but it refused to go away (*Nikkei Net,* December 9, 1999). Sakakibara became an even more vocal advocate after he stood down as vice minister for finance. He took up the idea in December, 1999, reasoning that "[r]eform of the IMF does not seem to be proceeding as the Japanese government had hoped" and criticizing the "inherent instability" in the liberalized global economy (Rowley 1999). The call was echoed by, among others, the Asian Development Bank, the Thai finance minister, Mahathir Mohamed, and Joseph Estrada.[4]

These calls in turn seem to have prompted even greater assertiveness on the part of Japanese finance officials. In late 1999, Kuroda Haruhiko, Sakakibara's replacement as vice minister for finance, caused shockwaves by recommending his predecessor as head of the IMF to replace Michel Camdessus. The job had traditionally gone to a European, with the head of the World Bank being an exclusively American preserve, but the Japanese argued that it was time for a greater Asian presence in international organizations. Sakakibara at first received the support of ASEAN and South Korea (_United Press International_, November 29, 1999). This proposal caused what can best be described as conniptions in Western financial circles but was only one of a series of Asian initiatives which had pushed Asian candidates for top jobs in international organizations.[5] The first had been as early as 1994, when Japan had supported a Korean as head of the WTO (Dawkins 1994). More recently, in 1999, Japan had supported a Thai, Supachi Panitchpakdi, for the same post. On all three occasions, European and American influence had prevailed to secure the position for a Western candidate, with Sakakibara's candidacy not seriously considered in the West.

But Kuroda did not stop there. Immediately after Japan withdrew Sakakibara's candidacy, Kuroda called for a greater Asian representation at the IMF, arguing that their voting power was not commensurate with their economic contribution, especially compared with the overrepresented Europeans. "A reassessment of the quota distribution to reflect changes in the global economy is urgently needed," he argued (Jacob and Tett 2000). Shortly afterwards, the Japanese caused more outrage in the West by proposing to double the capital base of the ADB, a move which would surely increase their influence within Asia, and which drew immediate criticism from the U.S. Treasury (Tang 2000).

Perhaps the most significant pan-Asian attempt to influence the international financial architecture occurred in May 2000 at the ADB meeting in Chiang Mai, Thailand. Here, the ten ASEAN countries plus Japan, China, and South Korea agreed to greatly expand the 1977 currency swap agreement in order to provide a liquidity pool upon which countries could draw to defend their currencies from speculative attack. The proposal was far from complete. Participants agreed that the present arrangement of $20 million was clearly inadequate, but although many agreed with Sakakibara that to be effective the facility had to be increased to at least $20 billion, no firm figures for an increase were specified (Crampton 2000). Nonetheless, the "Chiang Mai initiative" represented the first time that Japan and China had agreed on a concrete financial reform plan, and one of the first instances of extensive regional cooperation. As one observer put it, "The widespread dissatisfaction with the failures of the IMF and the World Bank to adequately respond to the 1997 Asian Currency Crisis could not be more explicitly expressed" (Fungladda 2000). At the time of this writing, the future of the Asian Regional Financial Arrangement (ARFA) is unclear, but it could well prove to be, in the words of an American banker, "[b]y far the most important post-crisis initiative to come out of Asia" (Roach 2000).

CONCLUSION: FROM COMPETITION TO COOPERATION

Asian suspicion of the Washington consensus has been made abundantly clear in the years since the Asian crisis hit in 1997 (see also the chapters by Cohen and Goyal). Yet East Asian attempts to influence the reform of the international financial architecture have met with little, if any, success. On one hand, the most radical reform—Malaysia's introduction of capital controls—appears to have been successful for that country, but has not been adopted elsewhere, despite some sympathy for the position. The most serious mainstream attempt at institutional reform, the Asian Monetary Fund, has so far been blocked by the West, although the idea refuses to go away. In part, though, failure also reflects divisions within the Asian countries themselves. China and Singapore have been hostile, or at best neutral, to the AMF. The failure of the AMF, at least in its 1997 version, also lends some credence to the view of Japan as a poor player on the international stage, strutting and fretting but accomplishing nothing. Japanese policymakers have been torn between loyalty to the United States and their desire to assist their Asian neighbors, and between their official commitment to liberalization and multilateralism and their traditional preference for stability and government management of the economy. Yet the events of the past three years give evidence of a genuine shift in Japanese economic diplomacy towards proactive initiatives (Grimes 1999). The first AMF plan of 1997 was an overambitious and botched proposal from which they quickly backtracked. Yet the New Miyazawa Initiative in 1998, Sakakibara's 1999 candidacy for the IMF, and finally the Asian Regional Financial Arrangement of 2000 were all diplomatic initiatives which may yet bear real fruit.

Regionally, we have seen how agreement on the problems of the Washington consensus have run into local rivalries, such as those between China and Japan, or Singapore and Malaysia. But Western pressure to block what regional initiatives are undertaken is already proving to be counterproductive, as Asian countries see such pressure, especially from the United States, as overbearing and self-interested. Thus, we are beginning to see the first signs of real regional cooperation. In summary, East and Southeast Asian acquiescence in the Washington consensus is at best contingent, and rests on very weak regional acceptance of its central ideological foundations.[6] East Asia's ability to cooperate is not yet sufficient to challenge the status quo. But it is stronger now than at any other time in the past half century.

NOTES

1. See Vogel 1996 and Laurence 2000 for competing interpretations of the process of Japanese financial liberalization. Vogel stresses the role of domestic politics in the reform process, and argues that Japan's financial system has been "reregulated" rather than deregulated. I instead emphasize the importance of international competitive pressures in bringing about a convergence of Japanese, British, and American regulatory styles.

2. The reference is to the case of Michael Fay, an American teenager who caused an international dispute when he was caught vandalizing a car in Singapore and given the standard sentence of six hits with a rattan cane—reduced to four following a personal appeal for clemency by President Clinton.

3. This was Diam Zainuddin, Malaysian special functions minister.

4. See, for example, Agnote 2000a; *Nikkei Net*, May 30, 2000; *Japan Economic Newswire*, May 26, 2000; *Nation, Bangkok*, May 6, 2000; *Bernama*, November 28, 1999.

5. See the *Economist*, March 24, 2000. Ironically, in 1986 the same journal had actually suggested a Japanese candidate to replace Camdessus's predecessor, Jacques de Larosière.

6. Greater intra-Asian willingness to cooperate also can be understood in balance of power terms, as a rational response to the United States' "unipolar moment." See the chapter by Armijo in this volume.

REFERENCES

Agence France Presse. ASEAN to Press for Major Role for Japan in Regional Monetary Fund. September 18.
————. 1997. China Cautious on Proposed Asian Monetary Fund. November 18.
Agnote, Dario. 2000a. Asian Monetary Fund Merits Serious Consideration, ADB says. *Japan Economic Newswire*, March 17.
————. 2000b. Sakakibara Stresses Need to Create Asian Monetary Fund. *Japan Economic Newswire*, May 5.
Ahmad, Reme. 1999. APEC Vow to Push Reforms. *Business Asia*, May 31.
Bernama. 1999. Estrada Backs Mahathir's Asian Monetary Fund Proposal. November 28.
Blaker, Michael. 1993. Evaluating Japan's Diplomatic Performance. In *Japan's Foreign Policy After the Cold War: Coping with Change*, ed. Gerald L. Curtis. Armonk, N.Y.: M. E. Sharpe. *Business Week*. 2000. IMF to East Asia: Oops! May 29.
Calder, Kent. 1988. Japanese Foreign Policy Formation: Explaining the Reactive State. *World Politics* 40 (July):517–541
Chang, Noi. 1998. Tarrin went to Tokyo and Will Go Again. *Nation, Thailand*, October 23.
Coyle, Diane. 1997. Japan Backs Asian Rival to IMF. *The Independent*, September 23.

Crampton, Thomas. 2000. East Asia Unites to Fight Speculators. *International Herald Tribune,* May 8.

Dawkins, William. 1994. Japan Speaks Up for Asia Region. *Financial Times,* October 25.

Dore, Ronald. 1998. Goodwill and the Spirit of Market Capitalism. In *Inside the Japanese System,* ed. Daniel Okimoto and Thomas Rohlen. Stanford: Stanford University Press.

Economist. 1986. Chicago of the Orient. July 19.

———. 1998. The Limits of Politeness. February 28.

———. 1998. The Worst Banking System in Asia. May 2.

———. 2000. Intrigue on 19th Street. March 24.

Fauziah, Ismail. 1997. Malaysia Acts to Keep IMF Away *Business Times,* Malaysia, November 24.

Financial Times. 1998. Japan's Injured Pride. November 19.

Frankel, Jeffrey. 1984. *The Yen-Dollar Agreement: Liberalizing Japanese Financial Markets.* Washington D.C.: Institute for International Economics.

Fujii, Yoshihiro. 1997. Can Mutual Trust Work? *Nikkei Weekly,* December.

Fungladda, Doungsuda. 2000. Nations Bolster Aid Network. *Nikkei Weekly,* May 15.

Grimes, William. 1999. Japan and Globalization: From Opportunity to Constraint. *Asian Perspective,* special issue on Globalization in East Asia 23, no. 4:167–198.

Group 21. 1999. Japan Must Introduce an Asian Currency. *Japan Echo* 26, no. 3.

Hatch, Walter, and Kozo Yamamura. 1996. *Asia in Japan's Embrace.* Cambridge: Cambridge University Press.

Hayes, Samuel, and Philip Hubbard. 1989. *Investment Banking: A Tale of Three Cities.* Boston: Harvard Business School Press.

Hirsh, Michael. 1998. Now It's Epidemic. *Newsweek,* January 19.

IMF Staff. 1998. The Asian Crisis: Causes and Cures. *Finance and Development* 35, no. 2.

Ishizuka, Masahiko. 1997. Japan's Economy Must be Model for Region. *Nikkei Weekly,* September 29.

Jacob, Rahul, and Gillian Tett. 2000. IMF Voting 'Should Reflect Power of Asia. *Financial Times,* March 22.

Japan Economic Journal. 1989. Tokyo Financial Market (Special Survey), summer.

Japan Economic Newswire. 2000. Think Tank Calls for Establishment of Asian Monetary Fund. May 26.

Janviroj, Pana. 1998. U.S. Stands by Fund Decision. *Nation,* Thailand, October 15.

Katzenstein, Peter, and Takashi Shiraishi, eds. 1997. *Network Power: Japan and Asia.* Ithaca, N.Y.: Cornell University Press.

Kawachi, Takahi. 1998. A New Backlash against American Influence. *Japan Echo,* 25, no. 2.

Khanthong, Thanong. 2000. Pushing for an Asian Lender of Last Resort. *Nation,* Thailand, May 6.

Kim, Stella. 1998. Among the Believers. *Time International,* October 26.

Kohr, Martin. 1998. A Poor Grade for the IMF. *Far Eastern Economic Review.* (January 15).

Kristof, Nicholas, and Sheryl WuDunn. 1999a. How the U.S. Wooed Asia to Let Cash Flow In. *New York Times,* February 16.

————. 1999b. World's Markets: None of Them an Island. *New York Times*, February 17.

Krugman, Paul. 1998. Asia: What went wrong? (online). Available from: <http:/MIT.hedu/krugman/www/DISINTER1>.

Kynge, James, and Gillian Tett. 1997. Asian Monetary Fund Debate Hots Up. *Financial Times*, November 14.

Kyodo News Service. 2000. Malaysia Breathes Life into Asian Monetary Fund Idea. May 17.

Laurence, Henry. 2000. *Money Rules: The New Politics of Finance in Britain and Japan.* Ithaca, N.Y.: Cornell University Press.

Lingga, Vincent. 1997. IMF Wants More Debate on Planned Asian Fund. *Jakarta Post*, September 26.

Mahathir, Mohamad. 1998. Trust Me. *Far Eastern Economic Review*, July 2.

Matthews, John A., and Linda Weiss. 1999. The Case for an Asian Monetary Fund. JPRI Working Paper, no. 55, March.

Mehta, Harish. 1997. Bangkok, Manila Step Up Calls for Asian Fund. *Business Times* Singapore, October 30.

Millman, Gregory. 1995. *The Vandal's Crown: How Rebel Currency Traders Overthrew the World's Central Banks.* New York: Free Press.

Miyazawa, Kiichi. 1999. Beyond the Asian Crisis (online). Speech to APEC Finance Ministers, Malaysia, May 15. Available from <*http://www.mof.go.jp/english/if*>.

Montagon, Peter, and Sheila McNulty. 1998. Don't Expect too Much: FT Interview with Lee Kuan Yew. *Financial Times*, November 17.

Nation, Bangkok. 1997. Initiative by Japan to form Regional Fund. October 7.

————. 1998. U.S. Finally Opens Up on Contagion. November 18.

————. 2000. Pushing for an Asian Lender of Last Resort. May 6.

Ng, Eileen. 1999. Chinese Premier Zhu Supports East Asian Monetary Fund Idea. *Agence France Presse*, November 23.

Nikkei Net. 1999. IMF Says it Opposes Creation of Asian Monetary Fund. December 9.

————. 2000. Task Force Debates Setting Up Asian Monetary Fund. May 30.

Nikkei Weekly. 1998. Japan Searches for clues to Asian Crisis. June 22.

Pharr, Susan J. 1993. Japan's Defensive Foreign Policy and the Politics of Burden Sharing. In *Japan's Foreign Policy after the Cold War: Coping with Change*, ed. Gerald L. Curtis. Armonk, N.Y.: M. E. Sharpe.

Richardson, Michael. 1997. Tokyo Defers to IMF on Regional Loans. *International Herald Tribune*, November 14.

Roach, Stephen. 2000. A New Asia Emerges. *Morgan Stanley Dean Witter Global: Daily Economic Comment*, May 10.

Rosenbluth, Frances McCall. 1989. *Financial Politics in Contemporary Japan*. Ithaca, N.Y.: Cornell University Press.

Rowley, Anthony. 1992. Capitals of Capital. *Far Eastern Economic Review*, June 25.

————. 1997. Asian, U.S. Officials to Discuss AMF. *Business Times*, Singapore, October 30.

————. 1999. AMF Idea Could be Revived to Combat IMF 'Complacency.' *Business Times*, Singapore, December 11.

————. 2000. SM Lee Doubts Efficacy of an Asian Monetary Fund. *Business Times,* Singapore, June 9.

Saeki, Keishi. 1998. Beyond Anti-Americanism. *Japan Echo* 25, no. 6.

Saito, Rieko. 1997. Asian Fund Scheme to Face Tough Going. *Japan Economic Newswire,* September 25.

Sakakibara, Eisuke. 1999. Reform of the International Financial System (online). Speech at the Manila Framework Meeting, Melbourne, March 26, 1999. Available from: *<http://www.mof.go.jp/english/if/e1e070>.*

Sawatsawang, Nussara. 1997. Asia Fund Proposal Not Dead Yet. *Bangkok Post,* November 21.

Segall, Anne. 1997. Europe Balks at Asian Crisis Fund. *Daily Telegraph,* September 23.

Shin, Yong-bae. 1998. PM Kim Bucks Government's stance on Creation of Asian Monetary Fund. *Korea Herald,* December 1.

Shiraishi, Takashi. 1998. The Currency Crisis and the End of Asia's Old Politico-Economic Setup. *Japan Echo,* 25, no. 4.

Steinfeld, Edward. 1998. The Asian Financial Crisis: Beijing's Year of Reckoning. *Washington Quarterly* 21, no. 3:37–51.

Straits Times, Singapore. 1998. To Japan's Credit. December 24.

Suzuki, Miwa. 1998. U.S.-Japan initiative Facesaving Measure. *Agence France Presse,* November 17.

Tadao, Chino. 1999. Restoring Asia's Growth. *Presidents and Prime Ministers,* 8, no. 2.

Takokoro, Masayuki. 1999. Japan and the Global Financial System. *Japan Economic Update,* Spring/Summer.

Tang, Edward. 2000. Good Ideas Stymied by Power Politics. *Straits Times.* May 10.

Teresa, Maria. 1999. East Asia Launches Closer Cooperation. *Japan Economic Newswire,* November 28.

Tett, Gillian. 1998. Japan Seeks Asian Monetary Fund. *Financial Times,* December 16.

Time International. 1999. Missed Opportunity. February 15, 42.

Vogel, Steven K. 1996. *Freer Markets: More Rules.* Ithaca, N.Y.: Cornell University Press.

Wade, Robert. 1998. The Asian Crisis and Western Triumphalism. Critique, *Japan Policy Research Institute* 5, no. 5.

Wade, Robert, and Frank Veneroso. 1998a. The Gathering Support for Capital Controls. *Challenge* 41, no. 6:14.

————. 1998b. The Resources Lie Within. *Economist,* November 7.

Xinhua News Agency. 1999. Malaysia Favors Free Market Without Currency Trading. September 2.

————. 1999. Estrada Describes Financial Crisis as 'Wake-Up Call.' October 21.

————. 2000. U.S. Cannot Force Asian Nations to Change. March 3.

Y., J. C. 1998. "U.S. Using Japan bashing to Undermine 'Asian Mentality': Economic Crisis Chance to Push Market Principles." *Nikkei Weekly,* June 22.

Zipangu Group, eds. 1998. *Japan, Made in the U.S.A.* Tokyo: Zipangu Publications.

Zysman, John. 1983. *Governments, Markets and Growth.* Ithaca, Cornell University Press.

Chapter 9

REFORM WITHOUT REPRESENTATION? THE INTERNATIONAL AND TRANSNATIONAL DIALOGUE ON THE GLOBAL FINANCIAL ARCHITECTURE

Tony Porter and Duncan Wood

In this chapter we examine the question of representation in the institutions concerned with the governance of global finance. We make two main points. First, and contrary to those who focus exclusively on economic or technical questions, we argue that representation must be addressed in discussions about the global financial architecture. Second, we assess the current state of representation in the relevant institutions, focusing especially on the role of developing countries, and find that the question of representation in the governance of global finance has been taken more seriously in the past decade and progress has been made. However there remain serious problems that need to be addressed.

THE IMPORTANCE OF REPRESENTATION

A hallmark of the contemporary era is the belief that those affected by government decisions should be represented in the policy processes that produce such decisions and that limitations on representation, such as exclusion of youth from voting or of nonexperts from science-based decisions, must be justified or compensated by alternative protections.[1] Representation is thought to be important for reasons of fairness, effectiveness, and legitimacy. For tasks that are too complex for citizens to manage directly, representation facilitates collective initiatives that take all citizens' interests into account and can thereby obtain widespread support among citizens for their enactment and implementation.

Generally, however, the emphasis has been on policy processes within the nation-state. Despite growth in the twentieth century in the application of such principles of representation to the participation of states in international institu-

236

tions, the practices and principles of representation internationally remain much less developed, with debates having focused on narrow questions such as who should represent China at the United Nations.

There are four main reasons for the lack of development of principles and practices of representation at the international level. First, many believe that international institutions have little policymaking autonomy and that individual sovereign nation-states retain control of their affairs. If this is so, then questions of representation are only relevant within the nation-state. Second, international politics has traditionally been more elitist and centralized than domestic policy areas: this view was successfully legitimized by claims that the public could not be involved due to the complexity and danger of the world outside the state's borders (Walker 1993). Third, many state leaders have been ambivalent or hostile to representation internally and have not been eager to see it expanded internationally. Fourth, one of the key aspects of international interdependence is international markets. Many believe that these operate best when they are free of government intervention. As part of the private sphere they are by definition free of the dangers of government wrongdoing that representation is designed to control.

These reasons for constraints on representation internationally are becoming increasingly irrelevant today. A growing number of policy decisions are being made in international settings. Although a state technically has the right not to participate, in practice its citizens are subject to effects from outside its borders and disengagement is too costly an option to consider. Both formal international organizations and more informal multilateral bargaining processes (Ruggie 1992) can develop an autonomous momentum, and thus it is important for those affected by policies developed in such settings to be represented throughout and not simply be satisfied with their government's formal right not to ratify and implement agreements. An increasing number of governments have committed themselves to democracy internally, and the representation of citizens internationally in nongovernmental organizations has been seen as important in areas where governments' commitment to democracy is seen as inadequate. It is increasingly clear that international markets have the types of public effects and need for rules that require government involvement. Thus, in general, the need and demand for principles and practices of representation internationally has increased.[2]

In looking more specifically at global finance, these and other reasons to be concerned about representation are evident. As we shall see below, traditionally international policies concerning the governance of global finance have been developed in settings that have restricted representation to officials of the Group of Ten (G10) or other groupings of the wealthiest and most powerful states or by elevating the influence of these states in larger organizations by weighted voting or other privileges. In the last quarter of the twentieth-century, first in the debt crisis of the 1980s and again in the Mexican and East Asian crises of the 1990s, it became clear that factors in developing countries were crucially relevant to the governance of global finance. Moreover, global finance and the arrangements for governing it had serious and sometimes catastrophic effects on citizens of developing countries. Thus the need to integrate developing countries into the international policymaking process became apparent for reasons of fairness, effectiveness, and legitimacy.[3] This was even more the case in the 1990s than the 1980s. In the earlier debt crisis financial flows were generally transferred through commercial banks headquartered in the G10 and it was possible for G10 states to exercise considerable regulatory control over the worldwide operations of those banks through their home offices (Kapstein 1994). In the 1990s portfolio flows carried out through decentralized arm's-length market transactions became much more important. Thus the active and legitimized involvement of emerging market states in regulation became a key issue.

Such legitimacy concerns have become increasingly important in recent years. One of the most telling criticisms of the international financial institutions over the past two decades or so has been that the programs they apply are designed to benefit the wealthy industrialized states, and that the costs have fallen on developing countries and their societies. By including a wider range of actors in decision making, it is hoped that the legitimacy of the international financial institutions will be improved in the eyes of state and nonstate actors alike.

As will become clear in the analysis that follows, some international institutions have chosen to adopt a broader definition of representation. For them representation in the reform process refers not only to the presence of developing states at the negotiating table, but also of nongovernmental actors. The World Bank in particular has identified the inclusion of societal actors in decision making as a key ingredient in the recipe for improving the international financial system.

There are many criteria for representation that could be developed and applied internationally.[4] For instance, one could weigh the relative benefits of a one-country, one-vote criteria against a representation based on population. However governance processes differ substantially across international issue areas and, given the difficulty of building international institutions, it is important to take seriously the need for processes to take into account and build on the institutions and practices that have come before. Thus we postpone a discussion of evaluative criteria until we have discussed the state of representation in global finance.

EXAMINING THE ARRANGEMENTS FOR GOVERNING GLOBAL FINANCE

The most important institutions for governing global finance have been the International Monetary Fund, the World Bank, the G7, the Basel-based committees, the International Organization of Securities Commissions, the Group of 22, and two new institutions created in 1999, the Financial Stability Forum and the

Group of 20. In this section we examine the status of representation in each, in chronological order of their creation.

The International Monetary Fund

Created in 1944 as an institution concerned with regulating the international monetary system, the International Monetary Fund (IMF) came under intense scrutiny during and in the aftermath of the crises that hit the global financial system in the 1990s. It was widely criticised following the Asian crisis for the nature of its lending practices and the conditionality that accompanied its loans. To many, it seemed as though the institution was merely continuing to espouse the Washington consensus that saw a standard package of solutions to any given crisis situation, a consensus that naturally stemmed from U.S. and other wealthy country domination of the institution's voting structure.

It is surprising, then, that the Fund has made few efforts to increase the level of participation by developing countries in major decision making in the organization. The IMF's focus has, instead, been on developing new instruments for surveillance, crisis prevention, and crisis management. Many of these instruments focus on the issue of transparency in developing countries and much of the emphasis is on adjustment within these same countries. Yet the question of participation and representation has received short shrift in the Fund, and the domination of the Fund by the executive board, and of the executive board by the United States and its G7 partners, continues much as before. As of the year 2000, the United States, Japan, Germany, France, and Britain held 39.67 percent of all votes in the organization. With an additional significant number of votes on the executive board accounted for by groups dominated by the other G7 states, Canada and Italy, the leading industrial economies clearly hold an unassailable position in the Fund in terms of decision making. The IMF also has been slow, in comparison for instance to the World Bank, to develop links with labor unions, nongovernmental organizations (NGOs), and other participants in global civil society (O'Brien et al. 2000).

The single change that is noteworthy in the Fund with reference to representation is the transformation of the Interim Committee into the International Monetary and Financial Committee (IMFC). The Interim Committee (or, to give it its full title, the Interim Committee of the Board of Governors on the International Monetary System) was established in October 1974 in an attempt to increase representation in IMF decision making during the fallout from the collapse of the Bretton Woods system. Made up of twenty-four representatives of countries and groups of countries in the same proportions as on the executive board, the committee acted as an advisory body to the board of governors. Its value stemmed from the mix of representatives from industrialised and developing countries, and from the fact that it represented every Fund member directly or indirectly.

The creation of the IMFC in September 1999 was significant for two reasons. First, the title change brought financial issues directly under the jurisdiction of the committee, recognising that the traditional focus on monetary issues had for long been an anachronism. Second, the advisory role of the IMFC was strengthened. Instead of meeting only twice a year as the Interim Committee had done, the IMFC is now required to hold preparatory meetings before its spring and fall sessions. Such preparatory meetings, it is argued, will allow for more wide-ranging discussion of contemporary issues and for introducing developing country concerns onto the agenda of the executive board.

In this context it is worth our while to consider the reasons behind the creation of the IMFC. In 1998 the *Financial Times* reported that the Group of 22 (see below) was seen by the then managing director of the IMF, Michel Camdessus, as a challenge to the authority of the Interim Committee. Unlike the Group of 22, the Interim Committee could claim to be truly representative of the full membership of the Fund. As Jean-Jacques Viseur, Belgian finance minister stated at the time, "No other international forum can match the breadth of the interim committee's responsibilities or strength of authority." (Chote 1998, n.p.). Camdessus argued that the interim committee should be made a true decision-making council, and it is here that the idea for the IMFC was born. The disappointing eventual transition to IMFC shows how Camdessus's ideas were watered down by the real decision makers in the IMF, the governments of the dominant advanced industrial democracies (Coleman and Porter 2000).[5]

Because of the relatively insignificant change in the IMF's decision-making process, developing countries remain marginalized in this central institution. However, it also can be argued that the Fund itself has become somewhat marginalized during the process of international financial reform. The creation of groups such as the G22, G33, and then G20 has provided alternative forums to the Fund for major financial and monetary decision making. Though these new groupings offer some level of representation for developing countries, they circumvent established decision-making processes, reduce the access of most developing countries (particularly smaller states) to the business of planning international financial reform and, perhaps, present a challenge to the authority of the IMF.

A final point that should be made is that continuing pressure has been applied by NGOs to the IMF and its sister institution, the World Bank (see below). Of note recently have been the efforts by Jubilee 2000 Coalition, an international nongovernmental organization committed to debt relief and elimination, to obtain the commitment of the world's major creditor governments to cancel the debt of the highly indebted poorest states. Though some progress has been made through the G7, Jubilee 2000 continues to press the IMF on the same issue. In September of 2000, during the annual meetings of the IMF and World Bank in Prague, the organization believed that it was finally being heard as Canadian finance minister Paul Martin seemed to publicly support their cause (Jubilee 2000 Coalition 2000). However, despite Martin's show of support for debt relief, no new initiatives emerged from the Prague meeting and other finance ministers expressed little support to reinforce Martin's enthusiasm. It would appear that NGOs continue to exert little influence over the development of Fund policy.

The World Bank

The differences in organizational culture between the Fund and its sister institution, the World Bank, have never been clearer than in their responses to the challenges of the financial crises of the mid and late 1990s. Confronted with the ongoing crisis in the international financial system, the Bank saw the question of participation in decision making as key. However, whereas the IMF made an attempt to broaden its supervisory mandate, and to increase the importance of the Interim Committee by changing its name and status, the Bank came up with an entirely different approach. In 1997 the World Bank began to move towards a development decision-making approach that stressed partnerships and inclusion. Rather than focusing on bringing developing country governments into decision making at the systemic level, the World Bank focused on decision making at the national and local levels, and on bringing in a wide range of social actors into the process. In January of 1997 the Bank published a task group report titled *Social Development and Results on the Ground* which commented on the "widespread recognition in the Task Group that . . . the Bank can have little impact acting on its own and simply adding to its agenda and capacity. In the future, it will need to put far more emphasis on partnerships. . . ." (World Bank 1997). The report put a great deal of emphasis on the role that civil society and NGOs play in development, and foreshadowed the eventual creation of a Civil Society Fund to assist in the creation of partnerships.[6]

The origins of World Bank president James Wolfensohn's newfound concern with civil society and NGOs seem to trace back to a rather singular event in 1994. At the annual meeting of the Bank in Madrid that year environmental protestors scaled the roof of the auditorium and proceeded to drop dollar bills inscribed with environmental slogans onto the delegates below. In an interview with the authors, Rossana Fuentes-Berain of the Mexican Newspaper *Reforma* noted that Wolfensohn was so shocked by the tenacity of the demonstrators that he committed to finding some way of harnessing and controlling this political energy (March 13, 2001). Subsequently, the Bank has tried to incorporate civil society actors into Bank processes.

Later in 1997, at the annual meetings of the Bretton Woods institutions in Hong Kong, Wolfensohn outlined what he termed the "Challenge of Inclusion," in which he called for greater involvement from, and dialogue with, a range of actors holding a stake in international development issues. Encouraging higher levels of participation in the Bank's programs from governments, aid agencies, and multilateral financial institutions can be seen as a move that fit closely with the broader systemic reforms calling for greater cooperation and coordination between the international financial institutions. However, Wolfensohn's plan went further to include a call for increased dialogue with nongovernmental actors and civil society.

The ideas contained in the the the "Challenge of Inclusion" were put into practice in 1998 in a series of consultations that took place throughout the year with governments, bilateral donor agencies, multilateral financial institutions, the private sector, academia, NGOs, and other civil society organizations across the Americas, Asia, Africa, and Europe. This consultation process was unprecedented in the history of the Bretton Woods institutions, and helped to confirm a fundamental change in the culture of the Bank that had been building since the early 1990s.[7] The findings of the consultation process were published in a Bank paper titled "Partnership for Development: From Vision to Action," which accepted the need for "broadening the dialogue between the country and its donors" on issues of aid and beyond (World Bank 1998a, 2). Among the major findings of the consultations was the widespread feeling of a need for greater interaction between the Bank and civil society, as well as a certain degree of skepticism as to the Bank's commitment to such interaction.

May 1998 saw the publication of the World Bank's *Social Development Update: Making Development More Inclusive and Effective.* NGOs and civil society again received a large amount of attention and the report noted that the levels of NGO inclusion in Bank projects had risen dramatically to 47 percent of all projects during 1997. More importantly, NGOs were included in the design stage of 60 percent of these projects, an increase from 22 percent in 1990. Opinion and information sharing with civil society was seen by the report as fundamental, and it noted a distinct improvement thanks to "a systematic dialogue with knowledgeable and influential specialists in the field from NGOs, academia, and other civil society organizations on a wide range of issues" (World Bank 1998b, 9). This improved dialogue, the report claimed, had led to a modification of Bank practices and a reduction in NGO criticism of the organization.

The issue of inclusion was reiterated and given greater depth later that year when Wolfensohn gave a speech to the annual meeting titled "The Other Crisis." The main thrust of this speech was to push for a more integrated approach to development and to stress the need for partnerships in development between donors, governments, and civil society. Following Wolfensohn's speech, the World Bank articulated a new approach to its development activities, known as the "Comprehensive Development Framework." The Bank has gone so far in its new approach as to publish a text titled *The World Bank Participation Sourcebook,* which, according to Wolfensohn, "presents the new direction the World Bank is taking in its support of participation, by recognizing that there is a diversity of stakeholders for every activity we undertake, and that those people affected by development interventions must be included in the decision-making process" (World Bank 1999, 1).

All these developments do not mean that the traditional control exercised by the wealthy countries has disappeared, as evident in the high-profile resignation in 2000 of the World Bank's chief economist, Ravi Kanbur, reportedly in protest over the refusal of the United States to accept his draft of the influential *World Development Report* due to its emphasis on empowerment (Atkinson 2000).

At the same time, it is important not to underestimate the significance of the sea change in World Bank decision-making philosophy that has been discussed above. Unlike the Fund and the other organizations examined in this chapter, the Bank has attempted to put a more human face on its lending activities, and to broaden participation beyond the state. Clearly, the most important decisions regarding policy are still taken by the Bank's major shareholders, but by recognising that *stakeholders* also have much to offer, the institution has moved far beyond its 19th Street sister. Indeed, the Bank itself recognises that it may have moved too fast in this direction, though not with reference to the IMF. The *Social Development Update* of 1998, mentioned above, noted that "concerns have been expressed by some Borrowers that the Bank may be running ahead of its partner governments in its dialogue with NGOs on policy issues and certain areas of strategy formation" (World Bank 1998b, 10). Most developing countries still have relatively underdeveloped civil societies, and nongovernmental organizations there do not have the access to government that we see increasingly in the industrialised nations. The Bank's enthusiasm for partnerships with NGOs in the developing world, while in theory a positive development, risks a backlash from governments if it is not handled diplomatically and in a politically sensitive manner.

The Group of Seven

During the 1990s it became apparent that the Group of Seven (G7)[8] was the most important locus of authority in the governance of global finance. Created during the 1970s in the wake of the collapse of the Bretton Woods monetary regime, the G7 has evolved from its origins as an informal summit of leaders discussing economic policy to become a more substantial location for developing international financial initiatives, with regular meetings of G7 finance ministers and central bankers and ongoing contacts between G7 finance officials in preparation for meetings. At the Halifax summit of 1995, in the aftermath of the 1994 peso crisis, the G7's involvement in reform of global financial governance was stepped up, and since then the G7 finance ministers have prepared regular progress reports on international financial reforms which are reviewed by the G7 leaders at their summits. The G7 leaders, by announcing priority initiatives in their communiqués, effectively issue directives to the IMF and other international financial institutions. The G7's importance is especially evident in the fact that it was the institution that, in 1999, launched the two new institutions that constituted the most significant institutional response to the financial crises of the 1990s—the Financial Stability Forum and the Group of Twenty, discussed below.

Unfortunately having the G7 as the preeminent authoritative body in the governance of global finance is highly problematic with regard to representation. There are many positive features of the G7. Its collegial style promotes pragmatic cooperation rather than rhetorical negotiation. Its small size, flexibility, and large joint political and economic capacity facilitate the exercise of leadership. The key and regular role played by high-level political leaders also contributes to its ability to get things done and makes it more sensitive to concerns of G7 citizens than might be the case with a process more dominated by bureaucrats. However, the G7, as starkly signalled by its name, cannot claim to represent anyone outside the seven wealthy countries that constitute it.

The deficiencies of the G7 with regard to representation have long been a source of criticism of the institution, but as it began to play a leading role in addressing the financial crises of the 1990s the lack of representation of developing country member states became even more problematic. Defenders of the G7 could argue that the G7 has no formal power, and that the policies to which it agrees are implemented through national governments or formal international organizations like the IMF where representation is more developed than in the G7. However, in practice the G7 has become sufficiently effective that it can devise quite detailed policy initiatives with global implications, such as the creation of the Financial Stability Forum, and muster the momentum to have these initiatives implemented. Recognition of the representational deficiencies of this process led the G7 to create the G20, as we shall see below.

The G7's twin organization, the G8, explicitly recognized the challenge of expanding the circle of consultation around the center of global economic decision-making in its 2000 summit communiqué. In part responding to criticism of the exclusive nature of G7 and G8 summitry, and in part as a reflection of the concerns of G8 member states such as Canada, the communique proposed, "In a world of ever-intensifying globalisation, whose challenges are becoming increasingly complex, the G8 must reach out. We must engage in a new partnership with non-G8 countries, particularly developing countries, international organisations and civil society, including the private sector and non-governmental organisations (NGOs). This partnership will bring the opportunities of the new century within reach of all" (G8 2000, Preamble, n.p.) It remains to be seen, however, how such inclusive principles will be applied in practice.

The Basel-Based Committees

The Bank for International Settlements (BIS), created in 1930 to deal with German reparation payments, has hosted a number of the most important groupings involved in the governance of global finance, as well as contributing itself to collaboration among central bankers on monetary and other matters. While the BIS has provided secretariats for these groupings, the most important of them have been mandated by the Group of Ten, which was constituted in 1962 to manage the General Arrangements to Borrow at the IMF.[9] As the BIS-based committees began playing a more prominent role, the United States overcame its scepticism about the organization and in 1994 decided to take up its seat on the BIS board of directors. Since then the membership of the board and the G10 have been identical. The G10-mandated, BIS-based Eurocurrency Standing Committee, formally set up in 1971 and renamed the Committee on the Global Financial System in 1999, was the first international grouping to be concerned with the growth of the Euromarkets. Since then the Basel Committee on Banking Supervision (BCBS), the Committee on Payments and Settlement Systems, and the International Association of Insurance Supervisors have been set up and are playing the leading roles in developing standards and practices in their areas of expertise.

The BCBS, set up in 1975, is the most prominent of these groupings and has gone the furthest in devising ways to involve officials from outside the G10. The three biggest accomplishments of the BCBS have been (1) establishing standards for bank capital adequacy; (2) agreeing on mechanisms, such as consolidated regulation through home offices of banks' worldwide operations, to try to ensure that lack of cooperation among regulators does not leave gaps or downward pressures on regulatory standards; and (3) compiling best practices for bank supervisors, notably in the 1997 *Basle Core Principles for Effective Banking Supervision* and the *Compendium* (BCBS 1997a). Beginning in 1980 with the Offshore Group, the BCBS has fostered linkages with groups of non-G10 bank supervisors in order to promote the dissemination of its standards and practices. By 1998 there were ten of these groupings, covering Latin America and the Caribbean, the Gulf States, Central and Eastern Europe, the Arab countries, East and Southern Africa, Southeast Asia, New Zealand and Australia, Transcaucasia, and Central Asia.[10]

The relationship between the BCBS and these regional committees varies. Some have been set up with the encouragement of the BCBS and do not have much capacity to take independent initiatives. Others, such as the Executives' Meeting of East Asia and Pacific Central Banks (EMEAP) Working Group on Banking Supervision are quite autonomous. The EMEAP Working Group, for instance, is part of a larger EMEAP project in which central bankers from the region cooperate and share lessons on a range of central banking issues. While the views expressed on the EMEAP website are compatible with those associated with the BCBS, there is little mention of the latter organization.[11]

During the 1990s the BCBS also began to involve emerging market regulators in its work in Basel. Its 1997 *Basel Core Principles* were developed by a group that included representatives from seven developing countries, and nine other emerging market countries "were also closely associated with its work" (BCBS 1997b, n.p.). The *Principles* were designed for dissemination in the developing world. Since then the Core Principles Liaison Group has continued to function and serve as a way to link the Basel Committee with emerging market regulators.

The other BIS-based committees have sought to involve emerging market regulators in working groups on an ad hoc basis and the BIS itself has taken steps to expand its membership, admitting an additional nine central banks in 1996 and 1997 and opening a Hong Kong office—the first outside Basel.

Despite these efforts to expand representation in the policy process associated with the Basel-based committees, it is clear that control over the process remains firmly in the hands of the G10 countries. The creation of regional committees provides a mechanism for the specific interests of non-G10 countries to be expressed but the participation of these countries in the development of standards is at the discretion of the G10 countries. In essence, the G10 countries have permitted non-G10 countries to participate in areas in which the latter are the major implementers or recipients of effects but not in more general global matters.

The International Organization of Securities Commissions

The International Organization of Securities Commissions (IOSCO) began as an inter-American organization in 1974, and thus from the beginning it had representatives from developing countries. As of 1999 it had 158 members, including 94 official securities commissions as well as private exchanges and associations and intergovernmental organizations. IOSCO has developed standards for securities regulation such as the 1998 "Objectives and Principles of Securities Regulation" and has encouraged compliance with its agreements through its regular "Report on the Implementation of IOSCO Resolutions" which monitors the performance of members (IOSCO 1998a, 1998b). Thus it is doing significant work, but is much more universal than the G10 committees in Basel.[12]

Representation has been enhanced since IOSCO deliberately institutionalized the participation of developing countries, in part through its regional committees but more importantly through the establishment in 1989 of its Development Committee, now called the Emerging Markets Committee (EMC). In its early years the Development Committee lacked focus and primarily promoted the growth of securities markets in developing countries as well as offering regulators from those countries an opportunity to talk about issues of common concern. More recently the tasks of the EMC have become more important, as evidenced in the closer working relations it has established with other bodies. For instance, in the mid-1990s the structure of the EMC was aligned more closely with the IOSCO's powerful Technical Committee in order to facilitate joint projects. In 1999 the EMC was invited to send a representative to act as an observer at the International Accounting Standards Committee on a committee working on accounting standards in emerging markets. It is also represented by its chair at the meetings of the Financial Stability Forum.

In 1999 the EMC held its own reunion in New Delhi, in addition to its gathering at the IOSCO annual meeting. The meeting endorsed the EMC report "Causes, Effects and Regulatory Implications of Financial and Economic Turbulence in Emerging Markets"(IOSCO 1999). The report differs from some interpretations of the crisis by stressing that the problem does not just lie with the quality of markets, regulations, and standards in developing countries but also with "role of investor behaviour within an environment of liberalised international financial markets in triggering and exacerbating the crisis" (8). It also criticizes the "one-size-fits-all" approach to crisis management and notes that "all parties must have an equal opportunity to participate in and present their views on these efforts" (IOSCO 1999, 66).

The Group of Twenty-Two

A prominent institutional response to the East Asian crisis of 1997 was the creation by the United States of an ad hoc Group of 22 process that ran from April to October 1998. Participants included fourteen emerging market countries, Australia, and the G7. Three working groups were formed, one on transparency and accountability, one on strengthening financial systems, and one on international financial crises, each jointly chaired by one developed and one emerging market country representative. In October each of the three groups issued a lengthy report on its area.

The creation of the G22 showed a recognition by the United States and the G7 that there was a need to incorporate emerging markets more directly into the policy process for reforming the international financial architecture. The G22 was more flexible than the IMF's Interim Committee (IC) both in terms of style (with the IC involving more formal presentations not well suited to developing a consensus on a complex report) and membership (with the countries most involved in the 1990s crises not necessarily at the table). The G22, it could therefore be argued, was effective in bringing together representatives that really mattered.

However the G22 was open to criticism of the arbitrary way in which its membership was chosen; the exclusion of certain actors from it, and its limited and one-off mandate. Other countries demanded to participate and eventually a G33, which brought in more European and other countries, was recognized.

Nevertheless there was much sentiment among policymakers that something more permanent and with a better claim to be representative was needed and this led to the creation of the G20 and the demise of the G22.

The Financial Stability Forum

At the beginning of 1999, after a brief consultative process and report by former Bundesbank president Hans Tietmeyer, the G7 launched a new international institution, the Financial Stability Forum (FSF). The FSF brought together twenty one representatives from G7 countries and fourteen representatives from the Basle-based and Bretton Woods institutions. Its goal was to facilitate the exchange of information and assessments among institutions and thereby to promote systemic stability. It has a small secretariat at the BIS and its first chair was BIS general manager Andrew Crockett.[13]

While the FSF was an important advance in integrating various policy areas such as banking, securities, insurance, official lending, and monetary and exchange rate matters, it was glaringly unrepresentative, with a national membership even more exclusive than the G10 committees in Basel. In June 1999 the G7 sought to address this deficiency by announcing that they were "broadening representation" by expanding the membership of the FSF to include Australia, Hong Kong SAR, the Netherlands, and Singapore and by indicating that non-G7 countries could participate in FSF working groups. However, these four additional members were hardly representative of the non-G7 world and, as with the Basel-based committees, the participation of others in working groups was at the discretion of the FSF members and therefore not a reliable form of representation. Indeed after the initial three working groups issued their reports in early 2000 it was not clear whether or how the non-FSF members would continue to participate in FSF work.

To its credit, the questions that the FSF chose to address in its working groups were controversial and important, including offshore financial centers, capital flows, and highly leveraged institutions (hedge funds). As well, the countries invited into the working groups were varied and not all ones that would be inclined to agree with G7 perspectives. For instance, the Capital Flows Working Group included, other than the G7, representatives from Malaysia, Brazil, Chile, and South Africa, as well as the World Bank, IMF, and BIS. Other developing countries included in the Working Groups or the Ad Hoc Task Force on Implementation of Standards were Thailand, Singapore, Hong Kong, India, and Mexico. Citizens of Sweden, Switzerland, and the Netherlands were also included in one or more groupings, at times as representatives of the BCBS. Thus representation was wider than one might initially have expected.

Despite these positive elements of inclusiveness, the FSF overall remains very unrepresentative and far short of what one would expect of the institution that is supposed to play a leading role in fostering global systemic stability.

The Group of Twenty

In September 1999, close on the heels of the FSF's creation, came the launching by the G7 of another international institution, the G20. First announced at the Cologne G7 Summit in June 1999, the G20 at its September creation had members from the G7, Argentina, Australia, Brazil, China, France, India, Mexico, Russia, Saudi Arabia, South Africa, South Korea, Turkey, the European Union, the IMF, and the World Bank. Indonesia was added shortly after the situation in East Timor had been sufficiently resolved.[17] Each member state is represented by its finance minister and central bank governor. The first chair was Paul Martin, Canada's finance minister. It had no permanent secretariat and was seen by its chair as a "virtual" institution—an institution "whose existence is not a bricks-and-mortar edifice staffed by international bureaucrats, but networks of national capitals" (Martin 2000a, n.p.).

Martin has noted that "best practices will not be implemented and codes will not be observed, if the countries that must adopt them have not had a 'voice' in their development. That is why the G20 is so important—because it brings key emerging market countries to the table with the G7" (Martin 2000a, n.p.). The fact that its member states represent 87 percent of world gross domestic product and 65 percent of world population is prominently noted in information provided about it (Martin 2000b). Moreover Martin has expressed a commitment to expanding consultations with nongovernmental actors: "I simply cannot emphasize enough the importance of the dialogue with civil society. It's certainly one we intend to pursue" (Martin 2000 b, n.p.).

There are a number of features of the G20 that suggest that the commitment of its G7 founders to meaningful involvement of non-G7 countries is genuine. First, in contrast to the FSF, it has permanently involved very large countries that no one could consider to be pawns of the United States or its G7 partners, including Russia, China, and India. Second, its process is designed to encourage the relatively equal and meaningful participation of its members, with only two representatives from each country permitted in the room at official meetings and with the use of e-mail and websites for communication as these are less constricting than the traditional reliance of the G7 on faxes. Third, Martin's selection is significant both because of his consistent support for increasing inclusiveness in the governance of global finance (as in Martin 1999) and because of Canada's record of support for multilateralism.

There are, however, some more ambiguous features of the G20 that could be seen as deficiencies with regard to representation. First, unlike the G7 there are no provisions for a G20 summit. Nor are there plans to fold the G7 into the G20. This signals the secondary and restricted role of the G20 as compared to the G7. Second, despite all the advantages for encouraging meaningful discussion of the G20's format, there are some costs in terms of representation as traditionally conceived. The emphasis on collegiality and practical tasks draws all participants into a joint process in which the possibility of citizens holding representatives accountable or groups of weaker countries allying in their citizens' common interest is reduced.[15] Third, despite the importance of G20 members there were, inevitably, many countries left out. Martin has indicated that the World Bank's inclusion is seen as a way to offset this but many would doubt that this is sufficient. Fourth, the G20's priority areas in its first year—stock taking on progress in reducing financial vulnerability, assessment of compliance with international codes and standards, reports on those codes and stability assessments, and an examination of differing exchange rate regimes—are all important but not as wide ranging as one might expect given the stature of its members. The major outcome of its first meeting, a commitment of its members to more intensive IMF examination of their national standards and practices, would not challenge the belief of those who fear that the G20 will just be a mechanism to foster support for existing policies favored by the G7.

Overall the G20 is an important advance in representativeness in the governance of global finance. Now that the commitment has been made to enter into high-level discussions with key developing countries it will be impossible to turn the clock back. Indeed the G20 can be seen as a recognition that the growing integration of emerging markets that was cited for other organizations above needed to be put on a more permanent footing. The G20, modelled on the G7, offers the possibility of offsetting the highly problematic exclusiveness of the G7's domination of policy formulation. Nevertheless it will take time before it is possible to fully assess the G20's significance. A different chair might push less actively for the G20 to play a prominent role. There are some countries, such as France, which are determined that the G20 not displace the IMFC which, formally, has a greater claim to be representative, and ultimately an alternative solution to the problem of representation may be devised. Despite these caveats, non-G7 actors are much better able to influence the policy process than they were before the G20's creation.

EVALUATING REPRESENTATION IN THE REFORM PROCESS

From the preceding description of changes in the makeup of international financial institutions it is clear that improving representation has been one of the values underlying the progressive reform of the international financial architecture. We must question, however, the nature and extent of such improvements in representation that have been witnessed over the past decade.

The criteria for such evaluation must be chosen with care. First we must ask how representation is structured. Is it universal, highly inclusive, or exclusive? Are representatives supposed to be delegates, that is, directly representing the desires and preferences of other actors, or are representatives included to inject some sense of the interests and challenges facing actors outside the policy process? Second, we should ask the goals of improved representation. Is it designed to appease those who are dissatisfied with the status quo? Is it designed to improve legitimacy? Or is it designed to improve effectiveness in the creation of new policy responses?

The first set of questions challenges us to think both quantitatively and qualitatively about the reform process thus far. Clearly representation in new committees has not been universal and the key committees in established institutions such as the IMF and World Bank remain quite exclusive. Select developing countries have been chosen for membership and participation in such groups as the G20 and Financial Stability Forum, and the criteria for their selection must be challenged. In the FSF, new member states were chosen for their status as "significant financial centers," but this excluded such major developing country financial markets as Mexico and Brazil, markets that clearly have a central role to play in crisis contagion. In the G20 developing states appear to have been chosen because of the size of their economies, a distinct improvement on the FSF but still excluding the vast majority of developing states, and in particular those that have small, weak, or highly impoverished economies.

The technical groupings that exist within the BIS and IOSCO respectively, though nonuniversal, do appear to have adopted principles of inclusivity. The BCBS in particular has taken concrete steps to coordinate activities with regional groupings of bank supervisors, whilst IOSCO has enhanced the participation of developing country supervisory bodies through the Emerging Markets Committee.

The IMFC is one committee that does seem to offer a sense of universality through delegative representation. The twenty-four members of the committee represent, directly or indirectly, the entire membership of the IMF. As a committee, the views of all members of the Fund stand a chance of being heard. The problem with this committee, however, is that it holds only an advisory capacity and real decision making power continues to rest with the executive board. While the executive board can also claim to represent all IMF members directly and indirectly through its twenty-four members, due to the principle of weighted voting the major shareholders in the Fund dominate.

The changes that have already taken place in the World Bank and have been hinted at by Paul Martin in the G20 regarding the participation of civil society in decision making and planning offer us a very different image of representation. In this image the concept of stakeholders replaces shareholders in development debates and policymaking. While this is laudable, it does appear to have come at the expense of greater inclusion of developing countries and their citizens in the Banks' inner circles, and may even pose problems for the Banks' relations with governments who do not share this very Western conceptualisation of decision making.

The answer to the second question is more difficult to discover as it is always problematical to try to ascertain intentions. However, the broadening of representation across the key committees and groupings in international finance has been aimed, it would seem, at both increasing legitimacy and improving effectiveness. In the case of the BIS-based committees, developing country participation was encouraged in the early 1990s as a way to improve information flows across not only G10 states but also developing country banking authorities in recognition of the highly interdependent nature of global banking. The G22, FSF, and G20, on the other hand, reflected the desire of the leading industrialized nations to legitimize their policy responses to the ongoing crisis in the international financial system. The World Bank is a good example of the combination of both aspirations—by including civil society it hoped to bring NGOs within the fold of the Bank and improve the effectiveness of Bank programs in the field. Such co-opting of NGOs appears to have reduced criticism of the Bank; whether or not effectiveness of Bank programs has improved will become evident in the years to come.

A key element in deciding the extent of representation in the reform process seems to have been flexibility. Clearly it would have been unworkable to attempt an architectural reform in the international financial system with the direct advice and consent of all member states in the Bretton Woods institutions. The G20 and its predecessors, though vulnerable to criticism of the arbitrary nature of their membership, were at least successful in coming up with policy recommendations in a relatively short time.

The major downfall of the attempts to broaden representation thus far remains the question of who is left out. The developing countries that have been included in the reform dialogue are the biggest, most dynamic, and most advanced of the developing world. They are the "emerging" markets. Here, it seems, the guiding principle for who is included is still a consideration of power and wealth. What about those states that remain mired in conditions of underdevelopment? Is the process of broadening representation based on a belief that all developing countries are basically the same, a surely erroneous assumption?

We note as well that there is a tendency in the reform process for expanded representation of less developed countries (LDCs) to focus on matters that are of specific concern to them while leaving the larger questions about the nature of the international financial architecture to processes controlled by the wealthy countries. The fundamental changes in the global financial architecture that have occurred over the past two decades—and not just those changes specific to developing countries—have had serious consequences for developing countries and thus they should be represented in the policy processes in which these fundamental changes are considered and initiated. It is not enough just to be *consulted* by the wealthy countries on these questions.

The following changes are illustrative of the ways in which these representational deficiencies could be addressed. First, the G7 and G20 could work to bring the latter up to the level of prominence of the former, initiating a G20 summit and altering the G20 agenda to correspond more closely to the types of problems on the G7 agendas. Second, the G7 representation in the Financial Stability Forum should be scaled down from three per government in order to permit meaningful permanent representation from developing countries. Third, the IMF and World Bank could be made more representative by, for instance, altering the methods of determining voting weights to reflect the greater importance of LDC stakeholders in the organizations and altering recruitment procedures to make the staff more representative (Woods 2000). While maintaining control over the use of the funds they supply may be a rationale for certain countries enjoying disproportionate representation in the IMF and World Bank, this rationale cannot logically be extended to new processes in these institutions that are concerned with architectural questions rather than lending questions. Fourth, an effort should be made to enhance the autonomy and capacity of regional supervisory organizations and to provide them more meaningful permanent representation on Basel-based committees to ensure that the weaker among them are able to intervene effectively in general policy discussions.

Powerful actors are often reluctant to share space in policy processes with weaker actors but in the issue area of global finance powerful states are unlikely to get the stability and the rules they desire without expanding the participation of developing countries in the system of governance, at least at the level of consultation. The benefits of such improved representation are likely to go beyond more effective LDC compliance and implementation that many officials stress: the types of policies and rules developed may be improved with more input from developing countries. It is not yet clear whether there is a "Southern consensus" that could be counterposed to the "Washington consensus" despite the efforts of some scholars to identify one (Gore 2000). Nevertheless, many policy ideas that have, in the wake of the 1990s crises, become the new conventional wisdom—such as concerns about the negative effects of hedge funds and other financial firms from wealthy countries, orderly sequencing of financial liberalization, and recognition of the merits under certain circumstances of capital controls—may well have been recognized earlier on, avoiding much hardship, if developing countries had been better represented.

Representation, then, remains a challenge for the international financial system. We cannot expect wholesale change overnight, but incremental steps are being taken to broaden the dialogue over financial reform. The inclusion of some emerging markets and a wider range of civil society actors shows promise for the future. We will have to see if the impetus of the past few years can be sustained as the threat of a major global economic crisis fades.

NOTES

Research assistance by Nisha Shah, Monica Otero, and Alfonsina Peñaloza and information provided by two G20 interviewees is gratefully acknowledged.

1. On exclusions, see Shapiro and Hacker-Cordón 1999. Compensating mechanisms can include systems of rights or bodies of law such as administrative law.

2. There are a several concepts that are related to representation. These include democracy (Coleman and Porter 2000), transparency, good governance (Woods 1999), ownership (Financial Stability Forum 2000, 11), and legitimacy (Porter 2000). It can be noted that transparency, good governance, ownership and accountability are compatible with market models of control while democracy, representation, and legitimacy are more exclusively political concepts. Discussing this broader set of concepts and the relationship among them goes beyond the scope of this chapter. It should be acknowledged as well that *representation* in politics, art, and other fields has been a key target of the literature on postmodernism. In our view, the postmodern alternative to representation—direct critical involvement—does not supplant the need for strong effective institutions adequate to contemporary international problems in which representation helps promote the interests and well-being of citizens.

3. "A strong sense of country ownership—including political commitment—is critical for fostering successful implementation of standards. . . . [A] sense of stakeholdership in the global financial system can be a strong motivation for implementing international standards. An effective way of achieving this would be to *involve a broad range of economies in the standard-setting process*" (FSF 2000, 10; emphasis in original).

4. For criteria relevant to assessing democracy, see Coleman and Porter 2000.

5. British Chancellor of the Exchequer, Gordon Brown, apparently argued against the change because of the changes that would be necessary in voting power allocation.

6. For an interesting comparative analysis of the World Bank's relations with NGOs, see O'Brien et al., 2000.

7. It was in the early part of that decade that the Bank began to work more closely with civil society representatives and local aid organizations.

8. With the addition of Russia, the Group of Seven in 1997 became the Group of Eight. However, in financial matters and at the level of finance ministers and central bankers, it is still the G7 that meets and makes policies.

9. The G10 is a grouping of representatives of eleven states—Belgium, Canada, France, Germany, Italy, Japan, the Netherlands, Sweden, Switzerland, the United Kingdom, and the United States.

10. Information on the Basle Committee on Banking Supervision is available at <www.bis.org> and from the Committee's *Report on International Developments in Banking Supervision,* issued approximately every two years.

11. Information on EMEAP is available at www.emeap.org.

12. Information on IOSCO can be obtained at www.iosco.org.

13. Information on the FSF can be obtained at www.fsforum.org.

14. "It was only after Indonesia held a democratic election that we invited it to participate in the G20" (Martin 2000b, paragraph 1030). Information on the G20 can be found at www.g20.org.

15. Woods (2000, 832) makes a similar point regarding the drawbacks of consensus decision making in the IMF and World Bank.

REFERENCES

Atkinson, Mark. 2000. Poverty Row Author Quits World Bank: US Secretary Accused of Attempt to Censor Report (online). *The Guardian,* June 15. Available from: <www.guardian.co.uk>.

Basle Committee on Banking Supervision (BCBS). 1997a. *Core Principles for Effective Banking Supervision.* Basle Committee Publications No. 30, September (online). Available from: <www.bis.org/publ/bcbs30a.htm>.

———. 1997b. Press Statement, September 22 (online). Available from: <www.bis.org/press/p970922>.

Chote, Robert. 1998. Group of 22: IMF fears loss of authority. *Financial Times,* October 5.

Coleman, William D., and Tony Porter. 2000. International Institutions, Globalisation and Democracy: Assessing the Challenges. *Global Society* 14, no. 3:377–98.

Financial Stability Forum (FSF). 2000. Issues Paper of the Task Force on Implementation of Standards March 25–26 (online). Available from: <www.fsforum.org>.

Gore, Charles. 2000. "The Rise and Fall of the Washington Consensus as a Paradigm for Developing Countries." *World Development* 28, no. 5:789–804.

Group of Eight (G8). 2000. *G8 Communiqué Okinawa 2000,* July 23 (online). Available from: <http://www.g7.toronto.ca>.

International Organization of Securities Commissions (IOSCO). 1998a. *Objectives and Principles of Securities Regulation,* September (online). Available at: <www.iosco.org>.

———. 1998b. *Report on the Implementation of IOSCO Resolutions,* September (online). Available at: <www.iosco.org>.

———. 1999. Causes, Effects and Regulatory Implications of Financial and Economic Turbulence in Emerging Markets (online). Report by the Emerging Markets Committee (New Delhi), November. Available from: <www.iosco.org>,

Jubilee 2000 Coalition. 2000. Cracks Open Up amongst Creditors on HIPC Consensus (online). Press release. Available from: <www.jubilee2000uk.org>.

Kapstein, Ethan B. 1994. *Governing the Global Economy: International Finance and the State*. Cambridge, Mass., and London: Harvard University Press.

Martin, Paul. 2000a. Speech to the House of Commons Standing Committee on Foreign Affairs and International Trade, May 18 (online). Available at: <www.fin.gc.ca>.

————. 2000b. Speech and responses to questions, in Evidence, Standing Committee on Foreign Affairs and International Trade, House of Parliament, Canada, May 18 (online). Available at: <www.parl.gc.ca>.

O'Brien, Robert, Anne Marie Goetz, Jan Aart Scholte, and Marc Williams. 2000. *Contesting Global Governance: Multilateral Economic Institutions and Global Social Movements*. Cambridge: Cambridge University Press.

Porter, Tony. 2000. The G7, the Financial Stability Forum, the G20, and the Politics of International Financial Regulation. Paper presented at the International Studies Association annual meeting, Los Angeles, March 12.

Ruggie, John Gerard. 1992. Multilateralism: The Anatomy of an Institution. *International Organization* 43, no. 6:561–98.

Shapiro, Ian and Casiano Hacker-Cordón, eds. 1999. *Democracy's Edges*. Cambridge: Cambridge University Press.

Walker, R. B. J. 1993. *Inside/Outside: International Relations as Political Theory*. Cambridge: Cambridge University Press.

Woods, Ngaire. 2000. The Challenge of Good Governance for the IMF and the World Bank Themselves. *World Development* 28, no. 5:823–41.

World Bank. 1997. *Social Development and Results on the Ground*. Task Group Report. Washington, D.C.: World Bank.

————. 1998a. *Partnerships for Development: From Vision to Action* (online). Report, September 24. Available from: <www.worldbank.org/html/extdr/pfd-vistoact.pdf>.

————. 1998b. *Social Development Update: Making Development More Inclusive and Effective*. Paper no. 27. Washington, D.C.: World Bank.

————. 1999. *The World Bank Participation Sourcebook*. Washington, D.C.: World Bank.

Chapter 10

THE EUROPEAN MONETARY UNION AS A RESPONSE TO GLOBALIZATION

Erik Jones

European debate about the architecture of global finance has become inextricably linked to the problem of state autonomy. The reason for this is simple. "Globalization" as a framework of integrated national markets for goods, services, and (most important) capital has replaced the embedded liberalism that supported the "golden age" of the welfare state (Ruggie 1983; Scharpf 1999). In the process, the natural order of things has somehow become inverted. Where embedded liberalism meant that market integration took place only to the extent that it did not conflict with the underlying values of separate national states, globalization implies that states must operate only to the extent that they do not hinder the functioning of shared (and integrated) markets (Ruggie 1995; McNamara 1998). The implications for policymakers are clear. Failure to heed this newly established hierarchy invites international financial crisis.

Or does it? Presumably if states could eliminate the threat of exchange rate collapse (and so shore up their attractiveness to foreign investors) then they could enjoy the benefits of liberalized capital markets without sacrificing domestic autonomy. Indeed, following much this sort of reasoning, the links between market liberalization and monetary integration are tight, both analytically and causally. Analytically, liberalized capital markets weaken state control over exchange rates and complicate the task of monetary policy coordination between countries. Causally, recognition of the threat posed by capital market integration to the European monetary system was an important factor in the political drive for monetary union during the late 1980s. As Tommaso Padoa-Schioppa explained in the introduction to his report to the European Commission, "The success obtained by persuading the Community that efficient allocation of resources and price stability come first is what today makes it necessary to verify the overall consistency of the Community's design for years to come" (1987, vi). Padoa-Schioppa's report did not itself call for a European Monetary Union (EMU).

However, it was clear in asserting that if the objective is "to successfully implement, and benefit from, full economic and financial integration," then "monetary union is the first-best solution" (p. 106).

But is monetary integration really part of the solution or part of the problem? Like globalization, EMU is often seen to subvert the basic principles of the national state. Where the state is inherently political, EMU appears wholly technical. Where the priorities of the state are national, the priorities of EMU are international (and internationally imposed). Where the focus of the state is on institutional arrangements, the focus of EMU is on market behavior. And where the state promises economic stability, EMU necessitates flexible prices, wages, and incomes. Small wonder, then, that many question whether the member states of Europe can reconcile their diverse social objectives with anything like a credible commitment to EMU and even suggest that monetary integration may be part of some larger neoliberal agenda (Richez-Battesti 1996; Luttwak 1997; Moss 2000).

The argument in this chapter is that the formation of EMU is about restructuring the financial architecture of Europe in order to enhance—rather than simply diminish—national autonomy. By implication, EMU functions—at least in part—to shore up and insulate Europe's member states during a period of necessary adjustment. The need for adjustment derives from the growing requirement for flexibility in the allocation of economic and political resources (Rhodes and Mény 1998). Such flexibility is necessary for market actors and state agents to meet a range of objectives in the provision of goods and services, private and public. In part, these objectives reflect the requirements of participating in an ever more integrated global economy (Berger 1996). In part, they also reflect the changing values and priorities of diverse European electorates (Inglehart 1997). However, that Europe's states require greater flexibility does not necessarily predetermine how such flexibility is achieved. EMU represents a common response to the problem of adjustment, but it does not preclude diversity elsewhere. Indeed, given different institutional starting points, it should be expected that Europe's member states will arrive at different formulas for enhancing flexibility at the national and local levels (Pierson 1998; Esping-Anderson 1999; Regini 2000; Scharpf 2000).

This argument is developed in five sections. The first section makes the broad claim that Europe's economic and monetary union effectively reconstitutes the compromise of embedded liberalism at the regional (European) level. The second focuses on the relationship between capital market integration and the development of greater flexibility in the current account. The third places current account flexibility against the background of broader strategies for macro-economic management. The fourth draws attention to the associated problems of volatility and risk when capital markets are integrated but currencies are not. The fifth section concludes by returning to the problem of reforming the welfare state.

EMU AS EMBEDDED LIBERALISM

The benefit of access to international capital markets is greater macroeconomic flexibility. Countries with access to international capital markets do not necessarily have to worry about the impact of macroeconomic policies on the current account balance–so long as they can borrow sufficient financial resources from abroad. The cost is increased risk and volatility. Countries that rely on capital inflows to finance deficits on the current account must face the prospect that international lending will dry up and so throw the overall balance of payments (and the exchange rate) into crisis. When countries cannot attract sufficient resources from abroad, they face an immediate need for structural adjustment— and one often accompanied by a collapse in the external value of the currency.

The challenge confronting national policymakers in Europe (as elsewhere) is to lower the cost without sacrificing the benefit. The problem is that different countries have different aspirations and confront different costs. At the same time, the existence of such differences constitutes a new problem in its own right. Variation from country-to-country raises fundamental questions about the equity and even utility of market integration. Finding one solution that fits all cases is difficult to say the least. Nevertheless, it is necessary if market integration is to be sustainable in the long run. And that is what the Europeans have tried to achieve through monetary union.

The founders of Europe's single currency hope to provide much the flexibility afforded by capital market integration, but at a lower cost. They also intend EMU to serve as a necessary bulwark for the completion of Europe's internal market. Such motivation is political to be sure. However, it is not altruistic and neither is it necessarily federalist. Rather, EMU represents an alternative form of "the compromise of embedded liberalism." Where the architects of the postwar order chose to limit capital markets in order to preserve domestic monetary autonomy while promoting free trade, the architects of Europe have chosen to eliminate national currencies in order to preserve access to international capital markets while laying the basis for a common market. The hierarchy of values is the same in both cases. Domestic diversity predominates over international conformity. All that has changed is the source of flexibility and nature of the constraint.

The interpretation of EMU as a new form of embedded liberalism is consistent with the history of European monetary integration. Countries within Europe have long recognized that differing domestic institutional structures have a powerful influence on the costs of doing business with the outside world. This is particularly true in the context of exchange rates, where the diverse impacts of volatility across member states have become part of the legend of monetary integration. The first serious proposal to create a monetary union in Europe— the Werner Plan of 1970—emerged from the exchange rate crises of the late

1960s and the monumental difficulties of creating a single system to protect French farmers and German manufacturers alike (McNamara 1993). Each subsequent phase has reiterated the importance of monetary macroeconomic stability both in its own right and in order to create a favorable environment for investment.

The argument that EMU operates as a form of embedded liberalism is also consistent with what Jeffry Frieden (1996) identified as "the impact of goods and capital market integration on European monetary politics" in his article by this title. Frieden's argument is that those countries that are most closely integrated have the greatest common interest in stabilizing exchange rates. His reasoning is that closer integration increases the importance of volatility in bilateral exchange rates such as between the member states of Europe. By implication, the relative importance of exchange rate volatility in other bilateral rates is lower. Thus while dollar volatility may be important for Europe as a whole (Belke and Gros 2000), it is less important for Europe's member states than volatility between them.

Having made the claim that EMU acts as a European compromise of embedded liberalism, however, it is necessary to illustrate two points: first, that EMU offers protection from the problems associated with capital market integration, and second, that member states retain the flexibility afforded by a relaxation of the current account constraint. The first point is most easily demonstrated during the immediate run up to monetary union. Europe's heads of state and government announced the values for their irrevocably fixed exchange rates in May 1998. Soon thereafter, the financial shockwaves of the Asian, Latin American, and Russian financial crises hit Europe. However, rather than forcing a change in the parities between European countries, the existence of these crises seemingly added to the rationale behind EMU. Even those countries such as Spain and Portugal that have displayed periodic vulnerability to adverse speculation in capital markets were able to retain their currency pegs. Moreover, they were also able to complete the process of interest rate convergence on European (German) norms. By December 1998, these countries no longer had to shoulder the burden of risk premiums for their access to international capital (ECB 1999, 43–48).

The protection afforded by EMU is also evident with reference to countries that remain outside, most notably the United Kingdom. Between January 1999 and September 2000, the exchange rate between the British pound and the euro appreciated by 15 percent while the exchange rate between the pound and the dollar depreciated by 13 percent. In effect, the European and American currencies traded places in their relative value toward the pound—with the British currency being worth $1.66 and 1.41 euros at the start of the single currency, and $1.45 and 1.63 euros twenty-one months later. Despite the apparent symmetry of these movements, however, the disparate impacts of this reversal of fortune did not cancel out. Instead large manufacturers, particularly in the automotive sector, began to clamor for rapid British entry into the single currency. They also began to redistribute some of the risks of currency volatility onto their suppliers (Toyota) and onto their workforce (Vauxhall). These actions resulted in a minor political crisis over British membership in EMU during August 2000 and may have contributed to a temporary revival of the Blair government's campaign for membership.[1]

The flexibility afforded by EMU is more difficult to establish. This is true both because monetary integration implies the transfer of monetary policy authority to the supranational level and because it builds on a foundation of integrated capital markets. The constraint implied by ceding monetary policy authority is tautological and therefore impossible to refute. The constraint implied by capital market integration is well established as well. In its simplest form, the argument is that states which choose to remove capital controls must inevitably select between exchange rate policy and monetary policy: Either monetary policy must be directed toward manipulating capital flows in support of exchange rate targets, or exchange rate targets must be allowed to respond to the flows of capital resulting from monetary policy changes (Andrews 1994). In this sense, the impact of capital market integration is both mechanical and direct. The more deeply capital markets are integrated, the more elastic are flows of capital with respect to changes in monetary policy variables and the more influential are international capital movements as determinants of national exchange rates.

CAPITAL MARKET INTEGRATION AND STATE AUTONOMY

Analysis focusing on the constraints implied by market integration poses a problem for most conventional stories about EMU. First, analysts must explain why industrial states chose to eliminate capital controls. The consensus is that while states might have opted for partial liberalization, they soon found themselves unable to prevent a wholesale integration of capital markets (Goodman and Pauly 1993). Second, analysts must explain why European states chose to prioritize exchange rate targeting over domestic monetary policy autonomy. Here the argument is driven by attempts to make the best of a bad situation: Europe's heads of state and government acknowledged the failure of Keynesian demand management as well as the apparent success of Germany, and so opted to pattern their institutions and behavior along German norms. (McNamara 1999). Third, analysts question whether monetary integration necessarily follows from capital market integration and, if so, whether any form of monetary policy coordination is sustainable (Cohen 1993, 1994). The apparent consensus around EMU is historically contingent (to borrow again from McNamara 1999), but the constraints implied by liberalized capital markets and monetary unions are permanent.

The relevant question to ask is why Europe's member states have opted for a system from which they cannot opt out. Again borrowing from Padoa-Schioppa (1987), the standard pro-European argument for monetary union is that only a single currency can ensure the benefits of capital market integration. Leaving aside for the moment the general welfare effects arising from the greater efficiency of deeper capital markets, this standard argument places the advocates of EMU in a difficult position: By promoting monetary integration they are also further constraining their room for maneuver in policymaking. This is not a necessary paradox, and policymakers may be capable of (altruistically) pursuing the common good even at their own disadvantage. Alternatively, politicians may be courting favor with the voters precisely by "tying their own hands" (compare to Giavazzi and Pagano 1988). However, it seems a difficult assumption to admit at face value, forcing analysts to posit the existence of "political influences" powerful enough to encourage politicians to override their material self-interest (Garrett 2000, 169). Therefore, without denying that capital market integration does impose some constraint on macroeconomic policy choices, it is useful to look for other implications of liberalized capital movements as well.

The starting point for this analysis is not constraint but empowerment. My concern is not so much how international capital mobility has affected monetary interactions between states, but rather how governments have taken advantage of integrated capital markets. While accepting that constraints do exist, the point to note is that international capital mobility increases the range of options available to macroeconomic policymakers. Not only do international capital flows promise to finance current account deficits, but they also provide alternative sources for domestic investment that might otherwise be crowded out by government borrowing (or that might fail to be "crowded in" by fiscal consolidation). Hence macroeconomic policymakers with access to international capital markets can afford to overlook important constraints—both external and internal—that policymakers with closed domestic capital markets must accept.

The greater macroeconomic flexibility afforded by integrated capital markets was immediately apparent after the 1973 oil price shock. Confronted with a high dependence on energy imports and a correspondingly low price elasticity of demand for energy, policy makers in advanced industrial societies relied on international capital accounts to finance inevitable current account deficits. The extent of this reliance was so great that already during the period from 1974 to 1976 foreign exchange reserves created in international capital markets took over from U.S. balance of payments deficits as the principal source of international liquidity (McCracken et al. 1977, 129). Meanwhile, the public sector share of gross domestic product increased in most countries and government borrowing increased as well. As a result, firms too increased their reliance on international capital markets as an alternative source of investment resources as well as opportunities. The volume of international financial transactions—and the macroeconomic flexibility they afforded—grew apace.

The implications of this new flexibility were not all salutary and neither were they easily reversible. Released from the tight confines of national capital markets, firms and other private actors began to whittle away at those restrictions on capital flows that remained in place. Meanwhile, governments benefitting from a relaxation of the short-run current account constraint confronted the tension between moral hazard and international creditworthiness. Although international capital flows can finance current account deficits, foreign debt must be serviced and ultimately repaid (Corden 1972, 30–34). Therefore, the problem with the liberalized capital markets of the 1970s was not that countries became hugely indebted to foreign lenders, but rather that governments did not use the breathing space offered by international capital flows in order to encourage the structural changes necessary to generate current account surpluses in the future (McCracken et al. 1977, 125–126). For many countries, the challenge was to create an environment suitable for investment or investor confidence. And in some cases—most famously Italy and the United Kingdom during the late 1970s—international lending threatened to dry up, facing the government with an immediate crisis in the balance of payments affecting both the current and capital accounts.

The experience of the 1970s left three important lessons behind. The first two are well known: Governments can liberalize international capital markets more easily than they can control them, and governments can ignore developments in international capital markets only at their own peril. The third lesson has had more obvious acceptance among economists than elsewhere. Simply, even governments with access to international capital markets cannot disregard the current account over the long run. This third lesson is supported by a powerful body of data and analysis (Razin 1995). Nevertheless, despite the strength of economic argument in favor of a long-run current account constraint, governments seem content to accept (and even encourage) long-term imbalances. Within Europe, some countries—such as Germany before unification, the Netherlands since 1982, and Belgium since 1985—have taken advantage of international capital mobility to support consistent current account surpluses. Other countries—such as Spain and Italy in the late 1980s and early to mid-1990s, and Portugal from the late 1980s onward—have run consistent deficits. There are clear advantages on either side. The surplus countries benefit from an export-led pattern of growth. The deficit countries can draw upon foreign capital for domestic investment. Persistent imbalances also entail costs. For the surplus countries the risk is that capital exports will undercut domestic investment (Bean 1989, 42). For the deficit countries the risk is that capital imports will do little more than fuel consumption. How these benefits and costs add up is a case-by-case consideration. In general terms it suffices to note that current account variability has undergone a step change at the European level.

Evidence for the change in European current account performance is assembled in tables 10.1 and 10.2. Both tables contain the average and standard deviation for the balance on current accounts as a ratio to gross domestic product (GDP) for the periods from 1960 to 1973 and from 1983 to 2000 respectively.

The period from 1974 to 1982 is omitted because of the powerful influence of the two oil price shocks (1973 and 1979). The countries are ranged from deficit to surplus, and clustered into "large" and "modest" groups. In comparing the 1980s and 1990s with the 1960s and early 1970s, three changes stand out: More countries are running average deficits; the extreme deficits and (particularly) surpluses are greater; and the variability (standard deviation) of national performance has increased in all but three cases—Portugal, Greece, and Spain. What is less apparent from the tables—but can be calculated from the underlying data—is that national performance during the earlier period tends toward balance (zero) while during the later period it tends toward imbalance. The conclusion, then, is straightforward: Under conditions of international capital mobility, the variability of national performance on current accounts has increased.

STRATEGIES AND OUTCOMES

Having established that there has been increasing variation in European current account performance, the next step is to explain how this change relates

Table 10.1 European Current Account Performance, 1960–1973
(Current Account Balance as Percent of GDP)

Country	Average	Standard Deviation
Large Deficits		
Ireland	−2.3	1.8
Denmark	−1.9	1.0
Greece	−1.9	1.3
Finland	−1.4	1.0
Modest Deficits		
Spain	−0.3	2.2
Modest Surpluses		
Austria	0.0	0.8
Portugal	0.1	3.9
Sweden	0.2	1.0
United Kingdom	0.3	1.0
France	0.6	0.5
Netherlands	0.7	1.5
West Germany	0.8	0.9
Large Surpluses		
Belgium	1.3	1.1
Italy	1.4	1.5

Source: European Commission

Table 10.2 European Current Account Performance, 1983–2000
(Current Account Balance as Percent GDP)

Country	Average	Standard Deviation
Large Deficits		
Portugal	−3.7	3.1
Greece	−2.5	1.2
United Kingdom	−1.1	1.5
Spain	−1.1	1.7
Modest Deficits		
Austria	−0.9	1.2
Germany	−0.6*	0.4*
Denmark	−0.6	2.3
Ireland	−0.3	2.9
Modest Surpluses		
Finland	0.1	4.0
Sweden	0.1	2.4
Italy	0.2	1.6
France	0.4	1.0
Large Surpluses		
Belgium	2.2	2.2
West Germany	2.5**	1.5**
Netherlands	4.4	1.3

* 1991–2000
** 1983–1994
Source: European Commission

to macroeconomic policy. My argument is that the most extreme cases of current account imbalance are the result (whether intended or not) of the prevailing macroeconomic policy mix. The level of demonstration at this point is only illustrative and not comprehensive. Rather than rehearsing a variety of policy scenarios under different regimes and using different models, my strategy is simply to establish the existence of policy combinations that (a) are not available in a world of closed national capital markets and (b) can explain the increasing divergence of current account behavior.[2] Because this is a general argument, the examples draw from both within and outside Europe.

Consistent Current Account Deficits

Examples of countries with consistent current account deficits include the United States in the 1980s and 1990s under a flexible exchange rate regime, and

Spain and Portugal in the 1990s under the fixed-but-adjustable regime of the European Monetary System (EMS). In all three cases, the policy mix combines loose fiscal policy with tight monetary policy. The effects of this mix are easiest to describe under a flexible exchange rate regime. The fiscal expansion increases domestic consumption and so draws down on the current account. Meanwhile, tight monetary policy raises interest rates and so attracts an inflow of foreign capital. Despite the deterioration on the current account, this inflow of foreign capital places upward pressure on the exchange rate and so induces an appreciation of the currency. This currency appreciation blocks off the use of relative prices as a means of correcting the current account and so prolongs and even intensifies the deficit. Nevertheless, so long as the country can continue to attract foreign capital, it can also continue to finance a deficit on current accounts. Therefore, over the short-to-medium term the stability of the policy mix is principally dependent upon the international creditworthiness of the country as well as its relative attractiveness to foreign investors.[3] Over the long run, however, accumulated foreign debts will have to be serviced and ultimately repaid. Therefore the long-run stability of the strategy depends upon the governments' willingness to use foreign capital to support domestic investment and restructuring in order to generate current account surpluses in the future.

The advantages of the policy mix are domestic. Loose fiscal policy fuels consumption, tight monetary policy reins in inflation, and an appreciating exchange rate improves the terms of trade (that is, allows for cheaper and more plentiful imports). In the event that the country also suffers from a shortage of investment capital, an additional advantage is the increase in foreign funds for domestic restructuring. The disadvantages of the policy are both domestic and international. Although the domestic economy experiences a boom in consumption, the lower price of imports ensures that manufacturing faces intense competition from foreign producers. Meanwhile tight monetary policy results not only in attracting capital from across the globe, but also in raising real interest rates. Funds for investment may be more available, but they are also likely to be more expensive.

The United States' experience during the 1980s and 1990s illustrates all of the hallmarks of the loose fiscal / tight monetary policy mix. Under the first Reagan administration, both real interest rates and fiscal deficits increased, leading to a massive inflow of foreign capital, a strong appreciation of the dollar, and a dramatic deterioration on current account. This strategy was both surprising and unwelcome. Not only did it seem to encourage a rapid "de-industrialization of America," but it also threatened the stability of the international economic system. As the decade progressed, concern that the U.S. economy would experience a hard landing rather than a smooth adjustment increased (Marris 1987). Meanwhile, the presumption was that the U.S. ability to sustain such current account deficits is a function of its unique role in the world economy. It is American hegemony in a less powerful and more decadent guise (Calleo 1992).

The argument here is that the policy mix is less a function of American power than of the integration of capital markets. Therefore it is possible to identify a similar strategy used by smaller countries as well. Spain and Portugal follow the characteristic pattern of the tight monetary / loose fiscal policy mix in the early 1990s: domestic expansion leading to a deterioration on current account financed by capital imports induced through relatively high real interest rates. Evidence for the Spanish and Portuguese policy mixes is assembled in table 10.3, which provides average data for fiscal balances, current accounts, nominal short-term interest rates, interest rate differentials with Germany, and real interest rates (GDP deflated) for the period from 1988 to 1995. In order to facilitate comparison, table 10.3 also includes U.S. data from 1982 to 1998. The data support the broad similarities between the policy mixes and current account performance in the United States on the one hand and Spain and Portugal on the other hand. In all three cases, persistent current account deficits were only possible as a result of foreign capital inflows, and therefore of capital market integration.

Despite the similarities, however, the experience of Spain and Portugal differed from that of the United States in three respects. First, the smaller countries benefitted from capital transfers and so did not rely solely on foreign borrowing as did the United States.[4] Second, the two countries did not undergo such a strong currency appreciation despite their reliance on capital inflows to finance deficits on current account. Third, both Spain and Portugal were subject to periodic currency crises as international lenders questioned whether and how long the tight monetary / loose fiscal policy mix could be maintained. These three differences reflect the importance of America's hegemonic position in the world economy to its ability to maintain current account deficits over the long run. Because of its economic and military might, and because most countries hold dollars as a reserve currency, the United States has a relatively easy time

Table 10.3 Countries with Consistent Current Account Deficits:
Period Averages (Spain and Portugal 1988–1995; U.S. 1982–1998)

	Portugal	Spain	United States
Government Deficit (% of GDP)	4.7	5.0	3.9
Current Account Deficit (% of GDP)	2.7	2.2	1.6
Nominal Short Term Interest Rates (%)	14.1	12.2	6.5
Real* Short Term Interest Rates (%)	4.2	5.9	3.4
Nominal Interest Rate Differential with Germany (%)	7.2	5.2	0.6
Real* Interest Rate Differential with Germany (%)	0.2	1.9	0.1

* Real interest rates are deflated by GDP.
Data source: European Commission.

attracting foreign capital and maintaining international creditworthiness. For Spain and Portugal, running consistent current account deficits is both more difficult and more volatile. Indeed, it may be possible only because where the United States can benefit from hegemony, Spain and Portugal can rely on their institutional and symbolic association with Europe.

Spanish and Portuguese participation in the European Union and specifically in the fixed-but-adjustable exchange rate mechanism (ERM) of the European Monetary System can account for much of the difference between U.S. and Iberian experiences. The European Union represents the source of much of the capital transfers to the Iberian peninsula—with the ostensible purpose of stimulating regional and structural reforms. Moreover, for both Spain and Portugal, the demonstration of a willingness to undertake domestic economic reform lent credibility to their participation in the EMS (Torres 1998; Calvet 1996). In turn, EMS participation enhanced the creditworthiness of both countries by reducing exchange rate risk, and so made them more attractive to foreign investors. Finally, once foreign capital inflows began to place upward pressure on the peseta and escudo, the intervention requirements of the ERM displaced responsibility for maintaining the system of fixed-but-adjustable exchange rates onto the weaker European currencies.[5]

The combination of macroeconomic policies, capital transfers, and EMS participation was not wholly stable. Both Spain and Portugal experienced sharp depreciations during the 1992, 1993, and 1995 currency crises within the ERM. Nevertheless, both countries were able to sustain persistent deficits on current accounts using foreign capital to stave off a crisis in their balance of payments. Moreover, reliance on capital inflows meant that the escudo and peseta tended to appreciate between crises even in the face of persistent current account deficits. At the same time, this tendency to appreciate was contained despite the strong inflow of foreign capital. Indeed, both currencies remained in the top of their intervention bands against the median EMS currency even during periods of gradual depreciation such as that between 1996 and 1998 (European Commission 1998, 158–159). Such a performance would not be possible without integrated capital markets.

Consistent Current Account Surpluses

Capital flows can offset consistent current account surpluses as well as consistent deficits. From an intuitive standpoint, however, the alternatives are not symmetrical. If a country is able to outperform its competitors either domestically, in the rest of the world, or both, why would investors—domestic and foreign—prefer to place their money elsewhere? Why would a government not encourage its successful manufacturers to repatriate profits and invest them at home? Alternatively, why should governments not allow current account surpluses simply to translate into ever increasing official holdings of foreign exchange reserves—a mercantilist war chest so to speak? The answer to the first and second questions has to do with relative returns on investment, while the answer to the second and third questions concerns the risk of domestic inflation. Capital will flow where the rates of return are relatively higher or the opportunities for investment are greater. By the same token, capital inflows—including repatriated profits and increased foreign exchange reserves—increase domestic liquidity.

If governments confronting a current account surplus do not take action, the likelihood is not only that capital will flow into the country but also that firms and workers will use their increased earnings to bolster investment and consumption. The result will be higher prices coupled with a change in performance on the current account. The logic of this mechanism suggests the paradox that governments hoping to run consistent current account surpluses may have to loosen domestic monetary conditions in order to hold down demand and stave off inflation. More generally, such governments must not only allow but also encourage international capital mobility.

Loosening monetary conditions to dampen demand and control inflation only represents a paradox when monetary policy instruments are directly and consistently assigned to domestic stabilization. When monetary policy instruments are assigned to influence international capital accounts the paradox is eliminated. All that is necessary is that the impact of monetary policy changes on the balance of payments as a monetary influence is greater than the direct impact of those changes on domestic monetary conditions—a point made implicitly in Mundell's (1960) early analysis of international capital mobility. However, the assignment of monetary instruments either wholly or principally to influence the capital account—like the constraint that monetary instruments must accommodate international capital markets—leaves open how the government will control domestic sources of inflation. Once again what is interesting is not so much the assignment of (or constraint on) monetary policy but rather the structure of the policy mix.

Examples of countries that have run consistent current account surpluses include Japan and the Netherlands throughout the 1980s and 1990s, West Germany before unification, and Belgium from 1986 onward. The macroeconomic characteristics of these countries are similar in that they combine tight fiscal policy, high domestic savings relative to investment, stable prices, and declining real wages. All four countries also benefit from nonmarket mechanisms for ensuring wage stability, ranging from direct intervention in wage negotiations (Belgium and the Netherlands), to concerted wage bargaining (the Netherlands and Germany), to institutionalized wage restraint (Japan). Data in support of this characteristic pattern is assembled in table 10.4, and includes the balance on current account, net national savings, the ratio of savings to investment, the average annual price inflation, and the rate of increase in real unit labor costs. Table 10.4 also provides comparable data from the United States as a benchmark for relative comparison. What the data reveal is that the four countries running consistent current account surpluses save more, invest (relatively) less, and have lower inflation and more rapidly declining real unit labor costs than the United States.

What the data in table 10.4 do not indicate is the extent to which the four countries running current account surpluses must manage macroeconomic (and specifically monetary) policy instruments with an eye to their impact on the capital account and on exchange rates. The empirical literature on the subject is substantial.[6] What it reveals is the complexity of the policy mix both at any given phase in time and across different time periods. Within the mix, monetary policy is not always and completely ineffective in the management of domestic demand.[7] Nevertheless, its use is not entirely transparent either. For example, Henning (1994, 134–170) outlines five phases in the evolution of Japanese monetary and exchange rate policy during the period from 1980 to 1992. The differences between the phases are categorical, and pivot around whether the yen should be made stronger or weaker, whether capital flows should be regulated or liberalized, whether interest rates should be raised or lowered, and whether the Bank of Japan should intervene in foreign currency markets. In each phase, however, the maintenance of the surplus on current accounts remains a priority and so at least some international mobility of capital remains a necessity.

As with the current account deficit, the advantages of pursuing a surplus are domestic while the disadvantages are both domestic and foreign. The advantages are also relatively concentrated in the tradable goods sector. Export manufacturers benefit from a relatively favorable real exchange rate, elevated profits, and from enhanced international liquidity. Meanwhile, the nontraded goods sector must labor under unfavorable terms of trade (fewer and more expensive

Table 10.4 Countries with Consistent Current Account Surpluses:
Period Averages (Belgium 1986–1998; Germany 1982–1990; Netherlands, Japan, and U.S. 1982–1998)

	Belgium	Germany	Netherlands	Japan	U.S.*
Current Account Surplus (%)	2.7	3.2	4.2	2.5	−1.6
Net National Saving (%)	9.0	10.3	9.6	17.2	5.5
Gross Saving/Investment	1.08	1.15	1.17	1.10	0.94
Net Saving/Investment	1.30	1.42	1.59	1.20	0.83
Price Deflator, GDP (annual % change)	2.6	2.6	1.8	1.1	2.9
Real Unit Labor Costs (annual % change)	−0.6	−1.0	−0.8	−0.5	−0.2

* The United States is a consistent deficit country presented here as a benchmark for comparison.
Source: European Commission

imports), constrained wages, and a relative lack of investment. Internationally, trade competitors are likely to view sustained current account surpluses as prima facie evidence of unfair trading practices. Such international concern is not wholly misplaced. Armed with access to international capital markets, states are empowered to sustain current account surpluses despite the constraints this may place on the exercise of monetary policy. Moreover, the evidence suggests that they have done so.

RISK, VOLATILITY, AND COST

Integrated capital markets offer the promise of macroeconomic flexibility, but only at a cost. The cost is expressed in terms of risk and volatility. Countries that rely on international capital markets face the risk that lenders will withdraw their credit or borrowers will default on their obligations. They also run the risk that sudden movements of capital between currencies will cause dramatic swings in exchange rates—altering relative prices in complete disregard for "the fundamentals" such as movements in relative costs. Indeed, given that goods markets play so little role in determining the value of exchange rates, countries run the risk that no matter how favorable their cost structures may be relative to their competitors—or how coherent their macroeconomic policy mix—a sudden or long-term movement of exchange rates may obliterate any advantage in relative prices (MacDonald 1999). Finally, countries run the risk that capital market and exchange rate effects will reinforce one another, with a credit crisis leading to an exchange rate crisis or the other way around, and so on. The permutations of such risks are vast, and each contributes to the volatility of exchange rates and interest rates.

In turn, this volatility is both self-reinforcing and costly in its own right. Investors estimating relative returns must bring forward their time horizons and so assume shorter positions which focus on shorter-term gains. Industries hoping to protect the value of their capital and output must either accept the cost of exposure to volatility, redistribute the risk onto weaker groups in the marketplace (suppliers, workers, consumers), or engage in financial hedging. The results of such distributive games are "negative-sum": everyone loses. Weaker groups must share in the cost of international exposure even if the focus of their activity is domestic. At the same time, the financial intermediaries that offer hedging contracts must cover their own exposure. In the end, the hedging instruments themselves become a focus for short-term investments and an additional source of volatility (Garber 1999; Watson 1999). The fact that forward markets consistently underpredict the scale of volatility suggests that inefficiency, and therefore cost, is somehow inherent to the system (Rogoff 1999).

The costs of capital market integration are systemic in origin but not in distribution. Institutional arrangements can influence both the allocation of risks and the nature of volatility. Similarly, institutions can influence the economic mechanisms that make risk and volatility important in the first place, changing perceptions or expectations and so moderating behavior. As a consequence, the negative impact of capital market integration is not everywhere the same. This is most obvious in the fact that different countries represent different risks for international investors and so must pay different premiums for access to international capital. There are premiums associated with the choice of macroeconomic strategy (sovereign risk), with the possibility of sudden movements in the value of the currency (exchange rate risk), and with the ease of getting into and out of the national capital market (liquidity risk). In turn, these premiums result in a higher cost of capital for some countries than for others.

The differences in premiums charged by international investors are obvious in any comparison between the industrialized and developing worlds. Where industrialized countries seem to be able to access international capital markets with relative impunity, developing nations do so only at great cost. Moreover, any attempt by developing countries to exercise the type of macroeconomic flexibility described above is likely to meet with disaster, as international investors raise the cost of borrowing exorbitantly or cut off lending altogether. The impact of different institutional arrangements on the cost of participating in international capital markets is less obvious in comparisons between wealthy middle powers like the countries of Europe. It remains important nonetheless.

Moreover, the imposition of premiums on the cost of borrowing is only one manifestation of the costs of integrated capital markets. Another manifestation works through the impact of volatility on investment in the real economy. The general claim is that investors confronting volatility in either interest rates or exchange rates will choose to defer their investment until markets calm down (Darby, Hallett, Ireland, and Piscitelli, 1999). By implication the expectation is that any relationship between volatility and investment will be negative—more volatility means less investment, and the reverse. In more specific terms, the impact of volatility on investment should be influenced by the importance of exchange rates or interest rates to the return on capital and by the ease with which investors can hedge, transform, or eliminate either a specific investment or their exposure to volatility. Thus we should expect investment in some countries to show a greater sensitivity to volatility than in others. This expectation is consistent with the assertion that welfare state institutions help to mitigate or redistribute exposure to risk (Rodrik 1998).

The different sensitivities of national economies to the problem of volatility is even more evident with respect to employment and unemployment. Again, in general terms, the argument is that firms confronting volatile interest rates or exchange rates may delay any decision to expand the workforce and may even be forced into redundancies. Thus, the general expectation is that employment growth will slow—and unemployment may even increase—whenever financial markets become volatile (cf. Gros 1998). Here too, however, national institutions will have a profound effect on the sensitivity of the real economy to volatility in financial markets. Because labor market regulations influence the prospects for hiring and firing, the term structure of wage contracts, and the nonpayroll cost of the workforce, they will also have an influence on how firms determine the appropriate strategy for responding to volatility.

CONCLUSION

Discussion of the cost of volatility necessarily returns us to the problem of welfare state reform. Differences in welfare state institutions explain differences in national responses to the problems of integrated capital markets. The greater the problems, the more important these differences become. However, eliminating the differences between countries will not eliminate the problems themselves. All it will achieve is a leveling of the playing field. And, in Europe, that is simply not the objective. Rather, the aspiration is to find a common solution to the problem of volatility—one that will preserve the macroeconomic flexibility afforded by capital market integration while at the same time making it possible to ignore substantial institutional differences between the member states. That common solution is EMU.

At this point it is necessary to concede that Europe's member states are all, from richest to poorest, engaged in some process of welfare state reform. However, such reform would be necessary with or without EMU, under segmented capital markets as well as in a globalized world economy. The reasons for reform have been alluded to in the introduction and can be related to changes in values, demographics, technology, and a host of other variables. It is also important to note that the method of reform undertaken in Europe is idiosyncratic—and deliberately so. The buzzwords adopted at the March 2000 Lisbon European Council summit center on "targeting," "bench-marking," and "shared-best-practice." These are terms for individual improvement within a collective process and not for convergence around a common norm.

What is unquestioned in Europe is that reform is necessary. Europe's member states have emerged from the sclerosis of the 1970s and early 1980s only to confront pernicious unemployment in the late 1980s and 1990s. The problem of this unemployment, more than anything else, drives the debate about welfare state reform at both the national and European levels (Jones 1998). Unemployment is also likely to dominate European discussions well into the future. What is clear is that Europe's leaders insist that EMU is part of the solution (Jones 2000). What is also clear is that the solution for Europe's unemployment problem is different from one member state to the next (Viñals and Jimeno 1998). For EMU to contribute to resolving Europe's unemployment problem it must be consistent with the wide variety of solutions that will be implemented at the national level. The analysis presented in this chapter suggests that it is.[8]

Indeed, if there is a dilemma posed by EMU, it arises from the excess of macroeconomic flexibility that monetary integration affords participating countries. The danger is not that countries will be unable to manage their economies. Rather, it is that they will take advantage of their relaxed current account constraints and strengthened creditworthiness to ignore already excessive imbalances. Indeed, evidence from the first two years of EMU suggest that this is likely to be the case.

For those countries in current account deficit, the challenge of attracting sufficient funds for domestic investment remains. However, the significance of this challenge is greatly overwhelmed by the elimination of premiums on the cost of capital. Just as during the early expansion of international capital markets, such deficits could result in enormous future burdens of adjustment. They could also destabilize European macroeconomic performance in the present. Therefore it is small wonder that Europe's heads of state and government would be so adamant about setting down rules to ensure macroeconomic stability under EMU. It is also small wonder that concern in Europe would focus on how such rules could ever be enforced and whether they will actually be obeyed.

For those countries in surplus, the difficulty of eliminating the inflationary potential of capital inflows remains as well. The point to note, however, is that such inflows present an inflationary problem only if Europe as a whole runs a current account surplus. If not, the extremes can balance one another out.

The point is largely theoretical. If the first twenty-one months of EMU are any indication, aggregate European current account surpluses are likely to be more than offset by capital flows from Europe to the United States (BIS 2000, 32). The preponderance of these flows explains the collapse of the value of the European currency since its launch in January 1999. Moreover, the flood of capital is so great that it has revived concerns about the differential impact of financial volatility across Europe's member states. EMU is only a partial solution to the problems posed by capital market integration: a regional bulwark within the larger architecture of global capital markets.

The greatest danger at the moment is not that EMU will collapse under the weight of internal division but rather that it will prove inadequate in the face of global forces. The experience of the Bretton Woods system is instructive on this point. The conventional wisdom is that Bretton Woods collapsed under the weight of excessive dollar liquidity. The United States ran balance of payments deficits both to ensure adequate provision of liquidity for international trade and as a symptom of fiscal imbalances resulting from the Vietnam War. In turn these deficits ultimately destabilized the whole of the exchange rate system (McCracken 1977, 12). This conventional wisdom may be deficient; however, it touches on a fundamental conflict between "the conditions for economic growth . . . and the practices of modern governments" (Keohane 1978, 109). Governments do not always exert self-discipline even when it is in their country's long-term self-interest. From the European perspective, the United States is viewed as continuously culpable of falling prey to short-term political pressures. EMU is in many ways not the first-best solution suggested by Padoa-Schioppa but rather a second-best alternative to a broader systemic reform. For most Europeans, any such transformation in the international financial architecture must begin with a reform of the United States.

NOTES

I would like to thank the students of the Institut für Politikwissenschaft at the Johannes Gutenberg Universität Mainz for their very lively and thoughtful contributions to this paper. Among my colleagues, I would also like to thank Leslie Elliott Armijo, Robert Elgie, Paul Heywood, Donna Lee, Kathleen McNamara, and Jonathon Moses. Any insights are theirs. The faults are mine alone.

1. Coverage of the political crisis around the automotive industry and EMU can be found in any quality newspaper from August 2000. The stories I relied upon were published in *The Guardian* on August 10. The displacement of exchange rate risk onto the Vauxhall workforce received somewhat less coverage. Macalister (2000) relates how Vauxhall activated a clause from its 1998 collective bargaining agreement whereby workers would forgo a £100 bonus if the value of the pound fell below DM 2.70 for two consecutive months. He also suggests that Vauxhall would continue to include such clauses in its bargaining contracts for the future.

2. Readers interested in deliberating different macroeconomic models are advised to consult Stevenson, Muscatelli, and Gregory (1988) and McKibbon and Sachs (1991).

3. The problem of maintaining creditworthiness (or credibility) is likely to be more easily resolved for rich industrial countries than for poorer developing countries. Hence many of the arguments here may have only limited application outside the privileged membership of the OECD.

4. Capital transfers played a particularly strong role in Portugal, accounting for more than 80 percent of net capital inflows during the 1988–1995 period as opposed to only 20 percent for Spain.

5. Most analyses of the asymmetric intervention requirements of the ERM focus on the privileged position of Germany given the relative strength of the deutsche mark. The point to note is that it is the position of relative strength and not the deutsche mark per se that is privileged by the intervention requirements. For a general analysis, see Gros and Thygesen (1998, 167–178).

6. See for example, Cooper (1968); Wadbrook (1972); Henning (1994); Kaltenthaler (1998); and Jones, Frieden, and Torres (1998).

7. Pooled cross-section time series analysis of the relationship between real short-term and long-term interest rates in the G7 countries indicates that monetary policy changes have a statistically significant impact on long-term real interest rates (and therefore economic activity) through their impact on short-term real interest rates. At the same time, this evidence suggests that accumulated current account surpluses have a significant negative impact on long-run real interest rates—as should be expected given the necessity for capital to flow in the opposite direct of the current account. See Sasaki, Yamaguchi, and Hisada (2000).

8. This is not to say, however, that national solutions for Europe's unemployment problem are going to be successful. Indeed, the danger is that the member states will fail and so undermine the legitimacy of EMU. For an elaboration on this point, see Jones (1998).

REFERENCES

Andrews, David M. 1994. Capital Mobility and State Autonomy: Toward a Structural Theory of International Monetary Relations. *International Studies Quarterly* 38, no. 2 (June):193–218.

Bank for International Settlements (BIS). 2000. *70th Annual Report, 1 April 1999–31 March 2000*. Basle: Bank for International Settlements.

Bean, Charles. 1989. Capital Shortages and Persistent Unemployment. *Economic Policy* 8 (April):11–53.

Belke, Ansgar, and Daniel Gros. 2000. Designing EU-US Monetary Relations: The Impact of Exchange-Rate Variability on Labor Markets on Both Sides of the Atlantic. Brussels: Centre for European Policy Studies. Mimeographed.

Berger, Suzanne. 1996. Introduction to *National Diversity and Global Capitalism,* ed. Suzanne Berger and Ronald Dore. Ithaca, N.Y.: Cornell University Press.

Calleo, David P. 1992. *The Bankrupting of America: How the Federal Budget Is Impoverishing the Nation.* New York: William Morrow and Company.

Calvet, Josep González. 1996. Le cas de l'Espagne. In *Union Économique et Monétaire et Négotiations Collectives,* ed. Philippe Ponchet and Otto Jacobi. Brussels: Observatoire Social Européen.

Cohen, Benjamin J. 1993. The Triad and the Unholy Trinity: Lessons for the Pacific Region. In *Pacific Economic Relations in the 1990s: Cooperation or Conflict?,* ed. Richard Higgott, Richard Leaver, and John Ravenhill. St. Leonards, Australia: Allen and Unwin.

———. 1994. Beyond EMU: The Problem of Sustainability. In *The Political Economy of European Monetary Unification,* ed. Barry Eichengreen and Jeffry Frieden. Boulder, Colo.: Westview.

Cooper, Richard N. 1968. *The Economics of Interdependence: Economic Policy in the Atlantic Community.* New York: McGraw-Hill.

Corden, W. M. 1972. Monetary Integration. *Essays in International Finance* 93. Princeton, N.J.: International Finance Section, Department of Economics, Princeton University.

Darby, Julia, Andrew Hughes Hallett, Jonathan Ireland, and Laura Piscitelli. 1999. The Impact of Exchange Rate Uncertainty on the Level of Investment. *Economic Journal* 109 (March):C55–C67.

Esping-Anderson, Gøsta. 1999. *Social Foundations of Postindustrial Economies*. Oxford: Oxford University Press.

European Central Bank (ECB). 1999. *ECB Annual Report. 1998*, Frankfurt: European Central Bank.

European Commission. 1998. Convergence Report 1998. Brussels: European Commission.

Frieden, Jeffrey. 1996. The Impact of Goods and Capital Market Integration on European Monetary Politics. *Comparative Political Studies* 29, no. 2:193–222.

Garber, Peter M. 1999. Derivatives in International Capital Flows. In *International Capital Flows*, ed. Martin Feldstein. Chicago: University of Chicago Press.

Garrett, Geoffrey. 2000. Capital Mobility, Exchange Rates and Fiscal Policy in the Global Economy. *Review of International Political Economy* 7, no. 1:153–170.

Giavazzi, Francesco, and Marco Pagano. 1988. The Advantage of Tying One's Hands: EMS Discipline and Central Bank Credibility. *European Economic Review* 32: 1055–1082.

Goodman, John B., and Louis W. Pauly. 1993. The Obsolescence of Capital Controls? Economic Management in an Age of Global Markets *World Politics* 46, no. 1:50–82.

Gros, Daniel. 1998. External Shocks and Labor Mobility: How Important Are They for EMU? In *The New Political Economy of EMU*, ed. Jeffrey Frieden, Daniel Gros, and Erik Jones. Lanham, MD: Rowman and Littlefield.

Gros, Daniel, and Niels Thygesen. 1998. *European Monetary Integration: From the European Monetary System to Economic and Monetary Union*. 2nd edition. London: Longman.

Henning, R. Randall. 1994. *Currencies and Politics in the United States, Germany, and Japan*. Washington, D.C.: Institute for International Economics.

Inglehart, Ronald. 1997. *Modernization and Postmodernization: Cultural, Economic, and Political Change in 43 Societies*. Princeton, N.J.: Princeton University Press.

Jones, Erik. 1998. Economic and Monetary Union: Playing with Money. In *Centralization or Fragmentation? Europe Facing the Challenges of Deepening, Diversity, and Democracy*, ed. Andrew Moravcsik. New York: Council on Foreign Relations.

———. 2000. The Politics of Europe 1999: Spring Cleaning. *Industrial Relations Journal: European Annual Review 1999* 31, no. 4 (December):248–261.

Jones, Erik, Jeffry Frieden, and Francisco Torres, eds. 1998. *Joining Europe's Monetary Club: The Challenges for Smaller Member States*. New York: St. Martin's.

Kaltenthaler, Karl. 1998. *Germany and the Politics of Europe's Money*. Durham, N.C.: Duke University Press.

Keohane, Robert O. 1978. Economics, Inflation, and the Role of the State: Political Implications of the McCracken Report. *World Politics* 31, no. 1 (October):108–128.

Luttwak, Edward. 1997. Central Bankism. In *The Question of Europe*, ed. Peter Gowan and Perry Anderson. London: Verso.

Macalister, Terry. 2000. Vauxhall Benefits from Sterling's Strength. *The Guardian*, August 24.

MacDonald, Ronald. 1999. Exchange Rate Behavior: Are the Fundamentals Important? *Economic Journal* 109 (November):F673–F691.

Marris, Stephen. 1987. *Deficits and the Dollar: The World Economy at Risk Rev. ed.* Washington, D.C.: Institute for International Economics.

McCracken, Paul, Guido Carli, Herbert Giersch, Attila Karaosmanogly, Ryutaro Komiya, Assar Lindbeck, Robert Marjalin, and Robin Matthews. 1977. *Towards Full Employment and Price Stability.* Paris: OECD.

McKibbon, Warwick J., and Jeffrey D. Sachs. 1991. *Global Linkages: Macroeconomic Interdependence and Cooperation in the World Economy,* Washington, D.C.: Brookings Institution.

McNamara, Kathleen R. 1993. Systems Effects and the European Community. In *Coping with Complexity in the International System,* ed. Robert Jervis and Jack Snyder. Boulder, Colo.: Westview Press.

———. 1998. *The Currency of Ideas: Monetary Politics and the European Union.* Ithaca, N.Y.: Cornell University Press.

———. 1999. Consensus and Constraint: Ideas and Capital Mobility in Monetary Integration. *Journal of Common Market Studies* 37, no. 3 (September):455–476.

Moss, Bernard. 2000. Is the European Community Politically Neutral? The Free Market Agenda. In *The Single European Currency in National Perspective: A Community in Crisis?,* ed. Bernhard H. Moss and Jonathan Michie. London: Macmillan.

Mundell, Robert A. 1960. The Monetary Dynamics of International Adjustment under Fixed and Floating Exchange Rates. *Quarterly Journal of Economics* 74, no. 2 (May):227–257.

Padoa-Schioppa, Tommaso. 1987. *Efficiency, Stability, and Equity: A Strategy for the Evolution of the Economic System of the European Community.* Brussels: European Commission, II/49/87, April.

Pierson, Paul. 1998. Irresistible Forces, Immovable Objects: Post-industrial Welfare States Confront Permanent Austerity. *Journal of European Public Policy* 5, no. 4:539–560.

Razin, Assaf. 1995. The Dynamic-Optimizing Approach to the Current Account: Theory and Evidence. In *Understanding Interdependence: The Macroeconomics of the Open Economy,* ed. Peter B. Kenen. Princeton, N.J.: Princeton University Press.

Regini, Marino. 2000. Between Deregulation and Social Pacts: The Responses of European Economies to Globalization. *Politics and Society* 28, no. 1 (March):5–33.

Rhodes, Martin, and Yves Mény. 1998. Introduction: Europe's Social Contract Under Stress. In *The Future of European Welfare: A New Social Contract?,* ed. Martin Rhodes and Yves Mény. London: Macmillan.

Richez-Battesti, Nadine. 1996. Union Économique et Monétaire et État-Providence: La Subsidiarité en Question. *Revue Études Internationales* 27, no. 1 (March):109–28.

Rodrick, Dani. 1998. Why Do More Open Economies Have Bigger Governments? *Journal of Political Economy* 106, no. 5 (October):997–1032.

Rogoff, Kenneth. 1999. Perspectives on Exchange Rate Volatility. In *International Capital Flows,* ed. Martin Feldstein. Chicago: University of Chicago Press.

Ruggie, John Gerard. 1983. International Regimes, Transactions, and Change: Embedded Liberalism in the Postwar Economic Order. In *International Regimes,* ed. Stephen D. Krasner. Ithaca, N.Y.: Cornell University Press.

―――. 1995. At Home Abroad, Abroad at Home: International Liberalization and Domestic Stability in the New World Economy. *Millennium: Journal of International Studies* 24, no. 3 (Winter):507–524.

Sasaki, Hitoshi, Satoshi Yamaguchi, and Takamasa Hisada. 2000. The Globalization of Financial Markets and Monetary Policy. *International Financial Markets and the Implications for Monetary and Financial Stability: Conference Paper No. 8.* Basel: Bank For International Settlements.

Scharpf, Fritz. 1999. *Governing in Europe: Effective and Democratic?* Oxford: Oxford University Press.

―――. 2000. The Viability of Advanced Welfare States in the International Economy. *Journal of European Public Policy* 7, no. 2 (June):190–228.

Stevenson, Andrew, Vitantonio Muscatelli, and Mary Gregory. 1988. *Macroeconomic Theory and Stabilization Policy*. Oxford: Philip Allan.

Torres, Francisco. 1998. Portugal toward EMU: A Political Economy Perspective. In *Joining Europe's Monetary Club: The Challenges for Smaller Member States,* ed. Erik Jones, Jeffry Frieden, and Francisco Torres. New York: St. Martin's.

Viñals, José, and Juan Jimeno. 1998. Monetary Union and European Unemployment. In *The New Political Economy of EMU,* ed. Jeffrey Frieden, Daniel Gros, and Erik Jones. Lanham, MD: Rowman and Littlefield.

Wadbrook, William Pollard. 1972. *West German Balance of Payments Policy: The Prelude to European Monetary Integration.* New York: Praeger.

Watson, Matthew. 1999. Rethinking Capital Mobility: Reregulating Financial Markets. *New Political Economy* 4, no. 1 (March):55–75.

AFTERWORD

Afterword

OF BUBBLES AND BULDINGS: FINANCIAL ARCHITECTURE IN A LIBERAL DEMOCRATIC ERA

Laurence Whitehead

This book provides an overview of the structure and dynamics of global finance at the end of the twentieth century. Under the twin pressures of scientific innovation and international integration the political economy of the world is changing faster than ever, and the balance between states and markets is being redefined. All this is happening within the broadly liberal democratic framework of norms and institutions that emerged reinvigorated at the end of the Cold War. Western governments and their policymakers tend to rely on the optimistic assumption that the tensions arising from rapid change can all be managed by sensible cooperation. If there are flaws in the existing "architecture" for regulating international finance, they can readily be corrected by expert analysis and rational redesign.

In this brief afterword I want to suggest that the changes currently in process are extremely dynamic and open ended. Institutional arrangements that seemed adequate for previous periods may embody assumptions that will be quite inapplicable in the near future. It may therefore not be possible to settle on a single fixed set of design principles (a "final architecture") that can be relied on to manage all the prospective tensions. When change is so rapid, and outcomes so fluid, it is easy to be overwhelmed by the pressure of immediate events. I attempt to counteract that tendency by invoking a very broad historical perspective. International finance has already undergone successive cycles of transformation. A glance at these antecedents reminds us both that all financial systems are socially constructed, and that when they fail to operate effectively or to generate adequate consent the costs can be very high.

However, according to liberal democratic principles, it may be possible to strengthen international cooperation and the regulatory framework governing international finance by reinforcing systems of authority based on widespread consent. Expert analysis will still be needed, but it can be channeled within a framework of enhanced dialogue and improved accountability. This is important, because when unexpected strains arise, consent will be required for the sacrifices and readjustments involved in containing them. It may be particularly important at the international level, where innovative forms of cooperation and regulation are most likely to be required, but where the principles of democratic legitimacy and popular consent seem most remote. The contemporary spread of democracy at the national level, combined with tightening of financial integration at the international level, makes the problem of legitimation a central issue in the study of international finance.

Reforming the "architecture" of the international financial system became a popular slogan in the wake of the various emerging market crises of the 1990s. This metaphor[1] suggests that by appealing to sound building techniques it must be possible to erect an edifice of rules, institutions, and procedures that will resist the laws of gravity and the pressures of time and events, so that international finance can be carried on without fear of collapse. There is an evident parallel between this metaphor and the language of "institutional design" that has gained currency in Anglophone political science over the same period. Similarly the "consolidation" of democracy invokes parallel imagery of political institutions fitting together into a robust structure of mutually supportive building blocks. All these construction-based metaphors convey the comforting impression that new social arrangements can be rendered permanent, functional, and indeed perhaps even beyond rational reproach, provided that the technicians who are in possession of the required theory and technical skills are allowed the freedom they need to apply their scientific expertise. The architecture metaphor actually goes further than this, implying by association of ideas that if the correct building principles are applied the result will not only be functional, but also aesthetically pleasing.[2]

This is a comforting imagery. But is it well founded? When political scientists such has Juan J. Linz and Arturo Valenzuela (1994) asserted that the best design principles for a new democracy involved parliamentarism rather than presidentialism, they failed to convince most constitution writers of their insight (and they never showed the courage of their convictions by arguing for parliamentarism in the United States). Against the physicalist metaphor of "consolidation" I have argued for the vitalist alternative of "viability" (Crabtree and Whitehead 2000). The present volume invites parallel questioning of the implicit assumptions associated with the notion of international financial architecture. Does the history of international finance uncover a reliable set of building techniques or design principles that can be relied on to deliver stability and functional effectiveness in the face of all challenges? Do the supposed experts in this field agree on the theory; also do they apply common standards as regards the technique; and do they possess the consensual understanding of the history that might validate their claims to authority? Is the negotiation of rules and procedures concerning international financial transactions an objective and impartial question of competence and good practice, like designing an archway? Or does it involve far more subjective components of interpretation, persuasion, and perhaps even intimidation, with compliance arising not so much from functional physical necessity but from convention, or indeed social control? Above all, given the multiplicity of conflicting social interests at stake (creditors and debtors, multinationals and microenterprises, finance ministers and farmers) how can consent be generated for a system whose specific outcomes may frequently be unpalatable (and even incomprehensible) to large sections of public opinion?

In a post–Cold War era characterized by widespread adherence to the principles of liberal democracy, consent may have to be secured through explanation and persuasion, rather than by mere imposition. On this view, any durable system of financial authority will henceforth need to be legitimized through some kind of democratic procedure of authorization and control. If the architecture metaphor is to be retained it should be on the understanding that sound financial structures require a triad of interrelated features—stability, effectiveness, and legitimacy. The legitimacy requirement means that technical expertise must be tempered by political accountability. For this reason, among others, one should not expect a unique "right design" to be the only possible option, universally applicable across time and space. Democratic authority is inherently provisional and subject to revocation. Whatever the rules and institutional practices in place at time t, they must be open to modification in the light of criticism from those affected, by time $t + 1$. Under liberal democratic conditions at the international level, as at the national level, there will always be a delicate balance to be struck between the requirements of financial credibility and those of political accountability. But to evaluate the present we need to see where it has come from. We need an historical perspective in order to gauge the direction and pace of change, but also in order to assess the foundations upon which construction would be based.

Until the Enlightenment, Western architecture was studied in accordance with a monistic doctrine that made it unnecessary to consider historical progression. Since the basic theory was timeless and unquestioned, contemporary structure could be studied side by side with counterparts from the Renaissance, and indeed from antiquity. It was only when the historical method of analysis was introduced that change, diversity, and indeed eclecticism supplanted orthodoxy. This shift in perspective meant that the structures architects built could now be studied in the light of the various ideals that inspired them, and not solely in accordance with some invariable conception of best practice.

There is a clear parallel here between the study of architecture and that of international finance. The monistic doctrine corresponds to the unquestioned orthodoxies of the gold standard. The range of monetary experiments that were attempted in the twentieth century (the "trial of managed money") reflected the diversity and eclecticism unleashed once that supposed naturalness came under critical scrutiny. Armijo's overview contains an instructive classification of financial history since the gold standard, identifying four contrasting periods. It is perhaps worth emphasizing that one of the key factors demarcating these episodes was international warfare. The gold standard was linked to British supremacy after the Napoleonic Wars, and ended with the Great War. The second period is simply the interregnum between the two world wars. Bretton Woods began with the defeat of the Axis powers, and came to an end as the United States lost in Vietnam. Of course the connections between warfare and changes in financial architecture require careful analysis, which cannot be undertaken here. The key point is that the succession of structural arrangements governing international finance has been discontinuous, and has reflected shifts in the global balance of power, as much as internal processes of reflection or debate among experts. Even if certain of these arrangements (notably the Bretton Woods system) can be viewed as the product of conscious design, the timing and much of the structure were heavily determined by more brutal power realities located outside the realm of financial engineering.

This volume is, of course, mainly concerned with contemporary issues rather than with historical analysis. The fourth of Leslie Elliott Armijo's periods—"post–Bretton Woods"—is therefore the one of greatest interest (see her chapter in this volume). But, as she makes clear, this is far from being a homogenous period, and indeed the pace of change may well be speeding up following the end of the Cold War, the reemergence of a more unified Europe, and the accelerated progress of capital market liberalization on the one hand, and of democratization on the other. For example, there were only about 30 functioning democracies in 1970, as compared to around 120 in the year 2000. Central banks have also proliferated (and changed their functions) as the international system has developed.[3] Clearly both democratization and the proliferation of central banks have been powerful tendencies reshaping the international system within which any future financial arrangements will have to be embedded. But it would be too simple to view these tendencies in a unilinear manner. After all, not so long ago every modern national state believed it should be equipped not just with its own army, law courts, parliament, and civil service, but also with its own telephone monopoly, airline—and of course, its own currency, regulated by its own central bank. These assumptions are all being rapidly undermined by liberalization and globalization. Why should central banks be different from telephone monopolies, once we view the ultimate user of both services as a mobile and deracinated individual consumer?

In a liberal democratic era a durable financial system must elicit voluntary consent from those whose monetary affairs it regulates. In this sense there can be no escaping the issue of *legitimation*, or the embedding of financial rules and institutions within systems of law, constitutional supervision, and, in the last analysis, of democratic accountability. However, financial systems derive their acceptability at least as much from the benefits they are thought to deliver as from the political legitimation they can invoke. In a market economy, it is no use issuing *assignats* (as the French revolutionaries did in the 1790s, only to end up with a worthless currency) and then expecting a distrustful populace to comply with your monetary decrees merely because the "representatives of the people" have voted them into law. During the 1990s a standard solution to this dilemma was to establish central bank independence within a democratic constitutional framework. The managers of each national institution would be chosen for their expertise and their good standing in financial markets, and would be appointed for long fixed terms to make them independent of the electoral cycle. They would also be given precise and narrow mandates (mainly concerned with inflation control) to reassure both citizens and markets that their potentially extensive powers would be used in a nondiscretionary and publicly checkable manner. The democratic legitimation of this system would arise from certain rules making them distantly answerable to an elected authority (usually the legislature). For example, parliament might be empowered to scrutinize the initial nominations of bank governors and to hold periodic hearings on their progress. The democratic authorities would retain the ultimate power to change their mandates, or even to revoke their charters, although this would be made procedurally difficult, and would be politically improbable so long as they retained market confidence.

This formula has provided a fairly coherent short-term answer to the question of how to reconcile market requirements for a sound and depoliticized national monetary authority with political requirements for democratic legitimation. But even within the confines of a single national polity the formula conceals some underlying difficulties that could still prove troublesome in the long run, notably concerning the way an exclusive commitment to a narrow domestic anti-inflation mandate may conflict with other broader concerns of monetary management, such as supervision of the banking system, avoiding exchange rate crises, and coordinating monetary and fiscal policy. In the absence of crisis, it may not be difficult to combine the forms of ultimate democratic accountability with the substance of institutional autonomy. But over the long run, and taking all existing democracies into account, it seems unlikely that such favorable conditions invariably hold. So in at least *some* countries elected politicians will probably have to decide whether or not to exercise their last resort authority in ways that would be regarded as intrusive by the partisans of technical insulation. After all, the potential for malfeasance is inherent in any institutional design which protests incumbents from external challenge. Even within the confines of individual countries it remains to be seen just how well the 1990s formula will withstand the tests of time.

The internationalization of economic exchanges and the liberalization of financial markets is beginning to forge a more globalized system of monetary regulation, with its international accountancy standards, its Basle formula for capital adequacy ratios, and its Financial Action Task Force against noncompliant monetary jurisdictions. Each individual monetary authority has to be viewed in this overarching context, and not merely in national terms. Everywhere the old ideas of national sovereignty are being eroded by commercial and financial interdependence. Even the Cubans have found themselves under pressure to turn to the IMF (from which they withdrew in 1963) for advice about how to restructure their monetary system to make it more compatible with international investment flows. Also, in the wake of the 1995 Mexican bailout, central bankers are finding it necessary to broaden and deepen their cooperation, in order to contain prospective future crises. Thus, in September 1996 the Bank for International Settlement (BIS)—the central bankers' bank—indicated that it would accept subscriptions from nine developing country central banks (including those of Brazil and Mexico) in addition to the funds subscribed by its thirty-two existing members. A "Financial Stability Forum" has recently been set up to allow national monetary authorities and regulators to work closely with international financial institutions on ways to anticipate and manage future financial crises.

Yet we should hesitate to infer from this that with the end of the Cold War there will now emerge a single, perpetual, liberal democratic institutional model of authority (including monetary authority). On the contrary, past evidence suggest that rapid technological and financial innovation—occurring unevenly across the surface of the globe—is constantly outstripping official efforts to regulate and stabilize financial systems. With international satellites about to provide home banking via the television screen, the very concept of a "national money supply" is currently under threat. Viewed from this perspective there are good grounds to doubt the immutability of classical central banks as pillars of the territorial nation state. But if the monetary authorities of the "third wave" democracies have to be overhauled in the same way that their state-owned enterprises have been, it is far from clear what the replacement design principles should be. The international orthodoxy of the immediate post–Cold War years was straightforward and uncompromising, but in the light of a decade of often disturbing experiences the original consensus has dissipated. Thus, for example, a 1998 World Bank report was obliged to concede the inadequacies of previous panaceas (rapid financial liberalization, pegged exchange rates, and so forth) and to acknowledge that "reliance on capital inflows exposes developing countries to external panics that may cause sudden and massive reversals in capital inflows, deep illiquidity, and strong contagion effects. Minimizing these risks and dealing more effectively with such financial crises would require a better architecture of the international financial system" (World Bank 1998, 377). Three years later no such architecture has yet emerged. The same report explained the limitations of financial regulation in individual developing countries in terms that could just as well be applied to the international financial institutions themselves: "It takes too long to develop supervisory capacity and skills. Moreover, supervisors are often unable to detect risky behaviour and take action against banks because the kinds of behavior tend to change over time and supervisors are not prepared for them. They may also be prevented by policymakers from taking action"(World Bank 1998, 139–140).

The notion that the international financial system needs a lender of last resort remains controversial. In principle a lender of last resort would be a ready source of (probably high cost, but unconditional) short-term credit to stave off episodes of market panic. This is in contrast to the present model, whereby the IMF provides highly conditional credit, for relatively long periods of time, at relatively cheap rates of interest. In any case, recent discussions concerning the appropriate role for the IMF and the other Washington-based international financial institutions have highlighted the scale of the new uncertainties (see the chapter by C. Fred Bergsten). One simple reason for doubt is that the lending capacity of the IMF no longer comes close to meeting the potential financing needs of the emerging economies. The Fund no longer has the resources to act as a global lender of last resort, given the huge expansion of private capital flows that has recently taken place. Moreover, it was designed to tackle the (public sector led) financial problems of the past, rather than the very different challenges of current (often heavily securitized and derivative–driven) international finance.

The new democracies in emerging markets provide a particularly vivid demonstration of the persisting uncertainties. Even when viewed in strictly political terms these are not fully consolidated regimes that have been stress-tested in adversity. If they are subjected to further banking and currency crises of the gravity experienced by Mexico and South Korea, such political fragilities could well be accentuated by economic stress. Argentina and Turkey are currently demonstrating this continuing potential for severe instability. Nothing has yet been done, in the wake of the recent emerging market financial crises, to provide robust reassurance against further episodes of this kind. On the contrary, it is now commonplace to assert that the international financial system as a whole remains in need of improved governance, greater transparency, and more generally a more solid financial architecture.

The combined banking and currency crises that have erupted in Mexico, East Asia, and Russia since 1995 have given rise to an intensified international debate about the appropriateness of the current mandates of the Bretton Woods institutions in general, and the IMF in particular. There have been high-level suggestions that the IMF took on inappropriate commitments, particularly in Russia and the Ukraine, and became involved in tasks that were beyond both its mandate and its competence. Fears have been expressed that if fragile governments come to believe that their monetary policy errors will be corrected by IMF rescue packages, this will induce moral hazard—the temptation to take risks on the grounds that the costs of failure will be assumed by others. This has led some to argue that there must be no more massive IMF bailouts, or at least that if these become necessary more of the costs should be borne by the private banks and less by the taxpayers who subscribe the capital for the Bretton Woods twins. Influential voices in the United States Congress and elsewhere have proposed that the IMF should limit itself to the tasks of anticipating, guarding against, and if necessary reacting to, future financial crises in emerging markets. There is little clarity as yet about how such reforms might work. Who is to control the decision making process? How far are Washington-based officials to be "insulated" from political pressures on the Bank and Fund emanating from its largest official shareholder? How can international financial institutions avoid *either* duplicating what the commercial banks can do better, *or* going against the commercial banks, and then failing to sustain their policies for lack of public resources?

The observation that IMF credits will only prove effective where they *supplement* what private capital might provide, without forfeiting the confidence of commercial operators, parallels the point that national monetary authorities traditionally needed to cultivate the confidence of a larger community of merchants and wealth holders. In market economies such financial institutions have never been self-sufficient bureaucratic agencies, in the Weberian mode. They have always acted as strategic centers operating within a broader and more decentralized nexus of financial interdependencies, and therefore at least partially dependent on market confidence. Architectural structures do not collapse because their critical components lose confidence in each other and so withdraw support, whereas financial structures rest on precisely such subjective social evaluations. In recognition of this, it has become fashionable to invoke "bubbles" as an alternative to the metaphor of architecture. But both are potentially misleading because they rely on materialist imagery to portray processes of social construction and interpretation.

At a more practical level, the Bretton Woods institutions derive their leverage from the support of key governments which are willing to replenish their capital if the need arises. But, in addition, and unlike the financial institutions of the pre-1914 period, they are not backed by the automaticity of a collective consensus that gold provides the ultimate store of value. Instead they exercise discretion based on their claim to superior knowledge or technical expertise about the nature of modern financial markets. Recent controversies over the purposes and activities of the Bank and Fund arise from the fact that this ostensibly neutral source of authority and correct action is increasingly contested. As private capital flows expand and substitute for official funding, and as a wider array of state actors, political interests, and civil society activists react to the consequences of globalization, these underlying assumptions concerning the Bank and Fund are increasingly contested. In a more "democratic" era, with financial discourse more focused on "transparency" (another questionably materialist metaphor for social practices), international financial institutions are being scrutinized not only over their expertise, but also over their political legitimacy. Both the World Bank and the IMF have recently demonstrated the difficulties involved in maintaining this delicate balance, as such pressures have mounted from both sides.

How can voters and citizens exercise their ultimate authority over the IMF, the World Bank, the Bank for International Settlements, or indeed the European Central Bank? If the answer is that they cannot, then it is open to question what consent they owe to the monetary choices made by these institutions. But the managers of global financial institutions are periodically required to take decisions with large distributional consequences. They need secure authority in order to act in a timely and effective manner, and as financial market liberalization progresses their tasks may become both more difficult and more urgent. The consequences of delay or mismanagement can be huge. In a liberal democratic system the voters may withhold their consent if such powers are deployed without apparent accountability or legitimation. In that sense Leslie Elliott Armijo is right to emphasize that democratic concerns can no longer be excluded from the discussion of international finance.

One small indication of these growing tensions was provided in 2000 by the unseemly way in which a new managing director of the Fund was appointed in replacement of the outgoing Michel Camdessus. A recent British attempt to promote accountability in the IMF sheds some light on the issues involved. The Treasury Committee of the British House of Commons published a report on the IMF in February of 2000 that was critical of British government secrecy with regard to U.K. votes in the IMF, provoking a government assurance that "the choice of the [new] Managing Director should be a much more transparent and openly democratic process" (U.K. House of Commons 2000, X). But of course the subsequent process by which Washington in effect vetoed the first German candidate for the post, after which a second German compromise candidate was accepted as part of a horse trade, revealed the huge gulf between such declaratory statements and the realities of international monetary diplomacy (see Kapur 2000). In view of this record of decision making in an agency that has made so much of the need to promote transparency and uphold models of good governance in the emerging economies, it may be hard to persuade new democracies to continue taking lessons in administrative or constitutional propriety from this source. More generally, this episode suggests that whatever the quality of democratic control exercised by national parliaments, there seems to be no adequate way of translating that sense of accountability upward to the international level.

Globally, democracy and liberalized markets may be in the ascendant, but the relationship between them is by no means stable or fully worked out. The interaction between information technology and economic liberalization is producing rapid and uncontrolled change in financial markets. If anything, proposals for political cooperation and reform to stabilize the world financial system are lagging ever further behind the pace of events. National political authorities may be more united around liberal principles than hitherto, and they may show a greater willingness than in the past to pool sovereignty and enter into durable cooperative commitments, though this may be truer in continental Europe than in other regions. But neither the nation-state nor emerging international institutional arrangements possess anything like the concentrations of power and purpose that underpinned the successful monetary authorities of earlier centuries. Nor are the comforting simplicities and reassurances of the international gold standard available as automatic disciplines or stabilizers when political authority fails or is abused.

I close with a brief examination of one implicit piece of the new international financial architecture: the seemingly ubiquitous recommendation from the international financial institutions that countries establish independent central banks. Hitherto the most encouraging evidence concerning the viability of an independent monetary authority in a democratic polity was confined to a limited number of favored national jurisdictions (such as the United States and Switzerland). But liberal internationalism now ambitiously proposes that these two desiderata can be reconciled beyond national frontiers, indeed throughout a global community of democratic nations bound together through integrated financial markets. How? With the passing of the international gold standard, and the discrediting of managed money formulae that became associated with high inflation, the liberal internationalism of the 1990s has been constructed around the establishment of a grid of independent central banks. In principle these operate according to rather standardized anti-inflation principles that are coordinated through institutional mechanics of mutual surveillance and market mechanisms of financial interdependence. But these are very abstract and mechanical principles that may not prove adequate to capture the interactions between "really existing" central banks, interacting responsively with the highly distinctive constituencies that nurture them and shape their respective outlooks. Consider, for example, the current predicament of the Bank of Japan. The BOJ is under unusual pressures as it struggles with deflationary forces that are not supposed to matter (from the view of Western orthodox opinion), and as it tries to adjust its relationship with the Japanese electorate and Japan's ailing conglomerates.

The belief in the efficacy of a global network of independent central banks assumes that the delicate balance between financial credibility and constitutional legitimacy that has been incrementally constructed in a few favored settings can now be replicated, generalized, and established on a much wider scale, across a much greater range of social and economic conditions. It assumes that not only strong national sovereignties, but also diluted and pooled forms of collective sovereignty, can be relied on to uphold and underpin such arrangements. It requires sustained coordination between such politically and socially distinctive entities as the Federal Reserve Board, the European Central Bank, and the Bank of Japan. This is an ambitious project (on the difficulties it faces see especially the chapters by Brawley, Laurence, and Porter and Woods). It will only be realizable—if indeed it is achievable at all—through careful institutional design and extended political cooperation. After all, not even the neoliberal theorists of "spontaneous order" deny that in the first instance economic and political liberalization needs to be consciously engineered. Only after a suitable constitutional framework has been established can the "conditions of liberty" flourish and self-propagate (note the introduction of vitalist imagery here). As we know from earlier, historical experience (notably 1914), even the more promising projects of liberal internationalism can end in failure. The unconsolidated regimes and fragile financial systems of many "third wave" democracies indicate that such dangers could still destabilize the current international liberalizing project.

As finance becomes more global, the management of the most important monetary issues requires a broad international perspective, and narrow national price stability mandates may become progressively less relevant. Of course when inflation control is at risk both markets and voters are likely to value such mandates highly. But at other times the main demands on monetary authorities (both technical and political) are likely to shift to other issues, such as exchange rate stability or the availability of adequate international liquidity, for which the 1990s formula is ill adapted. If national central banks are expected to focus exclusively on domestic price levels, how is the interaction between them to be coordinated with respect to such global financial concerns? On the other hand, if politically independent central banks instead shift their single-minded focus to the task of maintaining exchange rate stability, as has happened in most developing countries with fixed exchange rates, then the deflationary bias that this typically imparts to the national economy divorces the monetary authority even further from local political oversight and legitimacy.

In conclusion, the architecture metaphor directs attention to some vital requirements of a well-functioning system of global financial authority. But, unless we adopt an unusually liberal interpretation of *venustas* (attractive appearance), architecture is not much associated with democracy. Its merit is unconnected with its capacity to generate public consent. It may awe or inspire the populace, but they are outsiders. The designers and owners of great architecture are not—or not until very recently—thought answerable to them. An essential theme of this volume, by contrast, is that current and prospective global financial arrangements will require political legitimation. To the extent that the world has become more constitutional and more democratic, so too will these requirements. So the architecture metaphor needs to be tempered by other considerations. "Authority" is an alternative construct with a more explicitly social base. Democratic authority requires voluntary consent, which can be withdrawn if those holding it fail to sustain confidence or to persuade critics. It may have originated from an act of force, and it may endure for reasons of inertia, deference, tradition, and fear of change. But democratic authority also has a more positive content, which takes us further away from the connotations of "architecture." It must give reasons for expecting consent; it therefore educates participants into the justifications for particular social arrangements; and it thereby diffuses a sense of collective ownership and shared responsibilities. If this generates consent to and confidence in the status quo, then stability is reinforced. But there is also a price to pay for the benefits of democratic authority. Existing structures will be subject to external scrutiny and criticism. They may be held accountable for their failings, and they may be required to change, at the behest of outsiders. This is what democratic authority would add to existing global financial institutions. It should not be glossed over through overreliance on the metaphor of architecture.

NOTES

1. For an illuminating discussion of the way metaphors and analogies suffuse and structure social theory in general, and economic analysis in particular, see Mirowski 1994, especially chapters 2 and 19.

2. Morgan's translation of Vitruvius (1960) identified three interrelated features of sound architecture—*firmitas, utilitas,* and *venustas* (that is, structural stability, appropriate provision of space, and attractive appearance).

3. There were only 18 central banks in 1990, rising to 59 in 1950, 108 in 1970, and 161 in 1990. The current total is close to 200. See Capie et al. 1994.

REFERENCES

Capie, Forrest, Charles Goodhart, Stanley Fischer, and Norbert Schnadt. 1994. *The Future of Central Banking.* Cambridge: Cambridge University Press.

Crabtree, John, and Laurence Whitehead. 2001. *Towards Democratic Viability: The Bolivian Experience.* London: Palgrave.

Kapur, Devesh. 2000. Who Gets to Run the World? *Foreign Policy* 121 (November/December):44–53.

Linz, Juan J., and Arturo Valenzuela, eds. 1994. *The Failure of Presidential Democracy: Comparative Perspectives.* Baltimore: The Johns Hopkins University Press.

Mirowski, Philip, ed. 1994. *Natural Images in Economic Thought.* Cambridge: Cambridge University Press.

U.K. House of Commons. 2000. *The International Monetary Fund.* 3rd Report. London: House of Commons, Treasury Committee, February.

Vitruvius, Pollio. [1914] 1960. *Ten Books on Architecture.* Translated by Morris Hicky Morgan. New York: Dover.

World Bank. 1998. *Preventing Financial Crises in Developing Countries.* Washington D.C.: World Bank.

CONTRIBUTORS

Leslie Elliott Armijo is Visiting Scholar at Reed College, Oregon. Her research focuses on the political economy of finance, international and domestic, and the interaction of democratization and economic reform. Recent publications include *Financial Globalization and Democracy in Emerging Markets* (edited), "We Have a Consensus: Political Support for Market Reforms in Latin America" (with P. Faucher), and "Balance Sheet or Ballot Box? Incentives to Privatize in Emerging Democracies." She holds a Ph.D. in Political Science from the University of California at Berkeley. Her web address is: <www.mindspring.com/~leslie.armijo>.

Mark R. Brawley is Professor of Political Science at McGill University. His research interests include domestic influences on the desire to provide hegemonic leadership, institutions and rent-seeking, and also the interplay of political economic and security issues. He is the author of three books, the most recent being *Afterglow or Adjustment?: Domestic Institutions and the Responses to Overstretch,* and *Turning Points: Decisions Shaping the Evolution of the International Political Economy.*

C. Fred Bergsten is Director of the Institute for International Economics in Washington, D.C. and former U.S. Assistant Secretary of the Treasury for International Affairs. The latest of his 27 books are *The Dilemma of the Dollar: The Economics and Politics of United States International Monetary Policy* and *Global Economic Leadership and the Group of Seven* (with R. Henning). Recent position papers may be found at <www.iie.com>.

Benjamin J. Cohen is Louis G. Lancaster Professor of International Political Economy at the University of California, Santa Barbara. Educated at Columbia University (Ph.D. 1963), he has worked in the research department of the Federal Reserve Bank of New York, and previously taught at Princeton University and the Fletcher School of Law and Diplomacy, Tufts University. Author of nine books and over 200 professional papers, his recent publications include *The Geography of Money* and "Life at the Top: International Currencies in the 21st Century." His homepage is: <www.polsci.ucsb.edu/faculty/cohen>.

295

David Felix (Ph.D. University of California, Berkeley, 1955) is Emeritus Professor of Economics, Washington U. St. Louis, where he taught from 1964 through 1988. Prior to retirement his research papers and articles were primarily on economic development and economic history, with a Latin America focus. Since retirement they have been mainly on financial fragility and its international financial and real economic consequences. His email address is: <felix@wueconc.wustl.edu>.

Eduardo Fernández-Arias holds a Ph.D. in Economics and an M.A. in Statistics from the University of California at Berkeley. He is currently Lead Research Economist at the Research Department of the Inter-American Development Bank (since 1995) and previously worked at the International Economics Department of the World Bank. Several of his contributions to the debate over the international financial architecture are included in his book *Wanted: Global Financial Stability* (with R. Hausmann). Recent working papers may be found at <www.iadb.org>.

Ashima Goyal is Professor at the Indira Gandhi Institute of Development Research, Mumbai, India. She has earlier taught at the Delhi School of Economics and the Gokhale Institute of Politics and Economics. Her research interests are in institutional macroeconomics, development, the open economy and international finance. Recent publications include "The Money Supply Process in India" (with S. Dash), "The Political Economy of the Revenue Deficit," *Developing Economy Macroeconomics: Fresh Perspectives,* and "Do Foreign Inflows Let Expectations Dominate History?" She also writes a weekly column for the *Economic Times* of India. Several of her articles are available at <www.igidr.ac.in/~ashima>.

Ricardo Hausmann is Professor of the Practice of Economic Development at the John F. Kennedy School of Government at Harvard University. Former Chief Economist of the Inter-American Development Bank (1994–2000), he is also former Minister of Planning and member of the Board of the Central Bank of Venezuela. Recent publications include *Global Finance from a Latin American Viewpoint* (with U. Hiemenz), *Wanted: World Financial Stability* (with E. Fernández-Arias), and *Democracy, Decentralization, and Deficits in Latin America* (edited, with K. Fukasaku).

Erik Jones is Senior Lecturer and Jean Monnet Chair in European Politics at the University of Nottingham, and Professorial Lecturer at the Johns Hopkins Bologna Center. His publications include *The New Political Economy of EMU* (edited with J. Frieden and D. Gros), *Joining Europe's Monetary Club* (edited with J. Frieden and F. Torres), and *Disintegration or Transformation? The Crisis of the State in Advanced Industrial Society* (edited with P. McCarthy). He is also author of *The Politics of EMU.*

Henry Laurence is Assistant Professor of Government and Asian Studies at Bowdoin College, Maine, and was recently an Abe Fellow and Visiting Research Fellow at the University of Tokyo. He is the author of *Money Rules: The New Politics of Finance in Britain and Japan,* and has published on topics including on Japanese "sokaiya" gangsters, the Asian currency crisis, Korean unification, and satellite television in Asia. His current book project compares the British BBC, the American PBS, and the Japanese public television service NHK.

Tony Porter is Associate Professor of Political Science at McMaster University, in Hamilton, Canada. His books include *States, Markets, and Regimes in Global Finance; Private Authority in International Affairs* (edited with C. Cutler and V. Haufler); and *Technology, Governance, and Political Conflict in International Industries.*

Laurence Whitehead is Official Fellow in Politics at Nuffield College, Oxford University and Senior Fellow of the College. He is editor of *International Dimensions of Democratization: Europe and the Americas* and (with G. O'Donnell and P. Schmitter) also of the four volume series *Transitions from Authoritarian Rule.* Since 1989 he has been co-editor of the *Journal of Latin American Studies* and recently became editor of a new Oxford University Press book series, *Studies in Democratization.*

Duncan Wood is Professor Numerario and Director of the Undergraduate Program in International Relations at the Instituto Tecnológico Autónomo de México in Mexico City. He has published on developing countries and the international financial system, and on Canadian foreign policy. He is the author, with George MacLean, of *Introduction to Politics: Power, Participation and the Distribution of Wealth* and of *The Basle Committee and the Governance of Global Banking.* His e-mail address is <dunky@itam.mx>.

SUNY series in Global Politics
James N. Rosenau, Editor

List of Titles

American Patriotism in a Global Society—Betty Jean Craige

The Political Discourse of Anarchy: A Disciplinary History of Internaitonal Relations—Brian C. Schmidt

From Pirates to Drug Lords: The Post–Cold War Caribbean Security Environment—Michael C. Desch, Jorge I. Dominguez, and Andres Serbin (eds.)

Collective Conflict Management and Changing World Politics—Joseph Lepgold and Thomas G. Weiss (eds.)

Zones of Peace in the Third World: South America and West Africa in Comparative Perspective—Arie M. Kacowicz

Private Authority and International Affairs—A. Claire Cutler, Virginia Haufler, and Tony Porter (eds.)

Harmonizing Europe: Nation-States within the Common Market—Francesco G. Duina

Economic Interdependence in Ukrainian-Russian Relations—Paul J. D'Anieri

Leapfrogging Development? The Political Economy of Telecommunications Restructuring—J. P. Singh

States, Firms, and Power: Successful Sanctions in United States Foreign Policy—George E. Shambaugh

Approaches to Global Governance Theory—Martin Hewson and Timothy J. Sinclair (eds.)

After Authority: War, Peace, and Global Politics in the Twenty-First Century—Ronnie D. Lipschutz

Pondering Postinternationalism: A Paradigm for the Twenty-First Century?—Heidi H. Hobbs (ed.)

Beyond Boundaries? Disciplines, Paradigms, and Theoretical Integration in International Studies—Rudra Sil and Eileen M. Doherty (eds.)

Debating the Global Financial Architecture—Leslie Elliott Armijo

Political Space: Frontiers of Change and Governance in a Globalizing World—Yale Ferguson and R. J. Barry Jones (eds.)

Crisis Theory and World Order: Heideggerian Reflections—Norman K. Swazo

Political Identity and Social Change: The Remaking of the South African Social Order—Jamie Frueh

Social Construction and the Logic of Money: Financial Predominance and International Economic Leadership—J. Samuel Barkin

INDEX